h Media

Items should be returned on or before the last date shown below. Items may be renewed by personal application, writing, telephone or by accessing the online Catalogue Service on Fingal Libraries' website. To renew give date due, borrower ticket number and PIN number if using online catalogue. Fines are charged on overdue items and will include postage incurred in recovery. Damage to, or loss of items will be charged to the borrower.

Date Due	Date Due	Date Due
20. OCT 07	11. AUG	
16. FEB 10.		
10. MAY 10.		

Mapping Irish Media
Critical Explorations

edited by
John Horgan
Barbara O'Connor
Helena Sheehan

University College Dublin Press
Preas Choláiste Ollscoile
Bhaile Átha Cliath

First published 2007
by University College Dublin Press
Newman House
86 St Stephen's Green
Dublin 2
Ireland
www.ucdpress.ie

ISBN 978-1-904558-83-5

Cataloguing in Publication data
available from the British Library

Typeset in Ireland in
Adobe Garamond and Trade Gothic
by Elaine Burberry, Bantry, Co. Cork
Text design by Lyn Davies
Index by Jane Rogers
Printed in England on acid-free paper
by MPG Books Ltd, Bodmin, Cornwall

Contents

Acknowledgments

The editors would like to record the encouragement and support they have received from their colleagues in the School of Communications of Dublin City University and particularly that of the head of school, Brian Trench, who was responsible for the initial impetus for this project.

Contributors to this volume

PAT BRERETON lectures in film and media studies at both undergraduate and postgraduate level in the School of Communications and is head of SIM (Centre for Society, Information and Media) at DCU. He is particularly interested in new media literacy, and is editing a forthcoming volume of the new media research journal *Convergence* on DVD add-ons. His books include *Hollywood Utopia: Ecology in Contemporary American Cinema* (2005) and *The Continuum Guide to Media Education* (2001).

FARREL CORCORAN is professor of communication at DCU, where he has also served as head of the School of Communications and dean of the Faculty of Humanities. Before coming to Dublin, he studied for his PhD at the University of Oregon and worked at the University of New Mexico and Northern Illinois University. His teaching and research interests include: the political economy of broadcasting, media and cultural identity, global communication, European media policy, television and children, film and television audiences, mass communication theory, cultural memory, the impact of the internet on the mass media. He served as Chairman of RTÉ, 1995–2000, and is the author of *RTÉ and the Globalisation of Irish Television* (2004).

ROSEMARY DAY lectures in media and communication studies in Mary Immaculate College, University of Limerick. Her research centres on radio, especially community radio. She is author of *Community Radio in Ireland: Participation and Multi-Flow Communication, Droichead* (a handbook for Irish-language community radio broadcasters), and editor of *Bicycle Highway: Celebrating Licensed Community Radio in Ireland.* She is a founder of Radio Research Ireland (RRI), of the international radio research network (IREN), and is establishing a radio section in the European Communication Research and Education Association (ECREA). She is director of the Radio Research Centre in Limerick and is a founder of Raidió na Life, Wired Fm and Wired Luimnigh.

RODDY FLYNN is a lecturer at the School of Communications, DCU, where he is chair of the MA in Film and Television Studies. He is the author of two books relating to Irish film policy: *Cinema and State 1922–2005* (forthcoming) and (with co-author Pat Brereton) *The Historical Dictionary of Irish Cinema* (forthcoming).

DEBBIE GING is a lecturer in the School of Communications at DCU and head of the Media, Diversity and Development strand of SIM (Centre for

Society, Information and Media). She recently completed her PhD on masculinity in contemporary Irish cinema. Her other main research interest is interculturalism and media. She has published on the representation of marginalised groups in Irish cinema, interculturalism and multiculturalism in the Irish media, sound and the female voice in cinema, female violence in contemporary action cinema, and the consumption of mediated images of masculinity among teenage boys in Ireland.

JOHN HORGAN is former professor of journalism at DCU and a member of SIM in the School of Communications there. He has been a member of the Interim Commission on Broadcasting (1987), the Commission on the Newspaper Industry (1996) and the Forum on Broadcasting (2004). He is the author of *Irish Media: A Critical History* (2001) and *Broadcasting and Public Life: News and Current Affairs in RTÉ 1926–1997* (2004).

MIRIAM JUDGE is a lecturer on the multimedia programme in the School of Communications at DCU. Her research interests are in ICT in education and she has managed a number of research and evaluation projects in this field. She was a member of the steering committee for CASE (citizen and science exchange project), 2003–5, a cross-border action research project on science and citizenship involving secondary schools. She is currently conducting research on the Hermes Project, a thin client wireless broadband network involving nine schools in North Dublin and on the deployment of interactive whiteboard technology in Irish schools.

APHRA KERR is a lecturer in sociology and media at the National University of Ireland, Maynooth, and a research associate at the National Institute for Regional and Spatial Analysis. Her interests are in production, consumption and regulatory aspects of the media, particularly digital or 'new' media. She is the author of *The Business and Culture of Digital Games: gamework/gameplay* (2006) and has contributed chapters to *Understanding Digital Games* (2006) and *A Strategy Guide for Studying the Grand Theft Auto Series* (2006). She is currently working on a project examining transnational media practices by immigrant groups in Ireland.

PATRICK KINSELLA is a lecturer in the School of Communications at DCU. He has worked for over 25 years as a reporter, editor and producer in radio and television news and current affairs with RTÉ in Dublin and the BBC in London. In 1996 he co-ordinated a project to establish an independent inter-ethnic TV network in Bosnia-Herzegovina. He continues to write as a freelance journalist and broadcasting consultant.

PAUL MCNAMARA is a lecturer in journalism at the School of Communications at DCU where he served as head of school, 1995–2000. He was the founding president of the European Journalism Training Association [EJTA] and was one of the founders of the European Journalism Centre, Maastricht, Netherlands, where he served on the board of directors, 1992–7. His past research interests included international journalism education and paedophilic use of the internet. His current research looks at how journalists cover the European Union and its institutions.

MARK O'BRIEN is a Government of Ireland post-doctoral research fellow in the School of Communications at DCU. He is the author of *De Valera, Fianna Fáil and the Irish Press* (2001) and co-editor of *Political Censorship and the Democratic State: The Irish Broadcasting Ban* (2005). His teaching and research interests include media history, journalism studies, media policy and regulation, political communication, and media representations of crime and conflict. He is currently writing a history of the *Irish Times*.

BARBARA O'CONNOR is a senior lecturer in the School of Communications at DCU. She has an academic background in sociology and social anthropology and her research interests include feminist and gender studies, ethnographic and representational aspects of popular cultural forms and practices such as tourism, dance and media. She has published widely in these areas and is co-editor of *Gender in Irish Society* (1987), *Tourism In Ireland: A Critical Analysis* (1993), *Media Audiences in Ireland: Power and Cultural Identity* (1997), and *Irish Tourism: Image, Culture and Identity* (2003).

JOHN O'SULLIVAN is a lecturer in journalism, multimedia and related areas at the School of Communications at DCU and a member of SIM. A journalist for 21 years, he has worked in editing and reporting with newspapers, magazines and online ventures, with particular focus on ICT. Research interests past and present include journalism practice in online publishing, the migration of established media online, and design and format in print and online. He is currently working on a PhD thesis, investigating the interaction of economic models with journalism content online.

PASCHAL PRESTON is a professor in the School of Communications, and founder of the STeM research centre at DCU. His research interests include socio-economic and political aspects of new communication technologies and the changing role of information/knowledge functions. He is author of *Reshaping Communication: Technology, Information and Social Change* (2001).

HELENA SHEEHAN is associate professor in the School of Communications at DCU. She teaches in the areas of history of ideas and media studies. She is the author of books, *Marxism and the Philosophy of Science: A Critical History* (1985/ 1993), *Irish Television Drama: A Society and Its Stories* (1987) and *The Continuing Story of Irish Television Drama: Tracking the Tiger* (2004) as well as many articles on philosophy, politics and media in both academic and journalistic modes. She is currently writing a book on the tides of academe.

BRIAN TRENCH is head of the School of Communications at DCU, a member of the research centre, SIM, and a former full-time journalist, with experience in newspapers, magazines and broadcasting. He lectures in media research methods, science in society, science and media, and in journalism practice. His research interests are in public communication of science and technology and in online journalism. Recent publications include papers and book chapters on science information on the internet and science communication in the knowledge society. He is a member of the scientific committee of the international network, Public Communication of Science and Technology (PCST), and a former member of the government advisory body, Irish Council for Science Technology and Innovation.

IARFHLAITH WATSON is a lecturer in the UCD School of Sociology and a former president of the Sociological Association of Ireland. He is a member of the board of the International Visual Sociology Association and has been editor of the *IVSA Newsletter*. His research interests and publications are in visual sociology, minority languages and the media, and national identity and citizenship. He is the author of numerous articles in refereed journals and of *Broadcasting in Irish: Minority Language, Radio, Television and Identity* (2003).

Abbreviations

AMARC	World Association of Community Radio Broadcasters
BBC	British Broadcasting Corporation
BCI	Broadcasting Commission of Ireland
BFI	British Film Institute
BSE	Bovine Spongiform Encephalopathy
CCR	Connemara Community Radio
CE	Community Employment
CJD	Creutzfeldt-Jakob disease
CMC	Computer Mediated Communications
CNN	Cable News Network
COMTEC	Centre for Society, Technology and Media
CRÁCT	Comharchumann Raidío Átha Cliath Teoranta
CRAOL	Community Radio Forum of Ireland
CRC	Community Radio Castlebar
CSCL	Computer Supported Collaborative Learning System
CSCW	Computer Supported Co-Operative Work
DCU	Dublin City University
DES	Department of Education and Science
DVD	Digital Versatile Disc
EC	European Commission
ENSCOT	European Network of Science Communication Teachers
ESRI	Economic and Social Research Institute
FÁS	Foras Áiseanna Saothair (Training and Employment Authority)
FMI	Film Makers Ireland
GAA	Gaelic Athletic Association
GATS	General Agreement on Trade in Services
GATT	General Agreement on Tariffs and Trade
GDP	Gross Domestic Product
GII	Global Information Infrastructure
IBEC	Irish Business and Employers Federatuon
ICT	Information and Communications Technology
IDA	Industrial Development Authority
IFI	Irish Film Institute
INLA	Irish National Liberation Army
IPR	Intellectual Property Rights
IRA	Irish Republican Army
IRCHSS	Irish Research Council for the Humanities and Social Sciences
IRTC	Independent Radio and Television Commission

IT	Information Technology
ITAP	Interactive TV Authoring and Production
ITV	Independent Television (UK)
KbE	Knowledge-based Economy
LAN	Local Area Network
MMDS	Multipoint Microwave Distribution System
NAI	National Archives of Ireland
NALA	National Adult Literacy Association
NCCRI	National Consultative Committee on Racism and Interculturalism
NCTE	National Centre for Technology in Education
NICRA	Northern Ireland Civil Rights Association
NSM	New Social Movement
NUI	National University of Ireland
NUIM	National University of Ireland, Maynooth
OECD	Organisation for Economic Co-operation and Development
OfCom	Office of Communications (UK)
PA	Press Association (UK)
PRTLI	Programme for Research in Third-Level Institutions
PWC	Price Waterhouse Cooper
R&D	Research and Development
RDS	Royal Dublin Society
RIA	Royal Irish Academy
RnL	Raidió na Life
RTÉ	Radio Telefís Éireann
RUC	Royal Ulster Constabulary
SARS	Severe Acute Respiratory Syndrome
SDLP	Social Democratic and Labour Party (Northern Ireland)
SIM	Centre for Society, Information and Media (at Dublin City University)
SIP	Schools Integration Project
SPI	Screen Producers Ireland
STeM (DCU)	Centre for Society, Technology and Media (DCU)
STI	Science, Technology and Innovation
TCD	Trinity College Dublin
TD	Teachta Dála
TnaG	Teilifís na Gaeilge
TVWF	Television Without Frontiers
UCC	University College Cork
UCD	University College Dublin
UNESCO	United Nations Educational, Scientific and Cultural Organisation

UTV	Ulster Television
VCR	Video Cassette Recorder
VEC	Vocational Education Committee
VLE	Virtual Learning Environment
WAN	Wide Area Network
WFL	Wired for Learning
WTO	World Trade Organisation

Introduction

John Horgan
Barbara O'Connor
Helena Sheehan

Globally there has been an explosion of media studies in recent decades. When many now teaching this subject in universities were students, it did not exist as a formal subject. Coming to it, this generation brought to bear upon it the disciplines from which they came – literature, sociology, philosophy, psychology, history, politics and economics – reading and writing books that drew strength from older disciplines. Another generation takes media studies for granted, but still needs to draw from its origins in older disciplines. It is enmeshed in history, sociology, politics, economics and philosophy. It is in the grip of the same theories and tensions as other areas.

Media studies in Ireland has developed in dynamic interaction with the development of the discipline internationally. These decades have been times of debate in which different theoretical positions have vied with each other in all of these disciplines, old and new. The culture wars have raged in our universities, at our conferences and in our texts. Many varieties of positivism, marxism, postmodernism, neo-conservatism have contended for position at the theoretical foundations of media studies, cultural studies and science studies, as well as history, literature, philosophy, sociology and economics. Various theoretical positions as well as various topics are represented in this book.

While the book is structured in the rather traditional way of media studies – a section on production, one on texts and one on audiences, the editors' intention is to raise issues which cross-cut each section, while acknowledging that each is a partial account and that each can only raise and answer certain questions within the limits of its theoretical and methodological approaches.

Media studies in Ireland evolved as a result of intellectual scrutiny of media among media professionals as well as among university academics. *Irish Broadcasting Review* was the result of critical engagement by broadcasting professionals in RTÉ. The first academic centre of media studies was the National Institute for Higher Education in Dublin, now Dublin City University. The School of Communications began with a BA in Communication Studies in

1980 and has multiplied its undergraduate and postgraduate degrees in various aspects of media studies. The College of Commerce in Rathmines, now Dublin Institute of Technology, was also a pioneering centre as was University of Ulster in Coleraine. Other universities have taken the subject up to various extents and in various ways in the years since then. The Media Association of Ireland was an important vehicle for contact and cross-fertilisation among media professionals and media academics, as was the annual but short-lived IFI–RTÉ summer school in the mid-1980s. The Irish Film Institute was also an important base for screening and discussion of film and television.

Out of the IFI–RTÉ summer school came collected papers in the form of a book *Television and Irish Society* (McLoone et al., 1984), which was followed in subsequent years by a flow of books such as *Irish Television Drama: A Society and Its Stories* (Sheehan, 1987), *Media Audiences in Ireland* (Kelly et al., 1997), *Cinema and Ireland* (Rockett et al., 1988), *Transformations in Irish Culture* (Gibbons, 1996b), *Devils and Angels: Television, Ideology and the Coverage of Poverty* (Devereux, 1998), *Screening Ireland* (Pettitt, 2000), *Irish Media: A Critical History Since 1922* (Horgan, 2001), *RTÉ and the Globalisation of Irish Television* (Corcoran, 2004). There have been a number of others too, never more so than in recent years, and numerous articles as well, both in academic journals and in other magazines and newspapers. The journal *Irish Communications Review* has been a vehicle for much fine research and argument. The Irish Media Research Network has taken up where Media Association of Ireland left off, albeit with a hiatus between the end of one and beginning of the other.

There has also been a lively media discourse about media, although it has been intermittent. Television programmes reviewing television, such as *Down the Tube*, and radio programmes, such as *Rattlebag*, reviewing media and arts, have engaged academics, producers and audiences in evaluating media productions. The press too has played a role, in television columns, features and letters pages.

In many ways and through many media, Irish media have been mapped interestingly and intensively over the past few decades. We hope to contribute to that exploration here. The categories we have chosen are not airtight, as many studies combine investigations into several areas. Indeed, it is a most welcome trend that increasingly there are studies that combine all three.

Production

All media are produced in an identifiable economic, social and political context. The interplay between media and context is bi-directional, symbiotic: media influence society, and are engaged in the social creation of public and private versions of social reality, and are in turn influenced by the public and private agents whose perceptions they help to form. At the same time, the modes of production are subject to technological and structural evolution. While there is no established matrix for the analysis of these various forces, not least because the variables are so numerous and because they are continually changing and evolving, a number of key factors are involved.

The impact of globalisation and increased consumer choice on production has been marked in Ireland and is explored in some detail in a number of chapters. Although the response of Irish public service broadcasting has been to devote increased resources to the production of material with a high capacity to attract indigenous audiences, notably news, current affairs and drama, the continual threat to audience retention from well-funded external broadcasters with substantial budgets and high production values has led simultaneously to a substantial reliance on imported programming. Television stations in Ireland serve up a very different mix of programming from that in other European countries, with much more drama and far less factual programming or arts coverage. Some 54 per cent of the output from Irish channels was classified as fiction compared with only 15–33 per cent elsewhere. Much of the drama served up to Irish viewers is imported soaps, with one recent survey (Ofcom, 2006) noting the prominence of British programmes such as *The Bill* and *Eastenders* in RTÉ's schedules. Overall, some 46 per cent of Irish TV output is imported, a figure that is substantially larger than that obtaining in other European countries (Ofcom, 2006: 40), although this global figure conceals, and is to a degree distorted by, the fact that the only national competitor to Radio Telefís Éireann, TV3, has an extremely high percentage of imported programming, itself distorted by the fact that some imported programmes (such as international sporting events) can be classified under 'domestic production' if they are introduced by Irish commentators and accompanied by locally generated analysis. The issues raised by these trends, together with those connected with media agglomeration, the ideological shaping of global television, and the question of youth culture, are addressed in Farrel Corcoran's chapter.

Commercial profitability, in Ireland as elsewhere, remains an overriding consideration for all media, including public service broadcasting. The widening of consumer choice, particularly in broadcast media, together with the character of increasing urbanisation (involving lengthy commuting patterns), have in all probability contributed substantially both to the emergence of new forms of print media production and to the reorganisation of media content in older models, as well as to discrete patters of media consumption. The consumption of television in Ireland averages 180 minutes a day compared with a European average of 218 minutes (Ofcom, 2006: 40). National print media increasingly target a readership that attracts advertisers, leading to the paradox in which static or marginally falling circulations can be accompanied by increased profits – a trend which, common sense suggests, cannot be extrapolated indefinitely. At the same time, both older semi-urban communities (typically those served by a strong regional print media) and new urban satellite or commuter communities (increasingly served by niche, often free publications) demonstrate a high degree of resilience and profitability that can at times attract predators. The same is true of regional commercial radio broadcasting, where the growth both in the number and profitability of outlets has taken place on a scale and at a speed undreamed of in the period immediately preceding liberalisation in the late 1980s.

Journalism, the core content of most current affairs media until the end of the nineteenth century, has gradually been supplemented – some would argue supplanted – both by the spread of new technologies (film, radio and television, the internet) and by the accentuation of commercial pressures, which have in turn led to increasing concentration of ownership and to a blurring of traditional divisions between information and entertainment.

Nonetheless, journalism as such has, although its parameters are now more contested, retained a reasonably central role in media production. This can clearly be seen in the way in which national journalistic production is responding to the challenge of globalisation as seen in the ubiquity of transnational news organisations (CNN, Sky, BBC World) and the multiplicity of choices of broadcast news media now available to consumers from cable and satellite. National print journalism has shown itself to be relatively immune to globalisation pressures, at least in those countries in which strong national news media have remained in indigenous ownership (although even here commercial pressures continually threaten staffing levels and the quality of journalistic content), and in which these media have made effective compromises with the demands of the electronic era, principally the web. The growth of the inernet itself as a news medium, with the emergence of the phenomenon known as citizen journalism and the consequent issues for authenticity, credibility and accuracy, are creating a new set of problems with which traditional media are only just beginning to engage. The issues arising from these developments are dealt with in some detail in the chapter by John Horgan, Paul McNamara and John O'Sullivan.

The environment created by this multiplicity of factors has particular implications for the cultural strand represented by Irish-language broadcasting which, despite its relatively late initiation and sometimes episodic growth, has established itself at a level at which it cannot be ignored, although its grasp – both on audiences and on funding – is always to a degree problematic. Iarfhlaith Watson's chapter explores recent developments in this area and their implications.

Film is another major area, which is discussed in Roddy Flynn's contribution. This is another production area in which neo-liberal economic considerations bulk large, not least because of the high entry-level costs and the effect of globalisation on distribution channels. Irish public policy in this area may well be more developed than in others, partly because of the way in which a substantial greater degree of financial incentivisation (common to all European states but in varying degrees) does not appear to have eliminated domestic cultural inputs.

Here, as in many other areas, the Irish legislative and regulatory framework is of prime importance and, as this volume goes to press, that framework is under serious review. Although the parameters for the legislation governing the financing of film production appear reasonably stable, those governing both print and broadcast media are undergoing substantial revision. In relation to print, proposed legislation governing both media accountability and the rights and responsibilities of journalists looks set to alter radically the framework within which Irish journalists have plied their trade for more than a century. In broadcast media, the formulation of the proposed new Broadcasting Act will radically alter the balance of power as between broadcasters and regulators, and introduce new structures whose effects will take some time to make themselves felt.

Particularly in broadcasting, the relationship between domestic and international or global production remains obstinately, and perhaps understandably, asymmetrical. But this in turn generates a range of challenges both for those who shape the external production environment (legislators and regulators) and those more directly responsible for production and content. As explored in the chapter by Paschal Preston, these challenges revolve at least in part around the terms of the debate, which can be artificially constrained in such a way as to conceal their ideological and social implications. In particular, aspects of the public and political discourse about the nature and implications of the development of the so-called 'knowledge society' can be strongly, and perhaps negatively, influenced by the extent and direction of inward investment, leading in turn to challenges which the Irish state and its institutions may be ill-equipped to meet. In related areas, the need to cast a cold eye on technological determinism and to evaluate the autonomy and power of those working in what has come to be known as the 'information society' (and not merely in the communication industries) is being addressed only partially and slowly within both policy making and practitioner communities.

All in all, Ireland's position as a small, mostly English-speaking country, exposed to the winds of globalisation both in terms of ownership and of content is one which will demand, at the least, continued vigilance, and a creative, appropriate and well-financed response (not least in the education sector) to a rapidly changing, and sometimes threatening, environment.

Representation

A primary area of media studies has been the investigation of patterns of representation. Such studies focus less on production or reception than on the product itself, on the texts that are produced and received, that is, feature films, television serials, radio talk shows, newspaper columns and multimedia websites. These studies address the question of how media productions re-present the world. They therefore necessitate interrogation not only of texts but also of contexts, that is, both the media representations and the world represented.

The discipline of media studies internationally has done much to illuminate this process. Irish media studies have developed within this international arena, focusing on how Irish media have represented Irish society, but also participating in global theoretical debates and studying media representation elsewhere.

Studies of media representation have multiplied over recent decades. Different studies carve out the territory in different ways and pursue their exploration by different methods. Some take a theme, such as gender, and trace how it is portrayed in one or more media and/or genre. Others take a genre within a medium and explore the manifestations of several themes within it. Studies can be structured around theme (poverty, crime, royalty, republicanism), medium (press, television, radio, internet), genre (news reports, drama serials, talk shows, advertisements), auteur (Aaron Sorkin, Gerry Stembridge), place (Ireland, Britain, USA, South Africa). Not only are there various ways of structuring such studies, but there are also various methodological approaches and theoretical perspectives involved.

As to structure, in the section of this book devoted to representation, we look at representation in a number of ways. Three chapters organise their material primarily by theme, while two do so by medium and/or genre and then by theme. Patrick Kinsella examines the representation of political conflict on the medium of television within the genre of news and current affairs. He demonstrates that it is not only the political arena that is contested terrain, but the reporting of it as well. Where both producers and audiences have had divided loyalties and disputed versions of history, even concepts such as accuracy and objectivity have been consistently controversial. Mark O'Brien investigates the reporting of crime in newspapers. He disputes media portrayal of an evolution of Irish society from a safe and crime-free past to an unsafe crime-ridden present and considers a number of factors that contradict this simple narrative and disrupt the dominant discourse on crime statistics. Brian Trench focuses on science and technology and articulates a composite picture emerging from various media. He takes issue with a narrowly instru-mentalist or economist view of science as undermining public engagement with science and its social, philosophical and ethical implications, and as devaluing other forms of knowledge. Helena Sheehan takes one medium, television, and one genre, television drama, or even more specifically, one serial, and traces a number of themes, showing the shifting patterns of drama-tising class, gender, crime, religion, politics, business and multiculturalism. She looks at the evolution of *Fair City* over a period of 17 years and inter-rogates its resonance with the lived experience of city and nation over that period, showing a complex interaction of the codes and clichés of soap opera with the rhythms of social history. Pat Brereton zeroes in on Irish film and highlights certain characteristics of its treatment of the nation, the troubles, the landscape, the church. He highlights new paradigms of engagement among students, who often speak a different language and sometimes harbour contrasting pleasure principles to the established academy, and argues for a continuing need for creative and critical dialogue with new generations of students and audiences to reinvigorate the study of film.

All studies of representation, however, address the question: How do media productions represent the world? How are class, gender, race, nation repre-sented in newspapers, current affairs broadcasting, feature films, television drama series, radio talk shows, lifestyle magazines, video games, internet blogs? More specifically, how do these media represent Celtic Tiger Ireland, the post 9/11 war on terror, US foreign policy, Iraqi resistance, famine in Africa, university life, homelessness, unearned wealth, trade unions, teenage pregnancy, cancer? What images of working women, asylum seekers, priests, politicians, travellers, multinational executives are in play?

There are not only varying answers to such questions, but alternative, even antagonistic, approaches to answering such questions. Contrasting, even contradictory, methods are used. Positivist content analysis counts and codes manifest content, such as the frequency of acts of violence or the ratio of male to female characters, stressing material that is clearly specifiable and easily quantifiable. Its critics add that it is superficial. It glides across the surface of media representation, but does not penetrate to underlying assumptions of thought or overarching structures of power. Marxism, which sets texts in social, cultural, economic, philosophical contexts, makes explicit the implicit ideologies and situates them in a larger narrative. Its critics, however, argue that ideology is 'so yesterday' and that grand narratives are both unachievable and undesirable. Postmodernist approaches eschew both positivist statistical data and marxist ideological analyses and tend to look at texts in terms of their formal qualities and to emphasise the pleasure that putative audiences take in the text over the power relations involved in producing it or the ideo-logical positions encoded in it. It is hostile to realist modes of representation, to narrative structure, to rational coherence, to socio-historical analysis. It critics find its studies de-centred, ungrounded, bitty and inconclusive. You can find elements of all of these positions within these pages.

Most, however, agree that the coding and decoding of images is a complex and active process and one demanding serious investigation and analysis. Some areas, such as dramatisation (or lack of it) of university life, have received scant study, whereas other areas, such as women in soap operas, have received massive attention both abroad and here, including in this book. This is to some extent due to the influence of feminism, which has been a major force in media studies, and the traditional reputation of soap opera as a female genre. The study of gender and soap opera has nevertheless displayed all the same tendencies as other areas. Feminism is a theory and movement that cuts along different lines from positivism, marxism or postmodernism and so feminist studies split into variations of these positions. Postmodernists may wax esoterically about the pleasure that women take in watching soap operas as self-justifying and somehow subversive, but marxists think it is indulging consumption over production and an excuse for lack of real resistance. Meanwhile, positivists count heads in line with the current mania for metrics.

An area of particular prominence in Irish media and Irish media studies has been the struggle between unionism and republicanism and the resultant 'troubles'. The surrounding issues of divided communities, armed struggle and the peace process have preoccupied news coverage in print and broadcast media, documentaries, feature films and TV drama for some decades now. So too has Irish media studies tracked the representation of these processes and engaged in analysis of contrasting images of loyalists, republicans, paramilitaries, politicians, amid the stresses and strains of everyday life in fraught communities. This is reflected in various studies of news and current affairs, including that presented here by Patrick Kinsella. Other studies have dealt with the history of rich fictional evocation of the troubles (Schlesinger et al., 1983; McIlroy, 1998b; Pettitt, 2000; Sheehan 1987, 2004).

Reception

Reference to the audience in many media books is an afterthought, something to be considered only when the more important work of media production and textual analysis has been completed. The relative dominance of political economy and textual studies on Irish media has led to a neglect of an actual social audience – the people who are engaged in reading, listening, viewing, zapping and downloading, and numerous other communicative practices. However, this section on reception aims to counteract this tendency by examining audiences in a number of contexts and for a range of media, old and new. It hopes to demonstrate why audience research is important and the distinctive contribution it can make to our understanding of the role of media in contemporary Irish society and culture. Ireland is a media-saturated society – a society more dependent than ever before on mediated forms of communication for delivery of information and entertainment. Media are therefore so interwoven into the fabric of everyday life that it becomes increasingly important to repeat the classic questions 'What are people doing with media?' and 'What are media doing to people?' Even to attempt to answer these questions we need to know more about the role media play in everyday life, about access to media, how and in what contexts they are used, the rituals involved in media use, the impact of media on people's ideas and emotions, the meanings and pleasures which are negotiated around particular texts and practices, and the interactions between audiences, texts and technologies. These issues are addressed in the five chapters about audiences for radio, television, film, internet and print.

Since the early days of audience research, there have been a number of approaches to the study of media audiences. Back in the 1920s, for instance, the new mass medium of radio generated much debate about its effects. It was generally regarded as all powerful with the ability to directly transmit messages to a passive and gullible audience, an orientation that was later transferred to television. The moral panics about children and violence testify to the perceived power of the new medium on television audiences. But despite the changes in theoretical and methodological fashions, the issue of the power of media in terms of its effects and influences remains a central focus for audience research. Though now considered to be a more complex and less behaviouristic process than characterised by early theorists, we know that media continue to exert considerable influence on the ways in which we think, feel and act.

Is the figure of the 'couch potato', slumped, mindlessly watching whatever happens to be 'on the telly', a realistic portrayal of media audiences? Or are audiences actively pursuing their own interests in their selective media use? What is the relative power of audiences in terms of interpreting media texts? Most of the studies in this section assume an active or interactive audience engaging with various kinds of media while at the same time addressing the way power operates, in some cases in relation to control over media use (Kerr and Day) in other cases in relation to the text-audience dynamic (Ging and O'Connor) and in yet others in terms of the power of groups to enhance or block access to media (Day and Judge).

Media globalisation also raises issues of media power. What are the consequences for audiences of the current trend towards media globalisation and convergence? It has frequently been suggested that these processes lead to a situation in which audiences are little more than the passive victims of niche-marketing. There is also a fear that globalisation will result in the marginalisation and eventual disappearance of national and local media, and that fewer people will have access to democratic forms of communication.

Kerr addresses the issue of globalisation and the relationship between local, national and transnational media while Day's chapter offers an insight into the potential of local media. Media globalisation is also implicated in the construction of cultural identities and 'imagined communities' addressed in terms of gendered identities by Ging and in terms of cultural values by O'Connor.

These are distinctive accounts in that the studies of which they form part have different origins, objectives and foci. Yet they all acknowledge the legacy of a critical cultural studies tradition in both theoretical and methodological terms. They all regard audiences as being crucial in the circuit of media production and consumption and their research is embedded in a framework that acknowledges the importance of the media practice of audiences. These studies also use a broadly ethnographic methodological approach, all using qualititative interviewing and focus group discussion as a primary research technique.

It is almost a decade since the first compilation of research on Irish media audiences was published (Kelly and O'Connor, 1997) and it is instructive to see the new themes and issues addressed in this volume. A glance through the chapters in the audience section reveals that many of these chapters could not have been written a decade ago as they all deal in various ways with newness: new technologies, new genres and new communities – indicating the rapid pace of change in the media and more widely in the cultural and economic landscape. One of the striking changes is the fact that recent migration has led to an expansion of media aimed at a culturally diverse audience and Aphra Kerr's opening chapter on the use of media by Polish migrants confirms that we are looking at a more diverse media landscape than in the past.

Kerr engages with the dual process of audience fragmentation on the one hand and audiences 'increasingly in control of when, where and how they engage with media content' on the other. In a pilot study investigating migrants' 'media practices and experiences on the ground' she details the ways in which local and national media have catered for this new population, and the ways in which the new migrants use media from home, host countries and elsewhere to meet their informational and entertainment needs. She shows how consumption patterns are influenced by a range of factors from desire for integration/acculturation, to occupation, age, and including length of time residing in Ireland.

Kerr's findings appear to counter the fears of what used to be referred to as 'wall-to-wall Dallas' or media globalisation leading to audience homogenisation. She attests to the fact that there has been a proliferation of media production to cater for this new Polish audience and this can be seen as an example of where increased mobility leads to differentiation and pluralisation of media. The indications are that migrants' use of media and the 'imagined communities' constructed through media use are no longer embedded in any one place, although it appeared that the older migrants have more attachment to the Polish 'national imagined community'. But the younger migrants seemed to negotiate 're-imagined communities' on an ongoing basis through their selective use of national (Irish and Polish), local and transnational information and entertainment sources. Perhaps Kerr's study points to the need for a re-imagining of the national in the light of recent social and demographic changes in Ireland, and that it might be more useful to think in terms of a number of 'public sphericules' (Cunningham, 2001) as opposed to the classic 'public sphere' as theorised by Habermas (1989), since for certain groups that is less important than either local or transnational communicative networks.

Barbara O'Connor, too, addresses issues of globalisation and media use, but from a somewhat different perspective focusing as she does on the enjoyment of reality TV amongst young Irish audiences. Her study was motivated by what she perceived as a homology between the values constructed by reality TV, such as competitiveness, individualism, narcissism, acquisitiveness and those generated in a Celtic Tiger culture. She uses the example of viewers talking about their enjoyment of the transformations achieved in make- over shows; participants' appearance, behaviour and environment such as the home, to show that these shows about 'ordinary people' are used to negotiate ethical and moral boundaries around the self by distinguishing between acceptable and unacceptable transformation practices. O'Connor claims that, rather than being in thrall to the values of a Celtic Tiger culture, viewers are actually engaging in moral/ethical discussion around personal conduct and relationships much like viewers of soap opera. However, there are also indications that the shows were successful in making high consumption lifestyles more acceptable or even normative, which served to highlight the contradictory nature of viewers' engagement with reality TV.

The theme of identity construction is also the subject of Debbie Ging's chapter on audience responses to the film *Intermission*. She uses the film as an example of a recent cycle of Irish films dealing with criminal working-class and underclass masculinity and focuses on the meanings and pleasures of these films for a male audience. In combining textual analysis of the films with empirical audience research, she found that the constructions of masculinity within the film were variously interpreted by the focus group members in her sample. Social class was an important factor in determining interpretive strategies and pleasures, with the working-class group identifying most with the anti-heroes in conflict with the forces of law and order. Her findings challenge the common misconception amongst film scholars that representations of 'New Lad' culture are read in an ironic way by male audiences. In fact her findings reveal that, despite variation amongst class groups in terms of critical engagement with the film, all groups were relatively uncritical of the hegemonic codes of masculinity embedded in it.

Miriam Judge's chapter on the appropriation of new media technologies in schools is based on an evaluation research project in primary and post-primary schools on the 'Wired for Learning' initiative. The discussion revolves around the centrality of the role of teachers in the implementation of educational innovation and the obstacles to appropriation of certain elements of the learning package. Interviews with teachers revealed that during the pilot phase they found themselves 'grappling with a technology which stretched their fledgling technology skills to the limit' and which challenged their existing professional practices in a number of ways. Her findings are a challenge to technological determinists by demonstrating the importance of the teachers' gate-keeping role in the adoption or resistance to new media technologies in schools. In addition to its policy implication, Judge's study also raises the issue of whether we can continue to talk about audiences in the same way as before, given that surfing the net or sending an email may be a very different activity from watching television. The fact that we now talk about users of new media rather than audiences for new media means that there is a blurring of the distinction between producers and consumers of these media.

While Kerr's chapter refers to the possibility for migrants to have more control over media content, Rosemary Day's chapter takes this a stage further by advocating the potential of community radio to turn audiences into producers and to operate as a micro-public sphere in which a diversity of voices can be heard. Day's discussion is based on a ten-year study of the objectives, structure and functioning of community radio in the Republic of Ireland and might therefore also have been appropriately placed in the production section of this book. However, because of its focus on the relationship between producer and audience it addresses, it engages centrally with one of the key issues in audience studies. Her interviews with station personnel about their experiences lead her to the conclusion that 'best practice' in the areas of ownership, management and programming can ensure a process of empowerment of both geographical communities and communities of interest. However, Day is aware that access to 'the airwaves on its own is not sufficient to ensure that members of the public get to be heard' and she is also mindful of the possible conflicts of interest and power dynamics within local communities. She sees community radio in Ireland as part of other community efforts to build a more inclusive and democratic society. Her research is underpinned by the principle of the human right to communicate and in this sense is also about 're-imagined' communities.

Conclusion

The difficulties and opportunities facing researchers in Irish media are manifold. In its uniqueness as a small country, which speaks a world language though containing a significant minority language and also exhibiting a substantial degree of cultural specificity, Ireland offers major opportunities as an accessible, variegated, open and yet contained laboratory for the study of the many and subtle interactions between media, culture and society. At the same time, its modest dimensions make its complexities less easy to avoid, and cut off the escape route marked by comfortable generalisations. In Ireland, as elsewhere, production, representation and reception are continually finding new forms as the era of mass media dissolves, in an almost filmic sense, into the era of niche audiences, new patterns of commercial exploitation, and the erosion of boundaries and constraints that were previously considered almost immutable. Even as the power of multi-national media corporations seems to grow almost exponentially, it is continually being undercut by new media in ways that also raise the old issues of accuracy, authenticity and truth telling in a new dimension. In these areas, as in many others, media research in Ireland has fertile ground to explore.

Section One   # Production

Chapter 1

Irish television in a global context

Farrel Corcoran

This chapter will explore what has come to be known as cultural globalisation from a number of angles, with a view to developing a greater understanding of the global context of television in Ireland. First we look at the way in which global television has emerged since about 1990, as the process of vertical and horizontal integration led to the development of giant media corporations, larger than anything the world had ever seen before. This process of media conglomeration is particularly striking in its ambition to reach young people, with constantly evolving forms of entertainment and media interaction. The meaning of this global media structure and its impact on countries in different parts of the world have been expressed in terms of 'cultural imperialism' in the tradition of critical media research, but there has also emerged a competing paradigm centred on the concept of 'globalisation'. We examine the position of Europe within this global structure and whether it has yet emerged as a powerful new regional centre of television production, able to compete with the USA for global influence. Finally, we focus on Ireland, how it has been affected by deregulation in the media sector, whether its television system is able to function in a global context, and whether its media economy will be able to support the production of television content to meet Irish needs.

Media conglomeration

The key element in the architecture of global television today is undoubtedly the unprecedented spate of mega-mergers of giant media corporations that has gained momentum since about 1990. Most of these conglomerates are North American. A very few are European (Bertelsmann) or Asian (Sony). This increasing concentration of ownership has made it difficult to know which conglomerate owns which local outlet at any particular time, as media companies continue to use the courts and to lobby the US Congress to remove the last few legal restraints on ownership, what one senior American regulator called 'the cumbersome underbrush of unnecessary government

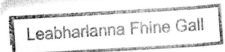

regulation' (Klinenberg, 2006). Despite corporate rhetoric to the contrary, the concentrated, conglomerated and profit-driven US media system, which forms the backbone of the global television system, is hardly the result of 'free enterprise'. It is the recipient of enormous direct and indirect subsidies and/or government-granted monopoly franchises. These include monopoly licences given to radio and television networks, cable and satellite monopoly franchises, magazine postal subsidies and copyright privileges, all of which suggest that, for these firms, the most important competition may well be in Washington, in obtaining the comfortable subsidies and licences that bring advantage over competitors (McChesney, 2006).

A few giant companies stand out from the rest. News Corporation, besides its global interests in newspaper, magazine and book publishing, and its port-folio of internet activities, is very active in film and television production and digital satellite broadcasting (Sky, Foxtel, BSkyB, DirecTV). A controlling interest is owned by Rupert Murdoch, whose global goal is to own multiple genres of programming, especially news, feature films, sports and children's entertainment, and beam them into homes in the USA, Europe, Asia and Latin America. Using a modest base in the Australian press, Murdoch entered the British media market in the 1960s and became a dominant force in North America by the 1980s, using the purchase of Twentieth Century Fox to launch the Fox Television Network. This has become an influential right-wing voice in the American public sphere, as well as a provider of material for News Corporation outlets in its satellite systems in other parts of the world. News Corporation's most recent global strategic move is to increase its access to the television market of the Indian sub-continent, to counter-balance the frustra-tion of the slow pace of its Star TV system's access to China. Between them, India and China contain two fifths of the world's population and a rapidly growing middle class with disposable income to spend on entertainment.

Other companies in the first rank of what has become a tiered global media market include Time Warner, Disney, Viacom and General Electric. With over 200 subsidiaries worldwide, Time Warner emphasises the production of television and film entertainment, as well as news and music, rather than the development of entire satellite systems. Time Warner is a major content supplier in virtually every medium on every continent. Its interests include a wide spectrum of magazines, internet sites, the whole range of Warner Brothers companies, the Home Box Office cable network, the news channel CNN and the Cartoon Network for children. Vying with Time Warner for the status of world's largest media conglomerate, the Disney Corporation shifted its emphasis significantly in the early 1990s from animation and theme parks to film and television, and quickly became a dominant global content producer in a wide range of entertainment. Disney became a fully integrated media giant with the purchase of the ABC Network in 1995, in one of the biggest acquisitions in business history. Generally regarded as the industry leader in using the strategy of global cross-selling and cross-promotion to maximise it revenues, Disney is active at a global level in book and magazine publishing, theme park operation and film production, as well as controlling ABC, ESPN Television, the History Channel and the Disney Channel.

General Electric has vast non-media holdings (in insurance, finance, health-care, military hardware, nuclear power, household appliances, aviation and locomotives), as well as a wide range of film and television production and distribution companies, including NBC, Telemundo, Universal Pictures, CNBC World and MSNBC. Viacom achieves its global reach through Paramount Pictures, Showtime, United Cinemas International and Blockbuster video and music stores, though its two main weapons in targeting global growth are Nickleodeon, a world leader in children's television, and the pre-eminent global music channel MTV. Viacom has had considerable success in finding inexpensive ways to customise programming and offer content in several languages for different regions around the world. Most of its world television entertainment ventures are aimed at children and young people, but it also controls book publishing via Simon and Schuster, Scribners and Macmillan. Because of the consumer power of the global youth market today and its inclination towards early adoption of new technologies, it is worth taking a brief close-up of some of the innovative ways being pursued by MTV for moving beyond traditional television.

Global youth culture

One of the greatest challenges for all broadcasters today is how to target young adult audiences, a key demographic for advertisers, with their content. Among global television companies, Viacom's MTV is one of the most successful in doing this. When it started in the US in 1981, many experts felt that a 24-hour music video channel would never work, even in what then was the niche environment of cable TV. But along with HBO and a few other companies, MTV legitimised what was seen as the very questionable model of pay TV. Twenty-five years later, its programming appears in 442 million homes in 167 countries worldwide, of which 88 million are in the US (Reuters, 2006).

Now a media giant in its own right, MTV is facing a business environ-ment dominated by the convergence of television with the internet, which creates a potentially new environment for music videos, music news and photos. Its competitors, as purveyors of youth-driven pop culture, include Yahoo, YouTube and MySpace. In 2005, it launched MTV Overdrive, a broadband internet video-on-demand service that already generates 1.5 million video streams per day. It targets university students through mtvU and mtvU

Uber and aims to increase opportunities not only for more access to content on its digital platforms, but also for interaction with it, by allowing viewers to upload their own content or watch behind-the-scenes footage during commercial breaks in musical events.

The strategy here is to build virtual worlds around MTV properties, deepen its connections with fans and move a generation ahead of what rivals are doing online. Its most recent innovation is the decision to build on the popularity of the teenage reality television show *Laguna Beach*, by pushing the boundaries of 'false reality' one step further, into a new interactive genre designed for what one executive called 'a group of people who are endlessly fascinated with watching themselves' (Siklos, 2006). 'Virtual Laguna Beach' will be an online service in which young fans can immerse themselves in virtual versions of the show's familiar seaside hangouts, by creating and controlling digitised, three-dimensional characters called 'avatars'. Other virtual worlds, combining the challenge of gaming with three-dimensional chat-rooms, are planned for launch in 2007, including a gay and lesbian site which will be designed entirely by its online participants.

New technology is also allowing television to become more mobile. MTV has become involved with Virgin Mobile to produce a suite of original, exclusive ring tones for the teenage phone market, and in the US it offers direct-to-consumer mobile content through its subsidiary Flux. Its new subscription music service Urge, which competes with iTunes, will be integrated into the next version of Microsoft's Windows Media Player. As a company built on bringing together pop culture and young people, MTV had ambitions in the online social networking boom too, until its parent company Viacom lost out to News Corporation in 2005 in the bidding for MySpace, where usage has quadrupled in less than a year. Global competition in an age with multiple delivery platforms involves gambling on finding the content that works best on a particular channel or website, and 'making it addictive for the audience, not just shoving another programme down their throat' (Reuters, 2006). A new example of this is the decision by Rupert Murdoch in August 2006 to start selling videos online from News Corporation's vast library of films and television entertainment (Bloomberg News, 2006). This service will be launched first on the IGN Entertainment website, and later on MySpace.com, where users will be able to transfer what they purchase to mobile devices using Microsoft's Windows system. There is increasing evidence that commercials are finally gaining traction in these social networking websites, where the emphasis is on commercials that are clever enough to be passed on, in ever-wider social networks around the world.

The sheer scale of new media distribution systems, exploiting the convergence of traditional television with the internet and mobile telephony, completely dwarfs anything we might see in a small country like Ireland, though Irish television still has to compete with global media companies for viewers' time and money, revenue from advertising and even access to the rights to broadcast popular genres of American and British entertainment. Analysis of the full range of these media giants has been well advanced in several academic studies (Herman and McChesney, 1997; Thussu, 1998, 2006; Hoskins et al., 1997; McNair, 2006) and in dedicated journals, especially *Global Media and Communication.* The increasing conglomeration of media companies is also tracked periodically in some news magazines (see, for instance, *The Nation*, 3 July 2006).

We now take a brief, historical look at how global television has been ideologically shaped by the utopian discourses emanating from global centres of power, and at academic discourses that organise the study of world communication around the paradigms of 'globalisation' or 'cultural imperialism'.

The ideological shaping of global television

When the global reach of television first became a real possibility, as an outcome of the Cold War 'space race' and American–Soviet investment in space technology, politicians and academics in the West began to weave visions of the kind of communication system that global television should become. The presidency of John F. Kennedy took the lead in driving its grand strategy forward with all the power of a utopian vision tied to new communication technologies. The imaginative force of Kennedy's New Frontier infused discussion of television in the early 1960s, when sales of television sets were escalating dramatically in the US and the American television networks saw their foreign earnings from programme syndication begin to match domestic revenues. Marshall McLuhan gave academic coherence to the Cold War rhetoric of global media. Diffused by American satellite technology, Western television would sweep scattered populations worldwide into a single, enlightening embrace: schoolchildren receiving space-based educational programmes in the classrooms of India, African farmers learning modern agricultural techniques that would defeat poverty, citizens of the Global Village espousing democratic values and strengthening the Free World against the perils of Communism. As a popular medium, television would shore up the restless, postcolonial Third World, win hearts and minds for the steady spreading of Western military and multinational corporation influence around the world. New Frontier global television rhetoric integrated into a single utopian project the economic interests of the largest corporations, taking aim at global markets, and American foreign policy in all its Cold War polarisation of Western freedom against Soviet totalitarianism. This dominant discourse of the time brought together into one seamless ideological whole the dream of enhanced global community and co-operation, with the imperial ambitions of the superpower struggle. It promised a better quality of life for all, at the same time as it locked in US hegemony. It was actually called the 'Free Flow' doctrine for many years by American diplomats, until a Third World revolt in UNESCO began to unravel it and use the new label 'cultural imperialism'.

Thirty years after Kennedy, the Clinton–Gore administration took an early lead in creating a political project out of the emerging popularity of the internet and the new opportunities opened up for global communication by the technology that could support broadband networks and digitise analogue television. Clinton's notion of the Global Information Infrastructure, promoted vigorously in the early 1990s, recaptured some of the Kennedy-era style of driving a political project forward with all the force of a utopian vision embedded, again, in new communication technologies. The GII project offered a new discursive framework within which to imagine the future, linked with the notion of the triumph of the West and the 'end of history' after the implosion of Communism. The idealised 'global society', now about to emerge with the worldwide spread of the internet, would caringly address public goals, but the means to address these would be private enterprise rather than state intervention. It would entail the global application of some key concepts, especially free trade without state barriers, and belief in the goodness of unrestricted competition in regulating 'the market'. Use of the term 'globalisation' began to become more widespread and it soon took the form of a research paradigm.

Before 'globalisation' began to dominate academic thinking about international communication, there was a strong commitment in research to the normative notion of the media nourishing a healthy, democratic public sphere, and to exploring how the actualities of international communication fell short of that ideal. Inspired by senior scholars like Herbert Schiller, Johan Galtung and Thomas Guback, critical media scholarship from the 1960s on began to focus attention on structural aspects of international communication, the dominant political and economic forces driving the global flow of information, from core to periphery and within peripheral regions, and the absence of any counter-flow back into core countries. Anglo-American news and entertainment were rapidly becoming ubiquitous. The global flow of news, for instance, inherited from nineteenth-century colonial news agency patterns and now being reproduced in television, meant that news is transferred to the countries of the South in such a way that primary importance is attached to issues the developed world sees as important. This criticism is still active. The structure of political and economic power exercised by the centre over the periphery results in the creation of certain aspects of the centre's value system in the periphery (Thussu, 2006: 51). Not only are local cultures in different parts of the world threatened by this global cultural hegemony, emanating from the centres of financial, technological and military power, but their problems, on the rare occasions when they succeed in catching the attention of core country media systems, are nearly always framed within the negative stereotypes of 'crisis news' (Schiller, 1969, 1976, 1981; Dorfman and Mattelart, 1975; McPhail 1986; Nordenstreng and Schiller, 1979, 1993; Gerbner and Siefert 1984).

Out of this 'cultural imperialism' paradigm emerged calls for a New World Information and Communication Order (NWICO), passionately debated in the Non-Aligned Movement, the UN General Assembly and UNESCO. Through reports and conference resolutions, delegations from developing countries argued that western hegemony in cultural trade was breaching their sovereignty and threatening their national identity (McBride, 1980). Western media organisations fought back and lobbied their governments to ward off any global policy moves that would limit their expansion. Tired of losing votes on these issues in spectacular ways in the General Assembly, Britain and the US abruptly pulled the plug on the NWICO debate by abandoning UNESCO in 1985 and leaving a huge hole in its budget. Cultural imperialism quickly disappeared off the agenda of UNESCO and academic attention began to focus on an emerging paradigm, loosely organised around the notion of 'globalisation', to which we will return below.

UNESCO has recently returned to some of these issues under the rubric of 'cultural diversity'. In October 2005, the Convention on the Protection and Promotion of the Diversity of Cultural Expression was approved by a vote of 148 member states to two (the US and Israel voting against it, in a pairing reminiscent of similar votes in UNESCO 25 years before). The Convention is a response to increasing pressure to subject the cultural services sector, including magazines and television, to the discipline of trade and investment treaties worked out at the level of OECD and the World Trade Organisation (Neil, 2006). As a new international treaty, the Convention is seen as a way to carve out trade in media from trade agreements like GATS, to promote cultural policies at a global level and ensure that disputes are adjudicated by cultural rather than trade experts. It would restore some element of state sovereignty over media policy in order to protect the diversity of cultural expression and strengthen recognition that the cultural aspects of development are as important as the economic aspects.

Ireland has a direct interest in this new development, since it has a history of supporting French arguments for preserving the 'cultural exception', when American pressure is applied in WTO discussions to remove what Hollywood sees as 'barriers to trade' and some European countries see as promoting and protecting their own audiovisual industries. The UNESCO Convention seeks to protect regulatory measures, content quotas, financial subsidies and public institutions (such as public broadcasters). For France, cinema-derived sub-sidies for its film industry are crucial. For Ireland, the protection of RTÉ and TG4 from predatory attacks is crucial. The Convention received strong inter-national support because of the widespread belief at state level that cultural homogenisation must be resisted, but it remains to be seen whether it will reduce the threat to cultural policies at the supra-state level of the WTO, where the interests of global media conglomerates have more influence.

Cultural globalisation

Not all academic discourse is based on critical media research, nor does it all support a cultural imperialist paradigm in explaining the global reach of giant media companies. Within social theory, a great deal of debate has centred on the term 'globalisation', the related notions of 'distanciation' and 'time–space compression', and the proposition that contemporary societies are undergoing rapid change that can radically increase feelings of uncertainly and risk (Giddens, 1990; Robertson, 1992; Harvey, 1989). International movement at several levels is undoubtedly a familiar experience for large numbers of people in the modern world: the movement of guest workers, tourists, refugees, capital investment, currency markets, clothes fashions, music, food tastes and so on. Social relations become more stretched across greater distances, radically freed in new ways from local contexts, and distance seems to disappear alto-gether at those moments when live, global television pulls together large numbers of people into the same real-time view of the fall of the Berlin Wall, or nose-cone views of 'smart' bombs doing their terrible work, or the collapse of the World Trade Centre in Manhattan.

Key to the 'globalisation' paradigm, which began to take root in corporate boardrooms as well as in parts of the academy in the 1990s, was the idea that global television trade has now become much more complex, with the development of satellite television and the advance of media privatisation and deregulation as guiding policy principles. The consolidation of geolinguistic areas of television consumption (Anglophone, Arabic, Spanish, Mandarin, Hindi and so on), it is argued, increasingly draws on large production centres now based in 'peripheral' countries, such as Egypt, Mexico, Brazil, China, India (Sinclair et al., 1996).

Meanwhile, audience research on trans-border television has suggested that audience responses to imported television, depending on the context of reception, are more complex and reflexive than are allowed for in discussions of cultural imperialism. Reception theorists argue that television viewers have sufficient cultural resources of their own to be able to withstand cultural hegemony associated with American television flows (Lull, 1995). Viewers are

able to see through the ideological connotations of globally distributed television, in ways that could not have been foreseen by cultural imperialism theorists
(Ang, 1985; Katz and Liebes, 1986). Some have argued, like Tomlinson (1991,
1997), that national cultures are no longer coherent and unified wholes, and
that cultural products adapt and mutate when they move between cultures in
ways that render obsolete critics' fears about cultural homogenisation and loss
of cultural diversity. There is no longer any natural relationship between
cultural and geographical territories, since new processes of globalisation are
bringing about 'deterritorialisation' (Garcia Canclini, 1995).

The main point of contention is whether this is actually what Schiller
(1991) called a 'post-imperialist era', as some globalisation authors argue. Is
there still a virulent form of Anglo-American hegemony in television that
imposes its shadow over all countries in proportion to their ability to resource
their own media systems? This is a question that has been raised in Ireland
from time to time in the 1990s (Government of Ireland, 1995). One answer is
that the scholarly emphasis on the 'interconnectedness' of a globalised world
and the creation of new, hybrid cultural spaces for bonding and solidarity, has
not only been overstated in globalisation theory, but 'fails to engage critically
with economic power' (Curran, 2002) and ignores the persistence in global
television of issues of domination. The very notion of globalisation can be
ideologically loaded with connotations of 'inevitability' and 'common sense',
and this can divert attention away from concerns about economic power by
suggesting that there is no longer a dominating or controlling centre in the
contemporary world. Focus on the central role of the US in the international
trade in media products is replaced by a view that North America is now only
one among many media production centres, situated in different world regions,
that exchange their products more or less reciprocally with one another, none
of them so much larger than the others that it could be said to dominate
them. In the words of Arjun Appadurai (1996: 31), 'the US is no longer the
puppeteer of the world system of images but is only one node of a complex
transnational construction of imaginary landscapes.'

Some critical communication scholars, such as Herman and McChesney
(1997), use the language of globalisation in a 'weak' sense, and their work can
be seen as modifications of the imperialist paradigm, because they are interested
in such global phenomena as the destruction of less profitable forms of cultural
production by large media corporations, and linkages between multinational
corporations and the political and military power of the state. The core propositions holding together the 'strong' version of globalisation are increasingly
being challenged, both for their theoretical contradictions and their failure
to remain robust when tested against evidence. Sparks (2005), for instance,
provides a succinct demolition of the main propositions of globalisation
theory: the supposed absence of a global centre of media production, the

argument that the Westfalian nation-state system is in terminal decline, the notion that globally popular cultural artefacts are no longer rooted in, for example, particular national (American) cultural taste patterns. The imperialist paradigm is clearly re-emerging, offering a different theorisation of the 'informational oligopolies' that have emerged over the last 20 years, 'reflecting the extreme culmination of well-established trends towards conglomeration, concentration, privatisation, deregulation and commercialisation, all at the political and commercial service of relatively tiny elites' (Boyd-Barrett, 2005: 18).

Europe and the United States

Despite the success of large regional television companies in Brazil, Mexico and elsewhere not only in dominating their own domestic markets, but also in exporting profitably to other world regions and even to the US itself, there is no doubt that the major US media companies dominate the new era of digital multichannel television and still have a pre-eminent place in world television markets. Europe is one world region where we might expect to find stiff competition emerging. If we look at the rankings of the top 40 audio-visual companies in the world today, however, we find that the US has more than double the number of entries (19) of its nearest competitor Japan (6), followed by Britain (5), Germany (2), France (2) and Italy (1) (*Variety*, 15–21 September 2003). Most of the European companies actually owe their presence in this ranking to strong performances only in their home markets. Their total revenue for 2002–3 is a fraction of what the US media conglomerates earned: $76.5 billion against $225.5 billion. Of the top seven global media corporations that have a truly global reach in film and television production and distribution, only one is European – Bertelsmann – and it has registered the slowest growth rate over the past ten years. The American companies in the 'first tier' of the global media industry have a very broad global span, including access to the huge media markets of India and China, representing two fifths of the world's population. The 'first tier' companies also have sole access to the US, the world's wealthiest media market. Chalaby (2006: 39) concludes from all this that while the achievements of European media concerns are impressive, they must be put in perspective. The American market is still out of reach for the vast majority of European media companies, which do not have the international scope to reach into the wealthiest layer of the world's media industry.

Multi-territory production companies are emerging in Europe, with the potential to export to the US (Endemol, pioneering developer of 'Reality TV', is a current example) but the market share of American companies in Europe still remains very high. This situation parallels the US domination of film distribution in Europe. The result is an $8.2 bn. deficit for Europe (2003 figures), a deficit that has grown by 70.5 per cent over five years. Add to this the fact that many of the new pay-TV channels emerging in Europe are owned by American conglomerates – Time Warner, NBC Universal, Cox Communications, Walt Disney, Comcast, Viacom and Liberty Global. A common strategy is to increase out-of-home revenue by localising television channels as much as possible, using several languages and a mix of dubbing or subtitles appropriate for each target market.

Should we see all this as cultural imperialism, or is that perspective still a 'deeply unfashionable problematic' (Tomlinson, 1997: 175)? Chalaby (2006) argues that, far from this being confirmation of a cultural imperialism argument, it actually demonstrates American success in mastering a new kind of global–local adaptation. The new pay-TV channels are hybrid cultural products, exemplified by MTV's success in mixing local music with American programming and video clips from global music stars. Discovery and National Geographic channels also get involved in local productions. Children's channel Jetix and Cartoon Network combine programmes from their large libraries' local European content.

But this welcoming of what Chalaby terms American 'cultural primacy' as a replacement for 'cultural imperialism' begs questions not only about the nature and quality of the content being produced for European audiences. It also raises questions about the economic impact of American dominance of European media markets especially those, like Ireland, with relatively small media economies that face both internal and external problems in formulating broadcasting policies. The limited national market in small countries poses an obstacle to the survival and profitability of their television production sector at an international level. Small national broadcasting systems like RTÉ have very limited possibilities for gaining any advantage in the European single market that the Television Without Frontiers directive was designed to encourage.

The conclusion has to be that Ireland and other small states have to react to global pressures under different conditions from those found in larger states. As Papathanassopoulos (2005: 48–9) argues, their policies have to take into account the interests of larger countries, rather than the other way round. Furthermore, they frequently have to face the inescapable television presence of a larger neighbouring country that speaks the same language. The implications of this phenomenon in the case of Ireland are explored by Corcoran (2004). We return to this issue below in the context of Ireland's cultural, linguistic and geographic proximity to Britain, and to European cultural politics, including the revision of the TVWF directive.

Television in Ireland

Ireland's positioning the global flow of television content must be seen primarily in relation to the small size of its population and the financial resources that can be carved out from the overall economy, to support at least an 'adequate' supply of television programming that is somehow 'relevant' to an Irish public sphere. Debate about what is both adequate and relevant has raged for years and deserves a full chapter in its own right. What we can say in general is that a combination of a weak television economy, an impoverished, run-down public broadcasting service, and an unregulated commercial television system can wreak havoc on the public's right to good information and entertainment that connect them with the culture they live in.

Ireland undoubtedly has a relatively weak film and television economy, with cinema screens dominated by Hollywood output and with a large number of television channels now dipping into a limited pot of advertising revenue. A. C. Nielsen, the official television audience measuring contractor, already measures audience size for 18 channels in Ireland, many of which are UK-based, all of them drawing advertising revenue through opt-outs for Irish viewers. The top dozen channels include RTÉ 1 and 2, TG4, TV3, BBC 1 and 2, UTV, Channel 4 and E4, Sky News, Sky Sports and Nickleodeon. Only the first four are regulated in Ireland. RTÉ 1 is still able to attract a third of the national audience during prime time hours (RTÉ, 2005) but this proportion is down from 42 per cent in 1998, just before the launch of TG4 and TV3. Dozens of other cable- and satellite-delivered channels are also competing for audience share, though this is not yet formally measured. When Digital Terrestrial Television finally rolls out, after the initial experimental phase that is scheduled to begin in 2007, that number will undoubtedly increase (for background to the development of digital television in Ireland, see Corcoran, 2004).

Ireland has a weak regulatory regime for overseeing the funnelling of money into broadcasting. The Broadcasting Commission of Ireland (BCI) is committed, like so many other European regulators influenced by the American *laissez-faire* model, to what is called 'light touch' regulation of how broadcasters' performance matches their promises, and to continually increasing the number of radio and television channels that must operate within this small media economy. Throughout the neo-liberal 1990s, the BCI was more concerned with the question of whether the market could sustain the growth of new broadcasting licences, rather than whether the Irish public sphere actually needed more radio and television channels. This tendency favours the agenda of the advertising industry and the business sector's appetite for more ways to access consumers, though the language used to justify it is often couched in terms of 'increasing viewer and listener choice'.

It remains to be seen what path will be followed by the promised new regulator, the Broadcasting Authority of Ireland, announced by the government in draft legislation in September 2006, as it sets out to oversee both public service and private broadcasting sectors in a unitary regulatory system. The challenge is made more acute by the fact that public broadcasting in Ireland is financed by a combination of licence fees and commercial revenue. In much of Europe, including Ireland, public broadcasting is now trying to withstand a combined ideological, political and commercial assault, driven by new lobbies, hostile to the idea of a licence fee, that have sprung up in the wake of deregulation. One hears more frequently the notion that paying for television from the public purse is becoming obsolete, that it should be replaced by direct subscription and commercial funding. The assumption that a market model is best, struggles for supremacy over the notion that an informed citizenry needs a healthy public sphere, nourished by a well-funded media space where public opinion thrives, where a diversity of viewpoints on life flourish in a broad range of fiction and non-fiction television genres. Many of the newly arrived channels interpret their relationship with their audience solely in terms of the demographic needs of their advertisers. Challenges to the very idea of a public culture have become widespread, as they have decades earlier in the evolution of broadcasting in the US. In fact, the local battles for advantage in contemporary Ireland resonate with all the public– private tensions that exist at a global level. How did we get to this juncture?

Ireland's proximity to Britain, and its sharing of a common language, are important historical factors in the relationship between broadcasters and audiences in Ireland. Overspill from transmitters in Northern Ireland and the west of England has been part of the Irish experience of television from the very beginning (Horgan, 2001). As new technologies of distribution arrived – cable, microwave, deflectors (legal and illegal) and satellite – British television channels reached ever deeper into Irish towns and countryside. A ministerial proposal in the 1970s to set up a second national television channel, which would in effect retransmit a selection of BBC programmes, was abandoned in the face of overwhelming survey evidence that most Irish people wanted a second RTÉ channel in preference to wider access to British television, however worthy the selection of content might be. A clear indication of how far broadcasting policy has changed since then – and perhaps also the structures of cultural nationalism – can be seen in the launch of TV3 in 1998, backed by a consortium of Irish entrepreneurs and CanWest Global, a Canadian media company based in Winnipeg, owning a string of television channels across Canada, as well as channels in Australia and New Zealand. Foreign ownership of TV3 took yet another turn in 2000 with the purchase of a 45 per cent stake in the company by Granada Television, which was then involved in a bid to merge with Carlton and become the backbone of a restructured ITV system in Britain.

Public service broadcasting in Ireland now found itself having to adjust to direct foreign investment in television in Ireland. RTÉ had already been operating for a long time in one of the most competitive same-language areas in the world, and holding its own in audience share. Competition from British channels, some of it the result of terrestrial overspill and some carried by cable, reduced the size of RTÉ's potential audience but did not seriously skew the field of resources available for public broadcasting. No other broadcasting interest was attacking the idea of public funding for television and there was no serious rival within Ireland for advertising revenue or the licence fee income. But in the 1990s, very active competition for television resources began to come into play. This happened first at the distribution level, with global companies arriving to expand both cable (US-based NTL and Liberty) and satellite (News Corporation's BSkyB) services. More Irish people are now able to purchase access to a range of non-Irish television channels via foreign-based distribution companies. Then some British channels began to sell airtime directly to advertisers for 'opt-outs' aimed at Irish viewers. For anyone watching these developments, especially those in the independent television production sector, keen to see if the media economy in Ireland would be able to sustain, even expand, the production of Irish content to counteract a rising imbalance between local and global news and entertainment, the arrival of TV3 was to be a massive disappointment (Corcoran, 2004: 216).

Conclusion

One positive development over the last decade has been the success of efforts to reduce disparities in television reception across the Border, a situation that left many people in Northern Ireland (especially in Belfast and parts of Counties Down, Antrim and Armagh) unable to receive very much insight through television into life in the Republic. This was because engineering restrictions placed on the power and orientation of antennae near the Border, such as Claremont Cairn, and the lack of RTÉ transposers within Northern Ireland, prevented the transmission of RTÉ programmes northwards. These restrictions were gradually eased, as a result of discussions at the Forum for Peace and Reconciliation, the Anglo-Irish Inter-Governmental Conference and especially during the negotiations that led to the signing of the Good Friday Agreement in 1998. The Irish language provisions of the Agreement also allowed for the extension into Northern Ireland of the signal of TG4 (which was launched two years prior to this as Teilifís na Gaeilge), where it now broadcasts to about 90 per cent of homes from Divis Mountain, a few miles outside Belfast.

The ending of what might be called a form of cultural partitionism is creating a genuine all-island audiovisual space that has the potential to increase mutual understanding between the different socio-political groupings on the island and accelerate the process of post-colonial reconciliation. We can get a glimpse of the potential here in Graham Spencer's study of the impact of television news on the Northern Ireland peace negotiations. Television has played a central role in political exchanges throughout the peace process, as political participants routinely used it as a communication conduit and 'signally system' (Spencer 2004: 605) to convey positions, responses and proposals as part of a process of dialogue, accelerating diplomatic communication and moving information in the direction of groups beyond the normal reach of governments. Television's reach into multiple audiences at once makes it a valuable mechanism for enabling parties to establish markers for where they may be headed, set out bargaining positions and exert leverage within the broader set of disagreements that separate them. Spencer concludes that the relationship between television news and the peace process is complex and subject to a range of variables, producing both positive and negative outcomes, but it can bring an emotional and dramatic power to diplomacy that often challenges political secrecy and intransigence.

The relationship between television in Ireland and television operating at a global level is obviously asymmetrical, because of Ireland's size. Global market forces are important in structuring this relationship, particularly the trend towards media conglomeration and the spread of the values linked with market liberalisation. Concentration of ownership has a major impact not only on television entertainment, but perhaps more importantly on the supply of international television news, a crucial resource for Irish people's understanding of the wider world beyond the island. Because of resource limitations, Irish broadcasters have only a limited opportunity to modify their dependence on the small number of wholesale services that dominate international news.

Global companies play an increasing role in the delivery of vast amounts of television to Irish homes, via cable, MMDS, satellite and broadband, and this role will change significantly as the switchover to digital television accelerates. Digital distribution systems are already having an impact on specific areas of audience interest, such as children's television. But European forces also play a role in shaping Irish television, including RTÉ's membership of the European Broadcasting Union, where public service values, as well as actual television programmes, are shared in a cooperative system, and European Commission directives like Television Without Frontiers, which urges quotas for European content.

One of the central tenets of globalisation theory is the notion that once-powerful production centres have lost their dominant position in the new global media structure, which has now become multi-nodal, offering greater opportunities for information flow to be diversified in many directions. Does this mean increased opportunities for Irish television companies to export television programmes to parts of the huge, wealthy Anglophone world? Attempts have been made in the past to find new audiences for Irish content, particularly through Celtic Vision and Tara Television. The former was launched in Boston in 1995 to relay mainly RTÉ programming, aiming initially for the East Coast of the US. This was a high-risk venture, given the difficulty of persuading cable operators to carry the new service, and it collapsed after a few years. Tara Television was launched in 1996 as a joint venture between RTÉ and United International Holdings/TCI, relaying a mix of RTÉ programming into Britain via satellite from Dublin. It was wound up in the High Court in 2002 after incurring losses of €17 million. This underscores the difficulty of generating some 'reverse thrust' in the process of globalisation. But it is possible that if there is sufficient political will to ensure that funding is always made available to resource a vibrant television production sector, more opportunities will arise for using new technologies to share local content with the Irish diaspora in various parts of the world.

Chapter 2

Irish print and broadcast media: the political, economic, journalistic and professional context

John Horgan
Paul McNamara
John O'Sullivan

The unique influences that have shaped the production of print and broadcast media in modern Ireland are a mixture of geographical, political, and cultural. In more recent times, there have been other influences, shared with media in the developed world generally: technological change, commercialism, and the enhanced competition, especially from niche media, in the digital age. Modern Irish media – in the sense of media aimed at a mass market rather than at a political constituency – date essentially from the establishment of the *Irish Independent* in 1905. Although the first radio station was established in 1926 by the new government of the Irish Free State, broadcasting was not effectively freed from the shackles of direct state control for another half a century (Horgan, 2001).

Penetration of the Irish market by British media, print and broadcast, has been one of the unusual features of the Irish media system. In the early years of the state various governments attempted, Canute-like, to turn back this tide with various forms of censorship. The digital revolution, and the internet in particular, have been the death-knell for this attempt to maintain cultural purity and commercial exclusivity, but a pattern had already been well established. The rising prosperity of the 1990s saw a series of fresh and aggressive assaults on the Irish market by UK titles, which now account for roughly one in four of every daily morning newspaper sold, and one in three of Sunday titles, where the market is especially competitive (Truetzschler, 2002: 1). Research carried out for the Commission on the Newspaper Industry (1996) suggested that Irish newspapers suffered from a number of competitive disadvantages, including a very high cost base. It also suggested that there was a substantial group of Irish media consumers – largely young, male, working class and in their twenties – who consumed little or no Irish media, preferring a diet of UK tabloids and, in broadcast media, the British ITV channel.

Nor has this competition been confined to popular or populist media. Its effects elsewhere can be gauged from the fact that approximately ten per cent of the total circulation of the *Sunday Times* was, by the middle of the first decade of the twenty-first century, accounted for by copies sold on the island of Ireland, North and South.

Throughout this period of increasing internationalisation and competition in the Irish media market, indigenous media have themselves been under-going a number of sea changes. In Northern Ireland, the confessional character of much of the print media, reflecting the deep religious and political divisions in that society, was unaffected either by the advent of commercial television in 1959 or by the change in ownership of the highly successful *Belfast Telegraph* in the 1960s, when it was purchased from its Irish family owners by the multi-national Thomson organisation (it was later to go through a number of other hands). In the Republic, however, the purchase of a controlling interest in the Independent group by the young Irish entre-preneur A. J. F. O'Reilly in 1973, and the transfer of ownership of the *Irish Times* to a trust in the following year, set the scene for a new fluidity in the media. Some newspapers died; new titles appeared, most notably in the Sunday marketplace, and competition became ever more intense, leading eventually to the extinction of the entire Irish Press group – then comprising three newspapers – in 1995.

This period of flux was accompanied by a reinvigoration of journalism, prompted in part by the high drama and politics of the Northern Ireland conflict which, in its most intense phase between 1969 and 1998, absorbed huge quantities of media resources and public attention. By the mid-1980s, in the view of one commentator, the quality of Irish political journalism had risen considerably. 'Investigative journalism began to develop from the late sixties, as it did also on television. A race of specialists appeared and multiplied – political correspondents, economic correspondents, experts on local affairs, health, education and so on. Their knowledge of their own subjects is impressive' (Chubb, 1984: 80). The same period, however, also spawned decisions by both Irish (1971 and 1972) and UK (1988) governments to restrict the freedom of broadcast journalists to report certain aspects of the Northern Ireland conflict. These restrictions remained in force in one form or another until 1994 and the legal framework under which they were implemented in the Republic was not finally removed until the passage of the 2002 Broadcasting Act (Horgan, 2004).

Another important influence on the production of print and broadcast media culture in Ireland has occurred via the media education system where journalism textbooks from Britain and the USA are widely used because of the dearth of Irish titles. This situation partly arises for reasons of scale. The total number of journalism students in Ireland at any given time does not justify, on financial grounds, the publication of an extensive range of Irish journalism textbooks. As a result, the influence of British and North American texts is significant. Journalism education at university degree level only came on stream in Ireland in the early 1990s, whereas journalism has been offered at third level in the USA for over 100 years, giving rise to an extensive back-catalogue of journalism textbooks and academic media analysis. Ireland is in the early stages of making good this intellectual lacuna.

The last quarter of the twentieth century and the early years of the twenty-first have seen the emergence of three distinct trends affecting both the production and content of Irish media. The first has been one of internal consolidation, the second has been one of increasing foreign ownership. The third – dealt with later in this chapter – has been technological and web-related. The first has been characterised by consolidation that has taken place particularly in the field of regional media, where an established proprietor like the Examiner group in Cork has moved to acquire media properties both in its own hinterland and elsewhere, and where existing regional media have consolidated their spheres of interest by launching different types of publication – often free-sheets – to offset perceived competitive threats from other titles.

The more dramatic trend, however, has been in the frequent acquisitions of Irish media, particularly but not exclusively regional print and broadcast media, by non-Irish interests. The national and regional broadcast media, after a shaky start following liberalisation in 1988, have become increasingly attractive to predators, and Today FM, the sole national commercial radio station until the expansion of Newstalk 106 in November 2006, has, together with a number of other regional print and broadcast media, been in the ownership of the Scottish Media Group for a number of years. This trend was discussed with some concern in 2003 by a Forum on Broadcasting, but, under EU law, which places few obstacles – apart from anti-monopoly legislation – in the way of the purchase of media entities within any EU state, is likely to continue. There are, it should be noted, some cross-media ownership restrictions, which prohibit media operators (defined as publishers, production companies, cable operators, etc., but excluding internet providers) from having more than a 27 per cent share in any broadcasting company. In these circumstances, the Broadcasting Commission of Ireland (BCI) has adopted a dual strategy. It takes into account the structure of the market when making licensing decisions and when ratifying (or declining to ratify) any major change in the shareholdings in independent broadcast companies. It has also created a significant regulatory framework in relation to content – notably in regard to the required proportion of news and current affairs – which is enforced on all broadcasting entities. In addition, the national Competition Authority 'when examining media mergers (in cooperation with the BCI regarding broadcasting, and with the [Department of Communications]), also takes into account any potential impact on the competitiveness of the market' (Kevin et al., 2004: 106).

The purchase of the important Leinster Leader group of regional news-papers by the UK-based Johnston group in 2006 was another indication of growing foreign interest in Irish media, and in the profitability in particular of regional media at a time when national media are facing increasing competition from digital rivals and from a fragmentation of the advertising marketplace. A similar trend has become evident in the print media in Northern Ireland, with the UK Mirror Group involved in purchasing one important title, and with consolidation of a growing number of regional titles under the ownership of the Alpha Group, controlled by the former Unionist MP, John Taylor, which has also acquired five regional titles in the Republic since 2003. Effectively, five companies now account for a substantial proportion of the regional press in the island, marking a dramatic change from the situation some decades ago in which most were controlled by small family-owned businesses, often allied with jobbing printers.

In the technological area, apart from web-related developments, the past decade has seen important changes. In relation to journalism practice and process, there have been major developments including the general acceptance of direct input and the new possibilities in relation to illustration, typography and layout. There has also been an accelerated rationalisation of plant and capacity in the print media, with both the *Irish Independent* and the *Irish Times* moving out of the centre of Dublin to printing plants on the outskirts of the city, where high-speed presses now produce not only their own titles but do contract printing for magazines and a number of regional titles. Similarly, UK-based titles have increasingly transferred and centralised the printing operations for the Irish titles on to greenfield sites in the Republic. The unit cost issue highlighted by the Commission on the Newspaper Industry in 1996 has generated one cost-cutting measure which would, at that time, have been greeted with incredulity: the *Sunday World* and the *Kerryman* – one a national Sunday tabloid headquartered in Dublin, the other a profitable regional published in the south west of the country, and both owned by Independent News and Media – are now printed on presses in Belfast which are home to the same organisation's *Belfast Telegraph* and *Sunday Life*.

The role in all of this of the Independent group has frequently given rise to comment. Its expansion into the regional newspaper market in Ireland – which is substantial – was actually organised before the O'Reilly acquisition in 1973 and before the development of strong competition legislation. It has been effectively precluded by competition law from increasing its share of the regional market, and it was prevented – also by competition law – from increasing a minority stake which it purchased in the *Sunday Tribune* as a way of defending its market share against the UK Sunday titles. It was briefly involved in the Irish Press group before the collapse of that enterprise (although this venture might have been adjudged anti-competitive by the Competition Authority), but has maintained a substantial share in the Sunday marketplace and – since the demise of the *Evening Press* – has an effective evening paper monopoly over much of the country with the *Evening Herald*. Its board has, however, capitalised on its substantial and reliable cash-flow to build up an extensive portfolio of overseas media properties, which makes it one of the most successful Irish companies in its field and which, on occasion, gives rise to fears about the implications, for media diversity generally, of its strength in the Irish marketplace (O'Toole, 1996). Its most audacious – and one of its most expensive – acquisitions, mentioned earlier, was that of the *Belfast Telegraph* in 2004, a purchase which might not have been permitted had that newspaper been operating in the same political, legal and fiscal structure as the titles controlled by the group in the Republic of Ireland. The group owns four of the 11 Irish national newspaper titles and has stakes in three others. More recently in 2006, it launched a free morning newspaper – *Herald AM* – to counter the threat posed by *Metro*, another free morning newspaper promoted by the UK Daily Mail group and in which the *Irish Times* also has a minority stake.

It is estimated that the Independent group publishes about 80 per cent of all indigenous national newspapers in the Republic (Truetzschler 2004: 124). However, this should be qualified by the important consideration that its position in the total marketplace falls short of dominance because of the large proportion of the Irish market accounted for by UK-owned titles. Its board has grown the business substantially since 1973 and it now operates on four continents in countries other than Ireland, such as Britain, South Africa, India, Australia and New Zealand. In 2004 it published over 165 newspaper and magazine titles which, taken together, had a weekly circulation in excess of 13.5 million copies. It also operated 53 online sites, which have 95 million page impressions per month in aggregate. The group's assets were valued at US$4.2 billion in 2004 when it had over 11,000 employees worldwide. In 2005 it posted an operating profit of €312 million.

It is credited with launching the so-called compact or dual edition of broadsheet newspapers. This innovation has increased circulation figures for *The Independent* in Britain, which is owned by the group, and the *Irish Independent* in Ireland. A convenient paradox is that the persistent – although reducing – losses at the London Independent can now be offset, for tax purposes, against the substantial profits earned by the *Belfast Telegraph* acquisition. The trust structure and the family trust ownership of a key 29.9 per cent shareholding in the Independent group would appear to insulate both these enterprises against any possibility of foreign ownership, but no such guarantees exist in the case of other media entities.

The liberalisation of the market for broadcast media since 1988 has been slower in the national arena than in the regional or local. The first national radio competitor for Radio Telefís Éireann, Radio Ireland, suffered a number of vicissitudes and did not achieve profitability for more than a decade, after several changes of ownership and re-branding (it is now Today FM). Plagued by financial difficulties, the national competitor for the State's public service television network, TV3, did not go on-air until 1998, and did not achieve profitability until 2005. The majority shareholdings in two of the national competitors to RTÉ are held by non-Irish companies. The third, Newstalk 106, is controlled by Irish interests but achieved national coverage only at the end of 2006. The majority ownership of TV3 is non-national.

The slowness with which national commercial broadcasting took root may partly explain the fact that – in sharp contrast to the situation in many other countries where market liberalisation has taken place – the channels operated by the national public service broadcaster, Radio Telefís Éireann, have maintained an exceptionally high market share – 40 per cent for the three national radio channels, and 43.2 per cent for the three national TV channels (including TG4, the Irish-language station) (www.Medialive.ie). Other factors have been a successful and proactive strategy adopted by RTÉ, enhanced by the rapid increase in population and household formation (and the associated increase in licence fee income) and a government decision to link the licence fee to inflation, subject to the achievement of certain performance targets.

The next phase of broadcasting development is the initiating of digital terrestrial television, piloted in 2007 and to spread throughout the country thereafter. The implications of this for broadcasting production are, as yet, unclear. The proliferation of channels in a content-intensive medium may result in the importation of more programming content and in the frequent rebroadcasting of material.

On-line journalism

Irish journalism and journalistic culture have yet fully to embrace the concept of online journalism, but, thus far, this has not been an unreasonable position to take. Criticism of classic media for failing to implement the latest interactive features or 'webby' content makes good copy for some 'with-it' media commentators and academics. Mark Deuze's classification of interactivity in on-liine media serves as a useful framework for conceptualising how journalism has responded to new possibilities, and it is tempting to take this a stage further with an approach that condemns new media laggards (Deuze 2003). But (and journalism students are sometimes quicker to grasp this) interactive technologies may not be the whole story, and many in the audience may not seek to contribute actively. As it is, print edition readerships have grown or held up well in recent years despite circulation declines in some titles, and publishers and journalists have not yet suffered the same shrinking of audience and defections to other media as seen in the USA – a shrinkage which has given an added impetus to the sometimes frantic and always expensive search for web-based solutions to revenue problems. It is this position of relative comfort that may have contributed to the opening of a gap between Irish online news and national news websites in Britain, locus of some of the radical developments in online news, and North America.

Irish journalists were among the pioneers among news outlets taking to the web, when the *Irish Times* first went online in 1994, with an ambitious vision to extend the nature and reach of its journalism. However, in the intervening period, the online arm of the organisation, rebranded as ireland.com, suffered cutbacks and lay-offs as part of a retrenchment that typified the global dot.bust reassessment of digital media. Now, in common with other national and many regional titles, its main activity is the re-purposing of existing content for consumption on PCs and other digital devices, with the principal added offerings of an extensive archive, as part of its subscription service, and breaking news. Similarly, RTÉ's news offerings online, while providing a vast resource of partially archived sound, vision and text, provide little more than heretofore generated by news producers. While Irish media clearly were aware of the strategic issues and the potential to move beyond the concept of an 'online newspaper', experience has demonstrated the durability of established modes (O'Sullivan, 2005a). This was not the vision of Peter Winter, quoted by the *Irish Times* in 1996, who commented:

> The first thing I did when I became interim CEO of New Century Network (an online development consortium of leading US newspaper groups) was to forever ban the phrase online newspaper. It is a bankrupt concept. It is highly fallacious and it is very dangerous to think in those terms. Replicating electronically what you do in print is a bit like taking a video camera to a Broadway play and imagining you are in the business of television production. This is a new medium. (Breen, 1996: 11).

News outlets figure prominently among native sites in Irish web audience rankings (and are also likely to be syndicated, for example via newsfeeds, in the web behemoths such as Yahoo! and Google), but it is clear that the market remains immature, with inconsistent and sporadic audience metrics and little progress towards the web's integration into media planning for advertisers, and with patchy adherence to auditing (Alexa Internet, 2007).

Irish media are not uniquely netphobic, and relative inertia in the face of high-blown rhetoric of radical media reform is characteristic of many news organisations internationally (Van der Wurff and Lauk, 2005). But leading players in so-called old media in Britain, whence much Irish news culture and practice thus far have been derived, have been busy experimenting. *BBC News*, the *Guardian*, *The Times* and the *Daily Telegraph* are all well advanced with significant offerings of content rich in hyperlinks, with blogs by editors and journalists, with citizen media, with opportunities for readers to comment and engage in meaningful debate, with multimedia, including podcasting by print organisations, and with ways of connecting with new audiences through the provision of links into social media. Simple expressions of how far things have come are the invitation to readers of the *Daily Telegraph*, heretofore perhaps perceived as the embodiment of waning values, to post its stories to such novel media exotics as del.icio.us, Digg, NewsVine, NowPublic and Reddit, or the *Daily Mail* offering readers a text form with selected stories in which they can post their comments. Relaunches of ireland.com, RTE.ie and Independent.ie show signs of a slow catch-up. Perhaps the most significant breach of old media mores has been the inclusion of journalists' blogs in ireland.com. And Independent.ie radically promises more opportunity to comment on stories, though it appears this has yet to be implemented significantly. For now, most changes are presentational.

Thus far, British-based publications that have launched Irish print operations or editions have not similarly extended their coverage on the web. The *Irish Daily Star*, the *Irish Daily Mirror*, the *Irish Sun*, and the *Irish Daily Mail* have chosen so far to maintain the online focus on their principal, British titles or digital spin-offs, although the *Sunday Times* Irish edition stories are carried on a (rather obscure) headline listing on the vast Times Online site.

Nor do Irish news consumers, becoming more at home in a media landscape where interactivity and intertextuality are the norm, have to look abroad to find new media features. If national media have been slow to adapt, the signs are that other sections of the new media ecology may move more quickly (and it may be remembered that national media were the last, by some distance, to make the investment and adopt changed work practices necessary to implement digital print technologies).

This overview does not afford space for a detailed taxonomy, but new developments can be observed at several levels. Within professional journalism, the specialist irishhealth.com has demonstrated its ability to augment conventional news and features with individual customisation, multimedia, and an array of interactive features, from personalised health calculators, to active discussions, to 'Rate My Hospital'. Niche publications with well-focused target audiences have long been a feature of online news, with entities such as the *Irish Emigrant* and the technophile electric news.net early leaders. As blogging, message boards, and government and corporate online publishing take root and grow, and as internet adoption accelerates with the switch to broadband, it is becoming clear that the colonies which Irish print and broadcast organisations have established online are at risk of becoming islands of static content, where reader or viewer comment is at best tolerated and at worst suppressed. The latter conclusion is supported by a comparison of broadcast media's vehicles of controlled interactivity, such as RTÉ's *Questions and Answers* on television, or *Liveline* on radio, with their websites, which do not permit audience input, even though the medium could so easily facilitate it.

Such a position may be anathema to online editors and other champions of new media, but the contrast certainly raises fundamental questions concerning core journalistic ethics and values. It is tempting to conclude that most practitioners are sceptical of any mission aimed at breaking the divide between audience and news producer, and integrating close scrutiny and dialogue, or of admitting bloggers to the fold, other than as curiosities worth covering as a news story. One of the most succinctly expressed responses to such a notion has been 'you don't hand the microphone to the rabble'. On a more prosaic level, journalists are also entitled to ask how they are to make the time for such activities. Such responses are not unique to Ireland, and are the subject of ongoing research that may formulate them more coherently, and there is an increasing body of literature that seeks to delineate the arguments in and around online journalism (Allen, 2005, Driscoll et al., 2005).

Ultimately, however, as with any other media, the discussion is touched in no small way by the peculiarities of Irish defamation law, which has seen the removal of message board facilities from the *Irish Examiner*'s website and the posting of strict notices to users of online fora such as boards.ie.

Journalism in Ireland

As the commercial and competitive aspects of Irish media assume greater importance in an increasingly globalised economy, more attention is being paid to the nature of Irish journalism, its special characteristics, its strengths and its weaknesses. These commercial pressures have had their own impact on journalism. Over the last two decades, there has been a substantial increase in business, personal finance, consumer, property, technology and travel news in print and broadcast media. Increased allocation of space in the newshole (the total space occupied by news) to specific commercial and consumer areas is often driven by their capacity to attract advertising revenue. For instance, the property supplements of national newspapers have grown in size and expanded their focus in recent years. One issue of *The Irish Times* in September 2006 contained 74 broadsheet pages of property editorial and advertising, a record for that newspaper.

The consumerist orientation of Irish society has resulted in noticeable increases in pagination in Irish newspapers. A snapshot survey by one of the authors of 11 national daily and Sunday newspapers published in March and April 2004 showed that, on average, each issue contained just over 100 pages, a clear reflection of a strong advertising market. Some newspapers regularly offer free music CDs or books at reduced cost to entice potential purchasers, increase circulation figures and consequently attract more advertising.

In some cases, commercial pressures to boost profits and shareholders' dividends impact on journalists when they are expected to increase output by cutting corners. This is achieved 'by employing journalists on short-term contracts, by demanding extraordinary rates of productivity - sheer volume of copy – from reporters, by reducing and, in some cases, effectively eliminating the sub-editing function – and so on. There is less on-the-ground reportage and research.' (Brady, 2004) The casualisation of news workers by refusing them security of tenure is often driven by economic factors. Tenured staff are more expensive and much more difficult to dismiss. Permanent staff are perceived to be in a better position to take an editorial stance independent to that of their news organisation than are freelance news workers whose contracts may be terminated at short notice and with relative ease.

Changes in media production, according to Tovey and Share, are 'not just a matter of technological evolution. Typically they are tied up with conflicts over power . . . public service broadcasters . . . have been forced to adopt the methods of commercial broadcasters, including new technologies and work practices.' They cite the work of Hazelkorn (1996), which examined changes in work practices at RTÉ. She found that:

- Demarcation between journalists, presenters and engineers had broken down, resulting in the elimination of some jobs and the creation of others, such as IT experts and 'multi-skilled' engineers;
- RTÉ used early retirement, redeployment, retraining and alterations to staffing structures to effect the necessary cost efficiencies demanded by competition and commercialisation;
- Casualisation and flexibilisation of the workforce enabled more people to make more programmes more cheaply;
- Women benefited disproportionately as the number of 'creative' and administrative jobs increased, whereas the number of male-dominated craft jobs declined;

- The amount of 'independent' production sector programming used by public service broadcasters increased;
- Such output typically involved cheap and cheerful infotainment fare such as entertainment news, and cookery, holiday and home improvement programming (Tovey and Share, 2000: 380–1).

This increasing commercialism does not, however, appear to have had a substantial impact on the ideological profile of Irish journalists themselves. According to Truetzschler: 'Most Irish newspapers are politically conservative and have a middle class orientation' (2004: 116). However, it is important to distinguish the political positions of journalists from those of the organisations that employ them. Corcoran (2004) conducted a survey of the political preferences of Irish journalists in 1997, based on a questionnaire developed by a team of international scholars led by Patterson and Donsbach. Their survey had been carried out earlier by teams of researchers in the USA, Britain, Germany, Sweden and Italy, and identified a number of trends. On the political spectrum, Irish journalists identified more with the left than the right. On a scale where right was seven, left was one and four was centre, the mean score for Irish journalists was 3.15. Only the Italian journalists considered themselves more liberal. The mean scores for the other countries were: Italy (3.01); USA (3.32); Germany (3.39); Sweden (3.45); and Britain (3.46). Whereas 11 per cent of Italian journalists placed themselves on the extreme left, only 3.6 per cent of Irish journalists did so. While 68 per cent of Irish journalists placed themselves left of centre, no journalist placed herself on the extreme right.

Irish journalists perceived the news organisations they worked for to be more conservative than themselves. Only the Italian journalists saw their news organisations as being clearly left of centre at 3.76. The other countries scored as follows: USA (3.98); Ireland (4.22); Sweden (4.22); Germany (4.27); and Britain (4.36).

Irish journalists saw themselves as substantially more liberal than their audiences. The difference between Irish journalists' mean position and that of their audiences was more than a full point (3.15 v 4.48). This was the largest perceived difference of the six countries surveyed. The only other country to record a gap of more than a full point was the USA (3.32 v 4.47). The gap between journalists and audiences was smallest in Sweden (3.45 v 4.11) with Italy and Britain showing slightly larger gaps (Corcoran 2004: 30).

The ownership of Irish media is in few hands and the editorial position of much of the industry is generally held to be centre-right. There is no correlation between Irish journalists' political beliefs and those of the news organisations for which they work. A more diverse ownership pattern in the media might give rise to a wider range of political positions therein. It would appear that Irish journalists' political partisanship is not relevant in determining the jobs they hold. Some 43 per cent of Irish journalists perceive a distance between themselves and their audiences and 44 per cent believe that journalists and the public do not share similar views.

> They see no reason to tailor their journalism so that it fits with the ideas and values expressed by the audience . . . a significant proportion of Irish journalists see themselves as having an agenda-setting role in terms of popularising ideas and values that may be at variance with the views of their audience (Corcoran, 2004: 35).

A comparison of which political parties were supported by the public and which by journalists indicated that the gap journalists perceived between themselves and their audiences was real. The support levels of the public and journalists respectively for Irish political parties in 1997 are shown in table 2.1.

Table 2.1 **Support levels for Irish political parties**

Party	Public Support (%)	Journalistic Support (%)
Fianna Fáil	44	5.6
Fine Gael	27	10.3
Labour Party	11	34.6
Progressive Democrats	4	2.8
Green Party	4	6.5
Others	11	2.8
No Preference	n/a	37.4
Totals (rounded)	100	100

Source: Corcoran, 2004: 36

Thus the largest party in the state, Fianna Fáil, was significantly under-represented among journalists and the second largest party, Fine Gael, was also underrepresented. Furthermore, the largest of the small parties, the socialist Labour Party, was significantly overrepresented among journalists. However, Corcoran notes that: 'the largest single group of journalists claim no party preference, probably because they see neutrality as a key element of their journalistic objectivity' (2004: 37). The degree to which this supposed neutrality can overlap with scepticism or even a predominantly negative attitude among print media journalists towards all political actors is explored in a later but no less relevant study which suggests that negativity could be interpreted 'as an indicator of increasing media malaise, in Ireland as elsewhere' (Brandenburg, 2005: 319).

In the early 1980s, Irish journalists were generally trusted and held in high esteem by the public. 'Compared with the British press, the Irish dailies are quite serious newspapers, nearer to the so-called quality British newspapers than to the populars' (Chubb 1984: 79). However, the situation began to change in the late 1980s when the British pop tabloids began to take a greater interest in the Irish market. They brought a different tradition, different practices and a different emphasis compared to Irish journalism. They pushed sport, sex and the cult of the celebrity and they pursued stories about the private lives of public people, something that had not been done previously in Ireland. One effect was to lower the reputation of all newspaper journalists in the eyes of the public. Broadcast and newspaper journalists are now viewed differently by the public. According to Coakley: 'a 1981 survey showed that the Irish were more likely than the "average" European to express confidence in the police, the civil service, parliament and the press (Fogarty/ Ryan and Lee, 1984: 179, 243) . . . By 2001, the position had changed . . . levels of trust in television and radio are high by European standards, but the print media are treated with some suspicion'. Eurobarometer figures indicated that, respectively, percentage levels of trust versus mistrust were: 78/18 for television; 77/19 for radio; and 53/40 for press. Newspapers in 2001 were treated with a significant degree of suspicion (Coakley, 2005: 57–8).

Irish journalists in general are a highly educated but predominantly middle-class group, according to Corcoran (2004). The fact that admission criteria to journalism and media degrees typically demand high previous academic achievement works against those from disadvantaged backgrounds. There is also resistance among some journalists to pre-entry journalism education at undergraduate or graduate level. They argue that journalism is essentially a non-academic pursuit, a trade rather than a profession. Some even suggest that the only education necessary for journalism is in skills-based areas such as shorthand and media production software. Corcoran's findings clearly indicate that the latter group is swimming against the tide. Mid-career training is not widely available to Irish journalists. The managers of news organisations are reluctant to fund such activities or grant news workers the time to participate in them. Where sanctioned, the emphasis tends to be on short how-to and technical courses rather than theoretical and reflexive ones, on developing production skills rather than reflective practitioners.

Media accountability

The traditional mutual wariness between media and other elites has been accentuated in recent years by the increasing propensity of the media to demand greater accountability from public figures, as well as by the trend – already mentioned – for the more populist media to explore the private lives of public figures (and occasionally their families) with less reserve than had traditionally been the case. At the same time, media generally have become increasingly irked by what they see as the restrictive nature of the laws on libel, aguing that these act as a curb on investigative reporting, and in this way affect the ability of the media to demand accountability from those in public life (Bourke, 2004).

Conversely, those outside the media have begun to draw attention to the fact that, almost uniquely in Western Europe at any rate, Irish media have few systems of accountability built into their own structures. Initially, this critique tended to be made by the trade union movement, particularly during a period of industrial unrest in the 1970s, when trade union leaders felt that the media were biased against them. More recently, the same sentiment has become more widespread among business and political elites, but it is expressed less frequently and with less force because politicians, in particular, to not want to acquire a reputation for media-bashing, given that the media are one of their key channels of communication with public opinion. Some of the harshest criticism, however, has come from within the media and, in one case, from a recently retired editor of the *Irish Times.*

> Journalism is one of the last functions without any system of public accountability – short of the courts – in this society. [Ireland] is the only western European state that does not have some sort of press council or ombudsman. As a result, Irish media can get away with a lot. There is little self-scrutiny. Supervision is frequently lax. Professional standards are sometimes low and are often tolerated on high. There is virtually no reference to international best practice . . . Most of the newspapers have learned how to say more or less what they want about people without getting themselves into legal trouble. A rich lexicon of journalistic euphemism (and some clever design stunts) have been developed that enables a publication to blast away at any chosen target – provided that considerations of fairness, propriety and balance can be put aside . . . Other considerations may be given short shrift – the methods employed by the journalist, the use of deception or illegality, the improper attribution of quotes, the eliding of the line between on-the-record and off-the-record, the invasion of privacy, hearing both sides of the story (Brady, 2004: 33).

Media accountability in Ireland has a varied history, and is different for the print and for the broadcast media. In the broadcast media, a Broadcasting Complaints Commission was set up by legislation in 1976, charged with examining complaints that broadcasters had breached any of the obligations laid on them under the broadcasting acts, particularly the obligations relating to impartiality. Despite its cumbersome procedures and the great length of time it took to arrive at decisions, this body achieved a certain measure of public credibility: it is required by law to publish its decisions in full in the

RTÉ Guide, which is owned by RTÉ and which is one of Ireland's largest circulation journals. Originally based entirely in, and staffed by, RTÉ itself, its administration and functions have now been transferred to the Broadcasting Commission of Ireland, successor to the Independent Radio and Television Commission which was set up to oversee the liberalisation of the broadcast media marketplace that was initiated in 1988.

In print media, although there is a substantial corpus of legislation governing its activities directly or indirectly, no corrective mechanisms of any significance exist. There is, within the National Union of Journalists, a procedure which hears complaints against members of the union for any alleged breach of professional ethics, but, in order to be processed, any complaint from a member of the public had to be sponsored by a union member. Not surprisingly, this mechanism has fallen into disuse. A number of newspapers, following practice in the USA, appointed 'Readers Representatives' in the early 1980s in an attempt to give speedy access by media consumers to an informal means of redress for innocent mistakes or editorial misjudgements. This initiative, however, did not really take root, and had been abandoned in all but a superficial sense within a few years. The debate has been a more live one at least since 1996, when the Commission on the Newspaper Industry suggested the appointment of a Press Ombudsman, who would have the dual function of (a) protecting media from expensive libel actions by affording complainants a low-cost method of securing correction, and (b) enhancing media credibility by importing a level of accountability into a profession that appeared increasingly to be guided by commercial instincts rather than by professional ethics.

While a number of public and private voices were raised in support of this concept, it evoked considerable hostility from the print media, where both proprietors and journalists felt that any statutory press council or press ombudsman would amount to an unwelcome curtailment by the state of the freedom of the press. The main pressure group for the print media in this instance, National Newspapers of Ireland, which had been campaigning for a number of years for reform of the libel laws, made it clear that even a hoped-for reform of libel would be too high a price to pay for the restrictions envisaged in any proposed press council. The existence of the voluntary Press Complaints Commission in the UK was held up as an example to be followed, rather than a council which would – both proprietors and journalists feared – be dominated by government

After some controversy, including the appointment of an Expert Group to examine the issues involved, government and industry agreed on an outline structure for a Press Council which would have independently nominated members but which would be recognised by statute – not least to protect it from actions for defamation which might be filed by journalists and others who might be the object of complaints from members of the public. Simultaneously, proposals to reform the law on libel were announced. Cabinet, however, felt that too much had been surrendered to the media, and instructed the Minister for Justice to prepare, in addition, a Privacy Bill, which was done: the original two-part understanding between government and media became a three-element equation, one element of which is seen by the media generally as seriously problematic. The texts of both a Defamation Bill and a Privacy Bill, introduced in the Dáil on 4 July 2006, were complex: lawyers described the Privacy Bill, in particular, as less a protection of individual rights than protecting 'the exercise, by a few, from a position of power and strength, of rights not realistically open to other citizens' (O'Rourke, 2006). Nonetheless, a Press Council has now been established by the industry, and the appointment of a Press Ombudsman is envisaged.

Conclusion

The pace of change in Irish media has accelerated out of all recognition in the last quarter of a century. The dominant mode of media landscape and its production and content has changed from static to dynamic. Issues which had not been raised before, or had been raised only fitfully, have surged to the forefront of public debate – issues of media diversity, media ownership, and media ethics among them. At national level, all media are facing new challenges, not least from non-indigenous and digital media, but also from an apparently inexorable trend of weakening circulation among national print media, despite increased investment and pagination. Further research is needed to ascertain the reasons for this vulnerability, or to evaluate, even approximately, some of the more obvious factors: the fragmentation of media audiences generally; a mismatch between media and public agendas; multiple and cross-ownership; de-regulation in the field of broadcast media; the migration of advertising to non-traditional media; and cost-cutting as a factor impinging on journalistic quality. Paradoxically, the regional media, both print and broadcast, show few signs of having been affected by these trends, and in many cases provide evidence of a vitality and profitability that does not seem to be guaranteed indefinitely to their national contemporaries. In all of this, the importance of economic factors is being recognised to a greater degree than ever before, and it may well be that media generally are disproportionately affected by any weakening of the strong economic cycle which has been apparent in Ireland – with a brief interlude in 2000–1 – since about 1995. Finally, current discussions about media accountability, which may in due course have substantial implications for both media production and content, indicate that a re-evaluation of the largely unexamined role of media in modern Irish society may be under way.

Chapter 3

Recent and current trends in Irish language broadcasting

Iarfhlaith Watson

Introduction

The last decade has proven remarkable for Irish language broadcasting. The most dramatic event was the establishment of an Irish language television station in 1996, but there have also been developments in radio and in programme funding in both the Republic of Ireland and Northern Ireland.

In the Republic of Ireland broadcasting in Irish is buttressed by positive attitudes towards the Irish language and the continuing role played by the Irish language as a symbol of Irish national identity. A majority of the population continue to regard the Irish language as an important component of Irish national identity. As a result, efforts by the state to promote Irish have been supported (or at least tolerated) by the public. Support is evident in people's declared willingness to send their children to an Irish-medium school (if there was such a school nearby) or people's willingness for the state to spend money on broadcasting in Irish (Ó Riagáin and Ó Gliasáin, 1984). This support appears to be quite normative insofar as the majority of the population who support the promotion of the Irish language believe that people should speak Irish – the emphasis here is on the word 'should'. In this context the existence of others who can speak Irish, as well as the effort by schools to teach Irish and the existence of Irish on television and radio (irrespective of the size of the audience) are sufficient for the purpose of maintaining the symbolic importance of the Irish language. In other words, the majority of the population are quite supportive of the Irish language – including broadcasting in Irish – but leave the actual practice of communicating in Irish to a minority.

As well as the majority of the population who support the symbolic existence of Irish, but can speak only a few words of it, there are two minorities who make use of broadcasts in Irish: one group uses the broadcasts to learn more Irish and another (about 10–15 per cent of the total population)[1] use them for entertainment or information. For these Irish speakers, their everyday use of Irish is functional not symbolic. Yet they are the embodiment of a national symbol. This nonetheless entitles them to no public respect, but rather occasional comments of equal measure of approval and disapprobation. The paradox between positive attitudes towards the Irish language and negative comments about Irish speakers may be because frustrations caused by learning Irish at school, which cannot be taken out on the Irish language itself, can be taken out on Irish speakers as the embodiment of the language.[2] A reason for this may be that the continued use of the Irish language, and not the individuals who speak it, is of symbolic importance. For the majority of the population, who do not speak Irish, the fact that some people continue to speak Irish is a more rational justification of Irish language broadcasting, which, to that majority, is primarily of symbolic importance. In other words, for the majority, the existence of Irish speakers is enough to keep the symbol alive. Beyond that there is a blinkered perspective. There is a hope that public investment in the Irish language is worthwhile – that Irish speakers actually speak Irish and that a reasonable number of people actually watch and listen to programmes in Irish. This means that there is very little desire that these audiences be measured.

In this chapter, although I shall provide some historical background, I shall focus on recent events in Irish language broadcasting. I shall place this discussion in the context of the role of Irish in national identity and I shall question the encroachment of a certain type of rationality, which emphasises counting and measuring, into most aspects of modern life, including broadcasting in Irish.

Irish language broadcasting in the twentieth century

From the beginning, the Irish language was part of the independent Irish state's effort to construct an Irish nation. This was part of the process of establishing its legitimacy. This effort included broadcasting programmes in Irish. There have been two aspects to broadcasting in Irish – providing a service for Irish speakers and encouraging people to learn some Irish or improve on or practise the few words of Irish they already have. Where these two aspects overlap or diverge is evident in the types of programmes broadcast. They overlap in programmes watched by Irish speakers of various abilities which entertain and inform Irish speakers while simultaneously promoting the use of Irish. The two aspects diverge in programmes targeted specifically at learners of the Irish language on the one hand, or at Irish speakers in a Gaeltacht (Irish speaking region) on the other.

In the decades after independence the emphasis was on restoring the Irish language to the position it had had as lingua franca several centuries before.

Restoration was part of the state's nation-building project. Although broadcasting in Irish was off to a slow start in the 1920s, during the following decades there were programmes in Irish such as *Is Your Irish Rusty?* and *Listen and Learn.* By the 1940s programmes in Irish accounted for ten per cent of broadcasting time on the national radio station Radio Éireann.

In the 1940s, broadcasting in Irish reached its zenith. Nonetheless Irish speakers were provided with a minimal radio service in Irish because the emphasis was on learners of the language. From the 1920s onwards there had been intermittent discussion of the possibility of establishing a separate Irish language radio station. One of the arguments against this was that radio ownership in the Gaeltachtaí (Irish speaking regions) was very low. When it was suggested that radios could be given away for free to the people in the Gaeltachtaí, it was argued that Irish speakers would be more likely to listen to the more popular programmes in English and that this would cause the English language to replace the Irish language in the Gaeltachtaí.[3] Several decades later in 1972 an Irish language radio station (Raidió na Gaeltachta) was established.

By this stage the technology had changed and radio had begun to be left behind by television. Domestic television broadcasting in Ireland had begun a decade earlier. Broadcasting in Irish was at an absolute minimum on the national television station during that decade and neither the function of teaching Irish nor of providing Irish speakers with a service was performed. By the 1960s the whole social, political and economic context had changed. The more conservative and protectionist ideology had been replaced by a more liberal ideology. The conservative ideology had been evident in many aspects of Irish society, including culture, politics and economics. The most relevant manifestation of this ideology was in the imposition of Irish on the public by means of the education system and radio. Although the conservative ideology had not gone, there had been a shift to a more liberal and social democratic ideology in which people were believed to have the right to certain choices. In the arena of broadcasting it was manifest in efforts in the 1950s to survey radio listeners. The survey results for Irish language radio programmes were never disclosed, but the evidence in the National Archives reveals that the listenership figures were very small indeed (see Watson, 2003: 33).

As well as being evident in counting and measuring, the new ideology was also manifest in the civil rights movement in the Gaeltacht. One of the results of this movement was the establishment of Raidió na Gaeltachta (see Hourigan, 2001). This was the first Irish language radio station and its emphasis was clearly on serving the Irish speakers in the Gaeltachtaí. This meant that there was a radical shift in one generation from a situation in which ten per cent of broadcasting time on the national radio station in the 1940s was in Irish (with a focus on learners), to a situation in the early 1970s in which a very low percentage of airtime on radio and television was devoted to Irish. With the emergence of Raidió na Gaeltachta there was a clear shift towards using broadcasting to serve Irish speakers rather than solely attempting to convert listeners to the Irish language. This shift away from compulsion, obligation and imposition was also clear in some of the changes made in the education system during the same period (see Kelly, 2002).

By this stage television was becoming the dominant broadcasting medium, and almost from the outset complaints were made that the Irish television station had too few programmes in Irish. As early as 1969 Doolan and others, who resigned from RTÉ, pointed to 'an leathcheal atá déanta le fada anois ar chláracha Gaeilge' ['the neglect from which Irish-language programmes have suffered' – author's translation] (Doolan et al., 1969: 295). By the 1970s there were organised public campaigns both to convince RTÉ to increase the amount of Irish on television and to convince the government to establish a separate Irish language television station. These campaigns continued until the early 1990s. Although some of the campaigners had campaigned for a Gaeltacht television station modelled on Raidió na Gaeltachta, the television channel which finally came on air in 1996 was primarily national rather than Gaeltacht, but it was based in a Gaeltacht locality and had some emphasis on the Gaeltacht in its programming.

Irish language broadcasting in the 1990s

The recent trend in broadcasting in Irish has been towards an acceleration in the quantity of Irish language radio and television programmes being produced, and in the number of radio and television channels on which these programmes are broadcast in both Northern Ireland and the Republic of Ireland. This increased programming has been focused specifically on Irish speakers, rather than on promoting the language amongst the rest of the population.

The most conspicuous development in Irish language broadcasting in recent years has been the establishment of TG4. The channel, which first came on air on 31 October 1996, was called Teilifís na Gaeilge (TnaG), but was renamed TG4 in a relaunch of the channel in 1999. The context into which TnaG/TG4 was born is radically different from the one into which Raidió na Gaeltachta emerged a generation earlier. The economic ontology of a neo-liberal ideology has gradually encroached on various political and social contexts to such an extent that it has led to the increasing individualisation of society. According to Silvia Carrel from the European Bureau for Lesser-Used Languages, 'the principle involved is to move closer to the citizen by satisfying his demands and respecting his rights, even from a linguistic point of view'

(Carrel, 1994: 16). However, this statement is more a reflection of the earlier liberal social democratic ideology. The intensification of the individualisation of society under neo-liberalism means that the individual, as the primary unit of society, is regarded as a rational actor whose actions are calculated. Often such calculation is synonymous with selfishness insofar as individuals are expected to act in their own best interests and those interests are understood as fundamentally economic. This is an 'instrumental rationality' (Habermas, 1979) or a means–ends rationality. There are times when individuals do not match these neo-liberal ontological expectations, for example when they act in their cultural, rather than economic, interests or when they act according to moral, rather than economic, principles. This mismatch between expectations and reality results in ontological dislocation. One manifestation of this dislocation is the tension between the various motives (cultural, symbolic) for broadcasting in Irish and the rational calculation of the success of its output according to criteria which differ radically from those initial motives.

In some domains, such as in business or bureaucracy, calculation and measurement are facilitative. If a business (perhaps even a broadcasting channel) has been set up to make profit, it makes sense to calculate the success of that business according to its profitability. Similarly, it makes sense to calculate the efficiency and effectiveness of a bureaucracy, such as a national health system, because without maximum efficiency and effectiveness people's health and lives are at further risk.[4] There are, however, other domains which have been invaded by this form of rationality, such as people's everyday lives, leisure activities or art (see Habermas, 1971).[5]

Another form of rationality which can be juxtaposed with rational calculation is rational debate. With this kind of rationality a course of action is decided upon, not as a result of measurement or calculation, but as a result of rational debate. The difference between the two forms of rationality is evident in the separate ontologies of many economic theories on the one hand and political and sociological theories on the other. The realm of politics, for example, has been invaded by instrumental rationality: rather than basing decisions on rational debate within the Houses of the Oireachtas (parliament), many decisions are taken outside these chambers. The government appoints an expert committee to make recommendations based on their rational calculations, and the Houses of the Oireachtas are treated as a rubber stamp rather than debating chambers. The difference is also evident in the media in the difference between the measurement-driven considerations of commercial broadcasting programmes and the democratic, cultural and educational considerations of public service broadcasting programmes. That tension is also evident in Irish language broadcasting.

I outlined above the shift that occurred in one generation between the 1940s and 1970s, from using Irish language broadcasting as an element in the policy of constructing an Irish-speaking nation to providing the Gaeltacht communities with a radio service in Irish, and also providing a minimal service on television for Irish speakers generally as well as for learners of Irish. In brief the shift of focus was mainly from nation to community. Another shift, which occurred in one generation, is evident when comparing Irish language broadcasting in the 1970s and 1990s. If the earlier shift in focus was from nation to community, the more recent shift has been from a focus on community to a focus on the individual. This focus is a more general approach evident not only in broadcasting but also more widely – for example, the focus on community was evident in various government efforts such as the establishment of Udarás na Gaeltachta in 1980 (its predecessor Gaeltarra Éireann had been established under the Gaeltacht Industries Act, 1957), or in the efforts throughout the 1970s to industrialise the Gaeltacht. This was clearly a manifestation of a focus of deliberation on how to facilitate the community. More recently the application of endeavours such as the Official Languages Act, 2003 to provide individuals with opportunities to use Irish is clearly a manifestation of a focus of deliberation on how to facilitate the individual Irish speaker.

This shift is not an absolute change, but rather a general trend. The focus on individualisation has meant an increasing emphasis on counting the number of individuals listening to radio or watching television. Such fixation on numbers can either distract the broadcaster from public service endeavours in a single-minded effort to maximise advertising revenue or it can help focus the mind on the best methods to fulfil the public service remit in a manner which attracts a large audience.

Irish language broadcasters are at a disadvantage in attracting advertising revenue because, while almost the whole population understands English, only 10 to 15 per cent of the population has relative fluency in Irish. This means that when, for example, Colum Kenny claimed that 'in July, its [TG4's] top 10 Irish-language programmes . . . were watched on average by 53,000 viewers' (Kenny, 2006) one is tempted to believe that this is in fact quite good given the small size of the Irish-speaking population. Irish language programmes on television are subject to this form of routine measurement because all the domestic television stations earn advertising revenue. For Irish language programmes the full force of market prerogatives are offset by public service obligations to the Irish language and dampened by public money acquired from television license fees and, in the case of TG4, direct state subvention. Although TG4 is not overly dependent on advertising revenue (more about money below), it has managed to increase its share of the national television audience each year since its inception in 1996. Starting from a very low figure of 0.3 per cent (a figure which has been disputed by TG4), its share of the national audience more than doubled the following year to 0.7 per cent, and again over the following three years to 1.5 per cent in 2000, and again to 3.2 per cent five years later in 2005. This percentage has been bolstered by the audiences attracted by the large number of English language programmes broadcast on TG4. Excluding *Euronews*, which is broadcast in the early hours of the morning, TG4 broadcasts for about 16 hours a day, about seven of which are in Irish. The large amount of broadcasting in English appears to be an intelligent technique of trying to appeal to the larger English-language market and thus hold on to some of that share of the market for programmes in Irish (most of which are subtitled in English). A very clear example of this type of follow-through audience is when the soap opera *Ros na Rún* (now broadcast on TG4) was first piloted on RTÉ1 after the main (English language) six o'clock evening news from 28 December 1992 until 3 January 1993. *Ros na Rún* attracted an average audience of 381,000 people or about a 12 per cent share of the national audience. The point is that *Ros na Rún* held on to an audience rather than attracting the audience all on its own. *Ros na Rún* has not attracted such a large audience in its years on TG4, primarily because TG4's potential audience is much smaller.

Even before TG4 began broadcasting it was announced that it would focus on young people (*Irish Times*, 17 April 1996). The emphasis on children has been very clear in the large number of cartoons produced in or dubbed into Irish, including very popular cartoons such as *Spongebob* and *Scooby Doo*. Anecdotal evidence suggests that children have been role-playing in Irish because of these cartoons. Those who were children when TG4 started in 1996 are now teenagers. The launch of the new teenage series *Aifric*, as part of TG4's ten-year celebration, suggests that TG4 is attempting to hold on to that audience as it grows up. The size of the project, which employs 100 crew and almost 150 actors, indicates the level of importance of this investment.

TG4 would not make such an investment lightly; in fact TG4 has claimed (www.tg4.ie) that it is one of the most efficient television stations in Europe because it broadcasts 16 hours of programmes a day for €28,000,000 from which it invests more than €15,000,000 a year in new Irish-language programmes from the private sector. According to TG4 this investment created 350 jobs in the independent film production sector. There are also 75 employees in TG4 headquarters. TG4 received this €28,000,000 from the government and commented that 'the channel's scope to develop and grow was constrained only by the limitations imposed by its ongoing low level of Exchequer funding' (TG4, 2006). The limitations of this funding are not restricted to the amount, but also to the manner of funding. That TG4 receives its annual subvention directly from government raises questions about its independence. However, TG4 also receives money from other sources, such as advertising, the Broadcasting Commission of Ireland, the Northern Ireland Film and Television Commission and in the form of programmes from RTÉ. The total received could come close to matching the government's subvention. For example, TG4 made €3,662,619 in commercial income in 2005 (TG4, 2006), was given the equivalent of €9,450,000 in programmes from RTÉ in 2005 (*Irish Independent,* 18 August 2006), was successful in having £3,000,000 worth of projects funded by the Northern Ireland Film and Television Commission in 2006 (*Sunday Independent,* 5 March 2006), and was awarded €3,000,000 by the Broadcasting Commission of Ireland for 16 specific projects (www.bci.ie).

The main Irish language television channel TG4 and the main Irish language radio channel Raidió na Gaeltachta both belong to RTÉ (the separation of TG4 from RTÉ will be discussed below). There is, however, a small Dublin-based independent Irish language community radio station called Raidió na Life, which began broadcasting in 1993. Raidió na Life was founded by Comharchumann Raidió Átha Cliath Teoranta (CRÁCT) and is primarily staffed by volunteers. In its application to the Independent Radio and Television Commission (forerunner of the Broadcasting Commission of Ireland) Raidió na Life stated that its programme policy was 'to reflect the broad range of interest of an urban population:– music alternative, Irish & European rock, traditional, jazz, classical and world: Talk: business, current affairs, environmental, local, international events, sports, arts etc. all through Irish' (www.irtc.ie [accessed in 2002]). It also claimed that its audience was 'Irish speakers of all ages, people interested in alternative music. Core audience of 14,000 in Dublin.' In the more recent application to the Broadcasting Commission of Ireland, Raidió na Life, rather than specifying a small core audience, pointed out that there were roughly 100,000 people in the Dublin region who claimed in the 2002 census that they spoke Irish every day (RnL, 2006). Its broadcasting hours, which a few short years before had been 4.30 p.m. to midnight on Monday to Friday and noon to midnight at the weekend, were extended through the night until 8 a.m. In 1999 Raidió na Life was awarded a renewal of contract for a further five years by the Independent Radio and Television Commission, but in recent years the Broadcasting Commission of Ireland has given it shorter contracts. The current contract is for one year and nine months. Because the station is mainly staffed by volunteers, it has provided a large number of people with radio broadcasting experience and some of them have continued in broadcasting in a professional capacity. In Raidió na Life's most recent application to the Broadcasting Commission of Ireland it lists 19 professional broadcasters who have worked as volunteers for Raidió na Life (RnL, 2006).

In relation to the two approaches to broadcasting in Irish (promoting the Irish language and service for Irish speakers), Raidió na Life clearly has as its objective providing a radio service for Irish speakers in Dublin. In relation to the ideological changes of recent decades (from community to individual), it is clear that Raidió na Life's objectives remain primarily in serving a community. Not only is it called a community radio station, but it is also owned by a co-operative (CRÁCT), and they argue in their submission to the Broadcasting Commission of Ireland: 'tá pobal na Gaeilge bunaithe cuid mhór ar ghréasáin úsáide a bhailíonn thart timpeall ar eagraíochtaí, agus tá beocht an phobail le sonrú iontu seo' ['the Irish-speaking community is based to a large extent on networks of use which are gathered around organisations, and there is evidence of community life in them' – author's translation from Irish] (RnL, 2006: 18).

As well as the dedicated Irish language radio and television channels, a small number of programmes have been broadcast in Irish on RTÉ's other radio and television stations and on the many independent radio stations throughout the country which are licensed by the Broadcasting Commission of Ireland.

Irish language broadcasting in recent years

Northern Ireland

In Northern Ireland it has been possible to receive RTÉ radio and television channels, including Raidió na Gaeltachta, for quite a few years. The BBC also broadcasts a range of programmes in Irish on both radio and television. For example, *Nochtú Uladh* and *Réalta agus Scéalta* (on BBC Radio Ulster), *Caschlár* (BBC Radio Foyle), *An Stuif Ceart* and *Srl* (on BBC2 NI) and learners' programmes on television and radio and information for learners on the BBC website, such as *Bitesize Revision GCSE Irish* and *Colin and Cumberland.*

Broadcasts in Irish are currently increasing considerably in Northern Ireland. As well as RTÉ television and radio (including Raidió na Gaeltachta) and BBC radio and television, a few independent radio stations broadcast programmes in Irish in Northern Ireland. At the time of writing, Ofcom (the Office of Communications), which provides licences to independent stations in the United Kingdom, had just awarded licences in Northern Ireland to three radio stations which broadcast at least some content in Irish. Iúr FM is a community station based in Newry, which proposes to have quite a few broadcasts (10 to 25 per cent of broadcast time) in Irish. Féile FM, which is based in Belfast and had been broadcasting for a short period of weeks each year was awarded a full-time licence. Raidió Fáilte, which is also based in Belfast, is a dedicated Irish language radio station, which had been broadcasting illegally in the past, but has recently been awarded a licence.

TG4 is also gradually being broadcast more widely in Northern Ireland. In the Belfast Agreement it was stated that the British Government will . . . explore urgently with the relevant British authorities, and in co-operation with the Irish broadcasting authorities, the scope for achieving more widespread availability of Teilifis na Gaeilge in Northern Ireland (Belfast Agreement, 1998).

In the Spring of 2005 TG4 was allowed to be broadcast via analogue terrestrial transmission to the Belfast area and to be available on Northern Ireland's Sky Satellite services.

The result of these current developments is particularly pronounced in Belfast, because TG4 is more readily available there, and the Irish language radio station Raidió Fáilte is a local station. In the past, people in Belfast were restricted to two dedicated Irish language radio stations (Raidió na Gaeltachta and Raidió Fáilte), one of which was a pirate station, and they will now have free-to-air access to a dedicated Irish language television station (TG4) as well as Raidió Fáilte which will have a licence. Broadcasting in Irish on BBC radio and television will continue, access to RTÉ television (which contains a few programmes in Irish) will be made easier, and some programmes in Irish will be provided by a few independent radio stations. The increase in the amount of programmes available in Irish on radio and television, which began in the Republic of Ireland in the 1990s with the arrival of TG4 (then TnaG) and of independent radio stations (most particularly Raidió na Life), has thus begun recently in Northern Ireland with the arrival of TG4 and of independent radio stations (most particularly the licensing of Raidió Fáilte).

In a similar fashion to the Broadcasting Commission of Ireland, the Northern Ireland Film and Television Commission funds Irish language broadcasting projects. In April 2004 the Secretary of State for Northern Ireland announced that there would be an Irish Language Broadcasting Fund. Six months later he announced that the Northern Ireland Film and Television Commission would administer it. Initially it was proposed that £12,000,000 would be made available over a period of three years to produce 90 hours of Irish language broadcasting a year and to reach an audience of 25,000 by 2007–8. However, soon after the announcement that the Northern Ireland Film and Television Commission would administer the fund it became clear that the British government's draft budget had accounted for £12,000,000 over five years rather than over three years. In 2005 the funding decisions awarded amounted to a total of £2,792,677 and at the time of writing £2,060,558 had been awarded for 2006, with the amounts for ten awards yet to be confirmed.

Republic of Ireland

The biggest recent event in Irish language broadcasting must be the separation of TG4 from RTÉ. Although TG4, from its inception, was under the statutory umbrella of RTÉ it was separately operated. TG4 (TnaG as it was called) was established under RTÉ ownership to avoid the need to pass special legislation. Although the Broadcasting Act, 2001 made the separation of TG4 from RTÉ possible, TG4 was not to be officially separated until April 2007. The separation process proper began when the Minister for Communications, Marine and Natural Resources (Noel Dempsey, TD) appointed Deloitte and Touche as well as William Fry Solicitors as external advisers to produce an implementation plan. This plan was then submitted to a Project Management Group comprising officials from the Departments of Communications, Marine and Natural Resources, of Community, Rural and Gaeltacht Affairs, and of Finance, as well as from RTÉ and TG4. At the time of writing the Project Management Team is endeavouring to formally separate the assets of TG4 and RTÉ. Although TG4 will be independent of RTÉ, RTÉ will continue to be obliged to provide TG4 with 365 hours of television broadcasting per annum.

In public RTÉ appeared to go along with the separation, although a private report from RTÉ to the Minister (details of which were exposed by Pól Ó Muirí in the *Irish Times* (Ó Muirí, 2005)) reveals an alternative agenda. In this report RTÉ promised to provide TG4 with more money if it were not made independent – the amount mentioned was ten per cent of the programme-commissioning budget – and simultaneously threatened TG4's current earnings. First, RTÉ argued that TG4 should be advertisement free and, second, RTÉ claimed that the EU Director General for Competition had 'raised significant questions concerning the nature of the funding of TG4' (Ó Muirí, 2005).

In recent years the BCI's Irish Language Advisory Committee has been promoting Irish language radio programmes, as well as offering training to Irish language presenters from commercial and community radio stations. The committee has also organised radio workshops for schoolchildren and initiated a project in which schools would produce radio programmes in Irish. The expansion in recent years of Irish language radio broadcasting appears set to continue into the future.

The biggest Irish language-broadcasting employer is TG4. Seventy-five people are employed in its head office and several hundred employed by independent production companies. TG4's head office is in the Connemara Gaeltacht in Galway and several of the independent production companies are based there too. With this level of employment in the area, one would expect the number of Irish speakers in this Gaeltacht to have increased between the two censuses of 1996 and 2002. This was indeed the case – there were a couple of thousand more Irish speakers recorded in the second census.

This did not lead to an increase in the percentage of Irish speakers in the Gaeltacht because the number of people who cannot speak Irish increased even more. The result is that the percentage of Irish speakers in that Gaeltacht actually decreased from about 82 per cent to about 78 per cent. This is reminiscent of the effect of the creation of jobs in the Gaeltacht during the 1970s.

The future of Irish language broadcasting

With the introduction of webcasting and podcasting the future of broadcasting appears to offer more flexibility. There are live radio and television webcasts in Irish as well as downloadable podcasts from radio stations and elsewhere. The most advanced Irish language webcast service is provided by TG4. It offers very advanced webcasting on its website (www.tg4.ie). As well as a live feed it has an extensive archive of their commissioned and in-house programmes. TG4's webcasting appears to be more comprehensive than other television stations.

In Ireland, thanks to TG4, Irish language broadcasting leads the way in television webcasting, but this is not the case with radio webcasting or podcasting. Although there are some radio webcasts and podcasts in Irish, they are trailing behind what is available in English from stations such as RTÉ. It is possible to listen to programmes in Irish live as they are broadcast by RTÉ's radio stations, including Raidió na Gaeltachta. Also Raidió na Life offers a live stream and, at the time of writing, is planning to offer podcasts so that people could download previous programmes and listen to them whenever they please.

Several podcasts in Irish, such as *Ar Muin na Muice* from Near FM or *An Líonra Sóisialta*, are already broadcast by seven radio stations, and also a few Irish language podcasts not connected to radio stations, such as Séamas Ó Neachtáin's *Cumann Carad na Gaeilge*. Overall, however, the Irish language appears to be trailing behind Scottish Gaelic in the number of podcasts, even though there are fewer speakers of Scottish Gaelic. Podcasting is in its infancy and many podcasts are transient and quite recent. In the future one would expect more podcasts in Irish. They are relatively cheap and easy to produce and one would expect an increasing number of Irish language organisations and individual enthusiasts to begin to produce them.

The other technology of the near future in Ireland is digital television. This will offer the opportunity to increase the number of domestic channels and might lead to a further increase in the number of Irish language television programmes. TG4 has considered establishing a second digital Irish language television channel, but it appears that, with the delays by the state in establishing digital television in Ireland, TG4 has had second thoughts about the second channel. Although digital television is not far off, a second Irish language television channel is off the short-term agenda. The effect of digital television in Ireland will be a further increase in the number of channels and therefore a further fragmentation of the audience.

Conclusion

The remarkable increase in the amount of Irish language broadcasting over the last decade is largely concentrated on TG4. There have been other developments in radio and television, but the preponderance of programmes in Irish are on TG4. Over the years RTÉ has moved Irish programmes on to its ancillary channel. With the establishment of RTÉ2, Irish language programmes were moved from RTÉ1 to RTÉ2. This has also been the case since the arrival of TG4 – there are now very few programmes in Irish on either RTÉ1 or RTÉ2. The result has not, however, been the ghettoisation of the Irish language, as was feared by Irish language activists in previous decades. The increasing size of TG4's share of the television audience, in an era of audience fragmentation, suggests that TG4 has developed a strategy which has countered the peripheralisation of Irish language programmes on a non-mainstream English language channel.

In this era of individualisation, Irish is increasingly treated, not as a community language, but as a language of individuals. This reflects the dominant neo-liberal ideology, but it also reflects the reality of the trend which has been ongoing since the foundation of the state – the shrinking of the Gaeltacht communities and their replacement by individuals spread throughout the rest of the country who speak Irish as a second language. Although there are still Gaeltacht communities as well as networks of Irish speakers in the cities and an Irish speaking community in Belfast, the majority of Irish speakers are isolated individuals who do not speak Irish regularly. Broadcasting in Irish is one way in which these communities and individuals are provided with a service in their own language and are brought together in a shared experience.

Individualisation is also evident in the shift from the use of broadcasting as a medium for producing an Irish-speaking nation to providing a service for Irish speakers. Over the past decade the increased availability of programmes in Irish on radio and television as well as in podcasts and webcasts has been mostly for Irish speakers, rather than learners. The trend has been, and looks set to continue, to provide programmes in Irish for Irish speakers (although podcasting has huge potential for learners' programmes). The audience for Irish language programmes is spatially fragmented because of the spread of Irish speakers throughout Ireland, but the use of webcasts and podcasts opens up an audience which is even more fragmented, both spatially, because of the global reach of the internet, and temporally, because of the possibility of watching or listening to a programme at any time.

TG4 is the principal element in Irish language broadcasting. The major developments in TG4 over the coming years will be concerned with its separation from RTÉ and its use of the potential within digital television and webcasting. The manner in which TG4 handles these developments will be the most interesting feature of Irish language broadcasting in the next few years.

Chapter 4

About Adam and Paul: film policy in Ireland since 1993

Roddy Flynn

It is hardly original to observe that Irish film policy has long been subject to the vagaries of the international film marketplace, given that, up to 1981, virtually all Irish film production activity originated overseas. Even the first Irish Film Board (1981–7) which became synonymous with indigenous cinema grew out of an attempt by the then Minister for Industry and Commerce, Des O'Malley, to find new ways to successfully compete for internationally mobile features projects. With the establishment of the film board in 1981 and in particular, after its re-establishment in 1993, it might have been assumed that the Irish state had, at least partially, wrested back for itself some degree of influence over the future of sector. As this chapter will argue, however, state policy since 1993 has, wittingly or otherwise, contrived to leave the Irish film industry more exposed to shifts in international terms of trade than ever before.

Film as an industry has been international since its inception. Although Hollywood has treated the entire planet as a potential distribution market since the 1910s, it was only after the Second World War that moves to organise *production* on a global basis began in earnest. The fact that some audiovisual industries outside the USA offered a greater degree of 'flexibility' (cost-effective labour and pliant trade unions, for example) than the domestic market, together with improvements in global transport and telecommunications networks, encouraged studios to engage in 'runaway' production overseas. The removal of 'artificial' national trade barriers under GATT and WTO rules gave further impetus to the internationalisation of production. In 1949, Hollywood saw 19 productions 'run away', a figure which rose to 183 by 1969 (Miller, 2005: 133). By 1998, $2.8bn worth of audiovisual production left the USA (Miller, 2005: 137).

In consequence it has become commonplace to discuss certain national audiovisual industries outside the USA in terms of how they facilitate the operation of this new international division of cultural labour rather than focusing on their contribution to indigenous film-making activity. Accounts of the audiovisual sectors in Canada and, more recently, in Eastern Europe now routinely assume that they are heavily integrated into the Hollywood-centred system of production. This chapter will suggest that the Irish audiovisual sector is also best understood in this fashion.

This was not, however, the vista that informed the key policy documents which initially drove Irish policy in the 1990s. In 1991, the Industrial Development Authority together with Temple Bar Properties, commissioned a report on opportunities for film-related job creation. The resulting document (produced by accountants Coopers and Lybrand, 1992) marked a sea change in Irish film policy in the emphases it granted to audiovisual production as, respectively, an artistic and industrial (read job-creating) undertaking. Notwithstanding film's cultural status, the arguments throughout the report for film industry support were couched in hard-nosed financial language, suggesting that any increased state investment in the sector would be more than compensated for by the tax returns to the Exchequer resulting from augmented production activity.

However, the report criticised previous approaches to developing and positioning the industry. Singling out the work of the Irish Film Board it noted that the decision to focus on low budget production with indigenous casts meant that, by definition, funding decisions had not been driven by commercial considerations, a difficulty exacerbated by a lack of understanding of and contact with the international film marketplace. Unsurprisingly, therefore, the report emphasised the need for the sector to become much more market-driven and to this end it made a series of recommendations relating to training, marketing and finance. Crucial amongst these was the identification of the Industrial Development Authority as the key body to drive the future development of the sector rather than – for example – a re-established Film Board. In a further nod towards commerce, the IDA were also invoked in the report's stress on the need to actively promote Ireland as a location for off-shore production. Given this, it is hardly surprising that the key recommendation coming out of the report focused on the market-oriented section 35 tax relief on film investment and specifically the need to make it more accessible to investors.

A month later, the producer's lobby group Film Makers Ireland published their own report (Film Makers Ireland, 1992) on the development of the independent television sector in Ireland. Given that the FMI report was informed by interviews with either the same individuals or individuals with similar production backgrounds, its conclusions closely echoed the Coopers and Lybrand Report. In particular the recommendations on section 35 were virtually identical.

Faced with two high profile reports in September 1992, the Taoiseach, Albert Reynolds, established his own special working group made up of film-makers, civil servants from the Departments of the Taoiseach, Industry and Commerce, Finance and Tourism as well as (amongst others) representatives of the IDA, RTÉ, the Arts Council, the IFI, Film Makers Ireland and the Irish Film Centre. Tasked with considering the conclusions of the two preceding reports, the group submitted the results of their deliberations in December 1992, although it would be the new year before its conclusions were made public (Special Working Group, 1993). With regard to the economic and employment potential of the audiovisual sector, the Group rehearsed the conclusions of the Coopers and FMI reports but also recorded some concerns from the Department of Industry and Commerce and from Finance. Industry and Commerce pointed to the high risk associated with film production and the need, at a time when the state's finances were being tightly squeezed, to ensure that resources were concentrated on those projects with the best chance of yielding *sustainable* employment. The 'sustainable' reference clearly expressed Industry and Commerce's doubts about the freelance nature of the industry and may have in part been influenced by the contemporaneous difficulties being experienced in the animation sector. For their part, the Department of Finance were at pains to stress that the film industry should not receive preferential treatment from the state because of ill-defined cultural or artistic characteristics.

Despite this the report argued that the international success enjoyed by Irish and Irish-themed films shot between 1986 and 1991 (i.e. largely non-Irish Film Board projects) had created a window of opportunity for Irish producers and directors. State intervention was essential to ensure that the momentum of activity within the industry did not dwindle to nothing.

Specifically, then, the report made five groups of recommendations, including inter alia: the need to amend the 1990 Broadcasting Act and to establish an Irish-language Television channel; the need to amend section 35; and the need to provide state subvention for developing and producing audiovisual productions. Of these, the discussions relating to tax breaks and state subvention were most significant. On tax, the group restated the need to extend section 35 to individuals and to increase the amount of film investment allowed for tax relief. With regard to state subvention the report stated that a majority of the group favoured some kind of annual subvention administered by a specialised Oireachtas-funded agency. However, rather than using the existing structures of the Arts Council or the Film Board, the group recommended establishing a new agency customised to the conditions governing film and television production in the 1990s.

The report went on make specific recommendations about the level of finance to be made available to the new agency and, critically, suggested that it be subject to periodic review. If after five years it was not considered to have been a success from a creative/economic perspective then the agency should be discontinued.

It is often assumed in reviews of the 1990s, that the policy changes actually introduced in 1993 – to which the subsequent leap in film-making activity is generally ascribed – grew directly out of the Coopers and Lybrand, FMI and Special Working Group Reports. However, key aspects of what Michael D. Higgins would introduce as the state's first Minister for Arts and Culture actually contradicted these reports.

Furthermore, as the 1990s segued into the twenty-first century, the assumption underlying of all these reports, that film policy was in large part about creating a sustainable domestic industry, would increasingly be undermined by de facto industry practice followed by subtle but discernable shifts in government policy.

The appointment of Michael D. Higgins at the newly established Department of Arts, Culture and the Gaeltacht in 1993 placed a figure with impeccable cultural credentials at the head of arts policy in Ireland. Despite this, Higgins's early pronouncements on film policy raised some concerns amongst film-makers: launching the Dublin Film Festival in March 1993, Higgins limited his ambition to having structures in place to promote a vibrant film industry by 1996 and would only commit himself to publishing a white paper on the subject within 12 months.

However, on 30 March 1993, Higgins was gifted a political opportunity which he seized with both hands. At 3 a.m. Irish time Neil Jordan accepted an Oscar for his screenplay of *The Crying Game* at the Academy Awards. Surfing the wave of public euphoria, Higgins secured cabinet approval to re-establish the Film Board without recourse to new legislation and at 7 p.m. the same day announced its immediate revival.

The decision to re-establish the Film Board effectively tore up the conservative chronology for the development of an audiovisual policy which the Programme for Partnership Government hammered out by Fianna Fáil and Labour over Christmas 1992 had envisaged. Although his opposite number at the Department of Finance, Bertie Ahern, deigned to announce alterations to section 35 in line with the Special Working Group's recommendation at his February 1993 budget, the Finance Act of May that year introduced three entirely new elements to the tax break:

- Section 35 was extended to projects where as little as ten per cent of the actual production work took place in Ireland.
- The annual investment ceiling was increased to £350,000 or up to £1,050,000 in a single project provided no further investment was made for three years.
- And – critically – individual investors were permitted to avail themselves of the tax break for the first time, by investing up to £25,000 per annum in productions certified by the Minister for Arts, Culture and the Gaeltacht.

Taken together with the 1993 Broadcasting Act which mandated RTÉ to commission programmes from independent production companies, by July 1993 Michael D. Higgins could reasonably claim – as he did at the belated launch of the Report of the Special Working Group on Film Production – that

> the main obstacles which hindered the growth of the film and audiovisual industry in this country have been removed. It is now the responsibility of the industry itself to respond to those favourable conditions and indeed deliver on the promises made their submission to the working group.

Even Higgins must have been surprised by the extent to which those promises were delivered on. The combined value of the 28 indigenous and off-shore productions cited by the Coopers and Lybrand Report as being shot in Ireland between 1987 and 1991 was £52.638m. That figure was almost matched by the 1993 figure alone – £50.5m – which would in turn be dwarfed by the figures for 1994 and 1995 when total audiovisual expenditure reached £133.1m. and £100.1 m. respectively. Although the equivalent of 480 full-time Irish jobs were created by independent audiovisual production in 1993, this shot to 1,291 in 1994.

The presence of overseas productions in particular accounted for the dramatic increases in the economic value of the Irish audiovisual production sector. Typical of this was the July 1994 arrival in Ireland of the $70 million production of Mel Gibson's *Braveheart*, lured from its Scottish location by a Department of Arts, Culture and the Gaeltacht promise not merely of access to section 35 funding, but also to 1,600 reservist soldiers as extras (reportedly for a nominal cost) and several historic sites and castles.

Despite the emphasis laid on his sympathy for the arts, Higgins's success in his early years at the department probably owed more to the extent to which he employed the rhetoric of the economic pragmatist to couch his arguments in favour of state intervention into the audiovisual sector, rather than arguing in primarily cultural terms. His comments during the first years of his tenure at Arts, Culture and the Gaeltacht demonstrate his recognition of the limitations placed on his freedom of action by the contemporary economic context. The dramatic cutbacks in public services and stringent controls on public expenditure which had been vigorously pursued since 1987 were still largely in place in 1993. It was not a time for arguing on behalf of largesse towards the arts on purely cultural grounds, a political point clearly recognised by Higgins:

> While I continue to promote my policy initiatives in the film area as primarily of cultural importance, I have made it clear from the outset that the significant range of direct and indirect State incentives which been put in place for the industry

must result in tangible return to the Irish economy in terms of employment and
value added (From 'The Development of the Film Industry in Ireland, Speaking
Note for the Minister (Michael D. Higgins)' addressing the British National
Heritage Parliamentary Committee 17 January 1995).

Higgins's language was also conditioned by the perception in some quarters
that film as a 'popular' art did not require state assistance. (This was reflected
in the manner in which the Film Board, which operated in the knowledge
that the Special Working Group had recommended that any new finance
institution should be reviewed within five years of its establishment, sought to
demonstrate its own commercial nous by reference to the – initially spectacular by state film body standards – recoupment rates on its investments.)
    Instead Higgins consistently associated himself with the annual report on
the economic impact of audiovisual production in Ireland produced by the
Audiovisual Federation of the Irish Business and Employers Confederation.
The report calculated whether the money spent on the Film Board and foregone by the Revenue Commissioners through section 35 was outweighed by
the income generated by the resulting increase in audiovisual production
(that is, testing the validity of the Coopers and Lybrand argument). The first
report concluded that this had indeed been the case: £700,000 had been spent
on the Film Board and £5.4m. had been foregone through section 35. But
£7.7m. had been returned to the exchequer as a result of the productions
examined, a net return of £1.6m. (Subsequent reports have – with the exception
of 1995 – consistently recorded net returns.) In short, although the report could
also point to other benefits accruing to Ireland as a result of these productions –
the transfer of skills to Irish crew working on overseas productions and even a
positive impact on tourist numbers, drawn by the images of Ireland seen
onscreen – the balance sheet surplus for Ireland Incorporated was the single
most important element.
    This approach allowed Higgins to sidestep the difficulties faced by the
first Film Board in 1987 which had been suspended explicitly because it had
failed to invest in sufficiently commercial productions. The broader focus on
overall film spending and revenue contained within the IBEC reports meant
that the spending by the second board was merely one element of a much
larger financial equation. If that overall equation resulted in an ongoing net
benefit to Ireland, then the commercial success or failure of any single element – such as the Board's investments – was much less significant, if not in
fact irrelevant.
    However, this did not prevent questions being raised about other aspects
of the film support infrastructure. In particular, abuses (perceived or otherwise) of section 35 by a series of productions and production companies in the
mid-1990s led the Department of Arts, Culture and the Gaeltacht to re-examine

the operation of the tax-break in 1995. They commissioned Indecon, a large economic consultancy, to advise as to whether section 35 was the most cost-efficient means of creating a sustainable film industry.

Indecon's conclusions (Department of Arts, Culture and the Gaeltacht, 1995) pointed out that section 35 benefited investors more than producers but conceded that the tax relief had nonetheless been a contributory factor in the post-1993 increase in production activity. However, the most significant Indecon finding was – IBEC figures notwithstanding – that tax foregone by the exchequer via section 35 had not been recouped through increased financial activity associated with the film industry. Indeed Indecon suggested that section 35 was costing the Exchequer approximately £5 million per annum. The Indecon report noted that IBEC's figures were arrived at by calculating the aggregate impact of all audiovisual production in Ireland, not all of which had availed itself of the tax incentive. Indecon argued that if one separated out these productions, then the economy experienced a net loss as a result of section 35.

Despite these misgivings Indecon did not suggest entirely removing the tax incentive. Instead, noting that 'on economic criteria it would be very hard to justify continuing the incentives in their present form' it put forward a series of recommendations designed to ensure that the tax break made a net contribution to the economy, including reducing the level of tax write-off available to private and corporation investors from 100 per cent of their investment to 80 per cent.

The Indecon conclusions were clearly reflected in the January 1996 budget. Whilst extending section 35's operation until 1999, Minister for Finance Ruairí Quinn also announced modifications designed to target the relief on indigenous films. For the first time the amount of section 35 money that could be raised for a given film was capped at £7.5m. Since no more than 50 per cent of a given total budget could be sourced from section 35, this was intended to limit the tax break's application to sub-£15m budget films (that is, budgets more in keeping with indigenous film-making than overseas projects). Quinn also sought to make section 35 more cost-efficient from the point of view of the exchequer: as recommended by Indecon, tax relief for individual and corporate investors was reduced from 100 per cent to 80 per cent.

The response of some elements of the industry to these changes was to assert that they would lead to a collapse in overseas activities coming to Ireland. Although a Department of Arts spokesman characterised such comments as basically hysteria, the Department still felt it necessary to organise a Michael D. Higgins-fronted charm offensive in May 1996 to convince American film-makers that Ireland remained film friendly. Despite this, production levels fell, and only an increase in independent television commissions (significantly in October 1996, TnaG went on air) compensated for the decline in feature activity. The downturn drove Higgins to lobby his opposite number at Finance to alter the January 1996 strictures at the next budget, but with only partial success. Thus although Quinn increased to £15m. the amount of section 35 finance that could be raised per picture, this was conditional on raising at least half the funding from corporate (as opposed to individual) investors. This was not a trivial point, however. Since 1993, section 35 had increasingly become the exclusive province of the individual investor, who facing a marginal tax rate of 48 per cent as opposed to the 36 per cent corporation tax faced by companies (or 12.5 per cent in the case of some firms), had a greater incentive to take up tax incentives.

Nonetheless the 1997 changes appeared to achieve an immediate payoff: in March it was announced that Steven Spielberg's *Saving Private Ryan* would be partially relocating the filming of a Normandy Beach landings sequence from the UK to Wexford, for financial reasons. This was less a reference to section 35, however, than to the financial benefits deriving from more informal supports. In a repeat of the *Braveheart* stroke, 1,000 Irish soldiers were loaned to the production for the D-Day sequence.

That it remained necessary to go to such lengths to secure even an element of a large-scale production reflected the extent to which, increasingly, Ireland faced competition for mobile projects. This also clearly informed Higgins's June 1997 announcement of the establishment of an Irish Screen Commission, which though presented as for the benefit of all films shot in Ireland, was clearly understood by the Hollywood press as meant to 'market the country as a film location and facilitate *incoming productions*' (*Hollywood Reporter*, 1997. Italics added).

Higgins would not remain at the department long enough to see the commission begin its work. At the June 1997 General Election, a new Fianna Fail/Progressive Democrats coalition replaced the Rainbow government of Fine Gael, Labour and Democratic Left. In a tacit compliment to Michael D. Higgins's success at the department, no other party manifesto had envisaged reversing the establishment of a separate Arts ministry: his successor, Sile de Valera conceded of Higgins that there was an awful lot they could agree on (White, 1997). Thus de Valera saw her main task as consolidating the gains of the previous years. To this end, in June 1998 she appointed a thinktank, chaired by entertainment industry accountant Ossie Kilkenny to assess strategies for the ongoing development of the audiovisual sector in Ireland in the context of the anticipated expiration of section 35, or, as it had become following the passage of the 1997 Taxes Consolidation Act, section 481. She also tasked the Group with the development of a decade-long roadmap for the development of the industry.

The resulting Kilkenny Report focused on the question of how to place on a more stable footing an industry which it described as being at a fragile stage of development (Department of Arts, Heritage, Gaeltacht and the Islands, 1999: 33). Although citing as strengths the talent pool available and the state's demonstrated commitment to the sector, the report cited a much longer list of weaknesses including:

- the failure to translate success in literary content creation to screen media
- the small size of the domestic market
- the project-by-project nature of production
- a lack of business skills
- lack of labour cost competitiveness/flexibility
- uncertainty as to the longevity of state support

The neophyte status of the Irish industry was characterised as offering an opportunity to correct these failings and avoid the tendency towards an artistic creative model which the report asserted had condemned other European industries to commercial obscurity. The report was built on the implicit assumption that Irish production companies could constitute the basis of a commercial industry, capable of competing successfully in an international market. To achieve this the group stressed the need to develop stronger production companies characterised by greater scale, capitalisation, business acumen and editorial expertise.

The strategies put forward for achieving this centred largely on the Film Board and section 481. With regard to the Film Board, the report proposed a significant expansion of the board's activities as the body best placed to improve script and project development, develop stronger indigenous companies and market Irish film both within and beyond Ireland. This was to be reflected substantial increase in its financial resources from £5.5m. in 1998 to £8.2m. in 1999.

The report also recommended retaining section 481 for at least seven years after 1999, since this would impose some market discipline on Irish production, and reinstating 100 per cent tax relief for sub-£4m budgets projects. Furthermore, noting that the film sector was still in a relatively early stage of development, the report argued that the section 481's retention could be justified as a support to an infant industry, 'irrespective of international developments' (1999: 71). However, this last reference hinted at the possibility that external factors were beginning to constitute a new rationale for maintaining the tax incentive, which had little to do with the industry's stage of development.

The Kilkenny Report would become a touchstone for assessing subsequent Irish film policy, although its stress on a commercially oriented conception of the Irish audiovisual sector to the exclusion of any substantive discussion of cinema as a cultural form saw it engender some (mild) criticism.

Sile de Valera wholeheartedly endorsed it stating that its conclusions and recommendations 'will form the basis of my proposals to Government . . . to thrust our industry forward through the next decade' (De Valera, 1999).

Despite this, the industry was somewhat disappointed by the response of the Department of Finance to the Kilkenny recommendations. Somewhat ominously, the opening section of the report had included a caveat entered by the Department of Finance's representative on the group which noted 'that the findings . . . and recommendations made by the Review Group do not necessarily reflect the views of the Department of Finance'. This caveat reflected in turn the views of the Minister for Finance, Charlie McCreevy, who had long advocated a fiscal policy of cutting government spending with a view to reducing income tax rates. From his appointment in 1997, he set out to reduce the exchequer borrowing requirement to zero and sought spending cuts accordingly. Thus although McCreevy agreed to extend section 481 (for five years rather than the Kilkenny recommendation of seven), he refused to reinstate the 100 per cent tax write-off.

Nevertheless, the years 2000 and 2001 proved highly successful for production. By the time, Sile de Valera left office after the May 2002 election, to be replaced by former Minister for Justice, John O'Donoghue, the industry appeared to be in good shape although a decline in indigenous production had become sufficiently serious by mid-2002 for the Film Board to introduce new schemes aimed at encouraging indigenous low and micro-budget production.

Ironically, when O'Donoghue was faced with film policy challenges, they emanated from within his own cabinet. From Autumn 2002 through until December 2003, he fought an ongoing rearguard action in the face of Department of Finance efforts to reduce state subvention to the Irish film sector. In October 2002, the Independent Estimates Review Committee, a Department of Finance body tasked with identifying €900m in savings on the December 2002 budget, expressed the view that the continuation of the Irish Film Board was 'unwarranted' (Independent Estimates Review Committee, 2002) suggesting that section 481 constituted 'sufficient financial incentive . . . to the film industry in Ireland'. In the event the threat to the board's existence was neutered even before the Review Committee's report became public, after O'Donoghue impressed upon McCreevy the need to retain the board. Yet scarcely had that particular danger been headed off than another arose. Having extended the operation of section 481 until 5 April 2005 in the wake of the Kilkenny Report, Charlie McCreevy, in his 4 December 2002 budget speech, announced the definitive termination of the tax break on 31 December 2004. In making this decision he was influenced by the deliberations of the Tax Strategy Group within the Department of Finance, which as early as 1999 had argued that the retention of section 481 could no longer be justified on the basis of the infant industry rationale.

McCreevy's announcement would engender a year-long campaign led by Screen Producers Ireland (the producers' lobby group) to reverse his decision. The arguments propounded and explored over the course of 2003 by SPI and the Department of Arts, Sports and Tourism constituted the most detailed dissection of film policy in the history of the state. June and October 2003 saw the delivery of two reports – one to SPI, the other to the Department of Arts exploring the case for continuing state fiscal support for the film industry after 2004. Taken together SPI/PWC constructed an argument which undermined the Kilkenny's Report's implied faith in the possibility of a commercial indigenous production sector.

The SPI/PWC rationale for retaining section 481 stressed its primary (indeed almost exclusive) role in attracting overseas production activity. Nonetheless by arguing that the net exchequer returns from international productions indirectly subsidised indigenous loss-making activity, both groups legitimated section 481's retention on the basis of its indirect contribution to national culture.

The reports both argued that McCreevy's implicit invocation of the infant industry rationale for section 481 in his 2002 budget speech failed to grasp the extent to which by 2003 the Irish film industry had become a node operating around the hub of Hollywood. SPI stressed that the prototypical nature of film production made it very difficult to predict market potential for any individual film project. Furthermore, since film production was a capital-intensive business, requiring access to substantial quantities of cash, the knowledge that even a relatively small percentage of the budget was available from soft sources such as section 481 had a disproportionate positive effect (Screen Producers Ireland, 2003: 34) on the decision by producers to make a film in Ireland. Taking up the argument, the Price Waterhouse Cooper report therefore concluded that had section 481 not been in place between 1999 and 2001, something in the region of €150 million in offshore funds would have been lost to the Irish economy. Similarly, the SPI report stressed that although in 1993 section 481 had lent the film industry first-mover advantage in terms of attracting highly mobile film capital, the subsequent decade had seen state financial support for film-making in the form of direct subsidy or tax incentives for private investment become the norm internationally.

Furthermore SPI also dismissed as irrelevant for film production the low rate of tax levied on corporate profits in Ireland, which had been so successful in attracting other industries to Ireland. In a tacit concession of the extent to which the Irish industry comprised companies producing films on behalf of other national film industries, SPI characterised Irish film production as 'a project based business where production is treated as a cost centre' (Screen Producers Ireland, 2003: 35) rather than a source of profit. This was not to suggest that films were not profitable but that profits would be earned by those who commissioned Irish companies to make films on their behalf (that is, major Hollywood studios who could use the leverage of their vertically and horizontally integrated structures to commercially exploit filmic properties across a range of media).

Having thus laid their cards on the table, SPI argued that removing section 481 would place Ireland at a disadvantage in competing with other potential locations. Both reports also hinted at the possibility that the loss of international work would indirectly hamper indigenous activity. Price Waterhouse Coopers concluded that offshore productions were more likely to make a positive return to the Irish exchequer than their often less well-resourced indigenous counterparts or co-productions. (Price Waterhouse Cooper, 2003: 34) The SPI report drew out the implications of this for indigenous production: 'Even in countries with relatively large domestic markets . . . viability of their domestic industry is only possible by accessing significant Government support and using the financial benefits flowing from international productions to support local productions' (2003: 34). In other words, given that state support of the film industry since 1993 had been pre-dicated upon the fact that the sector as a whole made a net contribution to the exchequer, the losses incurred by supporting indigenous activity could only be sustained politically if Ireland maintained a financial environment con-ducive to the large budget overseas projects which produced a net return for the exchequer.

These cumulative arguments had the desired impact: in his December 2003 budget speech McCreevy noted that having reviewed the case made to him by John O'Donoghue, 'film relief will be extended for a further period until the end of 2008, and that the ceiling per film will be increased to €15 million from 2005'. McCreevy's decision clearly represented a victory for elements of the film industry in Ireland. Yet the extent to which the 2003 debate on the pros and cons of section 481 had taken place without reference to cultural arguments was striking, especially given the indigenous cinema rhetoric that had characterised such debates in the early 1990s. The subtext of the debate suggested that even the Irish film industry itself had little faith in the commercial prospects of the indigenous film production sector.

The flip side of this was an acknowledgement of the extent to which the Irish film industry had come to constitute an element of the new international division of cultural labour. In the first volume of his *Information Age* trilogy, *The Network Society*, the Spanish geographer Manuel Castells describes the emergence since the late 1970s of a new 'informational' economy:

> It is informational because the productivity and competitiveness of units or agents in this economy . . . depend on their capacity to generate, process and apply efficiently knowledge-based information. It is global because the core activities of

production, consumption and circulation . . . are organised on a global scale, either directly or through a network of linkages between economic agents (Castells, 1996: 66).

In the period under review in this chapter, the structure and operations of the Irish film have increasingly come to exemplify the logic of this informationalism. As the rate of increase of Hollywood production costs has outstripped general levels of inflation, the incentive to stay abreast of production conditions overseas with a view to either reducing costs or accessing soft finances has also been developed. In the early 1990s, Ireland represented an opportunity for real cost-savings through not just the availability of section 481 finance but also less visible subsidies such as access to the defence forces and national monuments. However, as the 1990s went on, and other countries introduced similar initiatives, Ireland's competitive edge was progressively dulled. Charlie McCreevy's December 2003 extension of section 481 and the increased amount of money which could be raised per film using the tax break was a tacit acknowledgement of this reality.

As the years after 2003 have demonstrated, however, the gradual internationalisation of the Irish film industry has made it vulnerable to shifts in the international terms of trade beyond the control of the Irish state. Thus although 2003 proved the most successful year in the industry history, as major productions like *King Arthur* and *Tristan and Isolde* drove total audiovisual expenditure to €320.2m. a subsequent downturn drew attention to the significance of other factors influencing production levels in Ireland which had been partially obscured by the endogenous initiatives.

Key amongst these were favourable exchange rates, which though referred to by several producers and reports in the late 1990s were rarely subjected to close empirical analysis. In 1996 when US audiovisual expenditure in Ireland amounted to only €10m., the value of a dollar fluctuated between €0.75 and €0.82. However, as the dollar strengthened against the euro in 1998, rising to between €0.84 and €0.94, so too did expenditure in Ireland, reaching €47.5m. (At the same time the dollar weakened against UK sterling, making Ireland's geographically closest competitor a less attractive shooting location.) The dollar hit a 10-year peak against the punt/euro in June 2001 (when $US1 was worth €1.18). Such buying power made Ireland a very attractive location for the producers of *The Count of Monte Cristo, Reign of Fire* and *Veronica Guerin* all of which were shot in 2001 and 2002, with cumulative budgets of over $US150m. This was reflected in US spend in Ireland which reached €93.8m. in 2001 and a still substantial €58.4m in 2002.

After 2001, however, the dollar weakened: by 2005, it had become 30 per cent more expensive for Hollywood companies to shoot in Ireland than four years earlier. US spend in Ireland fell to €27m by 2004 as the dollar fell to

€0.75 by December of that year. The effects of this were felt throughout the Irish industry: employment dipped to less than the equivalent of 1,000 full-time positions for the first time since 1993 whilst Ardmore Studios had no bookings at all for the first six months of 2004.

Exchange rates were not the sole external factors contributing to the high level of US expenditure in the late 1990s and early 2000s. In April 2000, in a decision which went almost unnoticed outside the film industry, the Irish government finally signed up to the 1992 European Convention on Co-Production. As a consequence, although nominally competing for footloose productions, the fact that both of the main UK film tax incentives in the 1990s – section 42 and section 48 – were available to co-productions with relatively low levels of UK spend allowed US producers to structure projects which simultaneously availed of tax incentives in the UK and Ireland. This was regarded as a key factor in attracting major Hollywood films to Ireland (IBEC, 2005). Typically projects were shot in Ireland then edited in the UK: thus *King Arthur* in 2003 was largely post-produced in London by Cinesite Europe. This allowed the Bruckheimer company to use UK and Irish 'off-balance sheet financing' (tax breaks) to raise nearly a quarter of *King Arthur*'s $100m. budget. *The Count of Monte Cristo, Reign of Fire, Ella Enchanted, Veronica Guerin* and *King Arthur* (all co-productions with US majors or their satellites) also benefited from both section 481 and the UK incentives (www.world2000.ie).

However, in a further instance of the extent to which production levels in Ireland were vulnerable to external factors, the British Chancellor of the Exchequer Gordon Brown announced in early 2004 that both section 42 and section 48 would be replaced by a new structure and suggested that henceforth projects taking up British tax incentives would need to spend at least 40 per cent of their budget within the UK. The implications of this for Ireland were obvious. As the 2005 IBEC review ruefully noted, changes to UK film tax schemes were 'reflected in the number and volume of inward film productions shooting in Ireland'. Although in practice Gordon Brown's Spring 2006 budget set the minimum UK spend at 25 per cent rather than the signalled 40 per cent, other changes – notably the fact that British cast and crew working in Ireland would no longer be counted as British spend as had previously been the case – reduced the incentive to shoot such productions outside the UK.

The relative impotence of the Irish state faced with such exogenous pressures was acknowledged by John O'Donoghue himself. In July 2004, whilst asserting that the government had met its responsibilities in maintaining Ireland as an attractive film location, he conceded that

There is very little one can do about exchange rates and the value of the euro against the US dollar. I have no control over the fluctuations on the money markets . . . we can only control those things which are under our remit and maintain the highest standards in those areas in which we have power (O'Halloran, 2004).

Faced with a virtual halving of audiovisual expenditure in 2004 and 2005 as compared with the (admittedly spectacular) figures for 2003, the Irish state has attempted to fine-tune those measures that are within its gift in an effort to win back overseas projects. (In this respect it's worth mentioning that in 2004 and 2005 overseas funding for audiovisual production in Ireland fell to a quarter and a fifth respectively of the 2003 figure.) The most obvious mechanism is section 481: when the new €15m ceiling introduced by Charlie McCreevy in 2003 failed to have the desired effect, his successor Brian Cowan introduced further changes in 2006, allowing producers to avail themselves of 80 per cent of total production costs via section 481 up to a maximum of €35million. There has also been a new emphasis on promoting Ireland as a location. At the Cannes Film Festival in May 2005, John O'Donoghue announced that the Irish Film Board would shortly make arrangements to appoint a Deputy Film Commissioner, based in Los Angeles, to liaise with the major studios there and to effectively link these studios with the services and supports available in Ireland. Similarly, in July 2005 the Film Board announced the introduction of new management structure axing the positions of Head of Production and Development and Head of Marketing. But the board took the opportunity to entirely refocus the efforts of the marketing department on *attracting inward production*, with other marketing requirements (those related to promoting indigenous productions) being outsourced as and when needed.

However, the most practical initiative has also been related to the Film Board. In 2005 and 2006, Minister John O'Donoghue secured for the Board an additional €1.5m and €2.3m., to fund a new category of international production loans targeted at high-quality international production that can demonstrate a strong connection to Ireland (www.filmboard). Those connections have nothing to do with content: projects thus far taking up the scheme include *The Tudors* (a Showtime (US) production about the British royal family in the sixteenth century), *Northanger Abbey* (a Granada television adaptation of Jane Austen's novel) and *Kitchen* (which is set in a Glasgow restaurant and produced for the UK's Channel 5). Instead, announcements of Film Board involvement in these projects heavily stress the involvement of senior Irish crew and their economic impact: thus in addition to noting the €7.1 m. spent on Irish jobs and local goods and services, the press release for *Becoming Jane* revealed that the production accounted for approximately 820 hotel nights in Ireland (Irish Film Board, 2006).

There is nothing technically untoward about this re-orientation of the Board's spending. The 1980 legislation establishing the Film Board gave it carte blanche to do anything it saw fit in the interests of creating a film industry in Ireland. Actual practice throughout the 1980s and 1990s, however, assumed the board would concentrate on indigenous material. Thus when referring to the need for the board to balance its support for incoming productions with its role in promoting the indigenous Irish film sector in a May 2006 speech, John O'Donoghue was announcing a de facto shift in practice (O'Donoghue, 2006).

There is no question but that the Film Board's international loans have succeeded in bringing in new activity. Provisional estimates for audiovisual spending in 2006 suggest that total overall output will rise to €238m., a 50 per cent increase on the figures for 2005. Nearly two thirds of this (€155m.) has been spent on independent television production. Section 481 has also been an element in this. It is not a coincidence that the majority of overseas projects attracted to Ireland since 2004 have been television projects: the new tax incentives introduced in the UK in 2004 are not currently accessible for television production. Thus Ireland has again gained first mover advantage in that particular and currently lucrative niche market.

However, the television example again highlights the precarious nature of the current structure of the Irish audiovisual sector. Although in December 2006, the Film Board announced that new series of *Murphy's Law* and *The Tudors* would be shot in Ireland in 2007, the presence of such productions is reliant on Ireland's constant vigilance in the face of competing incentives elsewhere. In January 2007, an entirely new set of tax incentives came into effect in the UK and the government there was under pressure to further extend even those breaks for use with television production. The question ultimately posed then is that of how far future Irish governments will be prepared to go to compete in what has become an international incentives race and what the fate of indigenous production will be when and if a given Irish government decides that they can go no further.

Chapter 5

Ireland's way to the information society: knowledge(s) and media matters

Paschal Preston

'It is essential that we continue the drive to build a truly knowledge based society'
(Government of Ireland, 2006: 2)

'A knowledge society is about far more than commercial enterprise. It is inclusive, participative, concerned about quality of life and depends on the values people hold'
(Finbarr Bradley, *Irish Times*, 30 July 2006)

Introduction

Over the past decade, policy elites in Ireland, the EU and indeed worldwide, have appropriated the 'information society' or 'knowledge economy' as a meta-concept (or master-myth) in framing discourses on the distinctive features and direction of contemporary social and economic developments. This chapter interrogates selective aspects of such discourses, including their preferred definitions of knowledge and treatment of media services and other *soft communication* (i.e. non-technological) functions. It addresses the tendency of such discourses and related policy strategies, including those practised by key gatekeepers in Irish policy and university circles, to privilege certain kinds of knowledge functions whilst neglecting others. This implies a lack of attention to the expanding array of specialist knowledge functions, not least those directly related to new and mature media services, alongside the specific features of their role in socio-economic and cultural affairs.

This chapter engages with the national and international literature related to understandings of the overall contours and meanings of an evolving information society or knowledge economy and how these relate to the evolving role of the media, especially in the case of Ireland (Hereinafter the term 'Ireland' will be used to refer to the Republic of Ireland). In this chapter, in line with the practice of seminal theorists such as Daniel Bell, I treat the terms 'information society', 'knowledge economy' and 'post-industrial society' as referring to broadly similar conceptual and theoretical claims or phenomena. However, I emphasise that these three can and must be distinguished from the descriptive concept of an 'information sector' (Preston, 2001). The chapter addresses these issues by drawing on recent studies in the social science and humanities fields, including findings from research conducted by research centres based in Dublin City University.

The first section of this chapter considers aspects of competing conceptualisations of the information society and the role of knowledge workers or symbolic analysts in the contemporary era. We note a tendency to neglect the specific features of the media (public communication) services and the peculiar inputs and productions of media professionals as a specific sub-set of knowledge workers. This section identifies policy appropriations of the concept and critiques the growing influence of technology-centred and economistic models of the information society in recent times. Section two moves on consider the specific applications and implications of knowledge-economy discourses and developments in Ireland as well as some related policy issues. It also briefly considers aspects of the changing role and features of the media and 'soft communication' services, including the digital media sector. The conclusion draws out some implications for studies of the media sector, including the domain of digital media

The information society: contested concepts

Academic discourses

Daniel Bell is widely regarded as author of the most influential and sociologically robust versions of the orthodox theories of the information society (Preston, 2001). In his major thesis on the post-industrial or information society, Bell (1973) emphasises the rapidly expanding roles of relatively new 'knowledge-intensive' services and occupations. His empirical focus falls on specialist services and functions that grew relatively rapidly in the USA from the mid-1940s.

Yet, amidst the many developments and trends considered in this large work, we find that Bell accords no sustained attention to the media and cultural industries or related occupations. This silence is rather significant since these particular knowledge-based activities had been growing rapidly in the USA, especially in the period considered by Bell. A similar neglect can be found in Bell's subsequent major tome focused on the cultural contradictions of capitalism. In this case, the focus of Bell's particular critique of 'postmodern' culture is largely framed around high-art and other non-media forms of culture (Preston, 2001).

ety developments, were to be fundamentally 'market driven'. In effect, the cial role and protections attaching to public service broadcasting, long a minent feature of the media landscape in most European countries, were be increasingly regarded as atavisms within the shiny new technocratic ions of 'Europe's way to the information society' (Commission of the ropean Communities, 1995).

Furthermore, we may note that the EC's successive information society d knowledge-based economy initiatives have entailed large-scale policy bsidies and supports for the production of scientific and technological nowledge and for maximising the consumption and use of ICT goods and rvices. No similar supports were directed towards the forms of knowledge lost related to the development of the media and cultural services sectors Preston, 2001, 2003; Preston and Cawley, 2004)

Why and how such information society policies and discourses matter

What we observe here is not merely the construction of a distinct set of ideas for understanding the features of contemporary society but also how such discursive constructs play prescriptive as well as descriptive roles in the process of socio-economic development. In particular, recent policy discourses framed around the information society idea have played a key role in shaping and legitimating multiple new industrial and policy initiatives impacting on the information and communication services sectors.

Indeed, for the past decade or more, successive national and EU level public policies have played a major role in shaping the diffusion of new ICTs and related 'information society' developments more generally. Despite the neo-liberal rhetorics, with their fundamentalist emphasis on a 'market-driven' approach (Commission of the European Communities, 1994a), the influence of such national or supra-national state policies should not be underestimated (Preston, 2001). Quite apart from explicit 'information society' policy initiatives, such influences range from the much-extended sway of intellectual property rights, new forms of competition and privatisation policies, research and development and educational policies to new regulatory regimes for advertising, sponsorship and trans-national broadcasting. They also include public procurement or purchasing policies and the spate of 'eGovernment' initiatives, not least as the public sector became a very significant customer for new ICT related products and services since the dot.com bubble burst.

In this context, we must simply note and emphasise that state institutions have been a key force in shaping the design, supply and demand-side aspects of new ICT-related developments in Ireland, Europe and beyond. Alongside private-sector corporations operating in new ICT related sectors, state agencies have played a significant 'top down' role in shaping Europe's way to the information society. Furthermore, many user-orientated empirical

Such neglect is not confined to Bell's model. In many, if not most, other orthodox analyses of the knowledge economy originating outside the field of communication studies, we find that the media and cultural industries are either ignored or accorded peripheral roles relative to the privileged place of technological, managerial and other knowledge-intensive functions. Even when they are explicitly considered, the media and cultural industries tend to be treated as the mere objects of economistic or technological-determinist logics and relegated to the generic labels of *application services* or *content*, or even *software* (Commission of the European Communities, 1994b). In some such cases, the result has been bizarre forms of technological determinism sufficient to cause McLuhan's ghost to blush (e.g. Castells, 1996).

The autonomy and power of knowledge workers in information society

Since its first emergence in the mid-twentieth century, the information or knowledge society idea has always been closely bound up with debates concerning the changing class structures and power relations within the heartlands of industrial capitalism, especially those linked to the onward march of the so-called new professions, most of which first emerged around the turn of the twentieth century. These debates, in turn, linked the notion to the key international conflicts and issues concerning 'the politics of distribution' and the core ideological struggles in the context of the Cold War. No mean ideological commando in both the cold and class wars since the 1950s, Bell himself explicitly acknowledges that his writings on post-industrialism comprised but an extension of key arguments advanced in his prior work on 'the end of ideology' (Preston, 2001). Such background factors help to explain one important feature of Bell's and most other conventional information or knowledge society theories: the striking emphasis placed on the autonomy or freedom and power of knowledge workers.

Whilst Daniel Bell's book (1973) has subsequently proved to be the most popular and influential of the earlier academic contributions to the information society literature, it comprised but one of a swarm of works that were published in the 1960s and 1970s. At the same time it must be noted, if only briefly here, that Bell's work was not as original as its own text implies or as many subsequent contributions presume (Preston, 2001). Some key elements can be traced to prior work conducted in the 1950s by the economist Fritz Machlup and radical social theorists such as J. D. Bernal and C. Wright Mills – the latter, for example, provided an earlier and very different take on the role and autonomy of US knowledge workers compared to Bell. One common element comprises the information sector concept which framed key aspects of the empirical analysis that Bell mobilised in support of his own knowledge society thesis. In this light, Bell's substantive innovation was to harness the schema to a radical version of meritocracy, the autonomy of knowledge workers and related extensions of the end of ideology thesis. The information sector concept, however, can be usefully applied in studies of the evolving social division of labour whilst rejecting Bell's ideological baggage (Preston, 2001).

Policy appropriations: from information society to knowledge-based economy (KbE)

The first significant appropriations of the information society idea by policy circles can be traced to the USA during the late 1970s and early 1980s. This was the time when US foreign policy analysts concerned with international industrial and commercial strategies first identified the 'information society' idea as 'a strategic new element in the American global equation'. Indeed, these analysts defined the information society idea as one which well matched strategic US industrial and trade interests, serving to 'amplify American ideas and values in a more forceful way than has ever been done before' (cited in Preston, 2001: 73–4).

It is also pertinent to note that this was the time of the Regan administration and the final demise of the era of 'we're all Keynesians now' as Eisenhower defined it in the 1950s. More specifically, this period witnessed the rise of neo-liberalism as the guiding ideology and practice in US domestic and external policy affairs, especially as regards industrial and economic matters. Thus it is hardly surprising to find that in its subsequent career in policy discourse, the information society idea has often been defined or presented as if hard-wired to the core tenets of neo-liberal doctrines. By the early 1980s, high-level advisers to the first Thatcher government in Britain were also moving towards somewhat similar concepts and industrial strategies centred on the business of 'making a business of information' (ITAP, 1983).

Viewed in this light, the project for a global information superhighway proposed by the then US Vice-President, Al Gore in 1993–4 seems to have been somewhat less radical or original in scope and implications than he supposed or others have subsequently claimed. At the EU level, interwoven moves and narratives around the neo-liberal globalisation of trade and investment, the liberalisation of telecommunications and other services, alongside the issues of 'competitiveness', were brought together and explicitly linked to the information society idea through a number of key policy documents published in the 1993–4 period. The most significant was a report from the then powerful commissioner responsible for industrial and telecommunications affairs (Commission of the European Communities, 1994a). Often referred to as 'the Bangemann Report', this policy document had major and lasting influences on the framing of subsequent policies for information and communications technology (ICT) research and communication services, both at the EU level and in Ireland. Indeed, for some years following its publication, this report was repeatedly cited as a sort of bible or master text in other

Commission documents and by officials dealing with a industrial, educational and social policy fields. For exar invoked as a framework for an influential 1994 repor industrial and policy strategy for the audiovisual sector European Union's newly completed single market (Prest

Since 2000, there has been a distinct marginalisation of t *society* in favour of *the knowledge-based economy* in the fr policy discourses and practices related to research and ove economic development goals. These semantic shifts have b enced by the proceedings of the European Council meeting 2000 which adopted the ambitious aim of making Europe 't knowledge-based economy in the world capable of susta growth with more and better jobs and greater social cohesio of the European Communities, 2000a: 7). This goal has be expanding emphasis on the role of R&D for European co especially at the European Council's Barcelona meeting in heads of state and government committed themselves to inve cent of GDP in R&D by 2010 (Preston, 2003).

Media and related knowledge inputs and functions

The mid-1990s EC reports promised a significant expansion o employment in the media services sector as key features of 'Eu the information society' (Commission of the European Commu Indeed, they defined the media as important sources of 'high matter' jobs and promised that the numbers of such media professi double over the next five years (Commission of the European Co 1994b: 119). Similar views and themes were taken up by a subsequent EC reports and policy initiatives invoking the informat frame even if focused on more specific aspects of the media servi (Commission of the European Communities, 1994c).

These EC policy initiatives and discourses tended to be strongly by three distinct features or assumptions, all of which also applied quent developments in the Irish context. First, the overwhelming e continues to fall on technological knowledge, despite the fact tha revisions to the international industrial classification systems recognise science and humanities research fields as distinct and important in acitivities in line with policy recommendations made more than 15 ye (Preston, 1990). Second, the anticipated expansion of the media as source of employment and output growth in the EU area was view the direct or automatic effect of unfolding technological and netwo developments in the new ICT fields. Third, the role and functions o media and cultural services sector, like all other aspects of the informa

studies indicate how national and EU policy discourses have played an important ideological role in changing users perceptions and in stimulating their
purchase of ICT equipment and services, generally complementing the marketing operations of corporations involved in the supply of such products
(e.g. Silverstone, 2005; Preston, 2001, 2005).

Ireland's way: a knowledge economy hub?

Ireland and information society policy discourse
When and how did Ireland embrace the knowledge society? A more
historically nuanced account might well search for some point in the middle
ages when the island of saints and scholars starred as bright beacon for what
then passed as the 'leading-edge' of knowledge and learning in those dark ages
of European culture and civilisation. In terms of current technocratic definitions and discourses, however, we need only zap back to 1995 to trace the first
Irish official *information society* policy report. This was triggered not only by
the publication of the EC's aforementioned Bangemann report, but also by
the administrative and planning imperatives related to an impending Irish
presidency of the EC. Such was the context which prompted the relevant
government agency to commission a local university researcher to undertake
a study to scope out some of the policy ramifications of such relatively new-
fangled concepts in the Irish setting (Preston, 1995; 1997b).

From the mid-1990s, the information society idea began to permeate
policy discourses in Ireland and this was accompanied by a series of related
policy initiatives and the establishment of new institutions such as the
Information Society Commission. Since 2001, in line with EC-level fashions,
the term information society has been increasingly replaced by that of the
knowledge-based economy (KbE). Thus, we find that the latter term is now
generally invoked in Irish policy circles when framing plans and discourses
related to policies for fields ranging from research, innovation, industrial and
educational policies, as well as those for the electronic communication
services sector (e.g. Government of Ireland, 2006). Similar terminological
shifts have been evident in the policy discourses of other EU member states.
In Ireland as elsewhere, the fashion for the knowledge-based economy tends
to re-emphasise the importance of expanded investments in one specific
domain of technological knowledge (R&D) for national or European competitiveness. Otherwise, this terminological shift does not signal any major
break from the kinds of policy concerns and orientations that were previously
privileged in information society discourses.

Leapfrogging towards a global KbE hub or broadband basket case?
Our information sector analyses of employment structures indicate that
Ireland's economic miracle has been accompanied by a significant growth in
various kinds of knowledge- intensive occupations alongside the rapid rates of
overall economic growth of the past decade. But that does not imply a ready
embrace of contemporary claims that such changes signal that the Irish
economy has leapfrogged from late or lagging industrial status, or heavy
dependency on potentially fickle inward investments, to become a dynamic,
innovative hub of the global knowledge economy.

The analysis of employment structures certainly confirms that new ICT
activities, the leading-edge technology sector of the past decade, comprise an
exceptionally large share of the Irish economy. Yet that does not mean an
uncritical embrace of some of the wilder (hubristic) claims that have been
constructed around such facts. Take, for example, the much-celebrated claims
that Ireland is one of the largest exporters of software in the world, and the
biggest when weighted by size of economy. Analyses of the relevant information
sector data indicate that the impressive gross earnings from exports of software are matched by an almost equally large deficit in royalties and other
intellectual property rights (IPR) payments. In essence, such considerations
mean that Ireland's net performance is very much less indeed than the
headline-grabbing gross data suggest. In sum, such gross 'exports' earnings are
counter-balanced by the large outflows of royalties and IPR payments, as
elements of the repatriation of profits by multinationals leading to a
substantial diminution in the net or national income data.

Furthermore, whilst the ICT sector is but one sub-set of the global
knowledge-based sectors characterised by relatively rapid growth and/or
high value-added activities, it clearly commands a very significant share
of employment and output in Ireland. On the face of it, this is no mean
achievement given the sector's status as a leading-edge site for industrial
innovation and growth in recent decades. But despite its exceptionally large
role in the national employment and output structures, Ireland's indigenous
innovation performance in this sector remains very weak. The latter is
relatively weak when compared with the success of the older policies and
industries centred on the country's role as an export and localisation platform
for multinational corporations with respect to the EU market. Perhaps the
best reality check or crucial marker of the national economy's innovative
performance in the new ICT domain comprises the case of broadband
provision and use. As a complex new network system, a successful broadband
strategy requires multi-faceted innovative performance on the supply side as
well as in applications, demand and policy domains. Here, the conventional
metrics indicate that, despite its large ICT sector, Ireland's performance is far
from that of a leading edge economy. Its current status is less global hub but

more akin to serial fiasco, the 'broadband basket case of Europe' as one external researcher put it (personal communication; see also Preston et al., forthcoming).

Empirically grounded knowledge economy analyses serve to challenge some dominant understandings of the sources and status of Ireland's economic transformation since the mid-1990s. As regards the key drivers in the economy's shift from the slow to the fast lane, the much-cited role of a highly educated and knowledge-based workforce simply does not stand up in the face of comparative (international) scrutiny. However flattering or comforting it may be to those of us working in higher education, for reasons noted further below, this can only considered a second-tier factor in the recent performance of the Irish economy compared to other primary or top-level factors.

One primary factor here comprises the external boosts (not only in financial terms, but also with respect to organisational and other knowledge inputs) provided by inward investment. A second external factor, now subject to a distinct amnesia amongst the commentariat, concerns the significant inflows of EC funds up to the recent past, especially the crucial fillips to infrastructural and educational developments these provided through structural funds in the 1980s–1990s. A third comprises the crucial role of the Irish state overall, not merely the industrial development agencies, in fostering and readily servicing the multiple requirements of inward industrial investments. A fourth concerns the state's successful design and implementation of a peculiar neo-liberal regime for the control of labour costs via corporatist wage agreements alongside relatively minor concessions to popular social interests and liberal immigration policies. On the downside, however, compared to its success in the old Keynesian mode of regulation (as with the rapid state-led modernisation of telecommunications in the early 1980s), the Irish state appears strikingly inept when it comes to effective industrial strategies within the neo-liberal regulatory regime, especially in the case of key infrastructure domains such as telecoms (as in broadband), and also, as it now appears to be unfolding, in the case of Aer Lingus.

The 2004 OECD review of the Irish higher education sector provides another reality check to the hubris underpinning many recent constructions of the status and sources of Ireland's dynamic knowledge economy. Contrary to all the 'world class university' rhetorics that now pervade the strategy and mission statements of such institutions, this report revealed that the Irish university sector is very poorly funded relative to that in most other OECD countries. Instead of responding to the report's recommendation that this underfunding be addressed as a matter of priority, the government has dithered and delayed, failing even to maintain the major annual competitive research fund (PRTLI) which was simply cancelled for three successive years. At a time of unprecedented levels of state revenues, this signals a certain lack of 'world class' strategy or understanding at the higher-levels of research and education policy, concerning the basic practicalities of realising the state's declared goals of establishing and maintaining major centres of research excellence. This response to the OECD report also seems to signal that, in practical and material terms, the Irish state really places little strategic importance on the past or future role of the higher education sector as a crucial driver in Ireland's industrial development.

The way ahead: technology-centred foresight and fixations?

Information sector analyses underline the continued dependency of the Irish economy on inward investment and the relative weakness of indigenous industrial innovation, especially when it comes to goods or services that are internationally tradable. This is well illustrated by what is usually defined as Ireland's major high-profile corporate success story of the past decade, for it is clear that Ryanair's rapid growth is based on old-fashioned price competition. The past decade of Ireland's boom and 'way to the information society' has not produced any significant success story based on the kinds of the indigenous product or process innovations identified in the knowledge economy literature, or found in other small countries such as Finland with its Nokia (Castells and Himanen, 2002).

Of course, the relative weakness of indigenous industrial innovation has long been recognised as a feature of the Irish economy, but it has taken on a new prominence amongst the industrial and policy elites in more recent years alongside frequent invocations of the imperative to 'move-up the value-chain' in the face of declining national price competitiveness, especially in terms of wages and salaries. Such considerations are part of the national development plan and its implementation through new strategies for research, education, telecommunications and other sectoral areas (Government of Ireland, 2006). The key challenges are usually defined in terms of a paradigm shift in local enterprise culture towards more indigenous technology-based innovation alongside subsidising multinational corporations to locate some of their research activities in Ireland.

When viewed in the light of knowledge sector analyses, there are major questions as to whether recent and current Irish state strategies fully embrace the requisite paradigm shifts that their own definitions of the key challenges seem to imply. One strategic issue here concerns the extent to which state agencies concerned with research and industrial development are effective in transitioning to a new paradigm embracing both a much greater emphasis on indigenous innovation and a consistent knowledge economy framework. As regards the former aspect, there remains a distinct sense that they continue to be haunted by the ghost of their own [outstanding] success in the older strategy relying on inward investment. My own experience suggests that the inward investment mindset continues to predominate in the case of policy discussions and initiatives related to the media and creative services sectors. This also permeates the highly innovative strategy of seeking to subsidise and incentivise multinationals to locate R&D activities in Ireland since this also a highly risky strategy as it runs against the grain of long-established locational dynamics. Any substantive verdict on the effectiveness of this particular policy innovation depends on the findings of independent research, an undertaking that seems urgently required.

As regards the latter aspect, both policy discourses and initiatives have failed to make the requisite paradigm shift as they continue to conflate 'knowledge economy' with 'technology economy' in line with the 1990s policy tendencies discussed above. Indeed, current policies still seem to be locked in a older model of the high-tech economy, one which fails to take account of significant changes in the international division of labour, the increasing commodity features of much new technology and the role of bundling, or the expanding role of services as significant sites for industrial innovation. The key issue boils down to the continued privileging of technological research and the relative neglect of other new knowledge forms and research domains, not least those related to the media sector.

One glaring manifestation here is the notorious disparity in the respective research funding allocations made to the natural and physical sciences on the one hand and the social sciences and humanities on the other. These disparities have been amplified in more recent years by the massive increases in research funds for the former fields whilst the social sciences and humanities must make do with token crumbs. Whilst policy rhetorics occasionally remember to acknowledge that the latter are crucial in supporting industrial innovation as well as all-round policy and social development in the contemporary setting (Government of Ireland, 2006), these considerations are not extended the domain of material practices. The late establishment and subsequent low funding made available to the IRCHSS has done little to redress the growing disparities between the resources allocated to these two broad knowledge fields in the Irish context. The token-level funding made available to the IRCHSS only gives credence to the tales that its creation was simply to avoid the embarrassment of the Celtic Tiger being counted alongside Albania as the only members of the Council of Europe failing to establish such funding mechanisms for the social science and humanities fields

The particularly pronounced 'two cultures' divide in Ireland with respect to funding resources is closely linked to other non-material features of the national research and university setting. One is the manifest fear and paranoia that still pervades the Irish political and economic establishment with respect to the findings or challenges that may arise from anything that approaches independent socio-economic research. A second is the internal culture of governance and management in Irish universities where, at all levels, open debate and play of ideas is treated as something to be avoided at all costs rather than celebrated as the core of what such institutions are supposed to develop and encourage. The recent macho management posturing of university executives, triggered by government-led demands for competition and restructuring, seems likely to further repress the more collegial modes of university governance found in most other (north) European countries. Both these features are linked and illustrate that changing economic conditions do not necessarily or rapidly erode established cultural patterns, especially the unhappy convergence of the well-documented features of authoritarian Catholicism and the postcolonial state. Both run directly counter to the basic principles of meritocracy (whether applied to persons, ideas or policy strategies) and the importance of open debate and peer review by relevant experts (with respect to knowledge production, evaluation and selection mechanisms), which underpin the seminal models of an evolving knowledge society. These models presume the effectiveness and instrumental benefits of basic public sphere principles favouring the exchange of competing ideas, the associated emphasis on peer review and debate as selection mechanisms in the key decision making of knowledge production organisations, of which universities are deemed to be exemplars. The above-mentioned features of Ireland policy and institutional paradigm might well have matched the requirements of an industrial strategy primarily based on servicing the interests and needs of inward investment. But unless and until the clientilist features of the wider Irish political culture, not to mention the parallel absence of collegial modes of university management and governance are abandoned, then Ireland's prospects in emulating the indigenous innovation performance of other smaller countries will be much diminished.

Conclusion: some implications for the media sector

The chapter has considered how aspects of state agencies in Ireland, in line with EU and USA trends, have appropriated the information society or knowledge economy as master-myths when framing policy discourses on the features and direction of contemporary social and economic developments. We observed how such discourses and related policy practices emphasise technology alongside a fundamentally market-driven approach, constructing selective techno-economic logics as if hard-wired to the tenets of neo-liberalism. Yet, the related state policy initiatives are observed to play a major role in shaping those very same socio-economic developments. We observed that whilst the dominant strand of orthodox academic work on the information society tended to neglect the role of the mass media, the latter have been embraced by the subsequent policy discourses which frame them as major sites for new jobs, industrial and commercial exploitation.

The chapter also addressed selective aspects of such knowledge economy discourses and accompanying policy practices as they relate to the evolving role of the media and other 'soft communication' functions in contemporary society. This includes the tendency to privilege certain kinds of knowledge forms or functions whilst neglecting others. We noted how this comprises an especially prominent feature of the policies and practices of key gatekeepers in Irish research and industrial policy circles. Irish national policy discourses still tend to equate the knowledge economy with technology-based sectors – a tendency that well reflects (and helps to explain) the striking absence of funding for research in the social science and humanities fields for many years. One significant implication is that research, industry and educational policies have neglected the growing role of multiple specialist knowledge forms and functions, especially those cultural and creative knowledge fields which are directly related to industrial innovation and performance in 'new' media services domains.

This persistence of the tendency to fetishise technological knowledge when it comes to innovation in digital media domains is not confined to the Irish policy arena, but the problem seems to be particularly pronounced in this setting. One bizarre but peculiar feature of the Irish case is that the policy biases seem to be more informed by the presuppositions of actors based in state agencies than by the experience or expressed views of relevant actors based in the media sector.

Our information sector analyses indicate that the number of media and related creative knowledge occupations has grown in Ireland as in other EU countries. The 'media, creative and entertainment related' occupational category grew significantly over the past three decades. Indeed, over the 21-year period between 1981 and 2002, this occupational category increased its numbers by some 250 per cent, which was more than six times the benchmark increase registered for total occupations in the Irish economy over this same period (Preston, 2006). At the same time, however, we must note that the growth of the digital media domains remains relatively weak and patchy compared to the rich potential identified by several successive policy forecasts. In part, the realisation of such potential has been hindered by the features of Irish industrial and research policy discussed above – which the expensive inward-investment experiment that was Media Lab Europe so clearly illustrates.

But the relevant stakes for the media sector go well beyond the numbers of jobs, important though such considerations remain even in the 'new' Ireland. The combination of technology-centred and commodification logics, as described and prescribed by the neo-liberal knowledge society discourses, pose multiple implications for the media sector besides those discussed here.

In essence, they construct or reframe media services, journalism and other cultural activities as business activities no different from other sectors of the economy. The emphasis on economistic logics tends to neglect if not ignore the distinctive political and cultural role of the media in the struggles for a more democratic and just social order. Whilst they readily celebrate 'making a business of information' these discourses ignore the risks for a critical media or journalism culture capable of engaging with the shifting centres of material and symbolic power, including those identified by a former newspaper editor in the nineteenth century who advised that 'the first business of a newspaper is not to be a business'.

One of the major responsibilities of communication scholars is to address the downside threats of a media and journalism culture ever more subject to commercial criteria and orientated towards consumerism rather the goals of a more democratic order or informed citizenry. This chapter has indicated only some of the relevant challenges and barriers to such visions of future social development. Other aspects of these developments and challenges are addressed elsewhere in this book.

Section Two Representation

Chapter 6

War and peace on the screen: television representations of conflict in Ireland

Patrick Kinsella

'Audiences know what to expect, and that is all that they are prepared to believe in.'
(Tom Stoppard, *Rosencrantz and Guildenstern are Dead*)

Introduction

Northern Ireland is the very model of a divided society, with a population riven on the question of identity: British or Irish. In the nineteenth-century conception of nationalism, it is clearly not possible to be both; nor is it easy to be neither in the Northern Ireland context; individuals who refuse to identify themselves with one group or the other tend to find themselves classified anyway. While the two groups share a language, the different names for the place used by each group demonstrate the degree of mutual alienation: 'Ulster' or 'Northern Ireland' *vs* 'the six counties' or 'the north of Ireland'.

As so often in such disputes, religion is inseparable from the national question; one could read 'Protestant or Catholic' in place of 'British or Irish' above, but to describe the conflict as mainly religious would be to mis-understand the issue. Although much of the sporadic violence in Northern Ireland over the past two hundred years can be characterised as little more than the expression of inter-group hostility, the most recent phase of the troubles has articulated a political question: will there be an adjustment in claims of sovereignty?

Identity is so fundamental to our individual humanity that it is generally seen by conflict theorists as non-negotiable, unlike material interests over which bargaining and the establishment of common ground seem so much more tractable. Identity certainly generates the deepest emotions, including the will to fight, and in Northern Ireland it prompted from the 1960s to the 1990s one of the longest civil conflicts of modern times.[1]

Our purpose here is to examine the role of television in reproducing the conflict to its participants and other observers. The period coincides with the rise of television news as the predominant source of information about the world, including local events. In the 1960s, television was still new, and rapidly changing. Telefís Éireann had begun broadcasting in 1961 (and UTV in Belfast two years earlier). In Britain (and therefore in Northern Ireland), news bulletins were short, with limited use of pictures, until 1967 when the establishment of ITN's *News at Ten* made half an hour[2] the standard ration for prime time, and set the pace in use of film. It still took time to get pictures on air, because satellites were in their infancy and portable electronic cameras were in the future.

A beginning

Derry city centre. The front row of marchers begins to jostle with a disorderly row of RUC men. The black and white images show one of the leaders expostulating '. . . gentlemen, please. God save us . . .' when he is cut off by a blow to the stomach from police lines. We do not see whether it is a baton, a fist or a knee,[3] but we see his shock as he doubles up. The jostling intensifies, and now batons come down on heads. One cop clearly strikes a demonstrator who is walking away from the trouble. More blows, a young woman screams and falls.

This was Saturday 5 October 1968, generally held to be the start of the current troubles.[4] Television had been increasingly bringing conflict into people's homes, from the civil rights struggle in the United States, to protests around the world against the Vietnam War, and most recently the puzzling events of May 1968 in Paris. Now it was local. The Northern Ireland Civil Rights Association had been formed the previous year and there had already been a number of small protests and demonstrations about unfair housing allocations, limited voting rights and lack of jobs for Catholics. A march from Coalisland to Dungannon had passed off without significant incident. Now these were the first television pictures of violence meted out by police on Irish streets. Thanks to the courage and skill of cameraman Gay O'Brien of RTÉ, viewers in Ireland, Britain and around the world saw it all from the centre of the action. As the scene unfolds on screen, an officer clubs a man on the ground, and as he turns from his task we see his face. He observes the camera and walks quickly away. What did we see in his eyes? Rage or fear?

The local context is critically important for explaining the police action. The Derry demonstration had been banned by the Belfast government, not because of any direct threat, but because loyalists had arranged a counter demonstration (McCann, 1993: 96).[5] Although the civil rights campaigners at this stage asserted that their claim was merely for civil rights and justice, many Protestants saw it as a challenge either to their existing rights to jobs and housing, or increasingly to their status within the United Kingdom.[6]

A theoretical framework

It seems reasonable to assert as a general moral principle without further discussion here that violent conflict ought to be avoided if problems can be solved in a peaceful way, on the grounds that it imposes unnecessary human suffering. It further seems reasonable to take a position with the military historian John Keegan that, despite the little-understood human propensity to resort to violence, most individuals are generally reluctant to take the risks or bear the costs of exerting force in the pursuit of objects that might be attained otherwise, and that 'most human beings for most of the time co-operate for the common good. Cooperativeness must be taken as the norm' (Keegan, 1993: 79).

Our questions then are: How are people provoked or persuaded to fight? And how do the media contribute to the process?

It may be a caricature, but is useful nonetheless, to suggest that a model which many theorists have found useful in discussing the role of modern media simplifies society into three functional elements: the mass of citizens or public who produce goods, services and tax revenues; the establishment or elite who exercise power; and the media which communicate an account (or competing accounts) of events and commentaries thereon, providing the information on which citizens may base their opinions (Seaton, 1988). Different authors postulate various degrees of openness of the elite, and different degrees of autonomy for the media. Thus the elite may be more or less accountable and responsive to the wishes of citizens, there may be more or less competition for positions of power, and the media may be more or less independent and critical of the establishment in communicating a view of the world.[7] Of course, influence may be in more than one direction, to the extent that the media report on the activities and respond to the views of citizens generally as well those of the elite.

An extreme version of this model, propounded by Herman and Chomsky (1988) as 'the propaganda model',[8] asserts that the mainstream media are institutionally biased to serve the interests of the elite (which are generally in contradiction to those of the mass of citizens); the bias is due to systematic factors, including dependence on profits and advertising, dependence on and pressure from elite sources of information, and shared (anti-communist or pro-market) ideology. Herman (2000: 105) emphasises that this is not a conspiracy theory, but closer to a 'free market' model: 'The media comprise numerous independent entities that operate on the basis of common outlooks, incentives and pressures from the market, government and internal organizational forces'. One important prediction of the propaganda model is that mainstream media will only give space for debate about policy on key issues (such as war) where there is significant disagreement among members of the elite.

It is more generally accepted that messages generated by the media might contribute to social conflict by presenting some groups (religious, ethnic) as 'different' in some essential characteristics, thus exacerbating fear and hostility, and by presenting group interests as irreconcilable, and therefore non-negotiable.[9]

We can also identify four possible sources of media distortion. Again it seems reasonable to suppose that a distorted view of events makes it more difficult for citizens to make decisions based upon their real interests and may therefore increase the likelihood of conflict. The first source of distortion is outright propaganda. The others are gate-keeping, framing and portrayal.

Even where there is no deliberate intent to deceive, views of the world presented by the media may be distorted. Gate-keeping is a consequence of the fact that the time available for messages – news bulletins – is necessarily limited; even if we disregard the potential for inaccuracy in reporting, choices must be made of what events are reported because of limitations on the time available both to editors and audiences. Thus the media set a limited agenda for public discussion, 'forcing attention to certain issues . . . suggesting what individuals in the mass should think about, know about, have feelings about' (Lang and Lang, 1966, cited by McCombs and Shaw, 1972: 177. See also McCombs, 2004).

Questions of bias thus arise with regard to decisions about which stories to cover, with what prominence, and how often: does the agenda-setting function of the media present the 'right' menu of events and opinions? Different groups and different individuals will have agendas of what is important or interesting and worthy of attention, so conflict over the appropriateness of media agenda setting seems inevitable. For instance, how much prominence should be given to campaigns to establish the innocence of the Birmingham Six,[10] especially after their appeals failed in 1976 and again in 1988? Obviously, greater prominence would tend to cast more doubt (among those with an open mind) about the safety of the verdicts and to undermine trust in British justice, while antagonising viewers determined to support the British government in its struggle with the IRA. It was a topic to which Granada Television's *World In Action* programme returned again and again.

By framing is meant the device of fitting events into a narrative or context that allow a 'story' to be told. Any given facts can usually be presented in a range of ways: a bomb goes off; it can be framed as a terrorist act, expressing hate, or an act of war in pursuit of justice. According to Gamson and Modigliani, framing provides 'a central organizing idea or story line that provides meaning to an unfolding strip of events' (cited by Druckman, 2001: 227). It is quite common for indignant viewers to vigorously dispute the 'angle' taken on a story even where the reporter's facts are entirely accurate.

The issue of portrayal is a reflection of the status given to individuals or groups by the media. Public perception will be affected by the frequency (or rarity) of appearances, and also by the context in which they appear (as victim, hero, spokesperson or authority figure), and by the way in which they are described or characterised (whether by reporters themselves or by other interviewees). On a mundane level, senior trade union officials are variously described as 'trade union leaders' and 'union bosses', phrases which convey very different views of their representative status, and demonstrating how much depends on a reporter's choice of language. More importantly for our purpose here, the description of bombers as 'mindless', and of assassins as 'evil' may give some satisfaction to their opponents, but does nothing to enhance public understanding of motives and the underpinning causes of conflict.

Evidence on media effects

The conventional view is that television has enormous influence on behaviour and a great deal of effort has been expended in trying to measure its extent and direction. The direct evidence is far from clear, not least because of the difficulty in separating broadcasts from the myriad of other social circumstances that affect our decisions.

At the level of household behaviour, a study by Sanders and Calam at the University of Manchester found that parents who watched the 2005 ITV series on child behavioural problems, *Driving Mum and Dad Mad*, were 'less likely to shout at or hit their children, and were calmer and more confident in their parenting abilities'. As a result, of those children described as having 'severe behavioural problems' at the beginning of the study, 40 per cent had moved into the 'normal' range of behaviour as a result of changes in their parents' practices (Ward, 2006).

However, this was specific programming that aimed to entertain and educate, unlike news and current affairs which generally (at least in Britain and Ireland) aims to inform without being didactic or persuasive. The impact of television news coverage on political opinion and behaviour is not so clearly established, despite extensive research, particularly in the United States.[11] It seems obvious that television has an influence, but questions remain about the extent and mechanism, the degree of interdependence with other factors, and particularly about the predisposition of individuals to accept or reject particular messages or framings. In a survey of the literature, Livingstone suggests that the media are part of 'enculturation processes, which work over long time periods, and which are integral to rather than separable from other forms of social determination', and that the appropriate question is not 'how the media make us act or think but rather how the media contribute to making us who we are' (Livingstone, 1996: 421). The latter point of course is particularly relevant in conflicts over identity.[12]

The paucity of convincing measurement and the lack of a clearly understood transmission mechanism in generating media effects do not in the end absolve television and other mass media from complicity in the provocation of conflict. A well-documented and compelling case study is provided by the disintegration of Yugoslavia, with its official slogan of 'brotherhood and unity'. The calamitous wars of 1991–5 were preceded by the transformation of state controlled media into channels of relentless nationalist propaganda and disinformation (Silber and Little, 1995; Thompson, 1999; Buric, 2000). Perhaps an even more shocking example of direct media provocation was the role of state and private radio in organising slaughter in Rwanda in 1994, when an estimated 800,000 people were killed in a span of three months (Article 19, 1996; Des Forges, 1999).

Despite the uncertainty about the mechanism and extent of media effects, governments and other conflict parties believe television to have enormous influence, enough to justify manipulation, intimidation and censorship, as we shall see.

The long war

There is a widely held view, supported by a considerable body of literature (Curtis, 1998 [1984]; Miller, 1994, 1995; Schlesinger, 1987, 1991; Moloney, 1991; Purcell, 1991) that the British and Irish broadcasters were systematically biased in their coverage of the Northern Ireland conflict, and, in a role more or less predicted by the Herman and Chomsky propaganda model, took the side of the British state in its struggle against republicanism. Actually, the situation is a great deal more complicated, and a careful reading of the evidence shows the institutions were not so much a weapon, more part of the battleground of information and ideas.

The television landscape

There are four distinct audiences that concern us: viewers in the Republic of Ireland, viewers in Britain, and the two communities (Catholic-nationalist and Protestant-unionist)[13] within Northern Ireland. For most of the period 1968–98, these audiences were served by four television news broadcasters. RTÉ, based in Dublin, with a Belfast office from 1969 (Horgan, 2004: 75), covered the Republic of Ireland, with insignificant signal overspill into Northern Ireland. The north itself was served locally by UTV, part of the commercial ITV network, which also carried national bulletins from ITN in London; and the BBC, which also had both national bulletins from London and a locally controlled service in Belfast. From 1982, the second commercial company, Channel 4, began broadcasting from London.[14] The British channels have had a significant audience share in the Republic, mainly by means of cable.[15]

All four channels are public service broadcasters: RTÉ and BBC are both directly state owned and controlled, while the British commercial channels also have programme standards imposed by law. In the case of the BBC, its agreement with the Home Office requires the corporation to provide: 'comprehensive, authoritative and impartial coverage of news and current affairs in the United Kingdom and throughout the world to support fair and informed debate at local, regional and national level'. The BBC is barred from expressing its own opinion (other than on broadcasting) and must treat controversial subjects with 'due accuracy and impartiality'. The same phrasing was used in the Television Act establishing the ITV stations, but they were also required to avoid broadcasting anything which 'is likely to encourage or incite to crime or to lead to disorder or to be offensive to public feelings.'

In the Republic, the 1960 statute that created RTÉ ('the Authority') imposed a duty that 'any information, news or feature which relates to matters of public controversy or is the subject of current public debate . . . is presented objectively and impartially and without any expression of the Authority's own views'. The Minister for Posts and Telegraphs was given power to order RTÉ to 'refrain from broadcasting any particular matter'. The statute was revised in 1976 to require RTÉ to 'uphold the democratic values of the constitution', and to prohibit the broadcast of anything likely to incite crime or anything 'tending to undermine the authority of the State'. The power to issue censorship orders was also revised, but not removed until 2001.

Early days

The impartiality required of broadcasters was difficult to maintain in a society as bitterly divided as the north. Until 1969, for the most part, the solution was to ignore the divisions. The BBC tried to emphasise the positive aspects of community relations (where they could be found) and 'underplayed' the negative. Thus in 1959, after unionist outcry over a *Tonight* programme on betting shops in the province (and a BBC apology), the rest of a series of films on Northern Ireland by Alan Whicker was cancelled (Cathcart, 1984: 192–3). UTV at first produced only a five-minute unillustrated news bulletin, and its main current affairs output was an anodyne magazine programme, coloured by an apparent awareness that 'politics might be bad for business' (Butler,

1991: 106). During the 1960s competition between the BBC and ITV resulted in the devotion of more resources to television news, and a more robust attitude to reporting Northern Ireland problems, but even in 1967 the BBC was still adhering to the notion of a civic middle ground inhabited by both Catholics and Protestants, and UTV was opting out of transmitting programmes about the province made by other companies in the ITV network (Butler 1991: 108).

On RTÉ, news and current affairs was increasingly flexing its muscles and incurring government displeasure on a range of issues from housing to Biafra and Vietnam. But the head of news Jim McGuinness told fellow executives that RTÉ had been failing to cover Irish affairs effectively, and the first significant exploration of Northern Ireland issues was on *Seven Days* in July 1968 (Horgan, 2004: 53, 60).

The impact of violence

Broadcasters were ill prepared for the increasingly violent loyalist reaction to civil rights demonstrations, but responded swiftly. RTÉ appointed a full-time Belfast correspondent in May 1969 and other broadcasters also drafted in extra staff. But it wasn't just numbers. The BBC NI head of news recalled how a formerly 'undemanding patch' was overwhelmed.

> There was not the staff to cope with what was happening, there was not the experience to handle it, there was not the professional experience to understand it . . . there was a genuine fear of somehow misusing the power of broadcasting . . . that might just make things worse (Baker, 1996: 119).

That fear of consequences led to some decisions that were later reversed. When families were being burned out of their homes in Belfast, the BBC's Martin Bell was ordered to omit from his report the fact that they were Catholics (Baker, 1996: 120). But the pictures themselves were often enough to inflame matters. One journalist wrote how in the first days of inter-communal violence 'live coverage . . . of crude abuse and total disorder would, in a flash, empty the nearby pubs of the side being abused as men poured out to take part in the fight' (Kyle, 1996: 109). The panic response of the BBC senior editors in London was to adopt 'a temporary departure from normal journalistic considerations': the facts about rioting would be given, without pictorial coverage; 'extreme' street interviews were omitted; and Ian Paisley and Bernadette Devlin were banned. The policy was dropped not long afterwards, but existing policy requiring reporters to consult senior editors ('reference up') was restated and reinforced in 1971 so that 'senior professionals in the

BBC' could 'weigh the editorial value of programme material against the physical, political and legal risks in a sectarian environment affected by terrorism' (Cathcart, 1984: 279). Likewise, UTV temporarily reduced its own news output, and opted out of some 'sensitive' network programmes.

The tone of British television news and current affairs, at least until the British army was deployed in August 1969, tended to be favourable to the Catholics' grievances on housing, jobs and votes. The similarities with the black civil rights struggle in the USA were not lost on reporters 'parachuted in' from London, whether in the apparent justice of the demands being made, or in the hostility of the unionist and loyalist reaction (Kyle, 1996: 105–8). The unionists, who had for several years been highly critical of the BBC in particular any time divided allegiances were mentioned, became steadily more outraged to find themselves portrayed by most of the British media as 'bigoted and antedeluvian in much the same way as the South African regime . . . The civil rights campaigners were in contrast bathed in a white light of righteousness' (Moloney, 1988: 140).

The framing of the story changed radically after the army was deployed. Instead of 'justice denied', the story was now 'peace-keeping', and the British presence was portrayed as somehow holding the ring between 'extremists on both sides'. This ITV script was typical: 'In Belfast the British Army is once again back in the old routine. Men in the middle, keeping peace between two warring factions' (Thames TV, *This Week*, 18 September 1969, quoted by Butler, 1991: 108). But this framing was gradually replaced under the pressure of events. After the republican split between officials and provisionals in 1970, Belfast saw gun battles between soldiers and the IRA, with the first army casualties in 1971, and the dominant framing shifted from 'peacekeeping' to 'law and order'.[16] Butler recounts how the rise of the IRA polarised and simplified the issue for British-based reporters: 'The Provisional IRA was cast as the villain of the piece, and terrorism was viewed as the cause of the conflict. Moral simplicity has been a hallmark of British reporting ever since' (Butler, 1991: 110). Curtis adds that shortly after internment in 1971 the chairmen of both the BBC and the Independent Television Authority pledged that impartiality did not extend to the IRA in its battle with the British army and concludes 'The commitment to non-impartiality meant that only one side of the story could be told, and that the views and experiences of a large proportion of nationalists were now taboo' (Curtis, 1998 [1984]: 10). This is not fully borne out by what was actually broadcast. In December 1971 the BBC successfully resisted intense pressure from the government not to broadcast a long television debate on *The Question of Ulster*, which, to the outrage of unionists, included participants from the Republic. Nevertheless, journalists did feel intimidated and limited in what they could do, one writing that important questions about why Catholics supported the IRA 'cannot be asked by BBC employees' (cited by Curtis, 1998 [1984]: 14). There may be an element of campaign rhetoric here. As time went by, and despite caution on the part of BBC and ITV editors, and despite continuing pressure from the government and manipulation of information by the army and government, significant programmes reflecting republican opinion and exposing abuses by the authorities *did* get broadcast. For example in 1977 *Tonight* put out a compelling account of 'inhuman and degrading treatment' of prisoners by RUC interrogators, just as the European Court of Human Rights was considering a case against Britain, during which the Attorney General had stated that abusive practices had been halted. Naturally, the broadcast provoked intense criticism of the BBC from unionists, the RUC and sections of the British press, especially when another RUC man was shot dead by the IRA eleven days later (Kyle, 1996: 111–16). The same year, and to equal criticism from the same quarters, Thames TV broadcast an account of the conditions of IRA prisoners in the Maze prison.[17]

So, while Curtis lists over 50 factual BBC or ITV/Channel 4 programmes about the north that were postponed, cut or cancelled from 1968 to 1988, in the same period an incomplete catalogue by Heathwood[18] lists over 90 documentaries and investigations – excluding news – with subjects including 'shoot-to-kill' policy, the hunger strikes, lethal use of plastic bullets, and security force collusion with loyalist murder gangs. This is not to claim that the BBC and ITV were always successful in meeting the standard of 'due accuracy and impartiality', but it gives a more nuanced picture of the public service broadcasting organisations as contested terrain rather than the 'mechanism of control' (Schlesinger, 1991: 21) seen by some.

RTÉ, censorship and the 'silencing project'

The crisis in the north also exposed deep divisions in southern society, creating difficulties for RTÉ in upholding the requirement to be 'objective and impartial' that were possibly greater even than those of the BBC and ITV.

Firstly, reunification of the island as a republic was a national aim, set down in the constitution and very widely supported by the public and politicians. What sharply divided people was the matter of whether physical force in attaining it was justified. Even after seven years of bombings and shootings, one in five adults surveyed said they supported the activities of the IRA, and another one in five was 'neutral' (Davis and Sinnott, 1979, cited O'Brien, 2005: 49). From the beginning, the government was not willing to tolerate the use of the airwaves to justify violence or to frame events in the north as a liberation struggle. Yet what did 'impartiality' mean, other than allowing all sides to explain themselves, especially in the absence (until the Broadcasting

Act was amended in 1976) of any ban on incitement to crime? When informal meetings and discussions during 1969–70 (Horgan, 2004: chs 3–4) failed to ensure appropriate 'balance' in RTÉ broadcasts – meaning that unionist and British army viewpoints were not being heard, or that the IRA was being 'glamorised' – the government began to talk about using its powers. Much of the government pressure was over radio programmes, but the final straw was the RTÉ *Seven Days* television programme on 28 September 1971 in which the chiefs of staff of both wings of the IRA were interviewed on film, followed by a studio discussion with politicians. Three days later, the government ordered RTÉ to refrain from broadcasting anything that 'could be calculated to promote the aims or activities of any organisation which engages in, promotes, encourages or advocates the attaining of any particular objective by violent means' (Horgan, 2004: 99).

Despite the best efforts of RTÉ (Fisher, 2005), the government refused to clarify the ambiguities in the order, so RTÉ executives felt it was still permissible to interview paramilitaries, as long as the material did not 'succeed in promoting (their) aims and activities' (letter from RTÉ Authority cited in Horgan, 2004: 103). The following year, RTÉ radio broadcast a long account of an interview with the leader of the Provisional IRA, Sean Mac Stiofáin. It did not use his voice, but gave a more or less word-for-word account. In the ensuing row, the RTÉ Authority (board of directors) was sacked, and broadcast journalism entered the period that O'Brien (2005) calls the 'silencing project'. After a change of government in 1973, the order was clarified: it now banned interviews and *reports* of interviews with any 'spokesman for' the IRA, Provisional Sinn Féin and any organisation banned in Northern Ireland by the British government.

The orders created an intimidating atmosphere for RTÉ journalists, and there was much talk of self-censorship: Purcell (1991) describes how the ban on interviews was in practice extended beyond the immediate supporters of the IRA, and far beyond the issue of political violence, to cover industrial disputes, anti-drug campaigns and other local issues, if they included Sinn Féin activists.[19] Journalists and their trade union complained that many important stories were left untold because they were too difficult to tackle without including republican voices.[20] The effect was to demonise republicanism, if not to render it invisible on the airwaves. It was not until March 1993 that the Supreme Court ruled in a case brought by a trade union activist that RTÉ's interpretation of the order went too far in excluding individuals who were speaking for themselves rather than on behalf of banned organisations such as Sinn Féin.[21]

It is worth pointing out here that the British ban on broadcast interviews with Sinn Féin and others was in comparison merely cosmetic. It lasted from 1988 (just after the breakdown of secret talks between Sinn Féin and the

British government)[22] to 1994 (after the IRA announced a 'complete cessation' of violence), just six years compared to 23 years for RTÉ. Interviews with the IRA had already become virtually impossible since 1974 because of the requirement under the Prevention of Terrorism Act to notify the police about any knowledge of terrorist activity. But under the Hurd ban,[23] only *voices* of Sinn Féin (and other proscribed representatives) were barred. After some initial confusion, the BBC and ITV quickly resumed interviews[24] (with the tacit acceptance of the government); at first any provocative words were silenced and sub-titled on screen, later actors' voices were used over the pictures. When the person was speaking on issues not related to the 'war', their own voice was broadcast uncensored. Republican opinions and voices still reached audiences in Britain and Ireland via British television, but RTÉ could not even paraphrase what might have been said.

The limitations of television news: biased against whom?

In many accounts, the exclusion of republican voices from television, combined with the simplification of the conflict mainly to a 'law and order' or 'two tribes' frame from 1972 left viewers in Britain and Ireland bereft of the means to understand the underlying causes of the conflict. Leaving aside the fact that other means of information continued to be available, and that most people in the north itself continued to have a very clear understanding of the forces at work, it is clear that the conventions of television, and particularly of news bulletins, contributed to a degree of misunderstanding or ignorance outside the north. A dominant trend in the critical discourse about the media has been that television has not been impartial, but has taken sides in the conflict. For Miller (2002) and others, institutional bias produced a media environment that was unremittingly hostile to republicanism and favourable to British interests and unionist sensibilities. There are equally convincing alternative readings; Butler (1991: 115) suggests that at the very least unionism and loyalism were portrayed as the 'ugly' twin of intransigent republicanism, partly because of the 'pig-in-the-middle' framing of the British presence. Parkinson (1998) goes a great deal further, arguing that even after the civil rights framing of the conflict in the early days was replaced by a law and order framing, the media agenda was 'dominated by republican and "human rights" issues, with loyalist concerns such as political isolation, deteriorating security and "border genocide", being largely confined to the periphery of national media coverage' (Parkinson, 1998: 75).[25] Parkinson concludes that much of the damage (in failing to influence British opinion) was 'self-inflicted': unionists offered a 'monotonous' and 'sterile' political message, and their propaganda was not as effective as that of the republicans; but he insists this was compounded by the media's simplified framing and unanalytical reporting of the conflict over most of the period and by a general lack of sympathy for unionism (Parkinson, 1998: 162–7).

It is tempting to draw from this divergence in the literature a conclusion that in the midst of conflict neither party will ever be happy with reporting that includes any reflection of the view from 'the other side'. Certainly, it is common to hear in television newsrooms in Dublin, Belfast and London that 'as long as both sides are complaining we must be doing something right.' But viewers generally, whether party to conflict or not, are being deprived if editors and journalists do not find a means to overcome the limitations of their medium.

The tyranny of pictures

The demand for visuals imposes on television news what Birt in *The Times* (1975) called the bias against understanding. He blamed it partly on the lack of time available for background explanation in bulletins, and also on television's need for *stories* as a means to carry an explanation.

> Making a film about homeless people is not an adequate way of approaching the problem created by our housing shortage. Nor is a film profile of a Catholic or Protestant family in Belfast likely to be by itself a useful starting point on the road to understanding what is happening in Northern Ireland.

Yet without pictures that tell stories, the visual medium finds it difficult to engage audience interest in issues: it might as well be radio.[26] This tyranny means that television news is more susceptible than other media to having its agenda distorted by spectacular events, so that 'terrorist' acts become a form of manipulation. In one example cited by McCafferty, during the winter of 1988–9 the British army was causing a lot of damage digging up kitchen floors while searching for weapons in Belfast. In reprisal, the IRA bombed army housing in Derry. Only then did RTÉ report what had been happening in the arms searches (McCafferty, 1991: 212).

Without context, the succession of violent incidents seemed inexplicable, other than as the evil of 'mindless' gunmen and bombers (Butler, 1991: 111). During the 1970s and 1980s the news from BBC NI and UTV became a nightly catalogue of local horrors: a bomb here, arson there, a body here; with no sign of progress, no sign of victory for anyone, much of the violence was ignored in London and Dublin newsrooms.[27]

Moloney (1988) believes coverage of the north was at its best until about 1974, characterised by all that is healthy in journalism: 'curiosity, indignation, scepticism and a wish to inform and explain'. He argues that after the loyalist strike brought down the power sharing experiment, and the conflict ground on year after year, many journalists became convinced that the problem was insoluble, and that audiences in Britain and the Republic were becoming tired of a conflict that had become 'a simple violence story as predictable, regular and despairingly intractable as the Middle East'. That attitude began to change only with Sinn Féin's success at the ballot box in the wake of the hunger strikes (1980–1); now again there was something for journalists to explain: if the IRA are nothing but criminals, why do people vote for them? (Moloney, 1988: 142–6)

The technology of picture acquisition (and how it was used) also had an impact in adding to the almost random differences in coverage of similar events. What cameras were available, and where were they? It was an editorial decision where to place cameras, but influenced by concerns for crew safety. In riots, Seaton records, BBC crews were generally behind the police or army line, while those from Scandinavian broadcasters were more often on the side of the protestors, making the conflict look very different to their audiences:

> They understood different people to be the aggressors and different groups to be the victims. Of course, neither view was wholly accurate. But 'point of view' was a powerful mobilizer of sympathies – sometimes inappropriately. The angle of shot can produce anger, identification, or empathy (Seaton, 2005: 225).[28]

Warnings about bombs gave time for evacuation, and also for cameras to get there for the explosion; spectacular, but often without context. The coverage of no-warning attacks often depended on chance. The Harrods bomb in 1983 claimed six lives, and was briefly enough covered with grainy, distant pictures of ambulances and shoppers clearing the area.[29] The following year five people died as a result of the attack on the Conservative Party conference in Brighton. The political target was more significant of course, but the picture coverage was both more extensive and more emotional because cameras and lights were already on the scene: viewers saw close-ups of the severely injured being rescued.[30]

From conflict to resolution

If coverage of the civil rights march on 5 October 1968 in Derry is taken as the beginning of the troubles, some take 8 November 1987 in Enniskillen as the beginning of the end. Eleven people died when the IRA bombed a Remembrance Day parade, and again, it was an amateur camera that provided more than ten minutes of harrowing footage of the immediate aftermath. ITN left out some of the pictures, and the BBC did not broadcast all the sound (of sirens and distressed voices). The event dominated the news that night[31] and for weeks afterwards. Parkinson argues that the story had a profound effect on audiences, and particularly on the British public who 'for perhaps the first and only time they were able to fully empathise with the civilian population of Northern Ireland' (Parkinson, 1998: 70). It was not merely the pictures that had such an impact, this time the framing of the story was different too: the dominant narrative was not 'law and order', but 'reconciliation', largely because of the emotional story of Gordon Wilson, who lay in the rubble holding his dying daughter's hand, and in an interview from his hospital bed called for prayer and forgiveness. 'The event was seen as so catastrophic by the media . . . that it was believed it would prove to be a watershed in the history of the troubles, with the acknowledged "decency" of the ordinary people somehow overcoming the evil forces of terrorism' (Parkinson, 1998: 70). It seems a naive reading to suggest that the media would radically change the framing of the conflict because of one person and some harrowing pictures; after all the media had used the reconciliation frame before with the 1976 'peace people' inspired by Mairead Corrigan, grieving for her sister's children.[32] There were cross community demonstrations against violence, widely reported with a great deal of media sympathy – but they all ran out of steam in a few months.

What had really changed in meantime was the balance of underlying forces. After years of abstention, republicans were winning elections – Gerry Adams was MP for West Belfast – and would soon be looking for ways to end the war. The unionists were still trying to come to terms with the fact that they had failed to overturn the 1985 Anglo-Irish Agreement, which allowed for Irish government influence on British policy in the north. Despite the continuing violence of the next few years, there was now another story to be told, and though the law and order and pig-in-the-middle framings continued to be used, the conflict-resolution story had basis in reality, however frail it was at first.

Facilitating peace?

Just as there are two views of whether television coverage of the conflict was systematically anti-republican or anti-unionist, there are now two views about the framing of the peace process itself. One view is that, as it became clearer that militant republicans were talking peace, first to the SDLP,[33] then to representatives of the British government, to the Irish government and finally to the unionists, the media moved further and further from the law and order frame, and adopted a sympathetic, peace-at-all-costs narrative. A number of factors are cited to demonstrate this:

- after the 1994 ceasefire, a new tone was evident in interviews, especially with Sinn Féin; they now tended to be longer, with less hostile questions (Lago, 1998: 679–82)
- continuing violence went unreported or under-reported, or at least given less prominence (Seaton, 2005: 147; McDonald, 1997).
- broadcasters willingly took on the role of 'megaphone diplomacy', relaying to each side what might not be sayable in formal talks (O'Farrell, 1998: 99).

We should hardly find it surprising that many journalists covering the conflict, especially the locals, saw it as their minimum duty to avoid derailing the process of reconciliation. One Belfast journalist told Wolfsfeld: 'I'm unapologetic in saying I want peace. I want to end all this violence, this war. I've seen it all. I've been to the bomb scenes . . . many of my school friends are dead as a result of violence. So I want to end it all' (Wolfsfeld, 2004: 180).

Yet sympathy did not necessarily translate into practical assistance. Spencer interviewed politicians involved in the peace process and journalists involved in reporting it. He records frustration among politicians trying to find accommodation with former enemies that television bulletins focused always on remaining divisions, and concludes that the simplifications sought and presented by television news actually made it more difficult to advance to compromise. Spencer found the 'megaphone diplomacy' function was better achieved through the press than through television news, and concluded 'Even though the dominant position was one of seeking to develop the peace process . . . (television) reporting was primarily interested in a breakthrough or a crisis, which represented the process as lurching from success to failure' (Spencer, 2000: 86). Even when significant agreements were being reached, television news sometimes had a disturbing tendency to ask which side had 'won'.

Conclusion

There is a final temptation to link the simplifications made by television news with the simplifications made *about* television news. It has been argued here that the model of the media generally, and television especially, as a mechanism of control is not particularly useful. The story selections, framings and portrayals in news bulletins often displayed hostility both to nationalism and to unionism. Even as consensus views were being broadcast, audiences were resisting and subverting them (Morrissey and Smyth, 2002: 36–7). There was under-reporting, but audiences were frequently complaining that there was 'too much about Northern Ireland' (or too much bad news or too much gore) on their screens. It is true, too, that the British state did not shy from using disinformation and intimidation in an effort to hegemonise its 'two tribes' and 'peacekeeping' version. But other parties were equally guilty of manipulation, including the ultimate manipulation of savage attacks on civilians. The propaganda model, applied to the case of public service broadcasting, shows not consensus within the media, but an often vigorous contest between the governing elite and the journalists and even senior editors. Of course, it would be better if journalists did not have to fight against restrictions imposed by the authorities in order to report conflict properly, but that has always been part of the job. As long as broadcasters are trying to reach an audience with divided loyalties and to speak to disputed versions of history, then 'objectivity' and 'accuracy' themselves will be controversial and television news and current affairs programmes will remain contested terrain.

Chapter 7

Selling fear? The changing face of crime reporting in Ireland

Mark O'Brien

Introduction

If newspapers are the first draft of history, then from looking at how some sections of the Irish media cover the crime issue one would be tempted to assume that the history of Ireland is characterised by a safe, non-violent, relatively crime free past and an unsafe, violent, crime-ridden present. The past – when streets were safer and front doors were left open – has, almost overnight, been replaced by an unsafe present where crime is tearing society apart. In the public imagination the island of saints and scholars has been supplanted by an island of thieves, murderers and sex offenders.

This chapter contends that this assumption is inaccurate despite its prevalence in public reminiscing and media concern about society being overwhelmed by crime. The perception of society as having evolved from being safe and relatively crime free to being unsafe and crime ridden is appealing but too simplistic. Like many assumptions it suffers from the defects of any rose-tinted view of the past and any jaundiced view of the present. There never was a golden crime free era – other than in the public's collective memory and media reminiscences.

Every generation fears the moral decline of the present compared to the comfortable certainties of the past. This chapter contends that the low crime figures of the past are inaccurate owing to the non-reporting of crime by victims and that crime levels were kept artificially low by mass emigration. It also contends that the way in which crime was reported – or rather not reported – by the media in the past perpetuated this assumption that post-independence Ireland was a virtuous idyll. It argues that various constraints impeded explicit media reporting of crime in the past so as to create an inaccurate public image of the types of crime then being committed. It further argues that the style of crime reporting that emerged from the 1980s onwards has helped foster the perception that present-day Ireland is a much more dangerous society than it was in the past. In stark contrast to the past, crime is now overly reported with every graphic detail being included in reportage. I conclude by arguing that the changes in the way that the media report crime, more so than any quantum increase in the crime rate, have created this perception of a safe past and an unsafe present.

Measuring crime – a perennial problem

Measuring the true extent of crime in any society is, and has always been, problematic. Ireland is no different in this regard. Up to the year 2000, crime, as reported to the Garda Síochána, was divided into two distinct categories – indictable and non-indictable crime. Indictable crime was the more serious, containing within its four subsections offences such as murder, manslaughter, firearms offences, rape, sexual assault, incest and kidnap. Non-indictable crime consisted of more minor offences, such as public order offences, driving offences, minor assaults and licensing law offences.[1] In 2000 the two categories were replaced by headline and non-headline offences. For the most part the new headings simply replaced the old ones but one big change was the reorganisation of the subsections within each category. Headline offences now contain ten subcategories of offences, as opposed to indictable offences, which contained four. This allows for a more detailed breakdown of offences in the official statistics. In quantitative terms, non-headline offences account for approximately three quarters of all offences in any given year.[2] Media attention, however, is almost exclusively devoted to levels of headline offences, and although this reflects their more serious nature, at least one analyst has concluded that this focus has resulted in the public being misinformed about the true nature of crime in Irish society (O'Connell, 1999).

While the reorganisation of garda statistics allows for easier analysis of individual offences, two facts should be borne in mind when reading these statistics. Firstly, they record only crime that has been reported, and secondly, they represent a count of the offences that have been reported and do not take into account population change. There are a plethora of reasons why a crime might not be reported to the gardaí: the victim may feel that the crime is not worth reporting or that, if it is, nothing will be done; the victim may know the offender and may not want to involve the gardaí; the victim may fear reprisals from the offender; the victim may feel that he or she will not be believed; or the victim may feel implicated in or stigmatised by the offence.

As regards the statistics themselves, when read and discussed in isolation – as happens for the most part in media coverage of crime – they give only a partial understanding of the crime issue. The statistics represent a count of offences that have been reported without any reference to population growth. Given that the issue of crime is a quantitative one, it follows that it can only be meaningfully measured and understood in comparative terms. Unfortunately the comparator adopted by most media is that of year-to-year increases in headline crime – without any reference to population increase or comparisons to other developed countries – comparators that indicate that Ireland has a lower crime rate (per head of population) than most other European countries. In one EU study Ireland had half the amount of recorded crime per head of population as the US and one quarter as much as England and Wales (O'Donnell, 2004). Relating crime figures to population change would give a clearer picture of crime in Irish society, while comparisons with other jurisdictions would also put the issue into a more realistic focus.

Much ado is made by various commentators about the low levels of crime in pre-1960s Ireland – a situation usually explained with reference to greater community solidarity, the influence of religion, the lack of luxury goods to steal and greater respect for the living person (*Irish Times*, 19 September 2004). Little or no reference is made to the reluctance or inability of certain individuals to report crime or to population change, despite these being critical variables in any realistic analysis. Firstly, only lately have the physical and sexual abuse of children, established beyond doubt as endemic in post-independence Ireland, been acknowledged and atoned for (Raftery and O'Sullivan, 1999). The victims of this abuse – children in the care of the state who were farmed off to religious orders to be cared for – were effectively voiceless. Victims of physical and sexual abuse while in institutional care were hardly in a position to report such crimes to the Garda Síochána. The reverence accorded to religious personnel by society and the fear of reprisal were more than enough to ensure the victims' silence.

It thereby follows that the crime statistics for post-independence Ireland are inaccurate about the levels of crime being committed. While some may argue that this relates solely to physical and sexual crime, one must also bear in mind the deaths (often unexplained) of children within the institutions run by the religious orders. Is it possible that these deaths might mean that the statistics relating to murder and manslaughter are also inaccurate? Much of this criminal activity has only recently become public knowledge and is only now being recorded in crime statistics simply because an offence is recorded when it is reported, which is not necessarily at the same time as when it occurred. These offences are not categorised separately and so it is difficult to quantify them. Sexual offences reported to the Garda Síochána grew from 397 in 1990 to 968 in 1998 and the Garda Síochána annual reports from 1996 to 1999 noted that the statistics on sexual crime were inflated by cases that had been reported 'several years after they have taken place' (Garda Síochána Annual Reports 1996–9). By late 2006, approximately 2,500 survivors of institutional abuse had applied to the Residential Institutions Redress Board for compensation (*Irish Times*, 13 October 2006). It follows that the non-reporting by victims of these crimes when they occurred means that the crime figures from that period are a distorted base from which to compare past and present crime levels and that the past was not the virtuous idyll people might remember.

Secondly, post-independence Ireland was characterised by high levels of emigration. From the late 1920s to the early 1960s, economic stagnation ensured that vast swathes of the young adult population left the country in search of a better life elsewhere. Between 1951 and 1961 alone, over 400,000 people emigrated and the 1961 census recorded an all-time population low of 2.8 million people. It is impossible that that this mass exodus of young adults did not contribute in some way to the country's low crime levels. Ryan (1990: 64) concluded that 'along with those who came to Britain seeking a better life, there came also the misfits, the psychologically disturbed and the criminal'. Such individuals were inevitably in trouble with the law and ended up in prison. In 1960 alone approximately 3,000 Irish-born males were committed to English and Welsh prisons and between 1960 and 1969 Irish nationals made up approximately 14 per cent of prison committals (Ryan, 1990: 64).

It follows that the high levels of emigration kept crime levels in Ireland artificially low. The economic boom that swept through Ireland from the early 1960s onwards changed this situation. As emigration declined, the population increased from 2.818 million people in 1961 to 2.978 million in 1971.[3] As the population increased, so too did the level of crime. Between 1966 and 1971 alone the number of reported indictable crimes doubled from 19,029 to 37,781 (McCullagh, 1996: 3). Alongside a swell in population therefore came an increase in crime levels – evidence perhaps that Ireland was a low crime society, not because it was an isle of saints and scholars, but because it was an isle of emigrants.

'Don't read all about it'

The non-reporting of sexual crime to the Garda Síochána and the influence of emigration on crime levels thus create an official picture of low crime levels in pre-1960s Ireland and contribute to the perception that the past was a safer place. But so too did the inability of the media to report adequately on sexual crimes that were reported to gardaí and the court cases that followed. In a study on how the print media reported on sexual offence cases between 1923 and 1974, Keating (2002) examined the garda statistics on sexual offences to determine the level of such offences and then conducted a search of local and national newspapers to determine the type of reporting that accompanied, or, as he found, did not accompany, such offences and resultant court cases. Keating (2002) identified a belief among clergy and politicians that the public needed to be protected from discussions about crime, particularly sexual crime, for fear that such discussions would corrupt susceptible people. The publication by British newspapers of crime stories, and in particular crime stories of a sexual nature, was debated at length by the Catholic Church-inspired Committee of Enquiry on Evil Literature. One member of that committee later recalled the discussion on 'harmful-newspapers which simply set themselves out to describe crime, particularly sexual crime, with every disgusting detail; newspapers which serve no useful purpose, without any literary merit for which anybody with an educated mind would care one jot' (Dáil Debates, vol. 26, col. 625, 18 October 1928).

The legislation that stemmed directly from the committee's report was the Censorship of Publications Act 1929, the debate on which was characterised by deputies lining up to criticise media coverage of crime. The Minister for Justice, James FitzGerald-Kenney, asserted that the bill's most useful function would be 'to prohibit the sale in this country of objectionable newspapers'. Kenny expressed concern about the cumulative effect of reading too many crime stories, noting that, 'when you find perpetually one heaped on another, when you find that the person who reads that paper has his or her mind from the beginning of the time he or she reads that paper until the end of the time steeped in the details of sexually unpleasant cases, it must have the effect of depraving that particular person's mind' (Dáil Debates, vol. 26, col. 624, 18 October 1928). Another deputy, Hugh Law, criticised what he saw as the ever increasing 'production of a kind of newspaper which specialises in sordid, evil, demoralising matter' and the 'glaring headlines which relate in every case to some sordid, disgusting crime, or to some other evil aspect of life'. He regarded it as 'demoralising that we should have the attention of the people continually directed to crimes of violence, to sordid, ugly, vulgar things' (Dáil Debates, vol. 26, cols 624–5, 18 October 1928). Deputy Michael Tierney declared that there was 'a kind of tendency among even quite respectable periodicals, even among the periodicals of this very great and sainted country, where the Press is beyond all suspicion, to specialise a little too much in the collection and publication of details of all kinds of sordid crimes apart altogether from sexual crimes'. Readers were thus 'compelled to wade through pages of headlines dealing with this horror that took place in Paris and that horror that took place in New York, or how this man has committed suicide in a slum in one city, or another man has cut his sweetheart to pieces in another city'. Tierney was in no doubt as to the effects of such coverage, asserting that newspapers that 'devote a large part of their space to the publication of details of crimes of cruelty and violence, are doing a good deal to lay the foundations for a later development in the direction of sexual crime' (Dáil Debates, vol. 26, col. 643, 18 October 1928).

As a result of such concerns several sections of the Censorship Act were geared towards sanitising the coverage of crime by the media. Section 7 of the act allowed the public to complain to the Minister for Justice if several issues of a periodical publication 'devoted an unduly large proportion of space to the publication of matter relating to crime'. The minister could then refer the complaint to the Censorship of Publications Board and subsequently ban the periodical if the board so recommended. This measure is still in force today. Once passed, several periodicals fell foul of this provision. In an answer to a Dáil question in November 1930, the minister indicated that he had banned six imported newspapers for devoting an unduly large proportion of space to matters related to crime (Dáil Debates, vol. 36, cols 719–20, 28 November 1930).[4]

But the act was also intended to curb crime coverage by indigenous media. In this respect, the legislature imposed constraints on the detail that periodicals could publish vis-à-vis court cases. Referring to judicial proceedings, section 14 of the act declared it unlawful to print or publish '(a) any indecent matter the publication of which would be calculated to injure public morals, or (b) any indecent medical, surgical or physiological details the publication of which would be calculated to injure public morals'.

It was not long before a newspaper fell foul of these new regulations. In 1929 charges of breaching section 14 were preferred against the proprietor and editor of the *Waterford Standard* over its reportage of an arraignment hearing against a local theatre owner who was accused of unlawful and felonious carnal knowledge and indecent assault against a 13-year-old girl in his employment. The paper had devoted its entire front page to the arraignment hearing and included some medical detail that had been presented in evidence by the prosecution (*Waterford Standard*, 28 September 1929). The inclusion of this detail in the paper's reportage was, the state argued, calculated to injure public morals. On conviction, the editor, David C. Boyd, faced a fine not exceeding £500 or imprisonment with hard labour for six months or both. In his evidence Boyd stated he had published the story in full in the public interest – it had always been 'the policy of the paper to give careful, verbatim, and authentic reports'. He denied that he published the details to deliberately offend public morals asserting that 'the medical evidence was reported in clean, scientific terms in which there was nothing smutty'. He stated that such cases did not get the publicity they deserved and asserted that 'Publicity is good for morality. What evildoers fear most in offences of this kind is publicity'. He also stated that attempts were often made to suppress reportage of such cases and that refusal to bend to such pressure resulted in commercial consequences for the newspaper concerned – most likely in terms of loss of advertising (*Waterford Standard*, 26 October 1929).

In the month between Boyd's reporting on the alleged sexual assault and his prosecution, the Bishop of Waterford had condemned the paper's reportage 'as an outrage on public decency and morality, which no mere purposes of market could for a moment justify or extenuate'. While this 'outrage' remained unatoned for, he warned, 'parents cannot be expected to admit the offending newspaper to their households with the implicit confidence which they may have hitherto entertained' (*The Standard*, 26 October 1929). Such a denunciation could hardly have helped Boyd's paper in terms of attracting advertising from Catholic businesses – a message not lost on other newspapers. When counsel for the prosecution accused him of 'pandering to the prurient curiosity' of his readers Boyd retorted that 'if only a summary of the case were published people would be more smutty in their minds about it. There would be more speculation in their minds as to what happened.' Boyd was found guilty and fined £25, and the judge, who had also presided over the original hearing, declared that the publication of the medical details 'was a scandal'. He noted that he had had the right to exclude the press from the original hearing and would have done so if he had anticipated reportage along the lines of Boyd's. After Boyd's conviction, however, he felt that such an offence would not be repeated by the press (*Waterford Standard*, 26 October 1929). This double blow to free reportage – from both the Church and the judicial system – sent a clear signal to all media proprietors, and while the potency of this signal cannot be measured at such a remove it can hardly have inspired adequate coverage of sexual crime and resultant court cases.

Such sensitivity towards crime reporting back then, as is still the case, probably had much to do with political expediency. Given the extent of sexual crime in the Free State, it is possible that there was a political motive, as well as a moral one, in keeping crime news, particularly news of sexual crime, out of the media. The extent of sexual crime in the Free State was brought home to the government in the report of the Carrigan Committee, established by the government in 1930. Part of its remit was to investigate sexual crime and throughout its hearings it received evidence of the levels of sexual offences being committed. In his evidence to the committee, the Garda Commissioner, General Eoin O'Duffy, stated that the corruption of children was an increasing problem and noted that:

> an alarming aspect is the number of cases with interference with girls under 15, and even under 13 and under 11, which come before the courts. These are in most cases heard of accidentally by the Garda, and are very rarely the result of a direct complaint. It is generally accepted that reported cases do not exceed 15 per cent of those actually happening (O'Sullivan, 2001: 189).

Outlining the extent of the problem, and referring only to cases in Dublin between 1924 and 1929, O'Duffy stated that for the reported defilements of girls under ten there were 13 prosecutions, for the 10–13 age bracket there were seven prosecutions, for the 13–16 age bracket there were 11 prosecutions, for the 16–18 age bracket there was one prosecution and for the offence of rape of over 18s there were seven prosecutions and 72 prosecutions for the indecent assault of females. As Keating (2002) asserts, O'Duffy's evidence clearly indicates that the extent of sexual abuse of children was known in government circles. The public were very much in the dark, however, about the extent of the problem. The report of the Carrigan Committee was deemed too damaging for publication. As one civil servant noted; 'the obvious conclusion to be drawn is that the ordinary feeling of decency and the influence of religion have failed in this country and that the only remedy is by way of police action. It is clearly undesirable that such a view of conditions in the Saorstat should be given wider circulation' (Keating, 2002: 166).[5]

The suppression of the report amounted to suppression of public knowledge of sexual crimes against children. Thus public discourse on sexual crime was curtailed by the suppression of an official report and the legal constraints imposed on the media. In his systematic search in national and local newspapers for reports of sexual offences and subsequent court cases, Keating found that while newspapers carried comprehensive and highly detailed coverage of everything from petty larceny to murder, reports of crimes of a sexual nature were 'noticeable by their absence' (2002: 160).

This scenario was brought about by the cumulative effects of the taboo nature of such crimes, the impact of the censorship act and the impact of *Waterford Standard* case. As Keating himself put it: 'From the evidence to hand there would seem to have been a general reluctance by local and national papers at the time to publicise cases involving sexual crime against children' (2002: 161). Indeed, as far back as 1942, one crime reporter bemoaned the extent of sexual crime being perpetrated and the failure of the press to report on this issue:

> Few vice cases are ever mentioned in the press. Indeed a screen of official secrecy seems to shroud the whole question. The arguments for and against the publicising of vice prosecutions are various. Some contend that to publicise them tends to deprave the young and ignorant; some argue that it lowers the standard of public taste; some argue that vice and crime always find imitators. The opposite viewpoint, which, I must say, is also mine, is that, provided press notices are judicious, publicity acts as a warning – especially when . . . exemplary sentences are imposed (*The Bell*, 1942: 183).

In the wake of the *Waterford Standard* case newspapers were careful about how they reported on sexual crimes, if they were reported on at all. While not overstating the effects of the case, it demonstrates the mood of the time as regards media coverage of crime. As Keating asserts, when sexual crime was reported on it was generally described as 'sexual assault' with no detail being given about the specifics of the offence itself. Such reporting was incapable of sensationalism, with people either reading between the lines or not. This sober and restrictive reporting of crime was also a product of the nature of reporting at the time. Reporters were anonymous in that the practices of attributing by-lines and photographs of reporters to their stories were unknown. This prevented reporters from developing a public or crusading persona. Also absent was the system of specialist correspondent (with the exception of political correspondents), which ensured that crime reporting was not the preserve of any one reporter. All of this lay in the future.

From under-reporting to over-reporting?

Throughout the 1960s, as Ireland opened up economically and culturally, a new social order began to emerge. An educated and affluent post-civil war generation began to make its voice heard, a generation unwilling to accept uncritically the received wisdom of doctrines of the past, whether political or religious. Along with the questioning of political and religious certainties came changes in the structure and newsgathering tactics of the media. Telefís Éireann arrived in 1961 and, for the first time, the public could see, identify and identify with reporters. Although most people would have been familiar with newsreels in cinemas, now news was visual in a much more everyday way.

Television could also report news much more quickly than newspapers. It was a radically changed media environment to which newspapers had to respond. While this response was gradual, newspapers began to change during the 1960s. The introduction of by-lines (and much later photographs) did away with the anonymity of print journalists and gave the public an idea of whose work they were reading. The 1960s were also characterised by the appointment of specialist correspondents, whereby reporters were assigned to specific news areas and encouraged to develop an expertise and cultivate sources in them. While the position of political correspondent existed in most national papers, the mid-1960s witnessed the appointment of reporters to specific beats, for example education, religion, business or agriculture. Crime reporting, however, remained part of the general newsroom beat. This specialised post would evolve later and would stem from the appointment of reporters to cover general law and order news. Such reporters were invariably called security correspondents, a less exciting title than that of crime correspondent which would emerge later.

State sensitivity about crime reporting was again heightened during the 1970s, when, as the northern troubles worsened, the state struggled with a spate of paramilitary crime. Between 1971 and 1981 the level of indictable crime doubled from 37,781 to 89,400 indictable offences. Between 1971 and

1981 crimes against the person (which included murder, manslaughter, fire-arms offences and kidnap) jumped from 1,256 to 2,478, while offences against property (which included armed robbery) jumped from 10,654 to 28,916 McCullagh, 1996: 3). Rather than hyping this real increase in crime levels as a threat to society, many publications found themselves being hauled before the Special Criminal Court on charges of contempt of court and being accused by politicians of being 'on the wrong side' in the fight against paramilitary crime.

In 1975 the Special Criminal Court declared itself 'scandalised' after the *Irish Press* published claims that gardaí had beaten up suspects. Its editor, Tim Pat Coogan, was prosecuted, but successfully defended the paper. In 1976 the editor of the *Irish Times*, Fergus Pyle, was similarly prosecuted after the paper reproduced terminology from a press release that referred to the court as a 'sentencing tribunal'. Pyle apologised to the court and the charges were dropped. *Hibernia* magazine was also prosecuted and forced to apologise after it published a reader's letter that referred to a trial with the word 'trial' in quotation marks. In 1977 the *Irish Times* incurred the wrath of the government after it published an extensive investigation into the alleged beating of suspects by gardaí (*Irish Times*, 14 February 1977). The 'Heavy Gang' exposé prompted the Minister for Justice, Paddy Cooney, to condemn the 'gullible and uninformed media' that had, as he saw it, been 'taken in by people whose interests are served by breaking down public confidence in the police' (Allen, 1999: 193).

It was in the 1980s, though, that crime reporting came into its own. The problems of social exclusion and disadvantage caused by the clearance of inner-city Dublin tenements and the creation of inadequately serviced sprawling suburban estates were reflected in a growth in drugs crime and anti-social behaviour in the form of joy riding. The growing problem of heroin became the focus of much media coverage, as did the emergence of criminal gangs involved in the drugs trade. In this respect the *Sunday World* led the way with its exposé on Dublin drug dealer Larry Dunne. *Magill* magazine profiled one of the city's most reclusive criminals, Martin Cahill, prompting RTÉ's flagship current affairs programme, *Today Tonight*, also to profile Cahill, with a harassed Brendan O'Brien pursuing Cahill around the streets of Dublin.

This new approach in crime reporting, profiling and door-stepping dangerous criminals for comment, marked a new departure in crime reporting, a tactic that gained currency throughout the early 1990s. By this time the media landscape had again changed. Independent Newspapers had changed ownership and in the early 1980s, following extensive market research, it was decided to reinvent the company's titles. The *Evening Herald* was the first to undergo a revamp with market research suggesting a more aggressive and competitive approach to newsgathering and the addition of new features. The image of the *Herald* as an inner-city working-class newspaper no longer cut it with advertisers and so, in 1982, it was re-launched as a tabloid aimed at a young, urban, middle-class readership.

As one study suggested, this new target readership was demographically most likely to be victims of crime, and so it was perhaps inevitable that the paper would put a special emphasis on crime coverage. A war on crime was declared and executives decided that the paper would concentrate on a select few aspects of crime – those affecting the paper's readers – on a regular and systematic basis. Independent Newspapers group news editor, Ray Doyle, stated on RTÉ radio that this policy 'had been established within Independent Newspapers by representatives of editorial executives at a very high level. It has been decided that we should engage in this war' (Kerrigan and Shaw, 1985: 19).

But, other than crime being an issue that affected its new target readership, why did the reinvented *Herald* choose crime as its unique selling point? Why not politics or sport? The answer may be that crime continually satisfies the media's demand for news like no other phenomenon. In their seminal work on news values, Galtung and Ruge (1973) identified several criteria that influence whether or not media personnel feel an event is newsworthy. Among the criteria were: frequency – the timespan needed for an event to unfold; amplitude – the dramatic affect of an event; clarity – the unambiguous nature of the event; meaningfulness – the emotional impact of the event; unexpectedness – the unanticipated occurrence of the event; negativity – the harmfulness of an event; continuity – whereby the event becomes a running story; and personification – whereby an event is held up as personifying the moral state of society (Galtung and Ruge, 1973). Galtung and Ruge argued that the more an event satisfies these criteria the more likely the event will become news.

Crime satisfies all these news values. The immediate – or here and now – element of crime fits the news production cycle; crime is dramatic and can be reported in a easily understood 'good versus evil' narrative; it is meaningful because people sympathise with its victims; it is unexpected and it has negative consequences; a running story may emerge from coverage of the investigation and subsequent court case; and isolated events, horrific thought they may be, are often held up as personifying how violent society has become. Equally important is the fact that crime is omnipresent. Unlike politics or sports, it does not have sessions or seasons. It is an all-year round phenomena and is capable of feeding the media's insatiable appetite for dramatic and negative events to report.

While this explains why crime becomes news, it does not explain how crime might be hyped out of proportion by the media. To explain this Galtung and Ruge (1973) argued that once an event became news, what made it newsworthy – its unexpectedness, its negativity – became accentuated. The cumulative effect of this process of selection and emphasis, they concluded, was to produce an image of society that was at variance with social reality. In terms of crime coverage, this would mean that more serious crimes, those that most matched news values, were over reported in quantitative terms, while the less serious crimes, those that were most common in society, but which did not fit news values as much, were barely mentioned thus creating a picture of a society being engulfed by serious crime.

Is there any empirical proof to show that such a process actually occurs? An analysis by O'Connell (1999) of 2,191 crime stories from four national newspaper titles concluded that rather than giving a representative picture of the offences occurring, the newspapers provided 'an almost chemically pure, unrepresentative picture of crime in Ireland'.[6] O'Connell's (1999) study identified several biases in the newspapers' coverage of crime. He found a bias towards extreme and atypical offences in terms of frequency. In other words, the least frequent but more serious offences, such as murder and sexual assault, featured in reportage most often, and the most common but less serious offences featured more rarely.

Comparing the reportage to garda statistics, O'Connell (1999) found that while murder accounted for .004 per cent of overall crime it accounted for 12.3 per cent of crime stories in the sample; armed robbery accounted for .9 per cent of overall crime but 15.8 per cent of crime stories in the sample. O'Connell (1999) concluded that the typical offences that appear in the print media appear rarely in official crime statistics and that the typical crimes that appear in the official statistics appear rarely in the print media. Along with this over-representation of serious crime, he also found a bias towards these offences in terms of newspaper space (word count), finding that the more frequent the offence the lower the wordage and vice versa. He also identified a bias towards stories involving vulnerable victims and invulnerable offenders. Stories involving victims aged under 16 or over 55, and stories involving females as victims received greater coverage in terms of word count. He similarly found that stories involving male offenders received more space than stories involving female offenders. Thus the print media had a preference for male adult offenders and female and either very young or very old victims (O'Connell, 1999). In his study O'Connell found that of the four papers sampled, the *Evening Herald* contained the greatest proportion of crime stories to other stories. Indeed, a previous study of public attitudes towards crime (O'Connell and Whelan, 1996) found that readers of Independent Group newspapers tended to have the greatest fear of crime, regardless of previous victimisation experiences. This result held up even when statistical techniques were used to control for educational and social class differences between newspaper readerships.

No one shouted stop

Along with this new emphasis on crime coverage came a new style of crime reporting. Throughout the late 1980s and early 1990s, the newspaper market became more competitive. The creation of Irish editions of British titles, in which four to six pages of Irish news were wrapped around content already produced for the British market, resulted in the dumping of low-priced hybrid titles on the Irish market. This upped the ante in competitive terms and prompted some Irish titles to respond with aggressive marketing tactics whereby, rather than the marketing being constructed around content, the content began to be constructed to fit the marketing. As ever, the all year round phenomenon of crime was an issue that provided endless marketing opportunities.

It was an era when crime correspondents and the criminals they were writing about were elevated to celebrity status. It was also an era when crime correspondents actively and publicly used criminals as acknowledged sources of information. The two newspapers that led the field in this regard were the *Sunday World* and the *Sunday Independent*.[7] Unlike previous generations of reporters who covered the crime beat, the public profiles of the crime correspondents of these newspapers were actively promoted in their respective marketing strategies and they became household names. Stories of how crime correspondents personally challenged and door-stepped dangerous criminals made for great marketing opportunities but whether this was the function of a crime reporter was barely discussed while the stories were forthcoming.

The shape of crime reporting changed too. The new style was very much centred on reports of the interaction that took place between reporter and criminal. This situated the reporter as a central participant in, rather than a mere observer of, an event. Such a scenario involved the use of the first person singular, a more intimate and involved style of writing very different from the detached and impartial style of crime reporting that had dominated Irish journalism until then. While this style of writing was engaging and dramatic, what it meant for objectivity and balance was not adequately discussed while the stories were forthcoming.

A new tactic, the use of codenames, to write about criminals without naming them was also adopted. Thus the public was introduced to a cast of characters such as the General, the Viper, the Coach, the Penguin, the Warehouseman, the Gambler, the Monk and the Boxer. While this tactic may have safeguarded the newspapers from libel proceedings and from prejudicing any trial, it is at least arguable that it also tended to debase crime reporting by turning it into something akin to an oddly cast journalistic soap opera. The use of apocalyptic terminology such as 'untouchables' and 'gangland' in media discourse about crime also became commonplace. The inclusion of personal and intimate details on the lives of criminals – their relationships, their sex lives, where they lived, what type of car they drove and where they went on holidays – also broke new ground and it is on this issue that the lines between what is in the public interest and what the public is interested in began to blur. While such information was of huge interest to a public hungry for salacious gossip, it is debatable whether such stories were in the public interest. It is also debatable whether stories on violent criminals belonged in the lifestyle section of a newspaper. What is certain, however, is that such content was highly marketable to a scandal hungry public.

The killing of the *Sunday Independent's* crime correspondent, Veronica Guerin, in June 1996 by the same criminals that she was writing about prompted a debate on the function of a crime reporter. Was it, as it had evolved in some newspapers, to personally confront dangerous criminals on their doorsteps on the basis of information mostly received from sources with their own agendas, namely other criminals and gardaí? Was it to bring criminals to justice on the pages of their newspapers if the Garda Síochána was incapable of securing the evidence to convict them in court? Or was it, as Vincent Browne argued, to hold public institutions, the police, the court system and the prison system, to account in their handling of the crime issue? (*Irish Times*, 28 June 1996). But as a colleague of Browne's pointed out, for the most part media outlets opt for 'certain "sexy" and potentially sensational elements in order to steal an edge over the competition . . . Crime exposés sell newspapers; exposés of injustice, as a rule, do not' (*Irish Times*, 22 October 1996).

There is no easy answer to all of this, but it is at least arguable that the new style of crime reporting had at least one blind spot. Such was the enthusiasm for dramatic stories of the criminal underworld that corruption within the Garda Síochána went unnoticed and unreported. It is instructive that no crime correspondent broke the story of the corruption within the Donegal division of the Garda Síochána. Instead it fell to two Dáil deputies, Jim Higgins and Brendan Howlin, to use Dáil privilege to bring the corruption to public attention. Likewise the findings of the Morris Tribunal that 'proper discipline has been lost from An Garda Síochána' is hardly a vote of confidence in the ability of crime correspondents to make the force accountable to the public (*Irish Times*, 20 May 2006: 1). Whether crime reporting, a potent mix of detective work, intelligence gathering and journalism, should be the preserve of one high profile reporter or be carried out by an investigative team to diffuse the risks involved was also discussed, although little has changed in this regard. Crime reporting is still mostly centred on the 'celebrity crime correspondent' model – death threats against at least one crime correspondent notwithstanding (*Irish Times*, 15 November 2003).

Conclusion

Although the media portray the evolution of Irish society as continuously moving from a safe and crime free past to an unsafe crime-ridden present, there are a number of factors that contradict this simple narrative. Firstly, in the past many victims of crime were unable to report their victimisation; secondly, mass emigration kept crime levels artificially low in the past; and thirdly, the restrictions placed on media reporting of crime in the past ensured that crime, particularly sexual crime, was not adequately reported. These factors mean that crime statistics from the past are an inaccurate base from which to compare present crime levels and that public discourse about the types of crime being committed was inhibited by lack of media coverage. In reminiscing about the past, present-day crime reporting overlooks these factors, just as it overlooks the continuing rise in population in favour of concentrating on the annual rise in crime levels as indicated by the garda statistics. In 2004 there was a three per cent increase in headline crime, but there was also a population increase of five per cent, a fact missing from most coverage, but which is a crucial factor in giving context to increases in crime levels. Similarly, Ireland's favourable international position in crime league tables is mostly ignored. So too is the fact that one is more likely to be a victim of a crime involving property than a crime involving physical harm. In the year 2000 crimes against the person accounted for 4.26 per cent of headline crime, while crimes against property accounted for 95.74 per cent. In 2005 the respective figures were 6.37 per cent and 93.63 per cent.[8]

The ignoring of such factors and the over-representation of headline crime in the media gives a distorted view of a society besieged by crime and have two direct consequences. Firstly, fear of crime is created among the public. A July 2006 Eurobarometer poll found that 54 per cent of the Irish public identified crime as one of the two most important issues facing the country. The European average was 24 per cent. Another Eurobarometer poll published in February 2006 found that ten per cent of the Irish public thought it 'very likely' that they would be victims of crime compared to an EU average of 6 per cent. In the same poll, 44 per cent of Irish respondents thought it 'not likely' that they would be a victim of crime, compared to an EU average of 63 per cent (Corrigan, 2006: 15). Secondly, this public fear of crime allows politicians who should know better to hop on the 'tough on crime' bandwagon. Rather than a rational debate on the causes of crime – say for example, on the merits of drug prohibition – what emerges is a concentration on the effects of crime and how more gardaí and more prison places are needed to police us from ourselves.

From media coverage of crime one gets the sense that risk is ever present, more so now than in the past. This is a narrative that gives a sense of continuity to crime stories – that danger is just around the corner and nobody knows who is going to be the next victim. In stark contrast, the consensus among criminologists is that the crime rate is fairly stable, when expressed as per head of population and when allowance is made for occasional fluctuations in individual offences, such as murder, that occur in every jurisdiction. The fact that Ireland has one of the lowest crime rates in Europe is a headline that has yet to make it on to the front page.

Chapter 8

Irish media representations of science

Brian Trench

Introduction

As science has come to play an ever more central role in contemporary societies, media coverage of science has received more attention, both within formal media studies and well beyond. Policy makers pursuing a strategy for a knowledge economy, and aiming to ensure a plentiful supply of scientifically and technically skilled workers, are concerned that media coverage should encourage young people in this direction. Scientists seeking to expand research programmes and build institutions with the newly available funding hope that the media will help win public support for their endeavours. Specialist science journalists, convinced that they have important stories to tell, argue for more space and airtime. Practitioners and analysts in the rapidly developing field of science communication scrutinise media reports for how they reflect or shape public attitudes and awareness.

Our focus is on formal studies of journalism and media and, in the present context, on the relatively new academic discipline of science communication. Media coverage of science has been the subject of many descriptive, analytical and theoretical studies, particularly over the past twenty years. These have been published in journalism and media studies outlets, to a lesser extent, and in those of science communication, to a much greater extent.

This chapter will review

- reasons for critical attention to science in the media
- issues and trends in international studies of science in the media
- resources devoted to coverage of science in Irish media
- past and present patterns in Irish media coverage of science
- how this coverage connects with policy perspectives on the knowledge society

Studies of media coverage of science (sometimes 'media science' or 'science news' for short) are generally founded, implicitly or explicitly, on two propositions: that science matters more in contemporary societies than in any previous age, and that mass media are the main source of information about science for the majority of the population. It is difficult to test either of these claims rigorously, but they seem plausible and, in themselves, they provide an adequate justification for this sub-sector of media studies.

Advanced economies, such as Ireland's, rely heavily on the application of science to products and processes: manufacturing, health services, transport, agriculture, and many more sectors draw more than ever on the formalised knowledge and know-how of science and engineering, and on the skills of those with that formal knowledge. As Ireland, in common with many other countries, commits itself to the pursuit of a 'knowledge-based economy', research and development (R&D) and the associated skills, are accorded a central place in public policy. A series of advisory reports and policy statements, most notably and recently the *Strategy for Science, Technology and Innovation 2006–13* (Government of Ireland, 2006), have reinforced that emphasis. Public funding for R&D has increased threefold over the past decade and, as part of the broader development of the country's scientific capacity, the government and other social interests with a stake in this endeavour aim to raise awareness of, and support for, science in the general population. They often look to the mass media, as well as to the educational system and direct promotional initiatives, to help develop that awareness. In some cases, as we shall mention later, they are willing to fund media activities with that purpose.

Many public issues that have received significant political and media attention have a science aspect, or are centrally concerned with science. Climate change, avian flu, nuclear energy, SARS, renewable energy, stem cell and embryo research, BSE, environmental tobacco smoke, and technically assisted reproduction are just some of the many issues around which science enters the mainstream of public life. As the examples indicate, it most often does so in relation to other activities and concerns such as politics, ethics, economy, public or personal health and quality of the environment. The complexity or uncertainty of the science in these and similar issues demand careful handling, and frequently more attention to fine detail than may generally characterise media performance. The exclusion or downplaying of such complexity and such detail risks disabling media audiences (who are also citizens) in making informed assessments and choices.

Science also finds public representation and public meaning in 'purer' states, that is, less directly associated with other domains of public culture than in the examples just cited. The results of basic research are also reported where they are seen to answer big questions about humanity, nature and the universe. The audiences for such media materials are indicated in the continuing strength of popular astronomy, as one of the last remaining fields of significant amateur endeavour in science. There, observation and analysis are of phenomena of almost unfathomable scale that purportedly reveal how the universe, earth, matter and life are constituted. But participation in public science goes wider, as shown in attendance at public lectures by high-profile scientists and sale of books for general audiences on big topics in science.

For professionals in the field, media coverage can be an important resource. Increasing specialisation within science and the continuing proliferation of scientific publications mean that scientists find it increasingly difficult to keep abreast of developments beyond (and maybe even within) their own discipline. It is widely recognised that much of the most important and interesting current science is being done at the margins of longer-established fields. Many research scientists need to know what is happening in neighbouring and some-times even distant disciplines. Though they may frequently complain about the quality of media coverage of science, scientists are active consumers of it.

In all of these contexts – economic, policy, democratic, cultural, profes-sional, and more – we may say that media coverage of science matters not just to those directly concerned with science but to many other groups in society and perhaps to society as a whole. In Ireland, where government policy makes an especially strong commitment to R&D and to a knowledge economy, it matters more than in most countries. Before considering this dimension and how Irish media perform on this account, we shall briefly review what inter-national studies say about media science.

Media science studies

Studies of science in the media are now a well-established field of research and reflection, strongly represented in journal articles, conference papers, book chapters and books. Indeed, it seems that analysis of science in the media receives disproportionately more attention than media coverage of business, sports, arts, entertainment, and other more visible media interests. The spur to this development has come from the emergence of science communication as an academic discipline and professional activity. Alongside the occasional analyses of media coverage of science topics that have appeared in the established publications of journalism, media and mass communication studies, many more have appeared in the journals, text books, readers and essay collections that have defined science communication from the mid-1980s onwards.

The origins of science communication are mixed, but have particularly strong roots in the natural sciences, that is, among scientists who took up the cause of public communication of science professionally or as an ancillary activity, with or without additional training and education. The impetus for increased activity came mainly from scientific societies and policy makers, and from publicists, strategists and others working with these interests. Science communication, in its earliest phase, developed in isolation from the already established academic disciplines of social studies and history of science, but also from journalism and media studies.

These factors influenced the conduct of science news studies. The primary concerns were with how information was processed (and supposedly distorted) in the transmission from science to public through the media. Deploying a linear model of communication and implicitly hierarchical concepts of popularisation of science, such analyses measured media reports against standards of accuracy and adequacy derived from science. Analyses of trends in the volume of coverage frequently included a claim that the volumes were too low, thus implying there was some 'proper' level. Analyses of editorial resources drew attention to the low representation of science graduates among journalists, producers and editors, and the consequent weak presence of qualifying information to set research findings and risk statements in the appropriate contexts. Such analyses were frequently book-ended with recommendations that media employ science graduates and/or ensure that science stories were handled by specialists. Other analyses sought to discern the stance of media coverage as favourable, or not, to science, and to track changes in these stances over time. More descriptive studies looked at the preferred themes and formats of science stories and their evolution. Examples of science news analyses representing all of these types can be found in the editions of the specialist journals, *Public Understanding of Science*, started in 1992, and *Science Communication*, renamed and reoriented from *Knowledge*, in 1995.

However, already by the early 1990s there were critiques of these tendencies from within communication theory and social studies of science. A critical analysis of the science and media studies underlined the hierarchical character of the dominant conceptualisation of the relations between the two (Dornan, 1990). A British sociologist identified the prevailing model of communication that underlay much of the practical action in science communication, or 'public understanding of science', as it was known in Britain, as a 'deficit model', that is, a model in which the target audiences are assumed to be deficient in understanding (Wynne, 1991; Wynne, 1995). This critique is still frequently referenced in discussion of science communication. A German sociologist contributed an empirical study of the different approaches taken by experts (mainly scientists) and journalists to their interactions that is frequently cited as a reminder of the social and professional contexts in which scientific information is handled (Peters, 1995). Other early analyses looked at journalist–scientist relations as an example of source relations more generally (Dunwoody and Ryan, 1987), emphasised the role of public relations in mediating science (Nelkin, 1995), reported on the practices and approaches of science journalists, noting that they saw themselves as journalists first, and specialists second (Hansen, 1994), or drew out the underlying heroic view of science in television documentaries on science (Silverstone, 1984) and in the profiles in the trend-setting Science Today section of the *New York Times* (Fursich and Lester, 1996).

As science communication has matured, it has acknowledged its relations with neighbouring endeavours and, drawing the lessons from studies such as those cited, and others, it has developed more completely contextual approaches both to the study and the planning of public communication activities. These take account, among other things, of the diversity of audiences, of the constraints of media production, and of possible multiple meanings of public science. However, the 'deficit model' has continuing influence and many conscious adherents (Wilsdon et al., 2005; Trench, 2006). Some studies of media science continue to highlight the deficiencies of the media, for example in reporting risk (Roche and Muskavitch, 2003), and to lament the inadequate account by media of scientific procedure (Kua et al., 2004).

Trends and resources

Contributing to public awareness of, and comfort with, science was at least part of the strategy of elite newspapers across Europe and North America in establishing special sections or pages on science, from the late 1970s (*New York Times*) and 1980s (Fayard, 1993). The *New York Times* set a high standard with its specialist full-time staff of 12 or more, and its wide pool of regular freelance contributors. It has increased its science coverage over two decades, while others have reduced theirs (Clark and Illman, 2006).

In television, a similarly high bar set had been set for longer by BBC's *Horizon* series, introduced in the 1960s, and equivalent programme series in the United States, such as *NOVA* and *Discovery*. While public broadcasters in many European countries have produced occasional documentary series, none has maintained the continuity and consistency of *Horizon*. BBC has also been a leader in radio, but the majority of public broadcasters in Western Europe maintain several weekly (even daily, in the case of three German broadcasters) programmes on science (Mazzonetto et al., 2005).

Irish media followed these trends very unevenly. RTÉ television has occasionally bought in or co-commissioned with European Broadcasting Union partners science documentaries, and it ran a weekly technology magazine programme, *Zero*, for a single series in the 1980s. But it was only in the context of a strong policy push to raise public awareness of science, and the provision of subsidies from the state agency Forfás, that RTÉ commissioned in 1998 a three-part series, *Big Science*, and, from 2004, an annual season of magazine programmes, *Scope*, for younger audiences. Whereas *Big Science* attempted to follow the example of *Horizon*, using sources in several countries to tell a large and complex story, for example of DNA analysis, *Scope* has devised an original and cheerful format that takes events or phenomena of known interest to its target audiences as a point of departure for exploration of its scientific and technological aspects. State subsidies have also fuelled an initiative by an independent television producer that sources and prepares science stories for supply to various television programmes.

For over a decade, RTÉ Radio 1 has maintained a continuing interest in science, broadcasting a weekly magazine programme on science under various names, most recently *Future Tense* and *Quantum Leap*. The format of these programmes is close to that of equivalent programmes elsewhere – half-hour in duration, with four–five interviews or reports on current or recently published research, featuring scientists as authors of new research, or commentators on the research of others, but also including items that consider the social and cultural contexts of science. The station has also broadcast occasional series on aspects of science, including time and time-keeping devices, various liquids, technological and scientific futures, individual scientists, big questions, and most recently major historical and current figures ('icons') in Irish science. This output has been largely associated with one producer and one presenter, perhaps pointing to the vulnerability of the broadcaster's commitment. Current affairs programmes have had science or technology contributors in the past, but now no longer. Under government pressure, RTÉ appointed to its newsroom a health and science correspondent, later an education and science correspondent, but the holders of these positions have been much more strongly focused on education/health than on science.

The *Irish Times* was alone among Irish newspapers to appear voluntarily aware of international trends. Taking over the editorship in 1987, Conor Brady undertook to increase the number of science graduates among the editorial staff and to introduce a weekly science page (Mulvihill, 1987). Brady had a name for the page, *Horizons*, and he was reported as saying – albeit indirectly – that 'the major political questions these days are scientific and readers should be kept abreast of developments in science in the same way they are informed of developments in other areas' (Mulvihill, 1987). The *Irish Times* appointed reporter Dick Ahlstrom as science correspondent; he became science editor in 1997, when the weekly Science Today page began publication. Science columnist William Reville had started his continuing residency in the paper in 1992, and he and Ahlstrom remain permanent features of Science Today. Ahlstrom is the only newspaper staff journalist in Ireland with a defined brief to cover the science beat, though this responsibility represents about half of his time allocation.

None of the other dailies has recognised science as a specific beat, though science-based stories do appear in their pages and correspondents specialising in health, technology and environment may, quite frequently, have to assess published research in their areas of interest. Many of the science stories come from news agencies and syndication services: John von Radowitz, science correspondent of the British-based Press Association, is perhaps the single most prolific (though usually unnamed) contributor of science news to Irish newspapers. The *Irish Examiner* draws especially heavily on the PA's services, while the *Irish Independent* derives most of its science news from the syndication services of *The Times, Daily Telegraph* and *The Independent* of London. The *Daily Irish Mail* and *Sunday Times* (Republic of Ireland edition) frequently carry reports generated by the science specialists on the staff of the parent papers, as well as science-based stories produced by generalist reporters with the Irish edition. The *Irish Daily Star* and the *Evening Herald* rely on the agencies for the science news they publish, generally brief, unattributed reports on newly published research. Popular science magazines, a key feature of media science in many other countries, have had weak presence in Ireland. The most recent and durable of several attempts to establish a national science magazine is *Science Spin*, which began publication in 2004. It has had significant sponsorship from state agencies and this support has become increasingly influential in the magazine's coverage. The much longer-established *Technology Ireland*, published by the state agency Enterprise Ireland, has, in its most recent makeover, been paying more attention to scientific research and to the political, ethical and other issues surrounding it than in some previous versions. This magazine is sold on subscription only.

Analysing Irish media science

A mid-1990s review of Irish media coverage of science noted that the science policy debate raging in 1993, when the Irish Research Scientists' Association was established, had been 'ignored' by political correspondents (Sterne and Trench, 1994). The initiatives in research funding taken by government in more recent years, up to and including the publication of the Science Technology and Innovation Strategy in June 2006 with a commitment to invest €2.7 billion over three years, have remained outside the political journalists' range of view. Major policy departures, representing historically giant leaps in public spending, have been confined to the margins of media coverage. I co-wrote that 1994 review while still active in science and technology reporting and in the representative organisation, Irish Science Journalists' Association. We claimed the media lacked the resources to analyse the issues raised in the scientists' policy campaign, and that the coverage of the debate (or lack of it) revealed a media 'blind spot'. We noted the heavy reliance on foreign sources – news agencies and news syndication services – for stories on (international) science and technology and the near-absence of stories based on Irish science.

The review linked the low level of media attention to science in general and science in Ireland in particular to 'the weak representation of science in public affairs' as well as to communication failures of the Irish science community. Both of these observations were to be echoed in official policy documents. The advisory report to government on science and technology, known as the Tierney Report, referred to 'the Irish media's low level of interest and expertise in covering STI [science, technology and innovation]' (Science Technology and Innovation Advisory Council, 1995). The subsequent White Paper on Science Technology and Innovation noted 'the weak representation of STI issues in public affairs' (Government of Ireland, 1996).

Our media critique defined the favoured categories of science and technology stories as concerning: 'environment, particularly climate change; sexuality, particularly new reproductive technologies; genetics, particularly engineering of the future child's characteristics; health, particularly cures for diseases; inventions, particularly gadgets with everyday applications' (Government of Ireland, 1996).

A snapshot of Irish newspaper science stories, taken in 2001, showed that these remained among the predominant topics in science and technology stories, as they do still today, though with subtle shifts in emphasis between them. The 2001 survey was conducted within the EU-funded ENSCOT (European Network of Science Communication Teachers) project that produced science communication teaching materials on several topics, including science in the media (Holliman et al., 2002; ENSCOT, 2003). The media studies module, which I co-ordinated, included demonstration content analyses, as teaching resources, of three main aspects of science coverage in 36 newspapers in five EU member-states: the reporting of various phases of the human genome project; the coverage in the sampled newspapers of a single selected item of science news from the journal, *Nature*; and the collection of all science stories published in the sampled newspapers over four days in April 2001. The Irish sample of nine newspapers included the *Belfast Telegraph* and *Irish News*, both published in Northern Ireland.

The survey of genome coverage showed that Irish newspapers paid significantly less attention to this story than counterparts in other European countries, up to and including the announcement of the working draft of the human genome in June 2000, orchestrated by US President Bill Clinton and British Prime Minister Tony Blair. The total number of items on the chosen aspects of the genome topic in the Irish press was less than half the number in the next-smallest collection (France) and less than one quarter of the number in the largest collection (Spain). If anything, the slight differences in the size of the individual press samples ought to have skewed the figures in Ireland's favour. Again in contrast with the other countries, Irish coverage barely mentioned local angles or comments and made passing reference only to critical social and ethical issues raised by the genome project and the manner of its public announcement.

The April 2001 'snapshot' of routine science reporting again showed a significantly lower level of attention to science in the Irish press than in the press of the other countries. In the case of two newspapers, *Evening Herald* and *Sunday Business Post*, no item met the relatively generous definition of science story ('a story that included a significant explicit scientific content, namely a reference or references to scientific findings, scientific research, scientific procedure, science as an intellectual activity or scientists in their professional capacity'). The snapshot survey also showed that a large majority of stories across the five-country sample were drawn from life sciences, particularly biomedical sciences; in the case of Ireland, this proportion was 87 per cent. The favoured topics were: in-vitro fertilisation, gene testing, cancer risks, HIV, vaccines, stem cell research and CJD. Only two items of the total 46 in the Irish sub-sample (both in the *Irish Times*) included direct interviews with Irish scientists.

Reviewing Irish science coverage by a similar method in 2006 showed similar results, though a rather larger number of science stories and an even stronger bias towards medicine. A contributor to that trend was the arrival in the Irish newspaper market of the *Irish Daily Mail*. Its market orientation to women is linked to a strong interest in health matters and, thus, to medical research. Over four days in July 2006, the five morning papers published in the Republic of Ireland (*Irish Daily Mail, Irish Daily Star, Irish Examiner, Irish Independent, Irish Times*) all carried every day at least one item that referred to scientific research or to scientists.

But the *Irish Daily Mail* stood out on several of those days for the number and prominence of such items and references. On two days, 18 and 19 July, that newspaper led with science-based stories, one on research indicating that sun cream offered less effective protection if rubbed in, rather than merely smeared, and another on plans to require the addition of folic acid to bread sold in Ireland. The *Irish Times* and *Irish Examiner* both reported the sun cream story on the day after the *Irish Daily Mail*.

Several other stories were shared by two or more newspapers in the sample: these included the competing claims of various scientists on the start of human life, covered in the context of a high court case on the ownership of frozen embryos (page 1 lead in the *Irish Examiner* on 19 July), and new disagreements among US Republicans about the funding of stem cell research, covered on one, two or three days, depending on the newspaper. Surveys of various kinds were the basis of stories in all of the papers: surveys on obesity (twice), heart disease, depression, dementia, sleep, Alzheimers were among those reported in the *Irish Daily Mail.* The *Irish Daily Star* reported surveys on asthma, obesity, sports injuries, alcohol and HIV, as well as those on sleep and Alzheimers. As these topics indicate, the vast majority of science-based or science-related stories came from biomedical sciences, confirming a broader, international pattern that has been named the 'medicalisation' of science coverage (Bauer, 1998).

The *Irish Times* contributed to this trend with the reports on medical research contained in its weekly health supplement (19 July) but it was alone among the five newspapers in reporting substantially on research by Irish scientists. The Science Today page featured research at Athlone Institute of Technology on hormone disruption in trout, at University College Cork on the behaviour of cancerous cells, and at Waterford Institute of Technology on genetics of pine martens. Professor William Reville's column described research on dinosaurs, reported in a year-old edition of *Scientific American,* one of Reville's frequently used sources for summaries of current knowledge on selected topics. One of this columnist's favourite topics is science and religion and specifically his restatement of the compatibility between the two. Columns on this subject invariably attract a lively, and mainly critical, correspondence from readers who frequently question the place of this philosophising in a science column.

The *Sunday Times* represents an exception to these general trends, but its mention here also draws attention to the difficulty of defining 'Irish media'. The Republic of Ireland edition frequently carries reports on Irish research across a fairly wide range of topics, but it also contains the book reviews, extended profiles and features, and other forms of science coverage from the newspaper's British-based contributors, who include leading popular science author John Cornwell and science essayist Bryan Appleyard.

The position of the *Sunday Times* also points to a possible way of understanding the relatively weak representation of science in the 'domestic' media: these media may have tended to see themselves in impossible competition with the major British television channels, radio stations, magazines and newspapers, which draw on the incomparably larger pool of scientific activity in Britain.

The particular status of the *Irish Times*, with its science editor, its science page, its editorial writers' interest in science policy, is by now well established. It is further underlined by its sponsorship of public science events and initiatives, generally undertaken in association with the Royal Dublin Society (RDS) or the Royal Irish Academy (RIA). Former editor Conor Brady recalled the *Irish Times*'s decision to co-sponsor with the RDS the Boyle Medal for Science as aiming to 'link the *Irish Times* to areas of activity across Irish society' (Brady, 2005). RIA members and scientists, Professors Dervilla

Donnelly and David McConnell, are members of the Irish Times Trust, McConnell being chairman since 2000.

The academy was a partner in the publication of *Flashes of Brilliance*, a collection of features and profiles on Irish science and scientists by Dick Ahlstrom (Ahlstrom, 2006). The publication was also supported by the Industrial Development Authority and a television documentary based on selected scientists profiled in the articles was produced with support from another state agency, Science Foundation Ireland. Thus, the *Irish Times*'s science reporting might be said to have been endorsed as 'official science reporting'.

Ahlstrom's introduction to *Flashes of Brilliance* acclaims the state's contribution to science's development, to 'new well-equipped labs, [and] lots of research activity', to Irish research's 'capacity to do world-class science', and to making 'the goal of a truly knowledge-based economic future that much more achievable'. Despite his claims about the social impacts of science, the profiles in this book include little on the social significance of the work described. The emphasis is strongly on the intrinsic scientific significance and the reader is asked to take on trust the value of the research as 'world-class' or 'leading-edge'.

These several elements of review of Irish media coverage of science indicate that this coverage falls, very broadly, into two main categories: one category is news reports on current international research, selected as dealing with matters of some relevance to everyday life, most often health; the other category is features on Irish science and scientists in which the science is presented as self-evidently valuable. Whereas the coverage in the first category is apparently aimed at the general reader, and plays on established news values, the coverage in the second is presented in spaces defined as being for the science-interested audience. We might say that the coverage in both categories presents science as remote – either geographically or culturally or both – and difficult to engage with.

While some of the coverage reflects engagement on the journalists' part, very little of that engagement is critical, that is, asking how and whether things might have been different. This marks out science coverage as distinct: the critical function of media in relation to politics, sport, arts, entertainment, health services, transport and many more domains of public life, is well recognised, practised and accepted. The possible role of the media as science critic was proposed two decades ago in Britain: the media were seen as having a responsibility to present science within the 'whole picture', to 'see the future', and to 'interpret science' (Goldsmith, 1986). That proposition is beginning to find greater resonance within the international science journalism and science communication communities, not least because of the growing evidence of scientific misconduct.

Describing the knowledge society

The media's apparent unwillingness to engage critically with the practice of science and with science policy in Ireland connects with their broad acceptance of the main tenets of the public policy commitment to building a knowledge society or knowledge-based economy. The Fianna Fáil and Progressive Democrat coalition governments of 1997–2007 have established the knowledge society as an unquestioned frame of reference for policy making. In a series of policy statements and policy advisory reports from government-appointed bodies, the reference to a knowledge society has become increasingly central. Business interests, representative bodies of the higher education sector, trade unions and community organisations subscribing to social partnership have followed the government lead and adopted the knowledge society commitment, with varying degrees of emphasis.

Among the media, the generally independent-minded *Irish Times* has for several years helped reinforce the government's policy priorities: an editorial of 2003 worried that 'too many write [science] off as tedious and difficult' and insisted: 'There is a hard-nosed rationale for tackling the problem, given the government's stated aim of developing a knowledge-based economy here, one grounded upon scientific discoveries, research and development (*Irish Times*, 2003a). The newspaper elsewhere endorsed the government's 'clear purpose' as being 'to foster a knowledge-based economy, one that makes the new discoveries and develops the innovative products as a way to protect our economic future . . . The government's aim is that Ireland become a source of knowledge in its own right, an originator of innovation and scientific breakthrough' (Ahlstrom, 2003).

Irish media coverage of the government's *Strategy for Science, Technology and Innovation 2006–2013* illustrated the commitment of some media to the prevailing policy discourse, but also the near indifference of others. The government invested significant symbolic forces in the strategy's announcement: six government ministers were present on a Sunday, including the Taoiseach, Tánaiste and the Minister for Finance. Indeed, the reports on RTÉ radio and television news drew attention to the number of ministers present. The next day's *Irish Times* led with 'Scientific R&D to receive €3.8bn over next 7 years', referring to 'remarkable levels of research spending', describing the policy document as 'a comprehensive strategy for the development of science', and underwriting the goal 'to help Ireland become a world player in research' (*Irish Times*, 19 June 2006). These claims were amplified in a three-part analysis on page 5 which referred to the 'staggering sums involved' and 'the clear-cut commitment by the Government to promoting scientific endeavour'. An editorial the next day (20 June), a 1,000-word comment from UCC president Professor Gerry Wrixon a week later (26 June) and a contribution from technology columnist Karlin Lillington (30 June) all underlined the paper's strongly positive evaluation of this government initiative. However, economist Professor Finbarr Bradley of NUI Maynooth was also given space (3 July) to question the logic of the policy for a knowledge society that underlies the science strategy.

The *Irish Independent* carried a page-one report, though not its lead, on the strategy's announcement. It reported Minister Micheál Martin's statement that the strategy was about 'jobs, jobs, jobs'. The paper published further reports inside, a welcome from UCD's Vice-President for Research, Professor Desmond Fitzgerald, and an editorial that was also approving, but drew attention to the higher levels of research spending in Britain and Sweden. By contrast, the *Irish Examiner* reported the strategy launch in a single, relatively brief piece in its business section that highlighted the commitment of €2.7 bn (over three years) rather than the higher figure of €3.8 bn (over seven years). It gave greater prominence in its general news section to a statement from Minister Martin ruling out embryonic stem cell research in Ireland and followed up this topic with a columnist's contribution two days later. The *Irish Daily Star* showed even less interest in the strategy launch: its page-eight report said that the strategy was aimed 'to help Ireland secure its position as one of the world's advanced economies'.

Conclusion

The media emphasis on economic, employment and expenditure aspects of science strategy follows the government's lead. The government-funded science awareness programme, Discover Science and Engineering, also has a labour market focus: it principally targets school students in an effort to boost the numbers of students taking science and engineering subjects and thus ensure a more plentiful supply of scientifically and technically qualified graduates.

This highly instrumentalist view of public awareness of science chimes with the view of scientific knowledge that underlies Irish policy for the knowledge society: knowledge is especially valued if it can be turned to innovation in the economy. Other forms of knowledge are correspondingly marginalised. In this restricted view of the role of science, there is little place for public engagement with the priorities and purposes of research or with its social, philosophical and ethical implications. Although the Taoiseach's foreword to the STI strategy claims that the 'people are at the heart of the knowledge society', the roles the people can play are very limited. Since 2000, when the 'turn to science' took effect with the establishment of Science Foundation Ireland and its €100-plus million annual funding, there have been no substantial discussions of this policy in the houses of the Oireachtas and not much more outside.

Wittingly or not, the media, in their celebratory or economistic relation with science, may be reinforcing the low public and political participation in the hoped-for knowledge society.

Chapter 9

Television drama as social history: the case of *Fair City*

Helena Sheehan

Prelude: stories and society

What can television drama tell us of the social history of our times? How do the dramatic scenarios constructed by television serials relate to the socio-historical world in which we live our lives? How do soap operas represent the social order?

Television drama is a processor of the collective images and ideas through which we as a society represent ourselves to ourselves and to others. There is a complex and intricate relationship between the production and reception of television drama and the larger pattern of experiencing and coming to terms with the world. Its stories both express and effect the pressure of a wider world. Examining television drama in terms of the stories a society tells about itself can bring to light much about the experiences, moods, concerns, hopes, fears and values of particular social forces in a particular culture at a particular time. If we engage in a systematic study of texts and contexts, we can discern recurring patterns of representation. If we trace such patterns over a period of time, we can discern shifts that reflect / refract our patterns of social experience.

Although television drama may indicate much about the texture of the times, it does not necessarily do so in a simple and straightforward way. Every drama, even if unintentionally, reveals something of the dynamics of the interacting nexus of forces in the society that has produced it. It often conceals a fair bit about it as well. Every story, at least implicitly, embodies elements of a worldview, in the sense that it symbolically conveys certain premises about what sort of world it is, about how the social order is structured, about what the rules of the game of life are. In doing so, it either acquiesces in the status quo or it queries it, challenges it, dissents from it or poses alternatives to it. It either exposes or eclipses the underlying structures of power. It either normalises or subverts the idealisation of such power, the taken-for-granted assumptions which legitimate dominant ideologies so that they seem to be only common sense. It either induces or inhibits the exploration of alternatives. (Sheehan, 1987) [1]

Case study: *Fair City* 1989–2006

Let us apply this type of analysis to a particular society and a particular television drama. To what extent can we look at *Fair City* in terms of the social history of Ireland in the years from 1989 to 2006? How far can contemporary Ireland recognise itself in *Fair City*?[2] (Brennan, 2003, Sheehan, 2004)

Fair City came into the world bearing an enormous burden of expectations. Since the demise of *Tolka Row*,[3] there had been a sense of a yawning gap in the picture of Irish society emerging from RTÉ drama. As decades passed, there was growing demand for an urban serial. Indeed there was almost a sense of desperation about it, a sense that it must happen and that it must succeed. Its mandate was to be urban, contemporary and hard hitting on social issues.

When RTÉ announced it in its autumn schedule for 1989, it was at the centre of anticipation, not only from the media, but also from the audience. Much effort and major investment had gone into its development. The documents in the archives refer to it as *Glasfin*, then as *Northsiders*, but by the time it appeared on the air, it was *Fair City*, from the song 'Molly Malone': 'In Dublin's fair city, where the girls are so pretty . . .'. The opening sequence evoked Dublin, beginning with aerial shots of the city, inserting scenes of O'Connell bridge, the river, a park, a schoolyard, a bookies, a pub, neighbours talking over hedges of corporation houses, finally homing in on the Drumcondra area, which was to be the fictional Carrigstown.

The pilot opened with a succession of breakfast scenes in a number of houses with a running thread of various characters commenting on the story on the front of the *Northside People*, featuring the first anniversary of the local community enterprise centre. As the day went on, these characters all converged on this centre. Throughout the day, there were scenes of Dublin as we knew it: Cumberland Street Labour Exchange, Grafton Street, Bewley's Café. In between there was much happening: people coming and going, phone messages being conveyed, characters gossiping about other characters, rows about relationships and about money. The pilot finished with a party at the centre ending in a punch up.

A flurry of reviews followed the pilot and RTÉ even did a vox pop on the streets of Dublin. Most people said that they could not make out what was going on. Some complained about the accents, speaking in the same accents themselves. The consensus among the critics, of which I was one, was that it had got off to a frenetic start, that it was not clear who was doing what and why, but that it was promising and should be given a chance. (Sheehan 1989, 2004)[4]

The pace slowed somewhat, sometimes to the point of the pedestrian. All sorts of things were tried, but the audience fell and the critics became harsher. Inside RTÉ, there was consternation, but also commitment to do whatever it took to fix it. Sometimes it seemed that the desperation to make it better only made it worse. It was trying too hard to be something without being too sure what that something was. It was too bitty. Too much happened for too little reason. It was too imitative. It was looking too much to *Eastenders* and not enough to contemporary Dublin. By the end of first series, the centre was burnt down and characters had to find alternative employment. The emphasis was more on personal relationships and less on community activities.

All through the series there has been much pairing and trialugating, a prime soap opera cliché. There were also revelations of paternity and maternity. So many parents and children manage to lose and find each other in soap operas. Incest scenarios loomed when Heather and Floyd and then David and Emma came under the spell of seductions forbidden to siblings.

There has been wheeling and dealing, in the beginning much of it revolving around Jack Flynn, the local shady entrepreneur, subsequently around Eamon Clancy, who disappeared leaving a string of bad debts, and latterly by Sean Mc Cann, Seamus McAleer, Bob Charles, Sylvester Garrigan, all on the spectrum from slightly suspect to seriously sinister. These days there are higher stakes: property development, insider trading, offshore accounts, high tech bank heists.

An extraordinary number of characters have owned their own local businesses: recording studio, coffee shop, hair salon, pizzeria, pub, bistro, law firm, computer business, garage, taxi operation, health club, night club, construction firm, classic corner shop, accountancy practice, not to mention the black economy operations: moneylending, drug dealing, smuggling, prostitution. Although most characters were supposed to be of working-class origins, not many have been wage labourers. Those that have been have worked primarily in the local businesses. Hardly any have belonged to trade unions – those who must have been by the nature of their jobs, for example teachers, rarely mentioned it.

There were comings and goings, births and deaths, windfalls and debts, rows and reconciliations, and so on, but there often seemed to be insufficient reason why. There were rapes, abortions, kidnappings, sexual harassment, blackmail, murder, but how dramatic any of it was depended utterly on how compelling was the characterisation of those involved and how convincing was the motivation for the acts committed. It has often seemed to be soap opera by the numbers.

Nevertheless, internal documents show RTÉ addressing the problems of *Fair City* in a forthright, perceptive, and sometimes devastating fashion (Sheehan, 2004). Whatever happened within the production process as a result of such a critique, it was not apparent to the viewer or critic watching the production much of the time. In autumn of 1993 when presenting my paper to the Imagining Ireland conference,[5] it still seemed that, although the opening sequence evoked Dublin, Carrigstown was more like a 1950s rural village than a 1990s city. Everybody lived in each other's pockets and knew each other's business. Nearly everybody worked in the immediate area. This was soap opera convention, but it was not urban life. The only serial to break with this was *Brookside* in its early years, where characters lived in Brookside Close, but moved about and worked in the larger city of Liverpool in a way that opened up new territory for the genre, even if it collapsed back into the genre convention in the ensuing years.

Those involved in the production of *Fair City*, to whom I spoke at the time, answered that the budget did not allow for location shooting. Although I thought that *Fair City* should have been given the resources for location shooting, I did not believe than this alone would solve the problem. Even without location shooting, dialogue could refer outward in a way that it rarely did. Characters could come and go from the larger city and world and they could read books and newspapers, listen to radio, watch television, communicate by phone and email. In countless ways, they could be constructed in a conscious and dynamic relationship to the wider world. For most of the first five years of *Fair City*, characters came and went, ate their pizzas and drank their pints, did their deals, had their flirtations and affairs, their births, marriages, separations and deaths in a so-what sort of way, without sufficient rhyme or reason, without specific texture, without particular perception.

I argued that *Fair City* and *Glenroe* needed to engage more vigorously with the society in which they were set and put a number of questions to those who made these programmes: What did Biddy and Bela think about the big issues of our times? Did anyone in Glenroe or Carrigstown have left- or right-wing views? Had anyone noticed that the map of the world had been redrawn? Did anyone notice that Ireland elected a feminist president? Did anyone vote? Were the residents of Glenroe and Carrigstown the only people in Ireland with no opinion on the X case? Were they the only ones in the country not to make remarks about bishops and babies? Was everyone a religious believer? Would world trade agreements or structural funds allocation affect them? Did anyone belong to a trade union? Did no local TD ever come into Teasy's or Mc Coys? Did no one go to TCD, UCD, DCU or any third-level educational institution? Did no one work at Intel or Aer Lingus or any large industrial enterprise? Why did such a disproportionate number of characters own small businesses and those few who worked for a wage work for them?

It was not that any one of these absences was that conclusive, but taken together they indicated what I found missing, at least the surface of what I found missing. Even staying on the surface, I indicated some characters that

I would like some day to see: a married laicised priest, a nun who lived in a flat after coming under the influence of liberation theology in Latin America, a trade union official, a programme manager, a multinational executive, a computer hacker, a philosopher (why not?), a novelist, a journalism student, a night cleaner, a carpenter who could only find work in the black economy, a person who was long-term unemployed, a punter who voted for the Progressive Democrats and thought that the *Sunday Independent* was the fount of all wisdom, a communist whose life came into crisis in 1989. I knew that adding such characters would not solve the problem in itself, but if their parts were written well they could open out the scenario to show the structure of the social order in terms of the rhythms of everyday lives.

I am happy to say that many of these absences became presences in due course, although I have never investigated whether I could claim any credit for it. Malachy, a married laicised priest, became a main character. Eoghan and Suzanne and Sarah were university students and Fiachra a university lecturer. Politicians began to appear in McCoy's pub, as did computer hackers, journalists, novelists, multinational executives and trade union officials. As to carpenters, construction was booming. Frank and Damien were painters and had plenty of work.

There were wage labourers, but there was still a tendency to convert them quickly to petit bourgeois people of property. Robin started off as a feisty female mechanic, but became a snobby landlady almost overnight. Mondo too was a mechanic, but set up his own company to manage property. Hannah was a school cleaner, but also had a share in sandwich bar. There was still much missing.

Coming at *Fair City* in the context of a comparative study of soap operas and society in 13 European countries in the 1990s, Hugh O'Donnell viewed these serials, not as texts in themselves, but as sites of an ongoing process of negotiation between producers and consumers taking place within a larger framework (O'Donnell, 1999). Each was part of a greater overarching narrative created simultaneously by all the soaps. Although competing ideologies were seldom explicated, he contended, this narrative unfolded within a Europe in which social democratic hegemony was on the defensive in the face of a neo-liberal onslaught. The tradition of public service broadcasting was challenged by the advance of new commercial channels and attitudes. He placed the soap operas he studied along a spectrum, with British soaps at one end as a refuge of the embattled social democratic world view and the newer German ones at the other end as the realm of a young affluent depthless consumerist culture in the mode of *Neighbours* or *Dallas*. In between the two extremes were all sorts of permutations, which was where he placed *Fair City*: 'the unconvincing upward mobility of *Fair City* in Ireland, where the economic opportunities opened up by the tiger economy allow erstwhile proles to open furniture-restoring workshops in lock-ups' (O'Donnell, 1999: 225–6). *Fair City* placed itself within the social realist tradition of British soaps, he argued, but failed to deliver anything like the level of social comment provided by its British counterparts. This, I would contend, overstated the level of social comment in the British ones and understated that of *Fair City*. Although he cited my own work in support of his negative evaluation of Irish television drama in general and *Fair City* in particular, I found myself on the defensive and inclined to argue that our soap operas should not be compared so unfavourably with those of other European countries, particularly with those of Britain, which I have watched consistently. I do not think that watching a few episodes in 1994 and again in 1997 is an adequate basis for judging such a long-running serial. It is difficult to feel the force of the distinction he articulated as: 'Whereas in the British soaps working class experience is *dis*placed into petit bourgeois class positions, in *Fair City* working class experience is *re*placed by petit bourgeois aspirations' (O'Donnell, 1999: 108). Explaining this in relation to *Brookside* and *Eastenders*:

> the isolated, embattled and inward looking group of people who populate British soaps can be seen to represent the very real and widespread disarray of the British working class . . . political issues raised by soaps such as *Eastenders* and *Brookside* are constantly deflected and contained by being placed firmly within the framework of the family . . . they are also structurally diffused by the atomised, fragmented and unorganised class position of the protagonists. This is largely what gives British soaps their simultaneously progressive and conservative feel.

and to *Coronation Street*:

> *Coronation Street* is set in a Britain which never was and never will be, a country of publicans and shop owners where problems from the real world are taken in, reworked and reconfigured: they are transformed from political issues to personal ones and dispersed into an unending flow of narrative. (O'Donnell, 1999: 210)

As to *Fair City*:

> It constructs, even if only by default (which is . . . what hegemony is about), the new neo-liberal consensus of classless individuals moving up the ladder of personal wealth (though never very far) thanks to their own individual endeavours. The real (and very obvious) imbalances of Ireland's tiger economy in the 1990s are nowhere to be seen. Economic power is everywhere in microscopic amounts in *Fair City*, but nowhere in substance: it is a placeless utopia, neither rural nor urban, but combining elements of the mythologies of both. (O'Donnell, 1999: 109)

Edward Brennan's PhD thesis on *Fair City* (2003) also looked to global power structures and the wider broadcasting environment and concluded that the form, content and current dominance of *Fair City* in indigenous drama is the product of RTÉ's dominated position in a global media field transformed by a neo-liberal agenda of commercialisation and deregulation, which is the source of many of *Fair City*'s expressive limitations, preventing it from representing or questioning political or economic structures, making it incapable of dealing in any depth with questions of institutional politics, consumption and production (Brennan, 2003).

While there was much in these assessments, I would argue that they are nevertheless not quite on the mark with respect to *Fair City*. The serial was initiated and sustained within the tradition of public service broadcasting and it came from an impulse to give dramatic expression to the realities of contemporary Irish society. It might have done so inadequately and given too much ground to genre clichés, but it has not given unequivocal expression to neo-liberal individualism. It has reflected commercial pressures and individualist values, but not unequivocally, not unquestioningly, not alone in the dramatic frame. The genre, I believe, does have the potential to reveal structures of power and *Fair City* does have its moments of exploring that potential.

Fair City has felt the pressure of all ideological currents in Irish society to an extent not always obvious in the text itself. My interviews and investigations into the production process at various intervals in its history have indicated much complexity in its construction. What has prevailed in *Fair City* has been a liberal social democratic point of view, no longer under strong pressure from the old right or new left and confused by the nature of the challenge from the new right. Not that those involved in its production would customarily speak or even think about the production in such explicit ideological terms. It has given expression, implicitly or explicitly to neo-liberal attitudes, in some characters and situations, but it has not constructed a neo-liberal consensus of classless individuals.

As the years have moved on, *Fair City* has evolved. By 2001 it was going out four nights a week with 28 writers, a large and efficient production team and peak audience of 750,000. In November 2006 it celebrated its 2,000th episode with an average audience of 450,000 per episode. A new opening sequence made in 1997 was a stylish evocation of the tiger city: panning over the pigeon house at dawn, the distillery, an older city street, people walking along the strand by Dublin Bay, the fruit stalls and bustle of Moore Street, O'Connell Street, the bridges over the shimmering River Liffey at dusk. Updated again in 2005, it featured the Lúas, the spike, the boardwalks, the café bars, but still the old flats, terraced houses and fruit stalls.

It has the look of a city that has come up in the world, as indeed it has. It shows too in the look of the sets and lives of the characters. They are less downtrodden, but not fabulously rich with unearned wealth. Most of them are working class in origin and have achieved a modestly comfortable standard of living through education and work and presumably through the rising tide lifting many (if not all) boats. People of many colours speaking many languages stream though the fictional Dublin as they do the real one.

It has come to have more of the look and feel of an urban space around it, more of a sense of characters moving through the larger city, although there are still too many of them who own and work in local businesses. Still, Suzanne and Sarah were going to university. More characters now live outside Carrigstown, but come there to work, while others live there and go elsewhere to work. There is some location shooting in shopping centres, night clubs, hospitals, parks, city streets. The outdoor set built on an RTÉ lot with houses and shop fronts, streets and bus stops as well as the studio sets for pub, bistro, shops, flats and offices that have an authentic look of contemporary Dublin about them.

There is also more of a sense of the wider world in the way the script refers outwards even when the cameras do not go there. It is intermittent and it varies with scriptwriters. Sergei, a Russian migrant, even gave the locals a lecture on perestroika. Suzanne arrived back home from Borneo with Bobby from Glenroe in toe to scrutinise Carrigstowners on their use of fair trade products. Kay and Charlie, like much of the rest of the world, read and discussed *The Da Vinci Code*.

In the earlier years a 'no politics, no religion' rule prevailed, but this is no longer in force. A certain caution in dealing with politics remains and the north is an area that is avoided.[6] The notion of politics running through the serial is quite vague, but occasionally something vivid breaks through. There are now politicians who are regular characters, local councillors and business-men who belong to 'the party'. Although the party is never named, it is unmis-takably Fianna Fáil.[7] The serial has edged into the territory of the tribunals and the political corruption exposed in them. Two local politicians have been exposed as corrupt, McCann and Mannion, although both escaped public exposure. Mannion lost a Dáil nomination to Dermot Fahy, owing to his corrupt relationship to the builder Seamus McAleer, but McAleer has continued to throw his weight around with politicians, newspaper editors and building workers.

Actual politicians and events have been mentioned, such as one character telling another that if he went to prison, it would not be to Liam Lawlor's cell.[8] During the 2004 election, the show invited all political parties to submit posters for use on the set during the campaign. Royston Brady was the only candidate for the European Parliament to do so, but several local candidates had their posters up too.

The serial has increasingly pushed up against the limits of what it could do. In 2006 a script was written for an hour-long special dealing with an al-Qaeda attack on Shannon airport. This was overruled by RTÉ management, who feared that it might offend the muslim community in Ireland. Although the massive demonstrations against the war in Iraq that took place in Dublin in 2003 were not referenced in *Fair City*, it emerged that Keith declined to attend a mechanics' course in Britain, because he was afraid of being arrested as he had deserted his unit of the British Army to avoid going to Iraq.

Sometimes there have been storylines that deal with politics in the more mundane sense, stories that situate the local community and its characters in relation to power and property. One was about the closure of the local library, which is basically about public property and who had control of it. There was a romantic connection between Dermot and Jo, a politically articulate woman who led the opposition to the party on this issue. Another instance was a local pirate radio station, which Dermot had closed down by the gardaí, after Charlie Kelly, feeling a sense of power as a local broadcaster, started giving out about certain politicians and naming him. Charlie went into oppositional overdrive and started citing the *Communist Manifesto*. He sat down with his pint in McCoy's and explained that state power equalled violence.

Another conflict was a rent strike and eviction involving private property. Tara McCann, sharing a flat with other twenty-somethings, worked for a (vague) charity and spoke of power and wealth and inequality in a radical way. Even when 'going girly' in an effort to attract Jimmy Doyle, she wondered if the £25 frilly top she had bought was made in a sweatshop where workers were paid 25p. Another struggle was over a proposal to resite the homeless shelter, which put couples Jo and Dermot and Kay and Malachy on opposite sides. Pearse from the homeless shelter was seen reading Michael Moore. The very existence of a homeless shelter as a recurring set or site of stories is a significant departure from soap opera cliché.

An important story reflecting the evolving relationship of Ireland to the politics of the wider world was the entry of a asylum seeker into Carrigstown. Ashti was a Kurdish teacher who fled to Ireland, feeling caught between the Turkish authorities and those in armed struggle against them. At first, the only work he could find was selling *The Big Issue* on the streets of Dublin. Then he came to work in Phelan's shop. It indicated the difficult lives asylum seekers left behind, in this case including torture, the ruthlessness of those who profiteered on their transit and the suspicions surrounding them on arrival.

The Udenze family arrived in Carrigstown on a more hopeful note. The storylines involving them orchestrated multiple points of view on the new population of Ireland, particularly on the multi-racial composition of it. Coming from Nigeria via Britain, the Udenzes set up shop and worked hard. Most locals welcomed them and rallied to their aid when they came under racist attacks from those who did not welcome them.

Those who were hostile were all single white males who had not made much of their lives. Morgan was the most conflicted, confused and redeemable. He believed that immigrants were responsible for burning down his father's laundrette and ranted against 'multiculturalism as the new religion'. He was doing a line with Suzanne Doyle, but his attitude to immigrants put that relationship under strain. Pete was ignorant, rude, without redeeming qualities, insulting immigrants, especially blacks, and did them whatever harm possible. Joseph was more vicious still, believing in not letting enemies know what he was thinking, just doing maximum damage to them. They were especially inflamed by the black male / white female scenario that arose when Louise Doyle took up with Joshua Udenze.

The Doyles were in a bit over their heads. They invited the Udenzes to dinner in an effort to be friendly, but found it very hard to carry on a conversation outside their normal register. When the attacks increased, Rita remarked to Sarah that there was never such trouble in the past as there was these days with more and more foreigners arriving. Sarah sardonically replied: 'I get it, that good old island of saints and scholars stuff. You know, we all used to be so happy together and we had absolutely no problems whatever . . . except for the north and the travellers and . . .'

The Udenzes also represented different points of view. The father Gabriel wanted to integrate with the local community as far as possible. He was inclined to assume the best until he had to deal with the worst. His wife Nina was at first reticent to mix and thought that their son Joshua was looking for trouble by dating Louise. Joshua assumed that it was his right to be anywhere and to do anything. He was quick to fight over any slight. Gabriel counselled him to be careful. Joshua called his father a coward. Meanwhile, Morgan, Pete and Joseph were furious that the Udenzes were moving into a new house on their road. They called Gabriel 'King Kong' and said that soon it would be impossible to walk down their own streets. Gabriel died at their hands that night, as they burned down the house with him in it. The locals came out in sympathy and erected a park bench in memory of Gabriel. Nina chose a poem of Pablo Neruda for the occasion of its dedication.

So there has been trouble in *Fair City* as there has been in our society. Not that migrants have been only a source of discord in the narrative. People of many nationalities have come increasingly into the serial in various roles. Eastern Europeans have come to Ireland and related to the Irish as lovers, gangsters, bouncers and building workers, while Irish characters have taken to finding a Russian bride on the internet and wheeling and dealing in Bulgarian real estate. 'Don't worry', Bob assured a client, 'the communists are gone'. Sylvester and Carol were heading off to Gdansk for some sort of mysterious nefarious business, prompting a remark 'I thought people only flew out of Poland'.

An Iranian prostitute was recently murdered by her patriarchal husband, who arrived in Dublin looking to take son from her. Her son was taken in by the family of an Iranian professor in a Dublin university. Iranians talk in cafés about where is home now after living in several countries. There is more and more discourse negotiating between cultures.

Character development has improved considerably. Some characters are still too bland, but some have edge and represent interesting dimensions of contemporary Ireland. Although they (or their writers) almost never articulate any sort of ideological self-consciousness, they nevertheless embody a number of ideological positions that play themselves out in both society and soap opera. Nicola Prendergast has been an excellent embodiment of the yuppie mentality. In contrast, other characters have given occasional expression to a social critique to the left: Charlie Kelly, Tara McCann, Malachy Costello and Barry O'Hanlon. This has never been developed very far, but there are hints that some scriptwriters have something they might want to say through them.

Not surprisingly, older characters represent traditionalist Ireland in a society not very respectful of its traditions. Mary O'Hanlon, now dead, was closer to the Irish mothers that populated *Tolka Row* and *The Riordans.* You could imagine her being able to talk to Rita Nolan or Mary Riordan and knowing where she was in the world. However, living in Dublin in the 1990s, she had no idea. Eunice Phelan, like Mary, found it impossible to be the matriarch she wanted to be and failed to have any meaningful influence on her sons. Her mind is a dustbin of contradictory half-baked ideas, mixing old-fashioned Catholicism with tarot cards, horoscopes, reincarnation and celebrity gossip.

The women have been relatively liberated, in the sense that none of them is a full-time housewife, living off a man's wages and a man's identity. Some are accomplished and ambitious. Others do not have glamorous careers, but they do a day's work, even if it is working behind the counter of a pub, sandwich bar or corner shop. There are lapses, such as Carol becoming a kept woman, whining about being bored watching Oprah all day and not even knowing that she had become a gangster's moll, and Tracey being seduced into prostitution through weakness and stupidity.

Going against stereotypes in their jobs were Robin, a car mechanic, Tess, a taxi driver and Karl, a male nanny. The discourse about gender and the workplace has been knowing, sometimes playfully, sometimes not. In discussing what sort of person their new boss might be, Niamh asked Paul if he would prefer a man or a woman. He replied that he wanted a man 'to keep the lad quota up' and added 'besides with a man there are no mood swings or hidden agendas'.

The kinds of relationships explored have been more various. Eoghan Healy was an important character in exploring alternative paths. He came into Carrigstown as a DCU student, working his way through university. He was on good terms with the females his age and attractive to them. He talked through his coming out with them. Carrigstown took it in its stride and he subsequently became a teacher in the local school. He was conscientious in his work and in his relationships, but this did not exactly reap rewards. He developed a relationship with Liam, who was bisexual and married and did not deal with him very honestly. Then he took up with Andrew, a fellow teacher, who had a partner dying of Aids, who wanted help to die. Andrew would not do so, but Eoghan did. Simon's relatives denounced Eoghan in a crowded school hall. Not only was his career as a teacher in ruins, but he was questioned by the gardai and the last we heard the case was being forwarded for prosecution. Moreover, Andrew was not supportive. What became of Eoghan and this case? He has gone from Carrigstown, but could he not send an e-mail to another character to let us know? Storylines involving Eoghan, particularly about his coming out, received particularly high ratings.

The norms of sexual morality have shifted dramatically in both soap opera and society. There might be stray eyebrows raised about Eoghan, but the dominant point of view of how his character and situations were constructed was that he was a person of high moral character, whereas those who messed with him were not. More recently lesbian characters have come on the scene: Ann, an old school friend of Kay, Chrisso, a butchy barmaid, who fancied Carol and tried to win her away from Shay, and Camille, a high executive in Transglobal, who entered into a marriage of convenience with Conor.

Conor proposed to Nicola that they carry on their affair, despite the shock to her upon discovering his marriage. He proposed a relationship of 'no conventions, no restrictions'. Nicola's assertion that it was against her principles did not come across as stemming from the sixth commandment, but from yuppie respectability and property relations. Nicola's mother spoke not of sin, but of not bringing her up 'to be a loser' and advised her 'to get the business side of it under control'. Her mother was not too pleased either when she had a relationship with a black doctor.

On abortion, there have been several stories. Niamh became pregnant by Leo and went to England to do what many Irish women have done, without much soul searching. A more maturely explored and morally nuanced story came when Kay and Malachy, who treated the news of pregnancy with joy, found themselves on the horns of an agonising ethical and emotional dilemma after the amniocentesis. The child would be severely disabled. With great regret, Kay went to England and had an abortion. Malachy could not accept it. The edgy painful relationship between them after it was dealt with in a protracted and sophisticated way, although it did not seem to be popular with the audience.

For most of the time, the characters have lived their lies outside the norms of Catholic sexual morality with very little in the way of moral discourse about it. The Irish state has legalised divorce, but the Church has not changed its teaching. This has not deterred characters from divorcing and hoping to remarry (Paul and Nicola, for example). The adulterous affair between Dolores in an advanced stage of pregnancy with Frank in the house doing work on new baby's nursery pushed at the boundaries of transgression. So too was Billy's view that 'sex is a commodity to be sold like anything else'. The steamy liaison between Sorcha, a secondary schoolteacher, and her pupil Ross, the object of her daughter's desire, went far into the breach. Ursula, a priest's housekeeper and secret lover, finally admitted that they had conceived a son.

Fair City has tacitly tracked the secularisation of Irish society. It is assumed that most of the characters are Catholic, but it impacts little on their lives. For many years, there was no parish priest as a core character. It was part of the back story of Barry O'Hanlon when the serial began that he had intended to be a priest and he has consistently acted as a sort of secularised variant. As with many ex-priests or ex-seminarians, the impulse to be responsible for others, to articulate higher values, was still there, with or without a deity. He was first the manager of the community centre, then a teacher and eventually head-master of the local school. He has received little appreciation for his efforts, had a series of ill-fated relationships, lost his job and had a nervous break-down. He is now a journalist.

The first time a priest entered Carrigstown as a core character was when Malachy Costello appeared on leave from the foreign missions. He had come from the Philippines and went off again to Brazil. He was one of those priests who believed that they belonged with the poor and oppressed. He was regarded by his order as a loose cannon and inclined to cross the line in relating religion to politics. His discussions with his religious superior and with various characters from time to time in McCoy's pub have been among the more reflective bits of dialogue to occur in the series. He is one of the most interesting characters that *Fair City* has developed. He became involved in a relationship to Kay McCoy and eventually became laicised and married. It was not happy ever after. He could not settle into private domesticity or confine his role in the community to being a publican. He still felt a sense of vocation and a pull to those struggling from below. He has devoted much of his time to running a shelter for the homeless. Now he has separated from Kay and is in love with Sue, a social worker.

The issue of clerical sexual abuse came to the fore in special episodes. The serial in recent years has broken from genre convention from time to time to deal with storylines which foreground a whole set of new characters and back-ground the regular ones. These episodes dealt with a troubled victim, his family, his abuser and priests on both sides of the debate about how the Church should deal with it. A Killarney priest made *Fair City* the subject of his homily, upset that the serial had portrayed a priest breaking the seal of the confessional.

The serial has reflected in many ways the declining position of the Catholic Church in Irish society. Religion has come into it more than before, tracking a tendency 'to tiptoe back to the churches',[9] registering it more as desperation or shallowness than a genuine return to the faith of our fathers (and mothers). Dolores, in her grief after the freak deaths of her two daughters and suicide of her husband, has become suddenly very religious, running to church, erecting a kitchy altar in her house, bringing God into all sorts conversations. What is interesting has been the reaction of other characters. Cleo, the homeless girl she has taken under her wing, tends to look at her as if she is crazy. Others look uncomfortable, humour her and move the conversation on as quickly as possible. Even the priest thinks her religiosity is unhealthy.

Characters who are religious in the traditional sense, for example Ursula, are thin on the ground. Even she had sex with a priest. Others express a vague belief in something out there, but most seem not to think about it most of the time, turning to the Church only for rites of passage. Even here, the ritual is undermined in a way unimaginable in earlier decades. In relation to the baptism of Ben, Heather expressed reticence about renouncing Satan, sceptically saying to Jo: 'Do you believe that?'

The health service was at the centre of drama in another special. It just seemed to be *Casualty* transported to Dublin. Besides, there needed to be a lot more extras to convey how bad conditions are in Mater A&E. One critic characterised it as 'a couple of episodes set in a hospital in which the poverty of the health service is cleverly mirrored by the quality of the drama'. He went on:

> The dialogue became a distillation of every phone-in radio show of the past five years, with those words punctuated only by much hamming. It would seem that, given RTÉ's limited roster of drama, it is now using *Fair City* as a catch-all, a place into which it siphons the issues it lacks the budget to address anywhere else. On each occasion, the soap creaks and strains under the weight. Too often it collapses altogether.[10]

There is a prejudice against issue-based drama, which makes it all the more important that it be done well or it lets itself in for such criticism of such issues. It needed more sustained and careful dramatic treatment.

The representation of criminality in *Fair City* has been in contrast to other dramatisations of crime and criminals of this period. There has been a persistent tendency in Irish film and television of liberal indulgence of lumpen life and a tendency to make criminality chic and cute. This was manifested in such 1990s Irish productions as *The General, I Went Down, Making Ends Meet* and *Ordinary Decent Criminal*. In *Making the Cut* and *Fair City*, RTÉ departed from this and gave a darker portrayal.

The characterisation of Billy Meehan was better grounded and more plausible. He was working class in origin, nice looking and could turn on a certain kind of charm when it suited. He played mind games on those he drew into his web and could change from the hail-fellow-well-met persona to an insidious intimidator in a flash. The pull of his psychological seductions and the ruthlessness of his purposes were clearly shown. There was a certain implicit sympathy for those he drew into criminality, Leo, Lorcan, Carol, Tracey, but they were not indulged as blameless and Billy was not indulged at all.

The storylines involving drugs, prostitution and murder were played out in overt reference to real events in the current affairs of the time. At one point Leo said 'Look what happened to Veronica Guerin' and a detective delivered a put down to Billy as 'You're not the general, Billy.' There was also a knowing reference to past and present media representations of law and crime. Pauline pleaded with Leo: 'This isn't *High Noon*, you know' and Billy in cajoling-menacing mode put it to Leo: 'It's not exactly *The Sopranos*, is it?' When Leo was released from prison, after being falsely accused of Billy's murder, he was interviewed by RTÉ's crime correspondent Paul Reynolds playing himself. Billy might be gone (and let us hope he does not come back from the television dead like Bobby Ewing or Den Watts), but even more sinister criminals have filled the space. The pubs and clubs of Carrigstown have detectives, journalists and even novelists investigating their activities.

Conclusion: *Fair City* and our fair city

So what sort of picture of contemporary Ireland has emerged from *Fair City*? It is not Dublin in the rare old times. It is not the fair city of fishmongers, of cockles and mussels, alive-alive-o. No, this is a Dublin of hotmail and health clubs, of sex in the city, of clubbing and cocaine, of refugees and racism, of crime and compassion, of poverty and property, of books and websites and universities. It was ready for the millennium bug and the euro changeover. These Dubliners live in a new millennium, a multicultural milieu. While some resist, most are utterly open to its possibilities. Its inhabitants are the true descendants of Molly Malone.

Fair City is a play of the codes and clichés of soap opera with the rhythms of our social history. Through a complex process and in its own rough and tumble way, *Fair City* has come to be an interesting representation of our fair city.

Chapter 10

Characteristics of contemporary Irish film

Pat Brereton

Preamble: *The Wind that Shakes the Barley*

Irish film studies has traditionally been dominated by literary, nationalist and artisanal analyses, which have helped to promote a nascent film industry. Now, however, with an increasingly competitive and globalised audio-visual market, film research is also using a range of well-established theoretical tools including narratology, genre and gender studies, alongside postmodern, cultural and reception studies, to explain changing audience pleasures and modes of consumption. This chapter will situate some of these broad critical trends as well as providing readings of some Irish films, so as to explore how contemporary texts can be characterised as part of an accented local film industry.

The Wind that Shakes the Barley, directed by the British veteran Ken Loach and set during the turbulent period of the War of Independence, has been the only Irish-based film to win the prestigious Palme d'Or. Loach and screenwriter Paul Laverty have succeeded in showing history as narrative, which they believe is also relevant to today's so-called War on Terror.[1]

The Wind that Shakes the Barley can be read as a historical and polemical counterpoint to the pro-Treaty Neil Jordan film *Michael Collins* and alternatively sets out to validate the class politics which were claimed to have been the raison d'être of the anti-Treaty position in the 1920s.[2] Loach's film presents a riposte to the illusion of historical consensus presented in *Michael Collins*. While Jordan's film appeared to justify the pragmatics of partition, Loach presents a counter vision that confidently reaffirms the republican revolutionary ideal, which until recently had been demonised as a result of the long-running armed struggle in the north.[3]

The opening cliché of a hurling match displaying the skills of the native sport, performed by locals in their working clothes, is somewhat reminiscent of a number of (GAA/Guinness and AIB bank) advertisements, in their depictions of heroic, even mythic celebration of competition, framed against the background of a touristic Irish landscape. The same hurley sticks are later used as surrogate guns for training purposes and, like the Irish language,[4] encapsulate a national identity and culture as both exotic and ethnic.

Echoing the rites-of-passage opening scenes in Fergus Tighe's minor classic *Clash of the Ash*, Damien O'Donovan (Cillian Murphy) plays a true Cork native and is individuated as a medical doctor who is about to leave for London to achieve his ambition. Initially goaded by his friends for such flight, Damien walks over to see his neighbours and pay his respects. While visiting, there is a sudden attack by the notorious Black and Tans, interrupting the personal and the domestic, as occurs in much historical romantic drama. Unusually, however, there is little individualisation of the colonial enemy, as the British soldiers demand their names and harangue them for congregating 'illegally' and playing their native sport. One man/boy (Michael-Lawrence Barry) refuses to obey and defiantly speaks his name in Irish, for which he is taken to a shed and killed off-screen, becoming the first martyr of the screen conflict.[5]

Apparently not yet convinced of the efficacy of resistance, Damien is determined to escape to England, but is again thwarted at the local railway station. British army officers want to get on Damien's train, but the native transport staff refuse, claiming that their union has forbidden them to carry the British army. This refusal has serious consequences, as the driver and steward Dan (Liam Cunningham) are badly beaten for their trouble. This cogent form of passive resistance inspires Damien, with its display of dignity and strength in solidarity. Consequently, Damien ends up resolving to defend his country and follow his brother[hood] – personified by Teddy O'Sullivan (Padraig Delaney). Taking the oath of membership of the IRA and affirming his blood brotherhood with Teddy becomes a moment of transformation and as sacred as any priestly vocation.

A number of skirmishes are played out in this relatively small budget production which was part financed by the Irish Film Board. The film portrays the IRA as a guerrilla force fighting a more powerful and experienced occupying army. Significantly, the brutalising effects of war are effectively articulated, as raw IRA recruits physically shake at the sight of the dead after an ambush. Notably, Loach speaks in interviews of his disgust at the Hollywoodisation of war, as cheap visceral entertainment. The ambush sequence, visualising this truth, is one of the most thought-provoking representations of the war of independence in Irish cinema.[6]

As is conventional in such resistance narratives and apparently endemic within the long struggle for independence in Ireland, there are traitors who betray their comrades to the coloniser. A young farm worker provides information that leads to the capture of his fellow IRA men. When exposed, the informer is executed by Damien, now the leader of the IRA flying column.

Such 'hard discipline' is needed to maintain an effective fighting force against a ruthless enemy, but Damien shows remorse for his actions.

British brutality is visualised most especially by the torture of Teddy, using rusty pliers to extract his fingernails, with such scenes drawing down much criticism from the right-wing press in Britain. In a very provocative review in *The Guardian* online on 19 June 2006, entitled 'We should have learned from Ireland', George Monbiot is very supportive of Loach. *The Times'* critic Tim Luckhurst compared Loach to Leni Riefenstahl, the controversial German filmmaker who allegedly supported Nazism: '[H]is new film is a poisonously anti-British corruption of the history of the war of Irish Independence.' Meanwhile, Ruth Dudley Edwards in the *Daily Mail* on 30 May 2006 described the film as 'old-fashioned propaganda' and a 'melange of half truths'. Loach's crime, according to Monbiot, is to have told the other side of the story – 'the torture and killing of the colonised is ignored or excused, while their violent responses to occupation are never forgotten'. Making a very pertinent contemporary reference to the Iraq conflict, Monbiot concludes: '[W]hen troops are far from home, exercising power over people they don't understand, knowing that the population harbours those who would kill them if they could, their anger and fear and frustration turns into a hatred of all "micks" or "gooks" or "hajjis".'[7]

At a formal aesthetic level, however, the overall diegesis and the episodic narrative structure seems unwieldy at times. Some scenes carry an excessive expositional format, presumably intended for non-Irish audiences. For instance, framed within one scene, a 'real' newsreel of the Treaty is shown in a small town cinema. As the screen audience of republicans smoke and hiss, a caption confirms that members of the Dáil would have to swear an oath of allegiance to the British crown and the Treaty could potentially copper-fasten the partition of the island. While verbally foretelling and foreshadowing the continuing conflict over the partition of Ireland – the dramatic strategy for explaining this is somewhat laboured and un-cinematic for contemporary audiences. This is followed by an overly contrived discussion around the politics of the Treaty. A range of views are put forward about the Treaty's legitimacy, but mostly in disparaging terms.

One of the least effective scenes is the historical recreation of a Sinn Féin court that is intended to represent revolutionary republican justice. This foreshadows later Civil War divisions between the ruthless but pragmatic leadership of Teddy, who sides with rich businessmen that support their struggle, as opposed to a more democratic and a bottom-up faction who promote a different form of universal justice. The [politically correct] female judge – countering the masculinisation of the revolutionary activists on the ground – hears a case of a businessman who was levying extortionate interest charges from an old woman and finds in her favour. Meanwhile, Teddy pleads the case for the businessman stating that the republican movement cannot survive without the support of the business elite. The sequence appears to insinuate that the future pro-Treaty side, personified by Teddy, are not fully committed to universal notions of equality and remain somewhat equivocal, with the ends frequently justifying the means. This perception is confirmed later with the pro-Treaty side visually accused of replacing one form of oppression by another, as they take on similar uniforms to the old enemy. We all know which side Loach and his screenwriter Paul Laverty are on, but such sequences could have been more dramatically integrated into the diegesis of the film, rather than remaining foregrounded as didactic sermons – but then maybe this is the point.

Finally, of course, there is a tragic and inevitable denouement. Damien continues the fight for the republic against the new Free State government. He is captured and sentenced to death by a firing squad led by his own brother Teddy. Reminiscent of the 1916 martyrs, Damien spends his last hours writing letters that affirm his love for his girlfriend Sinéad, alongside his country. Following his execution, Teddy, who is certainly not demonised like the British soldiers, yet remains underdeveloped as a character, brings his brother's final letter to Sinead, whom he encounters again in front of her burnt-out family home. She breaks down sobbing as the narrative falteringly concludes. This melodramatic mise-en-scène remains a transparent symbol of the break-up of an erstwhile coherent Irish national identity. There is no resolution or romantic personification as happens in much historical drama and for which Neil Jordan indulges within *Michael Collins* to help achieve a mass audience.

Evolution of a film literature

History has remained a major preoccupation as demonstrated by the evolution of an Irish film literature. It was not until 1988 when Kevin Rockett, Luke Gibbons and John Hill co-authored the seminal reader *Cinema and Ireland* that Irish film research acquired a definitive study. The book addressed the history and political economy of Irish cinema, the representation of political violence and the romanticisation of Ireland within film. The book helped to foreground the importance of the first generation of Irish filmmakers; particularly Joe Comerford, Bob Quinn, Pat Murphy, Thaddeus O'Sullivan and their attempts to challenge the status quo[8] and create an indigenous film-making practice.[9]

As the number of academics working in the area has increased since the 1990s, more general studies have emerged, dealing with the growing number of 'second wave' films since 1993. These include Lance Pettitt's broad review of film and television in *Screening Ireland*; Martin McLoone's well-honed *Irish Film: The Emergence of a Contemporary Cinema* and Ruth Barton's student accessible *Irish National Cinema*, all displaying an extensive overview of a large number of new Irish films.

In building a distinctive filmography of Irish cinema, these books naturally tended to endorse a national studies approach, often implying a preferred, even progressive, reading. McLoone, for example, convincingly endorsed the need for political cinema without always clarifying whether he remained convinced by 1970s avant-garde radicalism, alongside the efficacy and relevance of postcolonial 'third cinema' strategies. One wonders, of course, if there can ever be a consensual appreciation of what is good, much less progressive cinema.

Irish cinema was primarily critiqued by how it articulated or addressed cultural demands, rather than using other measures or values.[10] However, at a conceptual level and to affirm a basic truism, both from a production and a theoretical standpoint, Irish cinema does not come from a self-contained or enclosed space of the island of Ireland. Yet many critics continue to validate a range of idealistic and romantic tropes from the 1970s, when a localised and nationalistic project was unilaterally endorsed to help 'paint the world's screens green'.

Nation building and its related identity politics demand that Irish films are primarily critiqued through their manifestation of a unique cultural identity, but commerce and tourism in particular are also intertwined with such noble if illusive aims. In any case, all film production and consumption, not just those financed by the film board, help to constitute a mosaic of collective cultural consciousness and are therefore both legitimate and valid as a source of analysis within the canvass of national film study.

While academic output has continued to grow over recent decades, important links and comparisons were made with British film and television in particular, ensuring that indigenous analysis would become contextualised within a globalised mediated framework. Furthermore, international conferences in America and elsewhere ensured that large diasporic critiques of Irishness continued to develop, as evidenced through readers like James MacKillop's *Contemporary Irish Cinema*. Strong interdisciplinary connections have also been forged, particularly through studies of adaptations and applying a wider range of literary theory. Furthermore, Irish cultural studies and identity politics generally have also been very active in Ireland as elsewhere, with a recent growth in postcolonial, class and gender analysis, drawing on women's studies research.

Further evidence of the flowering of film studies in Ireland across interdisciplinary boundaries is provided by the growth of a number of doctoral student anthologies, emanating from annual conferences, over the last number of years. Film journals like *Cineaste* and *Screen* have also helped initiate debate and develop international dialogue, which has been greatly augmented at home by the now defunct *Film West* magazine, alongside the long-running *Film Ireland* which began as a members' newsletter for *Film Base*, an important production facility for prospective new film-makers based in Dublin. More conventional academic analysis has been facilitated by *Film and Film Culture*, initially published out of the School of Humanities at the Waterford Institute of Technology.

The 'troubles' is writ large across a large number of Irish films and has ensured that national identity questions have remained a central preoccupation in the literature as signalled by a growing bibliography. Even following the end of hostilities, political representations of Irish 'terrorists' on film, continue to attract strong academic interest.[11] Directors, Neil Jordan and Jim Sheridan forged their film careers and created some of their best work through representing this violence and national conflict, with Oscar winning films including Jordan's *The Crying Game* and Sheridan's *In the Name of the Father* – a very emotive exposé of the wrongful conviction and imprisonment of a number of Irish for the IRA bombing campaign in Britain.[12]

At present there are full-length auteurial studies of Sheridan and Jordan, alongside analyses of individual films, enabling researchers to uncover the often-contradictory influences within the production process, but there is always room for more insightful publications, particularly within audience and reception studies. It is frequently suggested that too much reliance is placed on British and other case studies, that they are directly applied to an Irish environment, without always testing or modulating their applicability or relevance.

National cinema as a foundational principle

Historical debates help students frame an appreciation of key areas of study, and in spite of some criticism, teaching and learning Irish cinema are best served by an appreciation and understanding of nationalistic and ideological debates before dipping into the dangerous waters of postmodern and post-nationalist discourses. Essentially students should address identity questions before moving on to other issues.

Furthermore, the study of Irish national cinema also benefits from looking into how other nationalities read and appreciate their cinema. Tom O'Regan's (1996) forensic examination of Australian cinema has some very interesting parallels with Ireland, insightfully suggesting that all

> national cinema analyses situate the cinema simultaneously as a natural object in
> the film world (its production and industrial context), as a social object connecting

and relating people to each other (its social and political context) and discursively through language, genre and knowledges (its representation) . . . The critic's problem is one of writing the national cinema as a hybrid form, the film worker's problem is one of coordinating it as a multifaceted entity . . . The national cinema writer must take on 'multiple and diverse points of view' (O'Regan, 1996: 2–3).

O'Regan goes on to affirm that for Australian (to which I would add Irish) cinema to 'function', 'it must be naturalised as an unexceptional part of the local and international cinema landscape' and crucial for this is the 'supportive and regulatory role of the state' (O'Regan, 1996: 10–13). Irish film analysis must juggle between all these aspects and strike a balance between the uniqueness of Irish film and its integration and comparability with other national cinemas.

In student discussions over the years, it has been suggested that rather than simply reflecting a uniquely nationalistic Irish identity, classic 'Irish' narratives like *Man of Aran, Odd Man Out, The Quiet Man* and *Ryan's Daughter*, are more indicative of a universal sensibility, adopting generic formats onto an indigenous Irish setting. The strategy of co-opting these externally directed films for an Irish cultural mindset fitted into the legitimate needs of Irish film criticism, which aimed at tracing its antecedents from within the very small pool of stories set in Ireland, coinciding with a more powerful earlier literary revisionist tradition. The burgeoning film industry was certainly co-opted to reflect the more established cultural nationalism incorporated by the literary tradition of Yeats and Synge most notably, who effectively mythologised the west of Ireland in particular. A difficulty with such a project is the implicit assumption that a burgeoning national cinematic aesthetic ought to project a normative template for what Irish film could or should do in the future.[13]

Rural romanticism and touristic spectacle

Luke Gibbons, most notably, remains preoccupied with this perennial aspect of Irish film success, as he critically excavates how the Irish rural romantic and its touristic pleasures continue to capture a global imagination. In Ireland, the topography of wild touristic sites remains etched on the tourists' imagination. Other critics like Ruth Barton and Stephanie Rains have also explored this phenomenon from a heritage and touristic perspective.[14] From the early roots of an Irish romantic vision, as developed by the American film company Kalem in the 1910s spearheaded by Sidney Olcott, to the indigenous 'amateur' production of the *The Dawn*, on to more classical outsider representations of rural Irish landscapes in *Man of Aran, The Quiet Man* and *Ryan's Daughter*, a predominantly rural and nature-focused image of Ireland was successfully represented and validated.

More recently however, most home-grown narratives appear less interested in valorising a touristic landscape and remain preoccupied with emulating the urban-based generic Hollywood product in their attempts to achieve commercial success.[15] Contemporary film-makers from the initiation of the second film board 'emulate a universal and materially wealthy, post-colonial, urban environment, which frequently ignores the past and re-purposes landscape for younger audiences rather than nostalgic, diasporic ones.' I continue by suggesting '[W]e need to excavate and discover new discursive images of Ireland, that go beyond the violent historical political "Troubles" and the more recent religious and sexual traumas of the past, which have preoccupied the postcolonial cultural mindset' (Brereton, 2006: 416). Mindful of the dangers of repeating existing forms of national amnesia, there are nonetheless numerous diasporic touristic stories that can it is hoped represent and embody the Ireland of the future.

This striving for commercial success essentially calls upon universalising mythic tropes of Hollywood, but critics will quibble – at what cost – citing their multiple reductionism and stereotyping. Yet, according to Jim Sheridan, *In America* for example, attempts to reclaim an Irish primitive form of spirituality, which existed before structured religion and Christian theology became the norm. Sheridan incorporates full use of mythic excess in many of his films, which at the same time makes them appealing to mass audiences. Such films have been criticised for 'collapsing into a kind of historicist nostalgia' through their 'essentially regressive ideologies' (McLoone, 2000: 120). However, I believe Sheridan's mythic repertoire, including the beautiful white horse in *Into the West*, symbolising emotional and spiritual freedom, together with the childish innocence embedded within *In America*, remain highly provocative and engaging for mass audiences. The old successful tropes have life in them still, as contemporary film-makers and audiences seek reviving models of Irishness.

Evolving representation of the clergy and farmers

I have recently become interested in how various professions have been represented on Irish film and the way their evolving historical agency can serve to encapsulate the changing cultural attitudes, values and beliefs throughout Irish history. For example, the current fixation with gangsters frames a reading of journalistic practices, using the tragic story of the murder of Veronica Guerin. Such films as *Veronica Guerin, When the Sky Falls* and *The General*, are based on how Guerin was assassinated by drug dealers in 1996. At the outset, this narrative is framed as a heroic story of self-sacrifice and plays into stereotypical clichés of usually male heroes fighting for justice that appeal to mass audiences.

Previously, two of the most contentious professions or vocations, which were central to defining Irish identity, included farmers and the religious vocation. Yet for very different reasons, both have now lost their central iconic status within contemporary culture.

In historical classics like *The Quiet Man* and *Ryan's Daughter,* representations of the clergy and religion reflected perceptions of the Church within the wider Irish society. These characterisations were certainly favourable, validating the great reverence ordinary people then held their Church. More recently an anti-Catholic backlash has come to the fore, precipitated by the numerous and well-documented scandals and exposures. Surprisingly, it took a long time for representations of institutional violence to be documented on film, as exemplified recently in *The Magdalene Sisters* and *Song for a Raggy Boy.* It is inferred by Horgan (2003) and others that such traumatic evocation assists in the therapeutic process of healing within Irish society.

The Catholic Church is represented in contrasting ways in *The Wind that Shakes the Barley.* Early on, one priest (played by Tom Hickey) hears the confessions of the rebels while they are still on the run, displaying tacit support, only to be subverted later on when another priest (Sean McGinley) preaches from the pulpit against anti-Treaty supporters, affirming how the Treaty was democratically voted in by a legitimate Irish government and that the British soldiers had finally left the country. But replying from the congregation, Damien speaks of how the Treaty was imposed on Ireland and that the country was still controlled indirectly by the British. Damien as spokesperson for the anti-Treaty side continues, in a public effort to contest the moral legitimacy and power of the priest, by concluding how the Church always sided with the rich, which is reminiscent of a similar scene from *The Field,* as his fellow comrades walk out of the Church, contesting the Church's erstwhile leadership and moral supremacy.

While Catholicism was traditionally a primary marker in Irish film, farming the land embodied the other historical pillar of national identity. Up to the 1960s, Ireland had been culturally defined and economically determined as a rural and agricultural based society. This social reality had been augmented by a long and troubled history of the island as a British colony and contested space, where her people fought for centuries to regain sovereignty and ownership of the land. In this revolutionary project, the land[scape] was also appropriated by romantic nationalists to affirm its unique beauty and as a bulwark in the cultural and political struggle for independence.[16]

One wonders, now that the economy has been transformed through a Celtic Tiger renaissance, continuing the erosion of population from the rural areas and the decimation of farming as a viable profession, whether there has been a rejection of such values, together with a form of amnesia towards the traumas of the past as signalled by the current preoccupation with contemporary urban-based generic cinema in Ireland.[17]

Some recent strategies in Irish film study

New scholarship remains the lifeblood of a continuing and reinvigorated Irish film studies. Recent approaches to Irish film include auteurial investigations, alongside narrative studies, together with more local cultural and nationalistic debates. Of late, more practical-based analysis alongside primary research into early history of Irish cinema are being conducted. I would highlight the recognition of accent as the most unique feature of contemporary Irish cinema, helping to reinvigorate a generic typology of Irish cinema. In his foreword to Ruth Barton's study of Irish actors, Luke Gibbons affirms that, more than any other attribute, it is through voice – 'the idioms of accent, the intonation of speech – that Irish actors bring the cadences of their culture on screen'. (Barton, 2006: xvii)[18]

Díóg O'Connell (2005), in her doctoral study of recent Irish film, grappled with the notion that the actual lack of success of many Irish films of late is influenced by deficiencies in script development and the need to hone engaging universal narratives, which do not necessarily conflict with strong local storytelling. The Irish certainly embrace storytelling as an intrinsic attribute of Irish culture, as colourfully affirmed by Jim Sheridan and his valorisation of the Irish storyteller's facility to tell universally appealing stories.

The narrative structure of *Into the West* which Sheridan scripted, for example, remains preoccupied with a universal childish imagination. The Disneyesque escape from the realities of life is necessary for its two heroes, who are forced to live in a high-rise tenement outside of the city, because it is against their true gypsy nature. The signifier used for fantasy and escape is provided by a beautiful and mysterious white horse called Tír-na-nÓg (land of eternal youth) given to the boys by their grandfather. Played by David Kelly, the grandfather looks every bit the old, pre-mass-media communicator of fantasy for a people oppressed by invaders and poverty, the ancient Irish *seanachai* (storyteller). Celtic stories like the one Kelly recounts concerning Oisin, who fell off his horse while helping another to move a stone and immediately disintegrates on realising his true age, function to reinvigorate youthful imagination. In this romantic fantasy, problems of social identity and survival encapsulated by the otherness of Irish travellers can be deflected within a hazy, warm glow of mythic heroism.

In this apparently postmodernist era, with notions of history and national identity producing much less consensus for new generations of Irish audiences and film makers, much to the chagrin of nationalist and other critics, new aesthetic strategies are being posited and tested. It would appear that less currency is given to the polemical and political agendas of the past, in spite of the success of *The Wind that Shakes the Barley*, which regard film as an important medium to educate and initiate a radical agenda for a new Ireland. New tools and methodologies of research and engagement are needed to understand and explain the more prolific and commercially driven second wave of film production, which is frequently dismissed as lacking in creative, much less nationalist, appeal.

How to carry out audience research in particular remains a major issue for the future, and I applaud with some reservations Martin Barker's endorsement of this methodology, by concluding in a review that all film analyses make claims about the audience, but seldom make this explicit. While he does not want audience studies to replace textual analysis, he suggests few critical theories actually look for evidence to explain audience pleasures that could underpin an investigation of film. Yet an assumption that empirical research would necessarily anchor, much less determine, film analysis is open to question. Nevertheless, as Kristin Thompson cogently affirms, if there is no connection with actual audiences, film criticism remains a 'barren venture' (Brereton, 2001).

To advance this project, academic study needs initially at least to re-focus on the bottom-up skills of textual analysis to capture and explain audience pleasures without regressing back to old formalist, anti-ideological aesthetic paradigms.

New media and film

In recent years there has been an explosion of low-budget horror production, together with other new forms of generic film-making in Ireland, facilitated by relatively cheap new digital cameras and technology. The DVD format in particular has helped revolutionise the consumption and reception of film in Ireland and elsewhere. Currently, the research centre for Society, Information and the Media (SIM) at Dublin City University is testing the hypothesis that DVD add-ons provide an easily accessible archive to frame interest and deepen insights and intertextual associations for film study.[19] For example, there are very interesting Irish documentaries available on DVD add-ons, including *Man of Aran*[20] alongside more contemporary material for *When Brendan Met Trudy.*[21] Students have easy access to this archival material from which they can hone their scholarly skills and help reinvigorate the discipline for the future. The utopian discourse surrounding new media suggests that it offers experiences and pleasures, which older media could not. Yet conventional Irish film study pays little attention to the influences of new media, much less to the study of non-standard, short or no-budget film-making.

With the mushrooming of university and college courses in film and new media, students are now beginning to construct new grammars of film making and consumption which need to be taken on board, both as an aesthetic format and as part of a culture industry which have a global, rather than a purely national reach.

Conclusion

Finally, gauging the actual or inferred pleasures audiences receive continues to be challenging for national and other mainstream cinema, particularly as signalled by the response of new generations to films like *Disco Pigs, Intermission, When Brendan Met Trudy, Adam and Paul* and many others.[22] While it is relatively easy to critique existing paradigms of engagement, it is much harder to produce fresh and insightful avenues for examining film, as it is being produced and consumed in this twenty-first century. Nevertheless, to avoid such a challenge would result in a failure to capture the creative and academic energy of students, who often speak a different language and sometimes harbour contrasting pleasure principles to the established academy. Consequently, there is a continuing need for a creative and critical dialogue with new generations of students and audiences to reinvigorate the study of film. However, once Irish film study continues to be passionate as well as critical of its pleasures, its future is assured.

Appendix

Filmography

1934
Man of Aran, dir. Robert Flaherty

1936
The Dawn, dir. Tom Cooper

1947
Odd Man Out, dir. Carol Reed

1952
The Quiet Man, dir. John Ford

1970
Ryan's Daughter, dir. David Lean

1987
Clash of the Ash, dir. Fergus Tighe
The Dead, dir. John Huston

1989
Joyriders, dir. Aisling Walsh

1991
The Commitments, dir. Alan Parker

1992
The Crying Game, dir. Neil Jordan
Into the West, dir. Mike Newell

1993
The Snapper, dir. Stephen Frears
In the Name of the Father, dir.
    Jim Sheridan

1996
Michael Collins, dir. Neil Jordan
The Van, dir. Stephen Frears

1998
The General, dir. John Boorman

1999
Angela's Ashes, dir. Alan Parker
When the Sky Falls, dir. John MacKenzie

2000
Country, dir. Kevin Liddy
Disco Pigs, dir. Kirsten Sheridan
When Brendan Met Trudy, dir.
    Kieron J. Walsh

2001
How Harry Became a Tree, dir. Goran
    Paskaljevic

2002
The Magdalene Sisters, dir. Peter Mullan

2003
In America, dir. Jim Sheridan
Intermission, dir. John Crowley
Song for a Raggy Boy, dir. Aisling Walsh
Veronica Guerin, dir. Joel Schumacher

2004
Adam and Paul, dir. Lenny Abrahamson

2006
The Wind that Shakes the Barley, dir.
    Ken Loach

Section Three   Reception

Chapter 11

Transnational flows: media use by Poles in Ireland

Aphra Kerr

For Thompson (1995: 149) globalisation means an intensification of 'social relations' and the 'growing interconnection of different parts of the world, a process which gives rise to complex forms of interaction and interdependency'. It is increasingly recognised that the media and communications play an important part in the globalisation process as people increasingly move from place to place, some prompted by necessity, others by curiosity, some for work, others for pleasure (Rantanen, 2005). Similarly Appadurai (1990: 296) notes that today's 'mediascapes' and 'ethnoscapes' are important dimensions of global cultural flows which contribute to the construction of 'imagined worlds'. Where once media and communications were for technological and legal reasons mostly coterminous with state boundaries and for business and social reasons coterminous with majority cultural and national practices, today deregulation of broadcasting and telecommunications structures and new technologies problematise traditional distinctions between local, national and global media and allow media to become, to some degree, 'deterritorialised'. Satellite, cable and internet technologies allow companies to broadcast, and audiences to receive, television channels and programmes from different parts of the world while the internet also enables multiple forms of communication, information searching, media production and distribution for those who can access and use the technology.

Where once media scholars in international communications conceptualised media flows between countries in terms of media imperialism, Westernisation/ Americanisation and cultural homogenisation, the growth of research on audience experiences in general and migrant communities in particular have called into question these assumptions. Such work has pointed to the multi-directionality of global flows, the growth of transnational, ethnic, diasporic and personal media and the complexity and in some cases the hybridity of identities. Further, audience researchers have found that the relationship between the global and the local is not necessarily a one-way street and that in certain contexts homogenisation is countered by processes and practices leading to differentiation and pluralisation (Sreberny-Mohammadi, 1996; Gillespie, 1995; Georgiou, 2005; Robins and Aksoy, 2001). Indeed, what is interesting here is the diversity of responses within 'national' audiences and the need to go beyond the national and the global as explanatory categories (Rantanen, 2005: 95). Gillespie (1995: 6) argues that the term 'diaspora' is a useful intermediary concept between the local and the global that helps to transcend national perspectives. While initially 'diaspora' connoted the Greek and Jewish diasporas, more recent work has highlighted its usefulness in terms of 'the scattering of populations to places outside their homeland' for a variety of reasons, from political to economic (Naficy, 2001: 14). Certainly the recent rapid growth of the Polish community in Ireland points to the confluence of economic and political issues at home in Poland, the wider enlargement process of the EU and the need for Ireland in the current economic climate to encourage increasing inbound flows of labour. While diaspora highlights the movement of people and their collective consciousness, the concept of 'trans-nationalism' attempts to map and describe a wide array of interconnections and flows between and across boundaries. Some of this work has pointed to the varying degrees of connectivity that migrants can maintain with their home-land and the degree to which they may develop dual or collective identities (Khagram and Levitt, 2004; Vertovec, 2001). The media and telecommuni-cations of course facilitate these flows and processes of identity construction.

While there has been some work on the use of media by Irish emigrants in the United States (Corcoran, 1993), little has been written about migrants' attitudes to and use of both Irish and ethnic media in Ireland, and their access to and use of media from their homeland. Research from other countries, however, has indicated that, for migrants, limited representation of their culture in the media in the new host country can lead to the use of more transnational media, both from the homeland and from other countries. Gillespie's work on television and Punjabi London teenagers found that they increasingly turned to global, cosmopolitan cultural resources and homeland media to overcome the lack of national representation or in some cases racist representations in the British media (Gillespie, 1995: 110). Her work points to the continuing importance of class politics and the nation state in the con-struction of 'new ethnicities' (1995: 208–9). Naficy's work on Iranian cultures in Los Angeles, meanwhile, differentiates between three types of minority television: exilic television, produced by exiles living in a host country in their own language; ethnic television, produced by the host country for its indi-genous minorities in the majority language; and transnational television, consisting primarily of products from the homeland in the home language (Naficy, 1993). For Naficy, exilic media help to maintain links with the home-land while also helping to develop a new sense of self in relation to consumer capitalism and a new 'exilic economy' (1993: xvi). This work adds an important new dimension to audience research focused on the mediating influence of context on the reception of media content and in particular the 'domestic economy' of the home (Ang, 1996; Silverstone and Hirsch, 1992). Much work has noted that the decoding, interpretation or negotiation of media texts are mediated by the consumption context as well as age, class, gender, ethnicity and race (Morley and Robins, 1995; Morley and Silverstone, 1990).

A focus on the agency of audiences and mediating social factors is not to ignore the political economic factors influencing the production, localisation and circulation of media texts. In the Irish context, American, British and Australian programming dominate terrestrial audiovisual programming. While global media corporations are adept at 'internationalising' or 'localising' their products, at least superficially, there is little need for Anglo-American and Australian companies to do so for the Irish market given their common linguistic heritage. The circulation of these international media texts in the Irish context exists alongside the growth of an increasingly concentrated but vibrant local radio and newspaper scene, the launch of a niche Irish language television station and in the past five years the growth of media content aimed at new immigrant communities (Gibbons, 1996b; Corcoran, 2004; Kirby et al., 2002; Watson, 2002). To this increasingly crowded mediascape one must add the internet. Often seen as the key transnational media technology, research has indicated that national, cultural and linguistic affiliations remained important barriers to the circulation of internet texts even as internet technology allows content to cross national boundaries with impunity (Kerr, 2000, 2003; Preston and Kerr, 2001). Further, such research points to the economic barriers faced by producers in small markets. For Irish new media producers, the small size of the Irish market was a strong disincentive to produce culturally specific content: tapping into the Irish 'diaspora' was more difficult that many expected and far from rewarding economically. More recent work on Irish new media users maps the complex web of media resources to which Irish audiences have access, while at the same time pointing to the continued pertinence of household structure, cost and local contextual issues in shaping that use (Kerr et al., 2006).

This chapter focuses on the sources, patterns of use and attitudes of Polish migrants in Ireland to the locally available mix of media and telecommunications. It also starts to explore the cultural implications of their media use. Does the available mix of media and communications help to preserve social relationships with friends and family elsewhere and a sense of Polish cultural identity, or serve to pluralise and develop new identities? More specifically, what role do transnational, international, national and local media play in the migration process to Ireland?

The Polish language mediascape in Ireland

Irish people are no strangers to migration but inward migration from other countries to Ireland is a relatively new phenomenon. In 2002 just over 91 per cent of the population were ethnically Irish and white. Since then the population has increased by 8.1 per cent, owing largely to higher rates of immigration from Europe and Africa and a smaller number of asylum seekers and refugees. Almost ten per cent of the workforce were foreign nationals by 2006 and for the first time the 2006 census included a question on ethnic and cultural background (Watt, 2006).

Ireland imposed no restrictions on the number of workers from the new accession states to the European Union in May 2004. Anecdotal evidence would suggest that Polish workers have formed a large part of the growing number of European migrants in the last two years. With a home population of almost 40 million and unemployment running at up to 18 per cent in certain regions this is perhaps not surprising. Their presence is felt and seen in Ireland in the Polish food available in supermarkets, the Polish drink available in certain pubs, the signage in the tax offices and last, but not least, the proliferation of Polish language media. Further, specialist agencies are placing Polish workers on farms and in the equine industry around the country and local print and radio media, such as *Roscommon Herald* and Anna Livia fm, are including Polish language content to attract this new audience.

The range and number of media outlets catering for the Polish community in Ireland have grown quite rapidly in the past two years, encompassing not only Polish language programming and newspaper columns in the Irish-owned national and local media, but also Polish-owned and locally circulated media produced in Ireland. Colleagues in NUI Maynooth (NUIM) have started to map the evolving field of Polish owned media produced in Ireland. These entrepreneurs produce a range of Polish language newspapers and magazines which are overtly commercial in the main, often charging both a cover price and taking advertising, and they source content and financial support from mainstream media and businesses both in Poland and Ireland (Titley, 2006).

The growth of Polish media in Ireland contrasts with the relative lack of own- language media for other migrant groups. Abel Ugba found few locally developed migrant media in Ireland in 2002 and he noted that many ethnic groups, like Africans from former French colonies, relied on transnational media produced by groups in France and Belgium. Ugba went on to develop *Metro Éireann*, one of the first multi-ethnic minority media newspapers in Ireland (Ugba, 2002). Ugba argued that the development of migrant media publications were 'a practical response of the immigrant communities to ineffective, imbalanced and inaccurate coverage of their affairs by the [Irish] national media'. Neither I nor my colleagues have conducted a systematic content analysis of Irish media coverage of the Polish in Ireland. However, interviewees in the current research project felt that while the Irish media focused on 'sensational' news overall, the national media were quite positive towards Polish immigrants.

In early summer of 2006 three Polish-owned, Polish-language newspapers were produced from Dublin, including the weekly *Polska Gazeta*, the fortnightly *Polski Express* and the monthly arts and culture publication *Szpila*. Over the summer of that year two new Polish publications emerged, the weekly *Zycie w Irlandii/Life in Ireland* and *Anons* while Autumn 2006 saw the launch of *Sofa*. *Szpila*, meanwhile, ceased publication in Autumn 2006. *Polski Express* was initially free but alongside *Polska Gazeta* and *Szpila* quickly moved to a mixture of cover price and advertising. Interviewees noted that the content of both *Polski Express* and *Polska Gazeta* would be of interest mainly to newcomers to Ireland and they made extensive use of Polish symbolism like the Polish flag.

A range of Irish media outlets also provide Polish-language content. At present the *Evening Herald*, a national evening paper, runs a Polish language supplement each Friday, local Dublin radio stations, for example Anna Livia, NEAR fm and Radio Sunrise, run shows aimed at the Polish community, and RTÉ at national level and Dublin City Channel at local level, are following suit with television programmes. Not to be outdone, local media around the country are also catering to the changing composition of their audience by the inclusion of Polish language columns in *Limerick Leader* and *Kildare Post* and others, and in radio shows. This attempt by Irish media producers to become more 'multicultural' is happening alongside the local Polish print entrepreneurship: both must compete with mainstream Polish media print and radio offerings available over the internet and Polish television available via satellite.

This mapping of the burgeoning Polish mediascape signals a diverse range of producers and media outlets but tells us little of the audience for such offerings, the meanings constructed by Poles in Ireland of these offerings or their impact in terms of acculturation or alienation. Interviewees from this research project indicated that both Polish and Irish local and national programmes and newspapers tend to treat the Polish audience as homogeneous, regardless of their class, gender, age or length of time in Ireland. The answers to such questions demand a more qualitative and interpretative approach, but also one which must overcome both linguistic and cultural barriers.

This chapter draws upon a pilot research project conducted over the summer of 2006 and funded by NUIM's summer programme for undergraduate researchers. This project aimed to explore the source, diversity and meaning of transnational media practices by Polish migrants to Ireland. This work builds upon a previous project funded by the NCCRI which explored a broad range of transnational practices of the Polish and Chinese communities in Ireland and was conducted by Katarzyna Kropiwiec and Ying Wang under the supervision of Dr Rebecca Chiyoko King-O'Riain from the Sociology department of NUIM (Kropiwiec and Chiyoko King-O'Riain, 2006; Wang and Chiyoko King-O'Riain, 2006).

This chapter draws upon four focus groups which were conducted in Polish by Katarzyna Kropiwiec and subsequently translated back into English. The focus group discussions concentrated on four areas: communication with friends and family abroad; keeping up to date with news from home; keeping up to date with Irish news, and use of Polish media produced in Ireland. The four focus groups were conducted with 16 Polish people, 11 males and 5 females aged 27–58 years. Half of the group were married but not all had their families with them in Ireland. (See table 11.1, p. 188). The profile of the group in terms of age and educational attainment corresponds to the profile of immigrants to Ireland more generally, although females were slightly under-represented (Barrett et al., 2006).

Three of the focus groups took place in Dublin, including one in the Polish Social and Cultural Association building on Fitzwilliam Square, and two others in private rented accommodation. One took place in a family home in a rural area of Co. Laois. All but two of the interviewees were working and these jobs varied from carpentry and construction to office work, computer assembly and farming. Of those who were not working one was retired and one had recently arrived and was searching for work. One interviewee was a stay-at-home mother. The maximum any interviewee had been in Ireland was five years and the minimum was three months.

Polish use of the media in Ireland

Given the number of interviews conducted across the four focus groups, we cannot draw generalisations either to the entire Polish community in Ireland or to other migrant groups in Ireland. Nevertheless, some interesting findings emerged. Overall we can say that for these interviewees the media, both old and new, have played and continue to play an important role in their migration to Ireland both in terms of maintaining links with their homeland and to a lesser extent in terms of learning about their hostland. Interviewees accessed a range of media content from local, national and transnational producers, both in Polish and in English. The use of particular media seemed to vary, depending on age, occupation and language skills, although it also evolved as the migrant's time in Ireland lengthened. Further, interviewees were outspoken in their criticism of the quality of local and national media services and content. Locally produced Polish owned media, as well as national media from Ireland, were constantly compared to each other and to media channels and content from elsewhere including the UK and the USA. It was clear that the frame of reference used for this unfavourable quality comparison was either Hollywood or BBC productions.

Interviewees used a wide range of media, not relying on one but rather changing to the cheapest and most convenient as their time in Ireland lengthened. For all but three of the interviewees the internet was the first port of call to try to find out about Ireland before they came, but once in Ireland they used Irish websites, newspapers, radio and television to acclimatise, source jobs and apartments and get used to the Irish accent (see table 11.2, p. ???). Indeed, use of local and national Irish newspapers (12) and radio (10) was relatively high for this group. When it came to television, three quarters watched it, although the programmes were from a variety of sources, including Irish, Polish, British and American. Less than half of those interviewed used locally produced Polish language newspapers and radio programmes and none of the group watched locally produced Polish-language television programmes broadcast on local Dublin cable channels. Use of imported Polish newspapers (1) and Polish television accessed via satellite (4) were low, although they had access to Polish newspapers via the internet. The internet, mobile phones and international pre-paid call cards were used to communicate with home and friends in other countries

The most striking finding to emerge from this study is the central importance of the internet in the lives of these Polish immigrants to Ireland and the intricate relationship between this relatively new medium and the established mass media. When the interviewees initially arrived in Ireland they accessed the internet at public libraries and internet cafes. For some this was replaced by internet at home once accommodation was secured. All but three of the interviewees used the internet regularly (more than once a week). Those that did not were male and working in construction and farm labouring. One of these commented that he hoped to learn how to use a computer now he was in Ireland.

The primary use of the internet was for communication with friends and family in Poland or elsewhere via a range of applications including email, internet chat programmes, internet telephony and to send text messages to mobile phones. The second use was to obtain news and information from home via websites, streaming Polish radio or reading Polish newspapers on the internet. Some used the internet to view webcam images from their home towns. They also used it to source information on Ireland. The third use of the internet for these interviewees was e-commerce: buying airline tickets, betting, buying stocks and paying bills online.

> I do a press review every day, even every hour when I'm bored at work. Usually it
> is onet, wirtualna polska, interia, gazeta, polskie radio (interviewee F, 27, female).

While intensity and extent of use varied by age, occupation, ease of access and
length of time in Ireland, all interviewees relied on the internet both to
maintain social relationships at a distance but also to seek information and
news from their homeland and about their hostland. What was interesting
was the emergent use of local-to-local links over the internet as well as the link
to their homeland. One interviewee noted that they had been in the country
for ten months and had internet at home so when they wanted to find out
something about Ireland they either went to friends or to the internet. The
internet was used to help children look up information on Ireland for
homework and to establish local networks with other Poles in Ireland.

Nevertheless, while interviewees relied on the internet for information on
Ireland they were critical of the quality of information provided by some Irish
websites. A few such as rte.ie (news) and service providers like daft.ie (accommodation) and fas.ie (jobs) were popular. Other websites were considered
'very poor' or 'very general like a company card'. The internet was not seen as
a very useful source of cultural or historical information on Ireland, particularly
on local towns and cities. One interviewee complained they could not find
the rules of hurling anywhere. In the absence of such sites people went either
to Polish or American websites.

> For me the internet is information. I have a theme I'm interested in and I put it
> into a search engine, mostly in Polish, more often in English, when I don't find
> information in Polish. Mostly pages in English, not Irish, because the Irish
> internet is so poor. Most of the pages are American (interviewee P, 30, male).

Interviewees also noted that while the cost of the internet in Ireland appears
to be comparable to Poland, especially when differences in wages are taken
into account, over half complained about the speed and quality of the
connections, both at home and in internet cafes. They also felt that many
internet cafes were of low quality in terms of the technology, support and
environment.

The second striking fact to emerge in this study is the low level of
transnational (that is, via satellite) Polish-language television viewing (3), and
the relatively low level of English-language television viewing despite many
having access to it (9). Only two of the interviewees had access to Polish
language television from their homeland in their Irish homes. For these two
men, aged 40 and 58 respectively, television helped to keep in touch with
sports and news from home and they noted that they did not really want to
learn about 'Irish' culture and that they found the Irish accent difficult to

understand. They had both been in the country for over two years and one was in fact retired. English language skills and age seemed to be at issue in these two cases but these were the exceptions in this study. The other interviewee who watched Polish language television went to Polish restaurants or the Polish centre in Dublin if he wanted to watch a particular event. None of the interviewees knew that Irish television channels were offering Polish language programming. Other interviewees had the equipment to access Polish television but kept it in the wardrobe and decided to watch English language television instead to improve their English.

Interviewees noted overall that they did not watch television very often and that they preferred to watch English-language rather than Polish-language television programmes. Low levels of television viewing in general related to a lack of leisure time. Most of the interviewees worked long hours and in their spare time they did housework, shopping and met friends. In their leisure time they read, listened to music on CD, went for walks, went to concerts or went to the pub, but most agreed they had very little time for television. Where television is watched it is usually English-language programming on Irish television stations and this is prompted by a desire to improve their language skills. They mainly watched American and British programmes including sport, cartoons, movies, news, and programmes like *Panorama*, *Friends* and specialist channels like Discovery. The range of programmes viewed also related to whether they had children or not. Irish-produced programmes were not specifically mentioned.

> Now I am working normal working time and we are at home together we actually don't switch on the TV. It's just standing here and getting dusty (interviewee o, 28, female).

While the low levels of television viewing, particularly of Polish television may be surprising, the high levels of radio listenership are equally interesting. Radio is of course almost ubiquitous and many spoke of listening to the radio in the car, at work and in shops, whether they wanted to or not. Almost half had listened to Polish radio programmes on local Irish radio channels like Anna Livia and two listened to Polish radio streamed via the internet and digital television. For Poles living outside Dublin these programmes were difficult to receive. There were mixed opinions about the Polish programmes on Irish radio with some admitting they were 'amateurish' and others that they tried to satisfy all Poles and ended up playing a mixture of classical, songs and disco/pop all in the same programme. Nevertheless the older interviewees liked the phone-ins from Poles living in Ireland and the variety.

> they talk in Polish and it's a variety . . . very interesting, I like it very much. (interviewee B, 40, male).

I think they were very unprofessional. They just talked rubbish. And there were greetings all the time (interviewee I, 27, female).

The younger interviewees preferred specialist music shows and late night Irish phone-in or 'talk radio' shows. They also liked 'Polish specials', for example when Irish radio shows adopted the Polish soccer team during the World Cup and asked Polish people to come on air and talk in English about their national soccer team. Finally, they liked radio to pass the time and get used to the Irish accent. The differences between older and younger interviewees in this regard are interesting and may signal a greater desire for recognition and acculturation by the younger interviewees.

When it came to newspapers, interviewees were also unanimous in their criticism of the Polish-owned Polish-language print media in Ireland and these criticisms related to cost, the quality of the content and the underlying political agendas. Of the 16 interviewees, five read Polish language newspapers produced in Ireland and most felt the quality of writing was poor and noted that the stories were often taken from the internet, where they had already read them. Those who had been in the country for some time felt that the stories were not interesting and were of use only to Poles arriving in Ireland. *Szpila*, however, the monthly arts and culture magazine, was singled out by some for its good articles and content and the *Herald* Friday supplement was also complimented: 'It's better than the other, typical Polish papers. More honest information' (interviewee A, 42, male). Other interviewees noted:

> They are very orientated on sensation. *Gazeta Polska* is really like, what's the name of it – *Super Express*, the Polish tabloid. *Polish Express* – 60 per cent of the articles is written by the editor and 10 per cent of them is signed with a pseudonym. I don't know if they don't have enough people. And everything is in the same tone. I don't like it at all (interviewee F, 27, female).

> *Szpila* is boring, there is nothing to read. *Polski Express*, I think it is a communist lecture, they criticise everyone except of the communist option from the Polish politics. I think they are leftist (interviewee G, 38, male).

> I think they could also write a bit about news from Poland. And they only write about what is happening here . . . but when someone does not have access to the Internet, and not everyone has, or can use internet, they would have the opportunity to buy a paper here with fresh news from Poland (interviewee I, 27, female).

Another interesting criticism expressed related to the commercial nature of the newspapers and some felt that the journalists and operators were not interested in good stories or the truth, only in profits.

> I think that Polish media, papers are interested only in profits from the commercials. And people who write for them are not experienced journalists, just people who happened to be here. Care for factual substance is on the last position, and the priority is how to make money on the commercial (interviewee F, 27, female).

Most interviewees would prefer to access newspapers from Poland and most access them to some degree over the internet. The purchase of Irish newspapers tended to be higher for new arrivals when they were searching for a job or accommodation. Once settled the interviewees did not buy a daily newspaper, preferring instead to read the daily freesheets to help improve their language skills and rely on the radio, which always tended to be on at work, and the internet.

Nearly all of the interviewees used 'top up' mobile phones and when they wanted to call long distance they either bought an international call card or phoned from a call shop which are usually co-sited with internet cafes around Dublin. Interestingly the mobile operators are aware of the extent to which the Polish migrants are using their services and are competing in terms of call rates to Poland for these customers. Texting is highly popular as a means of keeping in touch with friends in Poland and in other countries; phoning is still the main means of keeping in contact with parents and spouses in Poland. Interviewees agreed that the quality and cost of telephoning in Ireland was cheaper than in Poland.

Migration, the media and identity: negotiating difference

Most of the interviewees in these focus groups were enjoying their stay in Ireland and found the Irish friendly and helpful. Only one couple had experienced difficulties when their money had been stolen, but Polish friends had helped out and they had decided to stay on and give things another go. It is interesting to note that over time these Poles were relying less on Polish centres and Polish friends and were more confident to ask Irish people for help and information. This may not be the case for all immigrant groups or indeed all Poles. Indeed it was obvious that within the Polish community itself that interviewees made distinctions and the stereotype of a 'Franck' was often invoked. This stereotype applied to 'older men in jeans' who worked in construction and were frequent churchgoers.

General experiences in Ireland provoked much comment and comparison with home. Most interviewees were outspoken about the poor quality of public transport in Ireland, which they said was a 'tragedy' and a 'drama' compared to what they were used to in Poland. They noted that Irish food was generally of poor quality and they spoke of the slowness of certain institutions, especially banks. For most interviewees their experiences in Ireland were contributing to a greater understanding of Irishness, or at least of Irish institutions. Comparison between homeland and hostland was constant and it was even more complicated when things were compared to perceptions and experiences of other countries, either mediated or direct. This growing multifaceted sensibility was reflected in an astute questioning of institutions and the politics of media producers. One interviewee for example noted that 'as a rule media are serving the power . . . they are always distorted. The communism was lying to us and now democracy is lying' (interviewee A, 42, male). For another younger interviewee who was stopping going to Polish mass in Ireland because 'the priest is moralising that you should come to church on Sunday, not to work, although there is a double rate [to work on a Sunday]' (interviewee I, 27, female).

The interviewees in this pilot research project kept up to date with news from home primarily via newspapers on the internet and telephone calls. While transnational media available via the internet from Poland and locally produced Polish newspapers and events in Ireland helped to reaffirm their Polish identity and maintain communal connections in the host and the homeland, they were not consumed uncritically. Some interviewees were critical of what they saw as the traditional and conservative elements of their national culture and were keen to assert their difference from those elements. They were also critical of the undifferentiated approach to 'Polishness' adopted by some media producers in Ireland and the attempt by 'opportunistic' producers to make money by providing low quality productions and content.

What is striking when reading the focus group transcripts is that even in this relatively small group the degree to which interviewees used English language media or Polish language media varied. This variance can be linked to their desire for acculturation and/or their desire to maintain a sense of difference, but it is also linked to such things as occupation, length of time in the country, age, language skills and media quality. For some, Irish media were an important way to learn how to speak Hiberno-English and to understand Irish culture. This was particularly the case for those with children but also for young professionals whose jobs involved working or dealing with the Irish public. One interviewee noted that

> the media are very important in the beginning. In the beginning of your stay you don't know the culture, the customs, you know very little (interviewee k, 33, male).

> I listen to the radio to kill the silence and also to get used to the spoken language. When I came here I got the phone with radio to listen to the language a lot. And I switched from music to the spoken text all the time. And at home I listened to BBC. They were talking quite clearly (interviewee F, 27, female).

we insist on learning the language. We don't use the Polish TV, we don't use Polish radio, we don't use Polish papers. We use all that is Irish (interviewee J, 33, female).

However, some of the older interviewees displayed a desire to watch and listen to Polish media from their homeland. For these interviewees the media served to highlight their difference and did not necessarily help in the acculturation process.

It's not interesting for me. They have their own culture, their music. We are Poles and we like our Polish songs. And to change over to the Irish music, folk, no, no (interviewee C, 58, male).

the Irish accent is awful, I can talk much better to a Brit, American, Australian or other foreigner speaking English than with an Irish person. It depends on with whom. I can see that educated people here speak with a better Oxford accent. And the others speak awful and it's hard to understand them. And they pretend that they don't understand me or they don't want to understand me (interviewee A, 42, male).

Of course in many instances the English-language media being used by Polish immigrants to Ireland are not Irish produced or speaking what is called Hiberno-English. This is particularly the case with television where interviewees were watching American comedy series and wildlife programmes as well as British current affairs programmes rebroadcast on Irish television channels. With the internet there are only a few Irish websites of use and otherwise they use Polish or American sites. Thus the interviewees were consuming both American and British international content and transnational media content from their homeland and in the main the predominant Irish media content accessed was via local and national radio and the two freesheets *Herald AM* and *Metro*. The latter of course rely heavily on the international wire services for their news. It would appear that where the local and national media do not provide representation of sufficient quality, users will turn to other sources.

The media and transnationalism

We can identify four types of media producer providing content to the Polish community in Ireland. Firstly, there are local Polish language newspapers provided by Poles for the Polish community in Ireland. These may conform to notions of 'exilic' and/or 'diasporic' media, in that they are contributing to the development of a sense of the Polish community in Ireland and are clearly opportunistic attempts to create media businesses and products to ease the 'transition' for Polish migrants to Ireland. Initial examination of the content provided by these outlets appears to be subject to an implicit assumption by the producers that many Polish workers will return home, and that they have a constant need for basic information on Ireland and information about communicating, travelling and sending money home to Poland. Interviewees noted that the publications often sourced their content from the internet or direct from Polish media companies. The overall quality of writing and content was very mixed. Initial examination of the publications found that they took both Polish and Irish advertising. Thus the transnational and the national can be traced in the content provided by local Polish producers.

Secondly, we have local Irish media outlets specifically targeting the Polish minority in Ireland in the Polish language in certain regions, including Dublin and Limerick. These provide both information and entertainment but use is relatively low unless there is free access, as in radio. While the media producers are clearly attempting to become more multicultural, and in many cases hire Polish immigrants to present and write for them, the reaction of interviewees in this study was mixed, particularly in terms of the quality of the content provided.

Thirdly, we have the mainstream Irish media outlets targeted at the majority of the population and published or broadcast in English. These are again useful in the initial stages when new arrivals are looking for an apartment or a job. Newspapers in particular, even when they include weekly columns in Polish, become less useful once an immigrant becomes established. Over time interviewees moved to access free newspapers, motivated by language needs. In the case of television, most spoke of watching Irish television to improve their language skills but then tended to prefer imported international programming where the English was easier to understand. Irish websites were also seen as generally of poor quality and lacking depth.

Interaction with the national media in Ireland is limited in some cases for reasons of cost, a lack of time, remoteness and a lack of language skills. Where interviewees were accessing national Irish television channels, negative representations of the Polish community did not appear to be an issue. Those who did view Irish national television stated that they were keen to try to understand Ireland and to improve their language skills. This was particularly the case for those living in remote areas and with families. Key of course here is that no distinction is made in some cases between content produced in Ireland and content imported and rebroadcast from elsewhere – for example international content on national media channels – as long as it is in English. Interviewees preferred to watch international programming from America and Britain on Irish channels.

Fourthly, we have transnational media broadcast or distributed directly across borders without localisation, including satellite television from Poland and internet content. Polish satellite television was not extensively used by these interviewees, while content on the internet from a variety of sources was.

Interviewees spoke of doing regular news surveys of content from home and using internet technology to bypass more expensive national telecommunications and media costs in Ireland. Overall for these interviewees international and transnational media content accessed via the internet and television in Polish and English were key information and entertainment resources in the longer term, while local and national media content in Polish and English were useful in the initial transition period.

Clearly delineating the local, the national, the international and the transnational is problematic in terms of the media in Ireland where national terrestrial television schedules are dominated by international programming and advertising, while local media can carry both English language and Polish language programming or repackage content sourced over the internet. In fact it is useful to distinguish between international programming rebroadcast on national and local channels and transnational programming that is broadcast unchanged across borders. The distinction between international and transnational in terms of the media serves to highlight the economics and politics of cultural production in a small nation where economics of scale simply do not operate. It also highlights the differential flows of cultural products between countries which share a geo-linguistic or indeed a geo-cultural heritage (Hesmondhalgh, 2002: 179–80). When we are trying to understand the cultural implications of the changing mediascape in Ireland for Irish audiences, it is useful to identify the source of the programming in addition to the location of the producer and the language used.

The literature reviewed at the start of this chapter would suggest that consumption of transnational media plays a role in 'constructing and defining, contesting and reconstituting national, "ethnic" and other cultural identities' (Gillespie, 1995: 11). The findings emerging from this pilot study would suggest that local and national, as well as transnational media, are involved in this process to some degree. Interestingly, the use of the different types of media and different genres of content by these interviewees varied over time but was influenced as much by quality concerns as cultural ones. In this study international and transnational media content, provided by a range of producers, were used to improve language skills for the new hostland, maintain contacts with the homeland and engage with programming from a range of other sources. International and transnational content provided high quality content, in terms of production values, as well as a range of Anglo-American and Polish identities. Meanwhile local, diasporic and national English and Polish language media provided useful transition material for new arrivals but were seen as less useful for longer term emigrants, less professional, less oppositional/critical of host or homeland politics and as operating with a very narrow sense of Polish identity. More work is needed before we can understand the implications of these media flows for Polish migrants in the Irish context.

Table 11.1 **Profile of interviewees**

	Age	Gender	Status	Time in Ireland	Occupation
A	42	M	S	15 months	carpenter
B	40	M	M	5 ys	construction
C	58	M	M	2 yrs	pensioner
D	55	M	M	2 yrs	X
E	38	M	S	2 yrs	construction
F	27	F	S	10 months	recruitment
G	38	M	S	22 months	office
H	28	M	M	6 months	computer assembly
I	27	F	S	8 months	computer inspection
J	33	F	M	10 months	housewife
K	33	M	M	18 months	farmer
L	32	M	S	5 months	fixing lawnmowers
M	32	F	S	3 months	DTP
N	34	M	S	3 months	not working
O	28	F	M	10 months	engineer
P	30	M	M	10 months	sales assistant

n= 16

Table 11.2 **Source and use of media**

Source	Media, language and ownership	Yes	No	No answer
Ireland/Poland/ USA/UK	Internet, multiple	12	3	1
Poland	Polish television	3	13	
Poland	Polish newspapers	1	15	
Poland	Polish radio	2	6	8
Local Ireland	Polish newspapers	6	4	5
Local Ireland	Polish radio	7	6	3
Local Ireland	Polish television	0	14	2
Local and national Irish	Irish newspapers in English and Polish	12*	2	4
Local and national Irish	Irish radio in English and Polish	10	1	5
Irish/USA/UK	Irish television in English	9	5	2

n= 16
*= includes free newspapers

Chapter 12

Big Brother meets the Celtic Tiger?
Reality TV, cultural values and identities

Barbara O'Connor

During the televised final of the 2006 Rose of Tralee competition, one of the contestants, in conversation with the show's presenter, playfully suggested to him that the backstage activities of the finalists would make a great reality TV show. Her comment was striking in two ways. This long-running television programme is itself a kind of reality show as it combines elements of the game show with 'ordinary' young women performing in a relatively unscripted way in front of the television cameras. The popular entertainment show offers viewers the pleasures of 'people watching' and of predicting the winner of the competition who is temporarily transformed from an 'ordinary' young woman into a celebrity. In this sense it is a forerunner of reality TV as we know it today. The contestant's remark is doubly interesting in that she freely acknowledges that there is a gap between the performance for the televised final and the backstage performance of the finalists during their week's visit to Ireland for the competition. Her casual reference to the existence of multiple realities and the link which she makes between them and performance for television highlights how reality TV is currently an integral part of the contemporary Irish cultural landscape.[1]

First established in the Netherlands, reality TV has become one of the most popular genres with audiences in Europe, the USA and Australia over the last decade. In 2001 the first Irish produced reality programme, *Treasure Island*, had an average audience of 120,000 viewers while one of the most recent, *Celebrity Jigs and Reels* (2006), had an average of 595,000, giving some indication of the substantial increase in viewing figures over that four-year period.[2] An early attempt to define the genre by Kilborn (1994) as 'a hybrid mix of presenter talk, verité material, dramatic reconstruction and various forms of audience participation', is later acknowledged by him to be 'notoriously imprecise' (Kilborn and Izod, 1997: 157). And more recently still Kilborn (2003: 55) wonders how useful the term continues to be in the light of the phenomenal expansion of popular factual television across a range of subgenres. The difficulties of arriving at an accepted definition of the genre have been echoed by other writers such as Von Feilitzen (2004), Hill (2005), and Aslama and Pannti (2006). While a precise definition may be elusive, of particular interest for the discussion below is its novel focus on both 'ordinary' people and 'celebrities' acting in a relatively unscripted way in front of the television cameras.

The enormous commercial success of reality TV and its popularity with audiences has generated both popular and scholarly commentary, much of it negative. Indeed, the increasing space given to reality programming in television schedules has created quite a moral panic about its ill effects on viewers. Many critics, approaching the topic from a political economy or textual analysis perspective, see it as an integral part of the 'dumbing down' of television within a globalised production system, as undermining of democratic values, and of diminishing the public sphere. Andrejevic (2002, 2004), for instance, claims that the genre has emerged as part of a wider culture of surveillance characteristic of contemporary capitalism. Motivations for viewing and the pleasures derived from programmes such as *Big Brother* are dependent on the voyeuristic aspects of the show. Furthermore, he sees it as seducing whole populations into a culture of surveillance because, rather than being perceived as undesirable, it is understood by cast and fans alike as a means of achieving creative self-expression and authenticity. It promotes values of individual celebrity. Turner (2006), too, is critical of the celebrity culture that he claims is generated by reality TV. The media, he suggests, occupy the centre of symbolic production, and their content therefore has a powerful social and cultural impact. But since formats like reality TV are increasingly globalised, media conglomerates 'may be trading in constructions of identity that are dislocated from any social or cultural context' (2006: 162–3). He is critical too of the ways in which ordinary people turn themselves into 'media content through celebrity culture' (2006: 153) and of the fact that the primary focus is on private identity: the personal, the ordinary and the everyday. Reality TV invites participants/viewers to merge their personal everyday reality with that created publicly by television, resulting in television playing a primary role in constructing identities for viewers. The identities on offer he finds deficient in a number of ways. He claims that because the format rewards people who perform their ordinariness with some degree of specificity rather than people with talent or achievements, it promotes mediocrity and an inordinate desire for fame, especially amongst young viewers. Kilborn (2003), too, criticises the kinds of reality on offer in the genre as inauthentic and commodified. Mendible (2004), approaching the topic from a feminist perspective, suggests that the American dating shows generate humiliation as a characteristic mode of response for women.[3] The ethical concerns about the kinds of values promoted by the genre have been summarised by von Feilitzen

(2004: 12) thus: 'it encourages bullying, harassment and degradation, in that the programmes and audience humiliate and evict contestants, something completely contrary to ideals of tolerance, solidarity and peace in democratic societies'. Because much of reality TV is about the lives of ordinary people and can be relatively interactive, it is the genre where the crossover between participants and audience is most likely to occur and audiences are therefore often erroneously regarded as almost interchangeable with the show's participants. It is all too frequently assumed that the kinds of identities and values which are perceived to be generated by the genre will be automatically and unproblematically accepted and/or aspired to by audiences.

While critics of reality TV are numerous, more sanguine views of its role are held by other writers, principally but not exclusively those engaged with audience studies. Coining the term 'democratainment', Hartley (1999) proposes that popular television in general has become more democratic because it includes a more diverse range of voices of ordinary people than ever before. Examining the interactive elements of reality TV, other writers (Jones, 2003; Roscoe, 2001; Tincknell and Raghuram, 2002) have asserted that contemporary audiences are producers as well as consumers because they now have more power to shape and control what they view through voting, web discussion and so on. Feminist scholar, Van Zoonen (2001: 672) has welcomed the advent of reality TV as a televisual space where the distinctions between the spheres of private and public life can be transcended. Indeed, she likens *Big Brother* to a feminist project in that the purpose of both is to valorise the private sphere that has traditionally been associated with women. The popularity of reality TV she suggests is 'a nostalgic yearning for authenticity, for ties with others like oneself, for familiarity and communality, and for the social legitimisation of one's private experiences'.

Empirical audience studies, while acknowledging the complexity of viewer practices, have tended to highlight how they engage with the genre to construct and negotiate identities in a positive rather than a negative way. Hill (2005:184), for instance, has conducted one of the most comprehensive audience studies to date and has found that 'much popular factual television implicitly and explicitly addresses viewers about good and bad ways to live their lives'. Lumby's (2004) and Quin's (2004) research with teenage girls in Australia also claims that these programmes are very useful for learning social relationship skills and for negotiating acceptable kinds of identities for themselves.

As indicated above, the views on how reality TV influences cultural values and identity construction tend to be diametrically opposed. The discussion that follows takes up some of these issues in an Irish context. Casual observation of some reality programmes had led me to surmise initially that the emphasis on surveillance, on celebrity, competition and consumption in the shows would appeal in particular to younger audiences, not only because these are the target audience for reality TV but also because it seemed to me that these were the values and practices being increasingly encouraged and constituted in Ireland's highly competitive and individualistic economic and cultural environment. In other words, I had anticipated a homology between the dominant cultural values represented in reality TV and in what is commonly referred to as the Celtic Tiger culture. So I set out to investigate the motivations and pleasures of watching reality TV in an effort to assess the kinds of values and identities that were being negotiated around it.[4] The discussion below is based on focus group research with a small sample of young Irish viewers ranging in age from early teens to mid-20s.[5]

Real selves, fake selves and performing identities

The fact that reality TV focuses on ordinary people acting in front of television cameras has spawned much discussion of 'the self', particularly the possible gap between the 'performing self' and the 'real self' of the participants, or between the frontstage and backstage behaviour identified by Goffman (1966). The focus group discussions concerning participants in reality shows generated much talk about the self: ordinary selves and extraordinary/celebrity selves; performing selves and real selves, good selves and bad selves. The references to the self are useful to the extent that they imply both a sense of identity and a moral discourse including how we see ourselves in relation to others, how we should behave towards others, and how we would like others to act towards us. All of these elements were present in the focus group conversations.

Research to date has confirmed that one of the main viewing pleasures of reality TV is guessing when participants are acting for the camera or behaving naturally (Jones, 2003; Brenton and Cohen, 2003; Hill, 2005; Aslama and Pantti, 2006). Viewers to whom I spoke corroborate these findings and were clearly aware that editing, staging and performing for the cameras meant that 'the real' could no longer be taken for granted. Discerning 'the real' can be difficult and becomes a matter of negotiation with others as the following extract about a former *Big Brother* contestant indicates:

> I mean how much of it was putting on the 'dumb as dirt' . . . this girl was making herself seem so stupid and she's not, she's savvy, that girl is more savvy than she lets on. She's the only one that's had any career that's lasted and she's made a career out of seemingly being dumb (Breda: MTV group).

To which the other participant responds:

> Do you believe that? I believe she's dumb but I don't think she's as dumb as she lets on' (Adam: MTV group).

Spotting the 'true self' was seen as crucial to enjoyment. Indeed, some viewers commented that *Big Brother* had disimproved in recent years because they felt that changes in format such as the withdrawal of privileges 'makes it more fake' and 'there's too many constrictions put on people, they aren't really allowed to be themselves even if they wanted to'. However, a participant in another group expressed the contrary view that contestants will eventually reveal themselves on camera and that 'game planning goes out the window'. What is interesting in this context is not the differing opinions, but rather the desire by all three participants for visual indicators of 'true selves' and of 'genuine behaviour'. The same theme is taken up in connection with one of the contestants in the 2006 series:

> He just wrecks my head, he overreacts about everything . . . he actually said that he *was* acting, whereas some people are kinda loud, mad and themselves, *he's not being himself,* [my emphasis] he's being someone else (Alice: Schoolgirl group).

The diary room in *Big Brother* was another opportunity for viewers to distinguish between the 'performing' and 'real' self. Karen a member of the CS group commented that 'part of it is the diary . . . even though you know they could be acting, eventually you spot the people who are genuine and the people who aren't'. Mary, another member of the same group followed this with a comment on another former *Big Brother* contestant who 'was so ordinary, you could describe her as common' to which the first speaker replies, 'That's why people liked her, because she was just herself'. And followed again by the second speaker, 'She'd say things and you'd say "that was so stupid" but she was just being herself'. Simon, the third member of the group, then reflected that 'The ones who win are the most real, the most genuine'.

The constant references to 'being oneself' and being 'genuine' expressed above point both to a belief in, and a desire for, a 'modernist' sense of self. By this I mean that there is an essential core to the self outside the realm of performance (see Hall, 1992) and which can be contrasted to the 'postmodernist self' characterised as a series of performances which can be changed according to circumstance. Bauman (1996) names one of his four ideal typical postmodern characters 'the Player' for whom life is lived as a game and who might also ostensibly be the ideal *Big Brother* contestant. However, the distinction which the viewers make between the 'performing self' and the 'real self' would seem to counter claims that self-identity in the era of high or postmodernity is as free floating as some would suggest. In actual fact, audiences react negatively to characters that are seen to play the game too strategically as in the case of Nasty Nick in the first *Big Brother* series (see Hill, 2005). Not only do audiences dislike those seen to be motivated solely by winning, but in the case of my own study, they also claimed to identify most with the characters which they perceived as kind and good although simultaneously acknowledging that the 'bad guys' were needed to create tension. For example, the list of characters from *Big Brother* that the schoolgirl group liked included those who 'haven't got involved in any of the fights', are 'not mean', 'doesn't talk to anybody behind their back', and '[is always] getting stuff for people [i.e. obliging]'. Among the contestants they disliked, one was 'a bully', another 'too big for her boots', another moody, 'sitting with a puss on them all morning'. Other groups too, seemed to identify with the kinder, more gentle participants which would seem to indicate that the display of kindness, co-operation and empathy are at least as valued by audiences as displays of competitiveness, aggression and greed.

However, as one might expect, not all identificatory processes were as clearcut as the above. The same group displayed a certain ambivalence towards the contestants in the MTV show *Super Sweet Sixteen*, on the one hand, criticising the greed and rudeness of some of the participants celebrating their sixteenth birthdays but, on the other, identifying with aspects of the consumerist lifestyle portrayed:

> It's [the show] really good . . . there was one girl I remember one night and she just goes 'I'm sorry you didn't get an invitation [to birthday party] but that's 'cos I don't like you' [in American accent] . . . and she goes 'this probably cost more than my parents wedding but I don't care 'cos I deserve it' (Alice: schoolgirl group).

Later in the conversation about the show she talks about one of her reasons for liking it 'Fabulous life or whatever, I just want to see what they get with their money, what *you* could get'. Here we can see that having noted and criticised the culture of entitlement of the teenager in question, she goes on to talk about the pleasures of viewing and of aspiring to her lifestyle. The other members of this group had a similar double-edged response and ridiculed what they perceived as the more ludicrously extravagant aspects of the celebrity's behaviour:

> Britney Spears gets a plane to New York to have a coffee and the plane back to her house which is in . . . like Florida . . . or something like that. She could actually just buy the coffee shop and put it in her house. Yea, how difficult would that be! [general laughter] (Sarah: schoolgirl group).

This group also commented on another show in which the teenage participants were 'so mean, they'd be jealous of each other, would have to have the limelight of the party . . . they get private jets to New York and go to shop in Chanel and Gucci shops'. Here we may note that hand in glove with the criticism of what are seen as extremely pampered lifestyles is the easy familiarity with designer labels. At one level this group are critiquing what they regard as excessive consumption but at another are firmly embedded within the discourse themselves. Their response can be usefully compared with the more negative response of some members of the older groups who had seen *Super Sweet Sixteen* and who very clearly rejected not just the participants' behaviour but also the culture which creates it:

> I look at it and [say] 'thanks be to God I had the upbringing that I had, I don't want all that money'. I have huge issues with people who have a lot of money. I love going 'you stupid, spoiled brat, I'd slap your face if I was beside you'. (Breda: MTV group)

Or:

> I didn't enjoy that now . . . I saw it once, maybe twice and that was about it . . . they're just spoilt brats . . . it's a form of bullying as well . . . kids coming up begging for invitations to the party and 'No, why would I want you at my party?' and then you see the kid going off in tears (Aisling: accountant's group).

The different responses to *Super Sweet Sixteen* are just one example of the varying relevance of specific realities for each of the groups. The younger group enjoyed the MTV reality shows – seeing people their own age, looking at what they did, and aspiring to some of it. It may be that this group were also at an age where identity work – building a 'cool' yet popular image – is particularly important and reality TV is a useful source of information about fashion, friendships, sexual relationships and so forth (see Gotz, 2004). It is also interesting to note that this group talked most about participants/ contestants as role models and their conversation was peppered with American slang words such as 'homey'. It might be tempting, therefore, to suggest that it was the youngest group who were the most susceptible to the consumption messages in these shows. However, both Hobson's (2004: 144) and Lumby's (2004) research evidence from the UK and Australia respectively attests to the high levels of discernment of young teenagers about reality TV.

Another form of identification and source of enjoyment of celebrity shows was in seeing the celebrities as ordinary people and making comparisons between their own lives and those of the celebrities. For example one young woman liked to see:

> how they [celebrities] live day to day, what they do, to see what they do when they get up in the morning, how they live their life, how different it is; then when you get up to a nine to five job, put on your suit, go sit at a desk, work away, then go home (Eva: accountant's group).

Another male member of the group asks if it is really day-to-day stuff that they are doing to which Eva responds 'Oh, yea, you see them getting up and having their breakfast, you see her getting her make-up done, going to the hairdresser, see them meeting for lunch'. She is challenged again by another male group member asking, 'But if the cameras weren't there would she have behaved like that' to which she responds:

> That's the thing . . . I know its not totally one hundred per cent realistic but . . . it's the attraction, even if half of it is realistic, to see what she does to get her money and how hard her life is and stuff.

Here we see how realism is not an either/or category but rather a continuum. There also seemed to be a gender dimension here, as it was the females who talked about this form of enjoyment, and in this instance it was the male members of the group who challenged the 'realism' of the situations portrayed. A similar kind of enjoyment can be had from seeing how celebrities cope with the challenges they face and the tasks that they are required to perform. The schoolgirl group mentioned this aspect as one of the reasons for liking the celebrity shows:

> Sometimes they have to maybe eat bugs, they get different tasks and jump off big, huge heights, they're facing their fears . . . [you] get to see them eatin' worms and stuff . . . get to see what they're like in real life (Evelyn: schoolgirl group).

By seeing celebrity responses to challenges, the viewer gets to see what they are really like, their 'real' self. The viewing pleasure of seeing celebrities as ordinary people is part of the contradictory discourse of celebrity (see Turner et al., 2000) that simultaneously valorises their elite status and their 'ordinariness'.

Transforming the self: good selves, bad selves

Von Feilitzen (2004: 12) notes that reality TV has been accused of a litany of moral trangressions – 'striving for sensation by seasoning the contents with sex, nudity, promiscuity . . . bad language and racism . . . and of promoting new lifestyle standards that prioritise publicity, glamour, competition, heightened self-centredness, individualism and oppressing other people'. The genre is popularly seen as both reflecting and causing this ostensible decline in moral values. However, this view has been robustly challenged by Hill (2005: 121) who claims that morality is actually at the heart of the genre and that there is an 'ethical turn' in reality programming which is significant in that it illuminates ethical values 'as represented in the programmes and as discussed by viewers' (108). She focuses on lifestyle programmes and quotes Hawkins (2001: 418) to support the view that they are not just about giving technical advice but are 'at the same time ethical because it involves giving privilege to certain conducts over others, the classification of certain conducts as good'. However, there are differences of opinion about the ethical function of such programmes. Bonner (2003: 104) acknowledges that 'lifestyle programmes alert viewers to the existence of more products and services for their utility in the endless project of the self'. And Wood (2004: 57) suggests that 'infomercials propose various "self-improvements" that fit people into a reality that currently exists and in terms of which they are somehow or other deficient' and are thus 'self-help manuals for the victimized'. Alternatively, Brunsdon (2003) stoutly defends them against Jonathan Miller's accusations of 'kapok' and 'dumbing down' and suggests that they have also been responsible for a 'pluralling up' (2003: 18) by which she means that programmes include a far wider range of the British public than lifestyle programmes in the past and that there is 'a greater attention paid to the stuff of everyday lives' which is positive. Hill (2005: 123) sees tensions within the subgenre: '[o]n the one hand the content of much lifestyle programming is about individual ways to improve care of the self. On the other hand, the content of much health based reality programming is about how other people care for individuals in compassionate and responsible ways'. Hill's analysis is embedded within an 'ethics of care' and her discussion of the 'care of others' is based primarily on pet programmes where compassion and responsibility are represented and responded to by viewers in a clear-cut fashion. I wish to extend the discussion to include lifestyle programmes other than health or pet programmes, since I found that the viewers' discussion of the 'care of self' was also embedded within ethical and normative discourses about others. The focus group members used the stories, characters and situations in these shows to negotiate ethical boundaries between acceptable and unacceptable behaviour within the domain of personal relationships.

One of the main pleasures for the viewers was the potential for transformation of the shows' participants. These transformations were especially, though not exclusively, associated with lifestyle shows and could range from changes in appearance, such as a new hairstyle, make-up and clothes, to individual behaviour within interpersonal and family relationships, to change of home, to 'making a difference' to other people. In discussing the makeover shows, viewers distinguished between ones such as *Trinni and Susanna* and more extreme ones such as *The Swan*, the latter eliciting comments such as:

> it makes me sick to watch, . . . it's like, they're so unhappy with themselves, it makes me sad because they think that by changing their appearance 'Oh, hey Presto, my life's going to be brilliant again' . . . and they come out . . . and their

children don't recognise them . . . its so sad . . . its just so American, I can't watch it (Mary: CS group).

Note here the critique of the misguided value system of the contestants, of American cultural values more generally, and implicitly of a mother's (in this case) responsibility towards her children. A former teacher in another group comments:

> That's the one (The Swan) I used to talk to my students about, I just felt it was morally wrong, . . . not morally wrong, but just because you look better on the outside doesn't mean you're any happier; and there was this whole feeling like 'You're beautiful now, life is perfect' and it's not (Breda: MTV group).

Both of the comments above are a critique of the emphasis on outward appearances as opposed to the inner core. Others viewers regarded this emphasis on appearance as being typically American, 'That's really extreme, wouldn't get away with it in Europe (Sean: accountant's group) or, 'that's American, I don't think it would happen in Europe' (Adam: MTV group). Comments about the participants being 'freaks' or 'unstable', though not explicitly related to the fact that it was an American show, seem to mobilise a common Irish stereotype of the USA as a place where people have more money than sense.

The transformations effected in *The Swan* were also seen to destroy women's individuality and the 'perfect' results achieved were thought to be fake.

> What I don't like about *The Swan* is that all the women come out as carbon copies of each other (Breda: MTV group).

> Its just fake . . . They're too perfect lookin' 'cos they come out real skinny and perfect and straight and . . . I don't like that at all (Siobhan: schoolgirl group).

> They look nice but they just look fake, they look totally different (Anna: schoolgirl group).

Participants in the less extreme makeover shows such as *Trinni and Susanna* were perceived as ordinary women who did not have problems but who could gain in confidence and self-esteem from the makeover.

> And then they did this series where they went back to the people [who had participated in the original show] . . . and you know the change was incredible like, they might have gone back to their dowdy ways or whatever, but they have a lot more confidence, and more self-esteem, 'cos like clothes, fashion, how much it makes a difference to people (Jane: accountant's group).

The distinctions made between the outer and the inner self in the earlier quotes are now dissolved in the linking of appearance to feeling – how looking good is related to self-confidence. Part of the viewing pleasure is witnessing the transformation of 'ordinary people' and is stated explicitly in the following:

> That's the best part, seeing them coming out and you've seen them at the start. 'How are they going to do anything with them?' they come out and it's just on outfit, it's not a new face, they're just like you and me, they are ordinary people.

> . . . basically the woman has no clue how to dress, nor does she care, she's very happy the way she looks, Trinni and Susanna are going to make her look fabulous, women in their 50s, going through the menopause . . . looking like rag women and Trinni and Susanna just makes them over and makes them look nice and feminine again (Jane: accountant's group).

Another viewer speaks of the pleasures of *Faking It* in similar terms:

> There was a girl who was a concert cellist . . . and she became the DJ. . . . to be a DJ she had to change the way she looked, the way she dressed, the way she spoke, even like the way she walked and talked and acted because . . . like she was very kind of square because this is how you sit when you are in an orchestra and this is how you act . . . [followed later in the discussion by]
> Yea, there was a follow up to it . . . she still was in the orchestra but . . . at night time did DJ gigs . . . she couldn't dance . . .and they were trying to teach her how to move And she was like 'No, I play like this because that's the way I'm supposed to . . . So she was actually finishing her set and going out onto the dance floor and dancing . . . and they were going like 'Wow, this is incredible!'. Like she had never plucked her eyebrows and they got her eyebrows waxed . . . she had never kind of groomed herself 'cos it didn't matter what she looked like as long as she could play, and then she realised . . . I can be a girl and not be frivolous, and you know fake, I can be *me* and still *take care of myself* [my emphasis] (Breda: MTV group).

In the extracts above we saw how the (female) participants found these kinds of transformations so pleasurable to watch, and also the ways in which they negotiated one aspect of the 'care of the female self' through discussion of the shows. The issues they raised about acceptable transformations of physical appearance and behaviour have been central to feminist debates for a long time. Key questions in this debate include how 'looking good' is constructed, by whom and for what purpose, and the levels of autonomy which women have in defining what 'looking good' means and so on. The importance of looking good, being feminine and having confidence is acknowledged; implicit and explicit references to 'buying clothes' indicate the importance of consumption in 'looking good'. But they draw the line in relation to cosmetic surgical procedures that they regard as extreme, irreversible, homogenising, and rejected by some as typically American. Makeovers are best when they enable expression of the 'true self' and enhance ones individuality as opposed to turning women into 'Barbie doll[s]' as one viewer suggested.

The transformation theme is carried through into the discussion of other programmes and kinds of transformation. The following quote illustrates how a participant acted as a role model for one of the schoolgirl viewers:

> One girl she was quite big and she wasn't popular in school, but she'd loads of friends in her own little gang . . . and when she spoke [following her success], she said 'I'm doing this for all those girls who think I can't do this' . . . she was so..she was actually inspiring, brilliant, I thought. I would watch that and think, 'If they can do it, I can do it too.' (Anna: schoolgirl group).

Another viewer spoke of a contestant in *WifeSwap* who was a 'control freak', but who was sent to a house where she was required to look after six children after which time she realised that 'there was a value in noise and mess, and fun in noise and mess . . . the place could be cleaned up and that kind of thing' (Breda: MTV group). Viewing pleasures associated with transformation were also mentioned in relation to building/renovation programmes such as *Grand Design*. Simon from the CS group commented on how the content of these programmes is 'very ordinary, they're building a house but they make it seem very exciting'. His observation could be applied to much reality TV in the sense that one of its main attractions is the transformation of routinised everyday practices into something exciting.

Watching reality TV also enabled viewers to observe ways of life that they would not normally come across in the course of their everyday lives which makes them 'realise there was a whole other world out there' (Breda: MTV group) and that you get 'more of an awareness of the world kind of thing, what you had before was the Cosby show and things like that . . . now you get to see into other peoples' worlds in a real way'(Adam: MTV group). Not only were viewers interested in how diverse people lived their lives but they also got real pleasure from watching the possibilities for people to transform and change – 'Just seeing the journey that the people go on' (Adam: MTV group). These comments are not based on naïve assumptions about representing reality. As we saw earlier, viewers are well aware that these shows are constructed in particular ways in order to maximise conflict and excitement but, despite this knowledge, feel that they can give them an insight into the realities of other people's lives as the following comment on *Wife Swap* indicates:

There's always a spoiled one where the husband does everything . . . there's always a poorer family . . . but you can really get an insight into family life (Breda: MTV group).

What Hill (2005) refers to as the 'ethical turn' was also carried into discussion of other reality shows. For instance many of the viewers had a positive attitude towards shows such as *Celebrity You're a Star*, in which celebrity contestants raise money for their chosen charity. In this context viewers made a distinction between the motivations for appearing on a show, the positively assessed charity appearance, and the negatively assessed appearance for 'fifteen minutes of fame'. Of course, the ethic of charity may be a substitute for more radical transformations of society but it is – given the increasing strength of a neo-liberal agenda of social care – at the very least an acknowledgement that concern and care for others continues to be a public value which they support.[6]

At one level, the transformations we witness in lifestyle programming and in particular the emphasis on changing appearances, whether of the body, the house, or the garden, can be understood as the consequence of living in a 'presentational' (Silverstone, 1999:69) culture where the programmes encourage (sometimes) absurdly high lifestyle expectations. At another level they can be seen as mythic – as a replay of the Cinderella story adapted to reality TV where viewers wanted to learn more about how other people live, to empathise with them, and to see their potential for transformation fulfilled. The utopian desire was palpable in the vivacity and enthusiasm of the viewers as they relayed transformation scenarios to me. The focus group discussions indicate that these potentially contradictory responses can be elicited simultaneously.

Conclusion

This chapter set out to explore the viewing pleasures of reality TV amongst a small sample of viewers, specifically how the pleasures and forms of identity offered and generated by the genre might reflect the 'Celtic Tiger' economy and culture. I had initially, and prematurely, anticipated that the core values offered to and accepted by viewers would be individualism, competitiveness and conspicuous consumption. What I found was substantially different and much more complex. Viewers were very critical of displays of extreme individualism, competitiveness and conspicuous consumption in the shows. In exploring talk around the 'self', I found that there was a rejection of a postmodern sense of self constituted solely by performance, that viewers identified most with the 'good' characters, and those most likely to be criticised were seen variously as cruel, bullying, greedy and unkind. The discussion of the 'care of the self' was embedded in an ethical discourse about the 'care of others'. Viewing was frequently motivated by a desire to learn about the lives of people who are outside the viewers' immediate social circle. In talking about the shows the viewers were drawing boundaries between acceptable and unacceptable behaviours, and in this way negotiating norms in terms of personal relationships and of responsibilities towards others. In tandem with these critical and humanistic responses there also appeared to be less progressive tendencies towards the immersion in consumption discourses, the cultivation of the ethic of charity, the emphasis on property ownership and so forth. However, these tensions and contradictions call for much more detailed research before we can arrive at any definitive conclusions about how these shows function in terms of generating and disseminating ethical messages.

One of the primary motivations for watching the shows, according to respondents, was that they could be used as a 'coin of exchange' with work colleagues, friends and peers. In terms of their function in everyday life then, it is important to bear in mind that the individual responses which were elicited in the focus group discussions are part of a wider 'interpretive community' in which the contestants' characters, performances and actions are the subject of popular 'water cooler' talk and gossip very much like conversations around soap-opera (Scannell, 2002). Viewers used their own experience of social reality to engage and identify with characters, but also to judge and critically access them. It is through this constant exchange of views about the shows that ethical issues relating to the self and others are being continuously negotiated and that these 'interpretive communities' are simultaneously 'moral communities'. In this respect, reality TV, like television soap opera before it, offers a space where the distinction between private and public is transcended, where personal values are negotiated in a public domain, not just through the text itself, but also through normative talk within viewers' social networks.

In this sense then, the criticisms which have been levelled against reality TV by critics such as Turner (2006) and Andrejevic (2002, 2004) seem to be premature and overstated. While they are correct to claim that the increasingly globalised systems of contemporary television production will have economic and cultural effects, it is unwarranted to extrapolate from the 'assumed' and generalised audience inscribed within these macro studies to specific socially situated audiences. And it is premature to make judgements about the effects of reality TV in the absence of sufficient evidence from empirical audience research with viewers (and non-viewers). Furthermore, because much of the critical debate about reality TV has revolved around its relationship to more traditional documentary modes, it is usually positioned in terms of how it measures up to an 'objective reality'. If we adopt an audience perspective, however, we need to take account of the subjective reality of viewers since they will engage critically with the 'realities' represented by relating it to their own personal experiences.

From an audience perspective, this study has highlighted the fact that reality TV is bigger than *Big Brother* (or even *Big Brother's Little Brother!*) and that viewers may watch a range of sub-genres of popular factual television with different motivations, levels of engagement, and viewing contexts which will, in turn, influence the enjoyment and the impact they will have on specific audiences. For instance, in the context of my own research, the youngest group liked the talent shows more and the older age groups liked the property programmes, since each related in specific ways to the current realities and to their life-stage desires and plans. But within groups there was also a mix of regular viewers, occasional and non-viewers and changing levels of engagement and distance within groups depending on other things going on in their lives. Generational taste differences were also apparent as the viewers frequently mentioned their parents' antipathy towards *Big Brother* and similar formats, regarding them as a waste of time (see Scannell, 2002). It also appeared that there was a gender dimension to viewing which was not systematically addressed here. Is it significant that when reporting family viewing, that mothers were more likely to watch than fathers? Or the fact that in certain subgenres, the narratives and modes of address are similar to soap opera (as noted by Roscoe, 2001; Kilborn, 2003), traditionally constituted and viewed as a women's genre?

How similar are Irish audiences to audiences elsewhere? My findings corroborate studies such as Hobson's (2004) and Hill's (2005) with UK audiences in so far as viewers engage critically with the genre, learn from it and use it to negotiate moral boundaries. But there are a number of interesting questions arising from this research which would warrant further investigation of the relationship between the local and global. Turner suggests that because reality TV formats have become increasingly globalised that they are now disembedded from local cultural contexts. To what extent is this the case? While formats may be similar, it would be interesting to know what the most successful subgenres are in other European countries. For instance, does Germany have as many property-based shows as Ireland? Or, in audience terms, what are the implications of the fact that the shows spontaneously mentioned in this study were British and American? Or the fact that the youngest group were more critical of Irish reality TV than the older groups? Does this represent a further decline in the national imagined community historically constructed by Irish media and the transfer of viewership to a globalised media landscape? Before we can answer any of these broader questions, we need to know more about how particular audiences are viewing reality TV, the specific representations of reality that they 'are curious about, interested in, or care about' (Hill, 2005: 191), and the nature of the relationship between the realities of their lives and those of the people they are viewing.

Chapter 13

New lads or protest masculinities? Exploring the meanings of male marginalisation in contemporary Irish film

Debbie Ging

Introduction

In the last ten years, the Irish film industry has demonstrated increasing generic and stylistic diversity, resulting in a comparable diversification of male characters or types (Spicer, 2001) on the screen. This coincides with the emergence of new and often contradictory discourses on masculinity in western media culture generally, where categories such as New Man, New Lad, Millennium Man, Dad Lad, Metrosexual Man and, most recently, Menaissance Man attest to a disturbance in popular thinking about what it means to be a man (Beynon, 2002).[1] As well as accommodating non-normative masculinities, however, this period has also seen the resurgence of more 'robust' or traditional images of masculinity, often borrowed from bygone eras in which male identity was less open to interrogation (a time when men were men) and reappropriated for (post)modern consumption. These male types are particularly evident across a number of new (sub)genres in contemporary anglophone cinema, namely the British 'underclass film' (Monk, 1999), the new British gangster cycle, the American teen or 'gross-out comedy'[2] (Greven, 2002), the 'male rampage film' (Pfeil, 1995) and the American 'smart film' (Sconce, 2002). While their influence on recent Irish cinema is apparent and they have been theorised extensively from the perspective of masculinity by British and American scholars, there is no work within Irish film studies, with the exception of Pettitt's (2004) exploration of the gangster genre and Irish cinema, that tackles these films from this angle. This chapter maps out the rationale, methodologies and key findings of the first Irish study to step into this gap.

Approximately twenty Irish films made in the past decade revolve around themes of crime and social exclusion, and feature sympathetic male antiheroes who are variously marginalised, criminally active and ostensibly positioned in opposition to the status quo. These films include *I Went Down* (1997), *Crush Proof* (1999), *Vicious Circle* (1999), *Flick* (2000), *Saltwater* (2000), *Accelerator* (2001), *The General* (1998), *Ordinary Decent Criminal* (1999), *Veronica Guerin* (2003), *When the Sky Falls* (2000), *Last Days in Dublin* (2001), *Headrush* (2002), *Intermission* (2003), *The Halo Effect* (2004), *Adam and Paul* (2004) and *Man About Dog* (2004). *Dead Bodies* (2003) and *Freeze Frame* (2004) can also be loosely associated with this 'cycle' given their preoccupation with crime, while the comedies *Spin the Bottle* (2002) and *The Actors* (2003) tend more towards parody of underclass and gangster identities. That traditionally male-oriented themes and genres such as crime, thriller or gangster have become increasingly dominant in Irish cinema is not, of itself, especially remarkable, given that these genres are popular in a global market in which the Irish film industry is under increasing pressure to remain competitive. Nevertheless, the discursive constructions of masculinity that characterise these films constitute a significant departure from those that dominated Irish film-making in the 1970s and 1980s. Not only has the focus shifted from a concern with rural male characters in distinctively Irish contexts to urban, working-class masculinities in more universal settings, but there has also been a distinct ideological trajectory, whereby an unequivocally critical approach to patriarchal masculinity has given way to more ambiguous portrayals of machismo.

Taken together, the films and their protagonists are characterised by a number of recurring features. Firstly, they revolve around strictly homosocial spaces in which women are peripheral and the evasion of responsibility and simultaneous prolongation of adolescent pleasures are central. Perhaps most significantly, work and breadwinning, traditionally key signifiers of masculine identity, have been replaced by joblessness and social exclusion. While these themes partly evoke the gritty social realism associated with the films of Ken Loach and their attendant critique of social disadvantage, they are also associated with certain freedoms and their unhampered expression. Rather than problematise unemployment, the films – like their British counterparts *Trainspotting*, *Twin Town* and *Shopping* – tend to celebrate socially marginalised lifestyles as a subculture with obvious appeal to a 'post-political male audience' (Monk, 1999). For Messner and Montez de Oca (2005), the defensive rejection of work by men is also prevalent in American media culture, and can be attributed to processes of deindustrialisation and the perceived feminisation of the working world. This trajectory from working-class hero to underclass (anti)hero is most evident in contemporary Irish films such as *Accelerator*, *Crush Proof*, *Last Days in Dublin*, *Adam and Paul*, *Man About Dog* and *Headrush*. With the exception of *Adam and Paul*, liberation from conventional employment appears to masculinise rather than emasculate men: like Tyler Durden in *Fight Club*, Renton in *Trainspotting* or Matt in *Green Street* (2005), their rejection of consumer capitalism and involvement in dangerous or illegal activities serve as symbolic male rituals or rites of passage through which they achieve recognition and respect from their male peers.

In these films, alternative pursuits associated with working-class men have become the new signifiers of hard masculinity: fighting, twoccing,[3] joy-riding, bare-back horse-riding, involvement in criminal gangs, greyhound racing, hare-coursing, betting, drug- dealing and drinking in the street create new homo-social spaces in which the responsibilities of work, relationships and property acquisition can be avoided. Thus, while the increase in gangland murders and robberies in Ireland in recent years has sparked public fears about crime rates and policing, gangsters and criminals have come to achieve iconic status in a large number of Irish films, including *I Went Down, Flick, Saltwater, The Halo Effect, Dead Bodies, Intermission, Accelerator, Crush Proof, Headrush, The Actors, Freeze Frame* and *Man About Dog*. Real figures such Martin Cahill and John Gilligan have also been the subject of several films (*The General, Ordinary Decent Criminal, Vicious Circle, When the Sky Falls, Veronica Guerin*), echoing British cinema's fascination with the Kray twins and Glaswegian gangster Jimmy Boyle in films such as *The Krays* (1990) and *The Debt Collector* (1999). Elements of the new British gangster cycle and of Tarantino's work are also strongly evident in fictional films such as *Headrush, Man About Dog, Last Days in Dublin* and *The Actors*. According to Monk (1999), Chibnall and Murphy (1999) and Leigh (2000), the resurgence in popularity of gangster iconography is best understood as a response to (perceived) changes to the genderscape. As Steve Chibnall (2001: 2) comments, 'It does not take Sherlock Holmes to deduce that the gangster cycle might index wider gender anxieties and to relate these anxieties to both changing occupational structures and social expectations and to the demonstrable gains of feminism.'

Strong elements of the American 'smart film' and, to a lesser extent, the 'male rampage film' are also evident in the new Irish films. According to Sconce, smart films are defined by a particular set of themes and styles, and manifest a 'predilection for irony, black humour, fatalism, relativism and, yes, even nihilism' (2002: 350). Sconce sees in the ironic, 'fucked-by-fate' attitudes of these films' protagonists a form of political intervention, whereas others have dismissed them as revelling in a form of 'hipster anomie' that has anti-hegemonic pretensions but in fact espouses a reactionary politics of gender. According to Giroux and Szeman, films such as *Fight Club, American Beauty, Rogue Trader* (1999), *American Psycho* (2000) and *Boiler Room* (2000) inaugurate 'a new subgenre of film narrative that combines a fascination with the spectacle of violence, enlivened through tired narratives about the crisis of masculinity, with a superficial gesture toward social critique' (2001: 96).

Increasingly, this angsty preoccupation with the self is becoming evident in Irish male-oriented films such as *Last Days in Dublin* and *Intermission*, frequently played out through the juxtaposition of typically laddish pleasures with incongruously intelligent and articulate voiceover and dialogue. In a review of *Intermission*, Irish film critic Michael Dwyer (2003: 2) explicitly acknowledges the film's continuities with American 'smart film':

> Imagine a multi-charactered narrative odyssey such as *Magnolia*, shot through with the visceral energy of *Trainspotting* and laced with rich, dark Dublin humour, and you begin to catch the essence of *Intermission*, the sharpest, most entertaining Irish movie in years.

Finally, many of these characters exhibit a preoccupation with male suffering and appear to exhibit characteristics of what Connell describes as 'protest masculinities'. According to Connell, in the absence of a gendered claim to power, unemployed men frequently take up 'protest masculinities' as a way of reclaiming lost power. This often takes the form of drinking, violence and other anti-social or disruptive behaviour. The performance of a 'tense, freaky façade' described by Connell (1995: 111), and the 'frenzied and showy' nature of this protest is especially evident in Irish films such as *Accelerator*, *Crush Proof* and *Last Days in Dublin*. Clearly, therefore, the films may be read as indexing the very real problems experienced by socially excluded men in Ireland. However, these images can also function symbolically, whereby discourses of male victimhood are mobilised not in response to class-based oppression, but rather as a means of contesting the perceived excesses of feminism. According to Savran, the conflicted, masochistic male hero of American culture represents a new form of dominant masculinity, profoundly informed by the politics of Robert Bly's *Iron John* and the American myth-opoeic men's movement. Although several critics (Tasker, 1993; Pfeil, 1995) have argued that the heroes of the 'male rampage' genre (which includes *Fight Club*, *Falling Down*, *Face-Off*, *Die Hard* and *Lethal Weapon*) are contradictory, ambiguous and highly self-reflexive meditations on male power and powerlessness rather than unequivocal endorsements of the patriarchal order, Savran concludes that the new discourse of white male victimhood is in fact a strategy employed by middle-class men to recoup lost power, and is thus deeply implicated in what Nye (2005) describes as a wider 'episode of remasculinisation' that is currently taking place in western societies.

Spectatorship and speculation

How male audiences understand and engage with the new machismo of contemporary cinema is central to many of the theoretical debates outlined above. Clearly, much of the ideological elasticity which the films accommodate is attributable to their deployment of postmodern irony. As Hutcheon points out, irony is 'transideological' (White, 1973: 38), in the sense that it can be used to reinforce rather than to question established attitudes, depending on who is using or attributing it and at whose expense it is seen to be. Thus for Sconce (2002), the hyper-aware (non gender-specific) audience is politically engaged through irony. Similarly, David Gauntlett (2002) reads laddish irony as an expression of male anxiety in the face of change and a means of renegotiating masculine identity. For Monk (1999), on the other hand, the (male) audience is post-political, irony-blind and in search of symbolic refuge from the responsibilities of adulthood. Similarly, Giroux and Szeman (2001), and Chibnall (2001) perceive irony as crucial to the discursive space of 'Ladland', where it functions as a means of deflecting serious critique and enabling to men to bask 'in reflections of their own dumbing down as part of a refusal to examine their most deep-seated prejudices against women' (Whelehan, 2000: 66). In almost all of these debates, however, the audience is configured as a hypothetical psychoanalytic construct (Gauntlett, 2002: 40) and universal meanings are imposed on particular viewing situations (Walkerdine, 1986), bearing little relation to how meaning is generated in socially specific contexts of reception.

In the absence of qualitative audience research, therefore, most of what is written about the cultural competencies of male audiences and the meanings and pleasures offered by these films is highly speculative. According to Turner:

> Whereas television studies and areas of cultural studies have been raiding ethnographic methodologies for years, film studies has been relatively slow to use these methods to approach the analysis of Kuhn's 'social audience' – the actual spectators in the cinema (Turner 2002: 379).

As Hanke (1998: 185) points out, this is even more pronounced in relation to research on male film audiences:

> Apart from the tradition of film study which has theorized the male gaze and the male spectator, masculinity as a dimension to social audiences' reception practices remains invisible except in a few studies (Morley, 1986; Steinman, 1992; Fiske and Dawson, 1996).

A key objective of this study, therefore, having identified a significant metamorphosis in the discursive construction of masculinity in Irish film, was to ask what these narratives, genres and images meant to different sections of the male audience, and whether and how they resonated with their everyday understandings and practices of masculinity, or what Nixon (1997) refers to as 'wider gender scripts'. Given the ubiquity of irony both in the films and in the cultural and promotional rhetoric surrounding them, one of the study's core objectives was to shift the focus away from the text towards a consideration of irony as an interpretive strategy (Hutcheon, 1994), whereby the audience's ability to read irony was considered to be a crucial part of understanding the gender-political functioning of images of (hyper)masculinity in contemporary film. It is important, however, not to overestimate the potential of audience research. As Mayne has warned, reception scholars need 'to be careful of the appeals that are made in the name of empirical audiences or ethnography as the truth that will set us free from the overly abstract theorization of the past' (Mayne, 2002: 34). That said, while small-scale qualitative audience research cannot expect to provide the definitive answer to a set of untested and radically divergent hypotheses about the reception and decoding of irony, such studies are nonetheless useful in their ability to 'put flesh on a theoretical skeleton and show how a macrotheory can be revealed in a particular analysis' (Fiske and Dawson, 1996).

Mayne's discussion of the tensions between textual and audience research is especially relevant to any study that appropriates theories of the active audience in a film studies context without jettisoning an understanding of cinema as ideological. She contends that reception studies has been problematised by the 'temptation to see any response that differs slightly from what is assumed to be the norm or the ideal as necessarily radical and contestatory' (Mayne, 2002: 38), and argues that, rather than taking non-preferred readings as evidence of ideological resistance, negotiated readings should be regarded as the norm: 'It may well be more useful to designate all readings as negotiated ones, to the extent that it is highly unlikely that one will find any "pure" instances of dominant or oppositional readings' (Mayne, 2002: 39).

This point has special resonance in relation to debates about irony and the performance of male violence. Indeed if, as the rhetoric surrounding lad culture and male-oriented films suggests, the preferred or dominant reading of performances of male sexism and violence is an ironic one (in other words, it is understood as a joke about the 'pastness' of such behaviours which, in turn, renders their enactment both acceptable and humorous because it can still provoke disapproval – 'for men who should know better'), then audiences who detect but fail to infer irony (Ackerman, 1983) may in fact be generating even more regressive decodings than were intended, that is, when parodic or ironic hypermasculinity is (mis)interpreted as straightforward machismo. In the case of Lacey's study of British male viewers of *The Sopranos*, for example, the fact that respondents picked up on the masculinity-in-crisis subtext of *The Sopranos* may signal little more than their prioritising of a more recent discourse of hegemonic masculinity (the white male as victim of feminism) over another, more traditional one. Similarly, as Fiske and Dawson (1996) indicate in their study of homeless men watching *Die Hard*, certain images of violence and hypermasculinity may be understood progressively when viewed from the point of class, but as regressive in terms of gender.

Methodology

Four focus group interviews were held, each of which lasted approximately three hours and entailed a brief introductory session, completion of the questionnaire, a screening of the film *Intermission* and a focus-group discussion. Extant groups were chosen because it was considered that these groups would be used to socialising with one another and discussing films, television programmes and other aspects of popular culture. As Tobin recommends: 'if your research is on a topic that people commonly discuss with others, do group interviews. Popular media are social texts. A good portion of the pleasure and meaning we get from movies comes from talking about them' (Tobin, 2000: 141). As far as group-specific variables were concerned, the intention was to talk to men from different age groups, socio-economic backgrounds and locations with a view to determining to what extent and how these factors might be seen as influential in engendering a 'clustering of beliefs' (Schlesinger et al., 1998) among the groups. It was decided that selecting two groups of urban-based and two groups of rural-based men would best serve the research questions relating to issues of local, national and transnational masculine identity, while involving groups from different socio-economic backgrounds would enable the researcher to address the key concerns of the study, namely how representations of class and masculinity – and the relationship between them – were understood by these groups. Finally, although most of the participants fell within the target age bracket for the films under analysis (15–35), it was decided to involve a group of older men (37–50 years) to determine whether or not significant cross-generational discrepancies were evident.

The urban, working-class group comprised six participants on a Youthreach programme, a national, government-funded education and training programme for early school leavers.[4] The Youthreach centre is located in a socially marginalised suburb of north County Dublin which has experienced problems with drug abuse and unemployment since the building of an estate of high-rise flats in the late 1960s. Participants in this group had all grown up in roughly the same urban area, were aged between 15 and 18 and were all single. Their highest level of education at the time of data collection (2004) was the Junior Certificate.[5] The rural middle-class group was made up of five members of the University GAA Club.[6] These participants were all undergraduate students, though from different disciplines (Sports Science, Engineering, Computers), and were aged between 19 and 22. Most of these students come from a rural town approximately 70 miles north of Dublin, and one is from a small town in the South East. At the time of data collection, they lived in the student residence on campus in two adjacent apartments shared exclusively by male students. The urban middle-class group was made up of five university-educated men between the ages of 20 and 23, four of whom were in stable employment. This group grew up together in a relatively affluent, middle-class Dublin suburb. Three were working in office jobs, one was working as a hairdresser and one was completing his studies and working part-time. Finally, the rural, unemployed group comprised seven members of a rural men's group, as well as the group leader. This was a group for marginalised rural men who had become socially and geographically isolated from their families and the community through unemployment and family breakdown in a region adversely affected by rural depopulation and the demise of small-scale farming. They ranged in age between 37 and 50.

The film *Intermission* (2003) was selected because it is, in many ways, exemplary of the Irish cycle under analysis and also because it addresses many of the theoretical issues discussed above. Moreover, as the highest ever grossing Irish directed and produced film (€2.8m.), it was likely to have had the widest reach across Irish audiences.[7] The majority of study participants had already seen this film, which facilitated discussions about the original viewing event (where participants saw it and with whom, what they recalled about their viewing experiences, how theatrical audiences responded to the film) as well as consideration of participants' engagement with the film, and related films and issues, in the second, more artificial context of viewing. The research was partly grounded (Glaser and Strauss, 1967) in the sense that the researcher was open to the possibility of eliciting entirely new findings not based on existing hypotheses. However, while the focus group interviews were flexibly designed to accommodate spontaneity (or, as Fiske and Dawson, 1996, put it, to allow the researcher to 'be surprised'), they were also informed by a number of guiding questions whose intention was to determine whether and to what extent the appeal of *Intermission* to participants could be understood in the context of the various theoretical claims about masculinity, spectatorship, cultural competence and mode of address that have emerged from the literature.

Rebels with different causes

As far as general film-viewing patterns were concerned, all of the groups reported significantly higher levels of film viewing at home than in the cinema, irrespective of age. While American films accounted for the majority of participants' film-viewing, many British and Irish films were also mentioned. The older, rural-based participants said they rarely went to the cinema, watched very few films at home and did not display much interest in films featuring gangsters, criminals or working-class urban characters. The Youthreach group were the highest consumers of criminal and gangster films and of films which could be said to feature 'protest masculinities' (Connell, 1995). In spite of the fact that they had enjoyed only short theatrical releases some six to eight years prior to the time of data collection, both *Accelerator* and *Crushproof* were cult films among this group, who also cited classic youth, drugs or gangster films, such as *Midnight Express* (1978), *Cheech and Chong: Up in Smoke* (1978), *The Godfather* (1972), *The Texas Chain Saw Massacre* (1974) and *Scarface* (1983) among their favourites. While films such as *Snatch, Lock Stock, Reservoir Dogs, Pulp Fiction, Die Hard* and *Man About Dog* were popular among the GAA group, their preferred genres were action, comedy and sports-themed dramas. Similarly, gangster and underclass films were popular among the urban professional groups but they also displayed the most eclectic taste in films and had seen the widest range of Irish films. Thus, the cycle of films under analysis, while they did not account for the entirety of participants' film viewing, were regularly viewed and enthusiastically received by all of the participants in the 15–25 age group.

For the Youthreach Group, the Lehiff character (Colin Farrell) was the film's protagonist and it was the antagonistic drama between male youth and the forces of law and order which structured their understanding of the film, and which seemed to underpin their wider interest in gangster, criminal and underclass films such as *Snatch, Lock Stock, Mean Machine* and *Chopper*. Because of their prioritisation of the Lehiff/Lynch plot over other subplots, *Intermission* was seen as comparable with *Accelerator* and *Crushproof.* Much like the informants in Fiske and Dawson's study (1996), the participants in this group sought out moments of resistance against the *status quo*, in which their favourite characters were seen to win tactical battles, if not the final victory. What is of particular interest in the Youthreach transcripts is the fluidity with which discussions moved from an interest in films about local criminal gangs to true and fictional crime stories located elsewhere (*Snatch, Chopper, Mean Machine*), as well as the way in which real crime, fictional crime and news-mediated crime were frequently conflated. As Fishman and Cavender (1998) and Surette (1998) have argued, the emergence of new, hybrid genres such as the 'reality crime' show represents both a new genre of entertainment and a new kind of crime news. Their readings were the most real / referential and the least critical / ideological (Liebes and Katz, 1990).[8] The tendency among this group to fixate on real (referential and closed) forms of involvement anchored their understanding of Irish film in a pointedly local – rather than national – context, yet they regularly discussed the Irish films in relation to similar Australian, British and American films about criminal gangs. For these participants, the 'imagined community' of the nation state (Anderson, 1991), in whose construction the mass media play a crucial role (Morley 1996), was significantly challenged by another, class-based imagined community – that of working-class subcultural communities – supported by media practices that transcend or cut across national boundaries.

Overall, gender equality was not a conscious concern of this group and they did not appear to mediate their 'psychic alignment' (Walkerdine, 1986) with *Intermission* or the other films discussed along lines of gender. Class identity, on the other hand, was central to the meanings and pleasures that they derived from watching the film, as well as other films such as *Accelerator*, *Crush Proof* and *Adam and Paul*. These boys, who had left school early and were pursuing vocational training, could relate to *Intermission*'s portrayal of work and the attendant pressures of earning money. The manner in which these films position the spectator in sympathy with their unemployed, disenfranchised or disaffected male protagonists seemed to valorise their way of life: unlike the countless news reports and documentaries which problematise and arguably stigmatise socially marginalised communities, these films were understood by the Youthreach Group as normalising everyday issues and problems with which they were familiar:

Interviewer: You know the way they hate their jobs, is that realistic?
Tommy: Yes
Peter: Nearly everyone complains about their job
Ray: Yeah
Gary: Nobody really loves their job I don't think, not unless it is a good job
David: Not all people
Gary: In factories and
David: A lot of people love their jobs I'd say
Declan: Yeah if they have good ones, the ones that you want
Gary: The ones that you're stuck with that you have to do, they're the ones . . . working in McDonalds and all
David: Yeah but nobody says oh yeah I want to work in McDonalds

The engagements and identifications of the GAA Group with *Intermission* were significantly different. There was general consensus that Detective Lynch was the central character, followed by Lehiff and John, and the film was viewed primarily as a comedy. During the focus-group discussion, these participants derived considerable pleasure from quoting lines of dialogue to one another, and regarded Lehiff's tough urban (anti)heroics as both identifiable with and 'other': their performances of his character seemed to walk a tightrope between establishing him as exotic or different to them and yet also being interpellated by his worldview. Although they did not engage self-consciously with the preoccupations of lad culture, they mobilised its defensive rhetoric of harmless, blokeish fun, and comments such as 'just take everything with a pinch of salt', 'it's just a movie', 'don't read too much into it' and 'it's just a bit of crack' were commonly used to deflect serious discussion away from *Intermission*'s 'trouble spots', such as violence towards female characters and misogynistic comments within the film about Sally's 'ronnie' and the fact that her last boyfriend had tied her up and defecated on her chest. They thus appeared to conflate anti-effects rhetoric with discourses that are common to both postfeminism and lad culture, in which irony simply signifies a refusal to engage critically or seriously with anything that is considered 'non-pc'. For most of this group, the pleasures and meanings generated by *Intermission* were coterminous with the discursive terrain of lad magazines: it offered gross-out humour, a world in which work was not imperative, a sense of fascination and ludic involvement with Colin Farrell's iconic working-class image and the ability to circumvent the film's more serious comments on men and masculinity by foregrounding it as a comedy.

The Urban Professional Group differed considerably from both the Youth-reach and GAA groups, firstly in that their involvements with *Intermission* were considerably more critical or ideological, and secondly in that they identified (with) John and Oscar as the film's protagonists, who underwent a significant personal journeys within the film from emotionally and sexually repressed to emotionally mature, relationship-oriented 'new men'. Unlike the majority of the other participants, they demonstrated an awareness of what the film was trying to do which, in their opinion, was to show up traditional masculinity as macho performance and to valorise new mannism:

Graham: . . . the manager and eh Colm Meaney, they're both kind of the older men, they're trying to be real in authority and have all this power, and show that they're real masculine and you know, they're

Ryan: They're the bosses

Graham: Yeah they're hard and stuff . . . whereas the new lads are all kind of, they don't even care they're after the girls they just want to settle down and find someone, whereas the old supermarket manager and Colm Meaney are about concerning themselves with being hard guys or whatever and those two sets are opposed to each other.

For these participants, Lynch and the supermarket manager were laughable yet realistic figures who represented an outmoded machismo, while Lehiff was perceived to be a stereotypical 'eighties light criminal' whose primary function was as a 'link character' (Graham), 'just to move the story along' (Sean). It is easy to conclude that it was the Urban Professionals' espousal of a more 'progressive' politics of gender equality that foreclosed engagement with *Intermission* as a 'laddish' film. However, it also emerged in the discussion that they were ardent fans of British gangster films such as *Snatch*, *Lock Stock* and *Layer Cake* and of the television show *The Sopranos* and that they were keen readers of magazines such as FHM, Maxim and Loaded. Lehiff, however, was considered to be a 'wannabe gangster' and clearly did not hold the same exotic appeal as the slick, 'authentic' criminals of the London gangster films or *The Sopranos*, for whom they had huge admiration. Like Joanne Lacey's (2002) British informants, who considered *The Sopranos* to be much more glamorous than the eastend gangsters of *Lock Stock and Two Smoking Barrels*, the Urban Professionals regarded Lehiff as a kind of locally recognisable, small-time criminal with whom they did not wish to identify. As Sean commented: 'if you were on the bus and you heard lads your age talking about robbing something you'd be shocked . . . you wouldn't want to associate with them'. This stood out in contrast to the identifications suggested by the Youthreach group, who clearly aligned themselves on the side of the 'rebels' and even partly read non-gangster, 'prosocial' crime films such as *Veronica Guerin* from the perspective of the gangster characters:

Interviewer: And eh whose side are you on in the film?
Ray: The young fellows . . . you wouldn't be on the guards side . . . nearly all the films you wouldn't be on the guards side.

However, in spite of the 'progressive' discourses of new mannism through which the Urban Professionals mediated their readings of *Intermission*, their discursive citations changed significantly when the conversation switched to gangsters and to lad magazines:

Interviewer: Why are gangsters or the gangster look so central to lad culture?
William: I don't know but I think you're spot on there, I find it really interesting reading about articles like that, it's just when Graham was going on about articles he read in FHM, I remember some em that I've read in FHM and they would be gangster articles, particularly about that, and if I was to say, if I was flicking through it I would actually stop at eh, ah you know, some mafia assassin thing or the top ten mafia gigs or something like that . . . eh I don't know why it is but it's interesting.

Graham:	Like the Krays or something.
Sean:	I'd say it's because they're always dressed sharply, they have power, they have money, they generally have the good-looking girlfriend, and they're respected by all their peers.
Ryan:	Yeah it's easy success.
Graham:	Yeah.
William:	And it's not considered stuffy.
Graham:	Yeah and they didn't start out successful.
Ryan:	And they're tough.
William:	You can't see the work.
Graham:	Yeah you can't.

Indeed, it transpired that this group was by far the most disaffected by what they perceived as the evolution of sexist attitudes towards men. For example, they expressed indignation in relation to the way in which men were stigmatised for looking at images of naked women and for reading about sex, whereas women 'got away with it', thus echoing a rhetoric of disentitlement that is common both to lad culture and to the masculinist strands of the men's movement. However, rather than appropriating the evasive rhetorical device of describing lad culture as harmless fun or alluding to its sexism as ironic, they endeavoured instead to point out its more serious or 'middle-brow' elements.

Of all the men interviewed, the participants in the Rural Men's Group were the least engaged both with contemporary film culture and popular discourses on gender. Although many of these men had become socially marginalised through population decline, the rationalisation of community services and changes in family networks (North Leitrim Men's Group Research Project, 2001), they exhibited no evidence of psychic alignment with Lehiff, and they had little or no interest in contemporary crime and gangster films. However, while most of the participants in this group said they did not identify with *Intermission*'s urban location and characters or depiction of the criminal underworld, they felt it was an accurate depiction of Dublin, judging by what they read in the newspapers:

Interviewer:	Is it about a place or a life that you recognise?
Paschal:	I think it was more or less the typical criminal . . . carry on that's going on in Dublin that's more and more . . . we read about it . . . the typical kind of general type of stuff you know like the life in estates . . .

On the whole, they did not see the film as addressing men or masculinity but rather as a film about crime and working-class life in Dublin, and were somewhat uncomfortable with its violence and bad language. In the question-naires, one participant from this group commented that *The General* was 'too violent and disturbing', while another felt that it 'romanticised mass murderers'. This overtly critical attitude toward media violence was not evident in any of the other groups.

The politics of irony

Given the diversity of readings between the various groups not only of *Intermission* but also of a wide range of other Irish, British, American and Australian films, this study illustrates that evidence of divergent and non-preferred readings is by no means coterminous with ideological resistance, since viewers frequently exhibited negotiated readings that were simultane-ously uncritical of hegemonic codes of masculinity. The findings also suggest that the ironic machismo which characterises contemporary lad culture is rarely consumed in the hyper-aware manner suggested by theorists such as Gauntlett (2002) and Sconce (2002). Although the Youthreach, GAA and Urban Professional participants often demonstrated an awareness of the controversial or provocative nature of some of the texts discussed, there was little indication that they fully grasped the ideological dynamics of lad culture. In this sense, they identified the presence of irony or what Ackerman (1983) describes as 'detection' but they did not move to the second level of 'inference', at least in any recognisable or coherent way. Even the Urban Professionals, who were adept at pinpointing textual borrowings and exhibited highly constructional engagements, did not call to mind the hyper-aware audience of master semioticians envisaged by Sconce (2002). Similarly, the GAA participants, whose discussions most closely eclipsed the rhetoric of laddism, displayed no conscious, self-reflexive or 'smart' engagements.

These findings are supported by those of an earlier study (Ging, 2005: 41–2), whose male teenage participants 'appeared to have little or no conscious grasp of laddism's anti-feminist backlash politics'. This notable absence of what Hutcheon (1994) refers to as irony's 'evaluative edge' raises important questions about the ideological functioning of postfeminist images of and discourses on gender in contemporary film and media culture. Such findings indicate that, as borrowings from 1960s gangster films or 1970s soft pornography have become increasingly incorporated into the mainstream, their initially visible, self-conscious and parodic status has been slowly ingested to the point where the critical distance necessary for inference threatens to collapse. This research therefore poses a significant challenge to the argument that sophisticated levels of media literacy or cultural competence facilitate ideological resistance. In the contemporary discursive terrain of postmodernism and postfeminism, in which irony has become 'a commodity in its own right' (Austin-Smith 1990: 51, cited in Hutcheon, 1994: 28), irony has become less a self-reflexive commentary on the outmoded status of former gender codes and more a cue not to take the text seriously.

Conclusion

Magazine circulation, box-office figures and CD sales clearly indicate that the appeal of the New Lad – in all his cultural manifestations from latter-day 'wide boy', 'spiv' or 'chav' to underclass criminal, neo-gangster, white rapper or soccer 'firm' member – reaches far beyond those who consciously align themselves with or enact these particular social identities. In Irish cinema, the transition from upbeat portrayals of stalwart heroes overcoming adversity to more ambivalent preoccupations with 'anti-social' and underclass mascu-linities has produced a new range of masculine types (Spicer, 1991) including 'losers' (Messner and Montez de Oca, 2005), protest masculinities, small-time criminals and 'wannabe rebels'. These genres and characters provide varying real and symbolic pleasures and meanings for different male viewers, and are understood as representing struggles against a range of different threats, both real and imagined. For the Youthreach participants, narratives about working-class criminals or notorious crime lords were the stuff of local folklore. The awesome regard in which they held real criminals such as Martin Cahill (The General) and Mark Brandon 'Chopper' Read appeared to stem primarily from these characters' ability to outsmart the law and to triumph over adversity. As was the case with Fiske and Dawson's participants, the appeal of anti-heroes in indigenised gangster and crime films was that they valorised an often-maligned social grouping, thus consolidating their sense of identification with a vibrant urban subculture.

For the Urban Professionals and the GAA Group, on the other hand, issues of gender rather than of class appeared to mediate their interest in gangster cinema and other films featuring hard or socially excluded mascu-linities. Rather than symbolising class-based struggles against authority and the forces or law and order, the films functioned primarily as a fantasy about masculinity freed from the constraints of adult responsibility and political correctness, and they were perceived by these groups – both explicitly and implicitly – as continuous with the pleasures and rhetoric of lad culture. There was therefore substantial evidence among the Irish men interviewed of the phenomena described by Leigh, Chibnall, Monk, Pfeil and Savran, in which the trope of the victimised underclass male functions as a cipher for a range of anxieties and discontents that have little or nothing to do with poverty, unemployment or other class-based concerns. This echoes a similar trend in the United States, where gangsta rap has been appropriated by white, middle-class suburban males ('wiggers') to express a communal sense of anger and dis-entitlement in response to what is perceived as a world dominated by political correctness and a host of other infringements on male privilege facilitated by women's rights (Kimmel, forthcoming). As Kelley comments, black rap culture has been commodified to such an extent that the ghetto has become 'a place of adventure, unbridled violence, erotic fantasy, and/or an imaginary alternative to suburban boredom' (Kelley, cited in Duncombe, 2002: 154).

Recent Irish cinema's implication in a much wider process of commodifi-cation of male social exclusion thus raises important questions about the impact of these images and discourses on public perceptions of male working-class youth and, in turn, on young working-class men themselves. As Robert Connell's work on the functioning of male power and privilege has so cogently illustrated, subordinated masculinities such as black sports stars are frequently used as exemplars of masculine authorisation, even though the groups or individuals in question are excluded from hegemonic privilege. Even though the films' characters may be understood by socially excluded men as 'protest masculinities' and may offer recognition and valorisation of such identities by presenting a counter-discourse to the news media's demonisation of socially disadvantaged male youth (Devlin, 2000), their celebration of these ways of life as subcultural lifestyles runs the risk of essentialising and further margin-alising these groups. As Higbee has commented in relation to French film *La Haine*, such imagery risks contributing to the 'already exaggerated media representation of the disadvantaged urban periphery as the site of violence and delinquency which warrants the repressive police presence' (Higbee, 2001: 202). Indeed the extreme polarity that has come to characterise media representations of young working-class men – as lawless and dangerous in the news media, yet reified as popular cultural heroes in advertising and the entertainment media – may ultimately be serving the same purpose, namely to stigmatise and essentialise underclass masculinity as a social inevitability rather than a social problem of the state.

Although statistics show that patriarchy continues to benefit men, its 'linked pattern of disadvantages or toxicity' (Connell, 2005: 1808) have become increasingly apparent. When exploited for their ostensibly transgressive value, however, these patterns of toxicity are in danger of becoming both (mater-ially) trivialised and (symbolically) lionised. Although the working-class participants in this study showed themselves to be adept at relating the films they watched to the realities of their lives and at using these narratives to play out fantasies of counter-hegemonic rebellion, they were also the group which was the least defensive and most celebratory in response to these images. Rather than empowering them, therefore, it is arguable that the predominantly real (closed, referential) nature of their readings compounds their vulnerability and, ultimately, their exclusion from a middle-class dominated media which plays a significant role in shaping public opinion about (the causes and effects of) male social exclusion. This supports Charles Acland's (1995 cited in Shary, 2005: 25) claim that 'in depicting delinquency onscreen in dynamic and dramatic ways, most teen films are artificially providing rebellion for youth who are told that what they do outside the theatre will be of little conse-quence'. What the research suggests is that the criminal and socially excluded masculinities of contemporary Irish cinema, even though they offer potentially resistive readings from the perspective of class, are deeply implicated in the gender politics of lad culture and are primarily an example of patriarchy reformulating masculinity to meet the next historical turn (Hanke, 1998: 189). As Bell Hooks (1994: 177) claims in her analysis of gangsta rap: '[r]ather than seeing it as a subversion or disruption of the norm, we need to see it as an embodiment of the norm'.

Chapter 14

Teachers and the consumption of ICT: a sociocultural analysis of a technology-based change project in schools

Miriam Judge

Introduction

Since the mid-1990s, as the pace of technological change has accelerated considerably, and as western society in particular has entered a post-industrial era in which information technology (IT) rather than traditional industry has become the key driver of the globalised economy, the role that IT was expected to play in education has become increasingly significant. As IT tools and systems began to permeate work and everyday life on a scale heretofore unimaginable, it became clear that the information society and the knowledge economy had finally arrived. Their arrival threw down a gauntlet to educators, namely, how to ensure that schools prepare young people for a changing world in which IT literacy had, almost overnight, become an essential life skill. Across most developed economies governments in the USA, UK and the rest of Europe responded immediately with a number of high profile policy initiatives, designed either to introduce or significantly increase the number of computers in schools. Ireland, with its growing reliance on the high tech sector for jobs and economic prosperity was particularly aware of the importance of IT in education and it too acted quickly with the launch by the Department of Education and Science (DES) in 1997 of *Schools IT 2000: A Policy Framework for the New Millennium.*

Schools *IT 2000* which set out a clear policy framework for the integration of ICT (Information and Communications Technology) into first- and second-level schools represented the first major initiative by an Irish government to computerise the nation's schools. Given the ambitious nature of the initiative, a dedicated agency, the National Centre for Technology in Education (NCTE), was established to implement the plan. A major focus of *Schools IT 2000* was to explore innovative ways in which ICT could be successfully integrated into the school curriculum and schools were encouraged to establish best practice models across a wide variety of school settings including special needs, curricular and technical support. These projects were funded and supported by the Schools Integration Project (SIP) strand of *Schools IT 2000*.

As part of SIP, schools were encouraged to work in partnership with business, industry, the community and third-level institutions in the development of innovative ICT projects. A number of leading IT multinationals also became involved in different projects. One of the most ambitious projects to emerge from SIP was known as 'Wired for Learning' (WFL), a partnership project between IBM and the Department of Education and Science. The first phase of this project which commenced in 1998 involved five schools – three primary and two post-primary – based in Dublin and Cork. Three of the schools were officially designated as disadvantaged by the DES. A second phase of the project commenced in 2000 involving a further 17 schools in the Dundalk area. This chapter will primarily confine itself to discussing the findings which emerged from the five schools involved in phase one of the project which were the main focus of the longitudinal study I carried out during the period 1999–2002.[1]

In analysing the discourse which emerged during Wired for Learning's implementation, a number of themes, such as ICT integration, leadership, school culture and the challenge of innovation and change in schools, loomed large. This study of the Wired for Learning project also offers an interesting insight into the process of the 'appropriation and domestication' of technologies in settings outside the home, the traditional locus for domestication studies. While much of the policy documentation in relation to ICT in schools has, since the 1980s, been formulated from a technological deterministic perspective, an analysis of how ICTs are actually deployed or otherwise in schools (of which to date there have been very few studies either nationally or internationally), reveals a more intricate and diffuse picture. The ways in which teachers reacted to the Wired for Learning project and the Wired for Learning product itself, by deciding not to engage with some product features and reshape others to suit their own working conditions, challenge the technological deterministic notion that technologies shape society and institutions in a linear causal way and that societies have no choice about the technologies presented to them. Instead, as social shaping and cultural studies theorists argue, understanding the adoption or otherwise of technologies in society is a much more complex process in which users and social, political, economic and cultural factors influence how societies adopt, repurpose or even reject certain technologies.

The Wired For Learning project

The Wired for Learning project takes its name from the Wired for Learning web-based communication and collaboration system. This system was developed by IBM under its flagship philanthropic Reinventing Education programme which targets systemic, school-based change around the world. The Wired for Learning system is made up of a suite of tools or applications that support communication, collaboration and learning for the entire community – teachers, students, parents and mentors. At the heart of the system lies the Instructional Planner application which provides a suite of related databases that teachers can use to create instructional plans, teaching materials and conduct assessments.

Within the broader context of educational technology, WFL can be classified as a cross between a virtual learning environment (VLE) and a computer supported collaborative learning system (CSCL) underpinned by a range of computer mediated communications (CMC) tools, such as secure email, private conferencing facilities to support dialogue between parents and teachers, a discussion board facility for students known as Talk@ School and collaborative working areas for teachers and students such as 'Team Projects' and 'Teachers Lounge'. WFL shares many of the features of other well-known virtual learning environments such as Blackboard, WebCT and Moodle, which have been introduced to third-level institutions in recent years. As a CSCL system it meets all of the criteria discussed by McConnell (1994) who defined CSCL as any form of co-operative learning communication that occurs over a network of computers that exploits the storage, process and retrieval capabilities of the computer for teaching and learning. However, unlike standard VLEs which were primarily designed for the third-level sector, and particularly for the distance education community, WFL was designed specifically for primary and post-primary schools.

At a philosophical level WFL also differs substantially from these other systems. According to one senior developer of the system (Hall, 1996), it was specifically designed with education reform in mind. In this respect WFL is probably best categorised as an 'idea' technology which, according to Hooper and Rieber (1995), seeks to transform the established practices and beliefs of teachers unlike 'product' technologies which merely seek to support them. The Wired for Learning project was designed at its most fundamental level to promote change in the Irish education system through using the Wired For Learning platform as a vehicle by which that change could be delivered.

As with any innovative project, WFL met with a number of challenges which began to surface as the project was implemented, arising from the concerns of teachers directly involved in implementing it. For the schools involved the learning curve turned out to be extremely steep as teachers grappled at one level with an intricate technology system that stretched their fledgling technology skills to the limit, and at another level with an instrument of transformation that confronted their existing professional practices. Inevitably, the full assimilation of WFL into the modus operandi of schools was compromised both by the technical aspects of the system itself and more fundamental human issues relating to teacher autonomy and accountability, the management of change and the culture of schools.

Technical aspects

While virtual learning environments have become a standard technology feature in many third-level institutions today, back in the mid-1990s when the web was in its infancy such systems were virtually unknown. IBM's Wired for Learning platform was among the earliest of these systems to be introduced into the educational sphere. From a technical design perspective the origins of Wired for Learning are interesting in that it is an adaptation of an earlier system known as Lotus Notes, developed by the Lotus Development Corporation, which IBM acquired in 1996. Lotus Notes is a distributed client/server application which combines two technologies – shared databases and messaging (email) which support groupware. Groupware of computer supported co-operative work (CSCW) as it is sometimes called (Rodden, 1991) promotes working in teams and relies heavily on networks for the transfer of information among individuals and organisations. As many organisations adopted a team-based management framework throughout the 1980s and 1990s, groupware products like Lotus Notes that facilitated online communication, collaboration, and conferencing and work co-ordination became quite popular.

Although Lotus Notes predated the web, it is probably true to say that it had a natural affinity with it, as one of its greatest strengths was its capacity to transfer information over local area networks (LANs), wide area networks (WANs), telephone lines and the internet. Consequently as the web evolved, Lotus Notes evolved too, ensuring its compatibility with this emerging platform. But it was never a pure web-based application in the fullest sense as its design architecture was shaped by an earlier technological form.

This had implications for its sister product, WFL, which, sharing its design features, had the look and feel of a product which belonged in the pre-web era. This was problematic for schools for two main reasons. First of all, unlike their counterparts in industry using a product like Lotus Notes who had had exposure to different computer-based systems for 20 years or more, and who had become accustomed to the evolution of computer software and the inevitable user compromises (for better or worse) that accompany them, teachers had no such experience. Prior to Wired for Learning arriving in their schools, the majority of teachers had never in any capacity used a computer before. Simple things like learning to use a mouse and navigate around a keyboard were their most immediate and pressing needs. Yet their first real encounter with technology was with a system that was very powerful and technically sophisticated. This was inevitably a daunting proposition for novice computer users. Secondly, as their introduction to computers also coincided with the development of web browser technology and the explosion of the web, the web design interface became the de facto standard for them as to how they thought any piece of technology should operate – simple, straightforward, intuitive and easy to navigate. By comparison, the technological sophistication of WFL which had so many features and applications embedded within it overwhelmed teachers at the outset, which was compounded by the fact that they did not know how best to deploy it nor what the expectations of them were in terms of usage.

As they slowly began to experiment with different aspects of the system some of the product's technical shortcomings emerged. Although teachers agreed that the WFL software was easy to learn, they were highly critical of its interface design. The user interface and the architecture on which the product was built were invariably described as cumbersome, antiquated and in need of modernisation. The product was perceived as prone to technical glitches which they found frustrating and annoying. The lack of an inbuilt spell-check facility and the requirement to use HTML coding for some of the more advanced features of the product were also off-putting for many teachers. The filtering system in WFL's conferencing applications was described as poor and one principal even suggested that this was partly to blame for parents' reluctance to engage with the system's private conference application, which was designed to promote private online communications between parents and teachers:

> I think maybe the private conference facility is a bit clumsy for parents to use. It is not parent friendly. They have to go through too many clicks. Email is more accessible and maybe emailing has become so user friendly and popular nowadays that private conferencing is not as attractive. It's too clumsy as well because when you see you have new messages you still have to search for them. They are not on top as they are with email [i.e. when one opened one's message box new emails were not ordered on top, as has become the de facto email sorting standard].

Some teachers also felt that the WFL interface was too layered and overly complex and that it consequently involved too many steps to get to where you needed to go. For this reason they felt that the system was unsuited to the teachers' standard work environment where most do not have a PC on their desk constantly available to them as do people working in offices. Accessing

WFL for most teachers thus added an extra task to their already busy day, usually involving a trip to the computer room first thing in the morning, during break time or after school, which effectively meant that the time available for a teacher to log on to a PC in the course of the working day was limited. This logistical difficulty was exacerbated by the fact that once you logged on to WFL it took too long to find out if a new message was actually waiting for you because of the number of steps required. The lack of an 'instant messenger facility' was seen as a system weakness.

Another weakness identified related to the system's home page. The home page application was an easy to use design facility which enabled teachers and students to create a personal home page, similar to a web page encompassing text, images and web links. Unfortunately the system did not support saving home pages for later reuse. For many teachers this was a major flaw as they liked to use the home page facility for events that occurred each year in the school calendar such as Halloween, Christmas and Easter. They felt that it was a waste of valuable time having to recreate these thematic home pages each year when they could just call up what they had previously done and modify it to suit a new class and new school year. As one teacher put it, 'IT should be about making our work more efficient and streamlined, not reinventing the wheel every time we need to do something again'.

Part of the problem with some of the technical issues that emerged can be traced back to misunderstandings by schools in their understanding of what being involved in the WFL project would entail. They did not understand that it was a pilot project and that for the Irish school system WFL was still very much a product under development and not the finished article. It took a long time for schools to grasp that this project went beyond the philanthropic donation of large amounts of equipment to schools, and that it would require a significant research and development component involving them in testing out the WFL software, localising it for an Irish context and experimenting with it to their own advantage. Although teachers had been informed by the project partners[2] that they would be involved in the process of localisation, they clearly did not fully comprehend what this would entail in terms of the time commitment required of them personally and shifting project timelines which are an inevitable part of software product roll-outs. Furthermore, problems such as the delay in getting an Irish version of WFL and software bugs in new revisions of the WFL product which caused system crashes created further difficulties for teachers, resulting in a loss of confidence in WFL among teachers in some of the schools.

In fairness to the project promoters, an analysis of the early project documentation indicates that the decision by IBM and the DES to proceed with an American version of WFL in Irish schools and localise it as it was being used was identified from the outset as one of the risk factors which could impact on the success of the project. To manage this risk and limit its impact on schools, technical support was constantly available from IBM for the duration of the project and IBM endeavoured to resolve software problems as speedily as possible either over the phone or through site visits. However, in hindsight, it is clear that schools found the whole area of localisation difficult to understand and identify with, even though much of what occurred was typical of any product development/localisation process. But the problem was that teachers, not being IT experts, found the whole language of computers – 'bugs' 'fix packs', 'versions' etc. – alien, especially given their total unfamiliarity with technology prior to the arrival of WFL. As the ICT co-ordinator in one school commented, 'Although they were talking about these different versions, versions two, three or whatever, my staff weren't interested in all this, all they were interested in was in a version that worked'.

Anyone who has ever taught or who has observed teachers in action in a computer laboratory can understand why teachers reacted in this way. There is a huge element of disruption involved in moving students from their normal classrooms to a computer laboratory and then getting them settled and focused on a task. This pressure is particularly acute at post-primary level where teachers have only 35–40 minutes per class period and need to cover critical curriculum elements during this time. If computers start to crash, the whole lesson is disrupted, resulting in core course material not being covered which then has a knock-on effect later on. It is clear that this was not an ideal way to implement an ICT product in schools and that localisation and product development are probably best resolved in a simulated environment with a tried and tested stable platform before being rolled out to schools.

Teacher autonomy and accountability

It has long been acknowledged that 'teachers are relatively autonomous in their own classrooms in terms of the pedagogical approaches they employ' (Lynch and Lodge, 2002: 165). Unlike many modern working environments which emphasise the importance of teamwork and collaboration, the predominant organisational form in schools tends to be individualistic with teachers working in isolation from their colleagues with little opportunity to work together or exchange ideas on a sustained basis. As Maeroff (1988: 3) reminds us 'teaching more than many other occupations is practised in isolation that is at times crushing in its separateness'.

As a well organised and highly unionised group, Irish teachers in particular have enjoyed greater professional autonomy than their counterparts in the UK, the USA and Australia, where traditional teacher autonomy has been eroded by a series of reforms over the last 30 years or more which have modernised work practices and increased transparency. The sweeping nature of these reforms has not been without its critics with many teachers arguing that such reforms have merely increased the burden of paperwork and bureaucracy to the detriment of the core function of teaching. As Drudy and Lynch (1993) remind us, 'while the teacher unions are recognised as powerful educational players in the Irish context this is not the case elsewhere' (van Veen et al., 2001, cited in Lynch and Lodge, 2002: 165), creating a situation where the pressure to reform schools and teacher work practices has not been of the same magnitude as that experienced in other countries. This preservation of the status quo in teacher autonomy in Ireland had by the early 1990s led to a situation in which 'the single homogenous class and the instructional modes associated with it are not conducive to co-operative teamwork or to innovative approaches to teaching and learning' (OECD, 1991). Nowhere was the reality of this situation more clearly exposed than in the Wired for Learning project, where strong teacher resistance emerged to engaging with some of the core applications, namely Teacher's Lounge, the Instructional Planner, and Private Conferencing.

Teacher's Lounge
Teacher's Lounge was one of three collaborative applications within Wired for Learning. It was aimed specifically at teachers unlike the other two applications, Team Projects and Mentors@School which were aimed at students and outside professionals respectively. Teacher's Lounge was designed to meet the communications and collaborative needs of teachers in a private, secure online environment. In theory teachers could use this application to solicit help or advice from each other on resources, teaching strategies, creative ideas, classroom management techniques and other classroom-related topics. They could also use it for discussion topics posted by and responded to by teachers. Of all the WFL applications, Teacher's Lounge represented the quintessential groupware product with its emphasis on professional collaboration and teamwork modelled on the business and industry work environment.

Although undoubtedly a convenient way of gathering and sharing information among colleagues, it had one major flaw in that it assumed that the norms of industrial collegial practice were equally applicable to schools. This was not the case, particularly in Ireland, where there was no tradition of teachers collaborating with each other in any formal sense. If and where collaboration occurred it tended to happen in a more informal, ad hoc way with teachers consulting each other only on a need-to-know basis if and when a problem occurred. As a result teachers found it hard to see the relevance of the Teacher's Lounge application to their everyday working lives.

They also questioned the value of using an electronic medium for peer-to-peer communication as they felt that face-to-face communications was a far more efficient and immediate way of getting things done. They argued that it was much easier and more convenient for them to consult with a colleague over a cup of tea in the staff room, as they in any case congregated there every day at the same time, or to pop over to another teacher's classroom for a quick response to an urgent query. Using Teacher's Lounge by comparison meant a trip to the computer laboratory during break, logging on, typing in a query and hoping that at some time during the day the other teacher would have done the same and perhaps responded to the message, by the end of the day if you were lucky, by which time you had probably managed to resolve the issue yourself. Assessed in this light, Teacher's Lounge as a collaborative tool appeared wanting.

At a much more fundamental level, reaction to the Teacher's Lounge illustrated very clearly the strength and depth of Irish teachers' professional autonomy and an education system that neither encouraged nor created space for the development of a collegiate approach to teacher professional development. Expecting teachers to engage collaboratively via an electronic medium, when they had no tradition and experience of doing this beforehand, was an unrealistic expectation from the outset.

The Instructional Planner

Teacher autonomy and teacher accountability loomed large when it came to using WFL's Instructional Planner application. For the most part teachers were uncomfortable with the notion of preparing structured lesson plans and sharing them online for their colleagues either to use or to conduct peer review comments on them. Again, this application with its procedural, scientific and systematic approach to how lesson plans ought to be prepared was very much at odds with the traditional norms and practices of the Irish teaching profession. While Irish primary school teachers are required to produce regular lesson plans such as An Cuntas Miosúil (monthly plan) and An Scéim Bliana (yearly plan) for inspection by departmental inspectors, the scope and extent of these plans are very much left to the individual teacher's discretion and creativity. This is very different from the situation in other countries such as the USA and the UK where teachers are required to adopt a highly prescriptive and procedural approach to lesson planning in accordance with systematic instructional design principles.

When it came to lesson planning Irish secondary schoolteachers enjoyed even greater autonomy than their primary school colleagues in that they were not required to produce any formal lesson plans as such. This meant that the Instructional Planner section of WFL seemed quite alien to them as the observations of one school principal illustrates:

> I feel that writing lesson plans isn't part of the culture of secondary teaching in Ireland. Up until now you were king in your classroom. You did what you liked

as long as you prepared people for exams and they got through. You could effectively keep anybody out of your classroom, you could even refuse an inspector. If
lesson planning was part of the school plan like it is in England and America and
in primary schools, then it would be easier because people would see it as part of
their roles, whereas now they see it as an additional burden. I think that's where
the difficulty lies.

The discretionary nature of lesson planning in the Irish education system in
part explains why teachers did not engage with WFL's Instructional Planner.
Typically when questioned about this non-engagement, teachers invariably
responded with explanations such as 'lesson plans are such a personal thing,
that they're unique to each teacher so you couldn't possibly share them with
someone else', or 'At this stage of my life, after twenty years teaching or more,
I am not going to change to writing lesson plans, I know in my head what I'm
going to teach'.

But there were also other issues which concerned teachers, such as fear of
peer criticism, a reluctance to share lesson plans with colleagues and suspicion
of increased accountability. Some teachers felt that the introduction of WFL
was an attempt by the DES to bring in greater accountability through the
back door. As one vice principal commented, 'I feel that WFL is actually in
some kind of deep down way a system of making teachers accountable. It's a
way of getting at teachers – a form of public accountability.' Unsurprisingly,
therefore, many teachers were extremely defensive on this issue, arguing that
the public examination system was the norm through which their professional accountability was maintained and by which they were judged, and
that they were intent on keeping it that way. Not engaging with WFL's
instructional planning tool was one way of ensuring that the status quo would
remain intact.

Private Conferencing
The Private Conference application in WFL provides an online forum for
private discussions between teachers and parents, teachers and student or
teachers and other teachers. The system is configured in such as way that only
a teacher has the authority to initiate a private conference although parents
and students can request one. As WFL also provided other ways to communicate with students and teachers such as student emails and Teacher's Lounge
it was envisaged that schools would use the Private Conference application to
communicate mainly with parents. However, this application was highly
contentious and never took off.

This can partly be explained by practical problems that prevented communications happening. In the three schools located in disadvantaged areas it
was estimated that only about 18 per cent of homes actually had computers

and although computer ownership was estimated at 50 per cent in the other two schools, very few were actually connected to the internet. This was because Ireland's telephone system operated very differently from that in the USA where local calls and dial up internet access were free. In Ireland, however, local calls and therefore internet access had to be paid for. This made it very difficult and expensive for parents to communicate online when either (a) they did not have the means (a home-based computer) to do so, or (b) they were concerned about how dial up internet charges would add to their monthly household bills.

Where schools tried to encourage teacher–parent conferencing, parents did not respond in the way that the schools hoped which was partly blamed on WFL's interface design which was described as cumbersome to use and lacking the user friendliness of email. Cultural differences between the Irish and American education system were also cited. Some teachers believed that the idea of private conferencing with parents was more suited to big schools in large American urban areas like Boston and New York where teachers and parents rarely met, but not to Irish schools, much smaller in size and where, particularly in semi-urban areas, there is much informal contact between parents and teachers at local and community events. They also found that those parents who tended to respond to private conferencing were those who were quite involved with the school and their children's education and whose children were performing well at school. Consequently teachers argued that the conferences became a non-event and a bit meaningless and time wasting for both teachers and parents. Some also had sincerely held beliefs that electronic communications with parents were not the way to go. Teachers and school principals all agreed that parents would still prefer to meet with a teacher in person if they needed to discuss issues in relation to their child's education. In this respect face-to-face communication was deemed a more personable, practical, sensitive and convenient way of dealing with a child's development and progress and the method least likely to lead to misunderstanding and rift between parent, teacher and child. While undoubtedly these difficulties and concerns stymied the development of private conferencing with parents, this is only part of the story. The other part is bound up with teachers' fears of increased accountability, extra workloads and the traditional nature of teacher–parent relationships.

The extra workload demands of communicating electronically with parents loomed large in the minds of teachers. Many wondered where they would get the time to respond to parent emails, if it would make them busier and involve working after school hours to service these emails. Uncertainty existed as to how quickly they would be required to respond and if a parent would consider them unprofessional if they did not reply immediately. They were also very wary about putting down in print any comments about a child that might leave them open to a legal challenge. The dilemma of private conferencing from a teacher perspective is probably best encapsulated by one ICT co-ordinator who had this to say:

> We've had huge discussions around private conferencing and people are very wary of it. You have to be very careful of how you word things in print and be very careful about how you are portraying children no matter good or bad. And then there was the element involved in replying to parents and also if a parent conferenced you on a Monday night and you didn't get time to access that message for a week, would parents feel you were ignoring them. So between that and all the legal aspects around written information, teachers are just very wary about it.

The possible threat of a legal challenge as a result of electronic communications with parents left teachers feeling vulnerable and upset that their employers, the DES, had not taken a lead on this issue by putting a proper code of practice in place for communicating with parents. As one teacher commented, 'It's dead easy to say [to a teacher] private conference with a parent, but you need to protect the teacher. You can't just land something like this on a staff and expect them to accept it without putting a protection policy in place.'

One of the most interesting dimensions to the debate on teacher–parent conferencing concerns the traditional nature of parent–teacher relationships in Irish schools where most of the power resides with the teacher by virtue of his or her professional autonomy and status. At a time when the DES was attempting to increase parental involvement in schools, particularly in relation to policy decisions, WFL's conferencing facilities presented schools with an ideal vehicle to enhance parental involvement at a decision-making level in the running of schools and other educational matters. This never happened and in the few cases where schools experimented with communicating with parents electronically it appears that this exchange was confined to the age-old discourse between teacher and parent concerning the educational development of a single child. It would seem that using WFL to involve parents in the school decision-making process was a step too far for all involved as it required a departure in mindset about parental involvement which, if implemented fully, had the potential to threaten traditional power relations in the school. This in large part explains why private conferencing was so hotly debated in schools and why some schools clamoured for 'teacher protection' while other schools never attempted to provide parental training on WFL's conferencing facilities, nor involved their home school liaison staff, who had the most contact with parents on a day-to-day level, in WFL training.

Innovation and change in schools

The problems associated with innovation and change in schools have been well documented (Fullan, 1991; Cuban, 1993a; Sarason, 1996). Schools are fundamentally conservative organisations where the predominant organisational form 'tilts towards stability in classroom practice' (Cuban, 1993a: 18). This conservatism has largely been shaped by societal expectations about the function of schools, in how they should be organised and the role of teachers. This is why 'cultural beliefs such as that teaching is telling, learning is listening, knowledge is subject matter taught by teachers and books' and the sanctity of the 'self-contained classroom which separates teachers from one another' (Cuban, 1993b: 198) have dominated both popular and practitioner thinking about schooling for almost 200 years. In this respect it can be argued that teachers behave in accordance with the norms and expectations of society at large which in turn help us to understand why teachers often appear resistant to innovation and change.

This resistance is particularly noticeable when one examines the history of technology adoption of schools where, as Starr (1996: 51) points out, the 'history of education in the twentieth century is littered with mistaken forecasts of technological revolutions in education'. While in the past inadequate resources and computing complexity have been blamed on this failure, a more critical perspective has highlighted the need to adopt a more holistic approach to our understanding of the role of technology within the larger context of the culture of the school and the interaction between technology, the teacher and the learning environment (Sandholtz et al., 1997; Means, 1994; Knuffer, 1993; Cuban, 1993b). As Knuffer (1993: 173) reminds us, proponents of instructional computing have traditionally given 'short shrift to the role of teachers', focusing their attention primarily on student benefits, while paying scant attention to the teacher's role in the acceptance, implementation and outcome of educational computing, despite compelling evidence of the centrality of teachers in the implementation of educational innovation.

By making teachers and schools the primary focus of research attention in the WFL project, this research has attempted to redress the balance. As a technological innovation in its own right and as a vehicle through which it was hoped to achieve school-based reform, Wired for Learning illustrated the many problems associated with two key discourses in education, namely ICT integration in schools and change in schools. Change as this research illustrates quite clearly is difficult for all involved and creates many tensions for individuals and organisations. The process of change affects deep-rooted beliefs, attitudes and values which are ultimately linked with people's worldview. The introduction of ICT into schools at any level is laden with implications for change. An understanding of the complexity of the process of change and how to manage it is an essential component of the successful introduction and implementation of school-based ICT. This fact has largely been ignored by techno enthusiasts and policy makers alike in their quest to modernise schools by inserting computers in schools without paying due attention to the process of integration (Barto, 1996), which is where the problem of change begins to surface. The people most affected by the process of ICT integration and the problem of change in schools are teachers. It is they not policy makers who decide whether and to what extent computers will be deployed in the learning process. Ultimately the attitudes and educational philosophies that form part of the culture of schools which have been shaped by the 'crucible' of classroom experiences and societal expectations of schooling are a significant factor in whether computers will be used, and how they will be used in schools (Collis et al., 1996).

The issue is further complicated by the problem of change being intricately linked to the problem of power, which as Sarason (1996: 335) maintains 'suffuses all relationships in the culture of schools'. When this culture is threatened by change projects such as WFL, the basis of power which is normally submerged in cultural subsciouness rises to the fore. This can lead to a contested space when 'someone' decides that something will be changed and 'others' are then required to implement that change. This is particularly the case when people feel they have had no real say in the decision-making process or that their professionalism is being undermined by the innovation in some way.

As this chapter has illustrated, the discourse that emerged in schools in relation to some of WFL's core applications went beyond technology itself to encompass deeper and more wide-ranging issues, including the culture of schools, teacher autonomy and power and the implementation difficulties associated with school-based reform. Apart from the insights garnered into the complexity of ICT integration and the associated problem of change in schools, a more rarefied analysis of the WFL project offers some interesting insights into the ongoing academic debate concerning the relationship between technology and society.

WFL: a microcosm of the technology and society debate?

In attempting to make sense of the relationship between technology and society, academics have adopted a number of theoretical positions on this vexing question which are probably best summed up thus: does technology shape society or do we as users shape technology? The earliest and most predominant of these theories, technological determinism, largely ignored the role of the user, positing the view that technologies are intrinsically neutral artefacts which shape society in a linear causal way. Implicit in this perspective is the notion that technology has its own trajectory over which society (and thus the user) has little or no control. This argument has been challenged by the social shaping theory of technology and the cultural studies approach to technological diffusion and appropriation. Both turn technological determinism on its head by attempting to understand the relationship between technology and society from a much broader perspective by analysing the social, political, economic and cultural contexts surrounding technological innovation and the crucial role that users play in the 'domestication' process of technological artefacts once technologies are marketed and sold to them.

Social shaping theorists such as McKenzie and Wacjman (1999) challenge technological determinism by arguing that, because technologies are designed for a particular purpose they have inbuilt social and political properties which mean that technologies per se can never be neutral. The Wired for Learning software is a prime example of this. Built on a groupware model that encompassed many of the values of the industrial and business world it could be construed that it was attempting to inculcate elements of business practice into the administration and operation of schools, and in fact a number of teachers interpreted it in this way. Some felt that this was a corporate project which was attempting to make schools 'behave more like businesses' and had philosophical objections to the involvement of business in schools with one teacher commenting, 'I think even the name "Reinventing Education" kind of told a lot about what they were trying to do. Teachers don't want to be reinvented by a multinational.' Furthermore, WFL was not just a technology product, it was also an 'idea' technology explicitly designed to bring about school-based reform. So it had definite political intentions.

If the social shaping of technology theory helps us to understand more fully the socially and politically shaped nature of how technologies are developed, the cultural studies approach extends our understanding of this concept further by considering the social forces at work when technologies enter the user domain. To date most of the work on the appropriation of technologies by users, inspired by the work of Silverstone and Hirsch (1992) and Morley (1986) has focused on the home. However, as technology has become more and more pervasive in society, the domestication concept has broadened to become 'a whole theoretical approach to media and technology and its role in everyday lives of households, people, or other kinds of organisations' (Berker et al., 2006). From this perspective the deployment of ICT into schools provides a rich yet largely ignored domain where user appropriation and domestication studies can also be conducted as the WFL project demonstrates.

Many studies conducted on the use of technologies in the home, from television and VCR to computers, have revealed that users and not just technological artefacts themselves shape how technological innovations are accepted, rejected or even redefined by their users in ways unintended by their manufacturers. WFL is a case in point. Teachers rejected those elements of the product that most affected them in terms of change and which had the potential to undermine their professional autonomy and power, such as the Instructional Planner and Private Conferencing. Instead of using Teacher's Lounge as a collaborative and communications tool some schools used it as a repository for building school-based resources, a valuable exercise in itself, though not one envisaged by its designers. Similarly, many teachers displayed great imagination and flair in how they used the home page application in WFL as a tool for improving student literacy and encouraging the development of student projects. This went way beyond the intentions of the original designers of the product for this application. At the end of the day the elements of Wired for Learning that enjoyed most success in schools were those that seemed most relevant to teachers' everyday work, such as 'Team Projects', 'Events@School' and the 'Homepage Designer', reinforcing the notion that the more things change, the more things stay the same.[3]

Finally when it comes to discussing the relationship between technology and society, no discussion is ever complete without considering the gender dimension to this debate. Within technology studies the role of women is often overlooked, because they tend to concentrate on the role of the inventor who is usually male. Even studies conducted from a more sociological perspective have tended to portray women's experiences with technology in passive terms, as routine assembly or clerical worker at the receiving end of technological change, or as users of technology in the home where women gain 'little technological competence from their use' (Wajcman, 1991).

By virtue of their gendered composition which is now predominantly female, schools represent a unique social milieu in which to further our understanding of the relationship between technology, power and the role of women, not least because schools represent the only institution in society where women as a professional body command a lot of power.[4] If the WFL experience is assessed from this point of view, it could well be argued that women are not just passive recipients of male technological inventions as often portrayed, but rather that when they have the power, they will, as in this case, exercise their authority to accept, reject or alter technologies in accordance with their own beliefs about what works best for them and their pupils in their classrooms, under conditions of their own choosing.

Chapter 15

Listen to yourself: the audience as broadcaster in community radio

Rosemary Day

Introduction

What happens when the listener becomes the broadcaster? Mass communication, traditionally a flow of communication in one direction from a few
professionals to a large audience, can be transformed into a two-way or multi-
flow where members of the public broadcast to themselves. This is a dynamic
process with the potential for radical effects in civil society. When members
of the public decide the issues to be debated and the manner in which they
will be broadcast, and when they produce and present the programmes
themselves, that process itself is empowering. When the channel is owned and
operated democratically it operates as a force to democratise both communication and relations within the community. Although the effect may be
radical, the idea of public participation in the mass media is not a new concept. Mills called this 'public communication' (1956), Enzensberger termed it
'emancipatory media' (1974), those who follow after Habermas (1989) see it as
a 'micro–public sphere' (Keane, 1995; Halcli, 2000) but it has rarely been
experienced. Mainstream media, be they commercial or public service,
cannot, and are not expected to provide such open access to the airwaves. As
they provide the main experience people have of mass media, it is not
surprising that many people cannot conceive of communally owned and
listener-generated media. The traditional division of the discipline of Media
Studies itself into three areas of investigation – production, text, audience –
does not recognise the possibility of the listener becoming empowered to
speak. But what happens when the boundaries between the neat divisions
become blurred? How should a situation in which the audience are the
broadcasters be categorised, researched and theorised? These are some of the
questions which prompted a ten-year study of Irish community radio stations
(Day, 2007).[1] One aspect of that study was the provision for public participation by Irish community radio stations and it is the findings from this
research which inform the following discussion.

Traditionally, for radio, the audience member has been the listener. However, the relatively new sector of Irish broadcasting, community radio, turns that relationship on its head and works to facilitate the active participation of members of the community in the communication process. This chapter describes the aims and the practice of Irish community radio stations primarily in terms of public participation in the media. It explains how this participation is facilitated and how it should be evaluated. It investigates Irish community radio stations as facilitators of the human right to communicate. It explains why the other two sectors, public service and commercial media, do not, and should not, be expected to provide for such participation. It asks how the transformation of the traditional one-way flow of communication of the mass media into two-way and multi-flows can be both radical and empowering.

Community radio in Ireland

Over 20 community radio stations have received licences to broadcast in Ireland to date. Each of these is defined by the regulatory authority, the Broadcasting Commission of Ireland (BCI, formerly the Independent Radio and Television Commission, the IRTC) which states

> A community radio station is characterised by its ownership and programming and the community it is authorised to serve. It is owned and controlled by a not-for profit organisation whose structure provides for membership, management, operation and programming primarily by members of the community at large. Its programming should be based on community access and should reflect the special interests and needs of the listenership it is licensed to serve. (BCI, 2001: 3)

This definition emerged from an 18-month, IRTC pilot scheme for community radio in Ireland in the mid-1990s and was based on the discussions and reflections of the participants in the eleven community radio stations in that scheme. It covers the basic elements which a station must include in order for it to be licensed as a community radio station. It draws clear lines of demarcation between community media and the other two sectors of Irish broadcasting – public service (RTÉ) and commercial, independent stations throughout the country (such as Today FM, BEAT FM or Highland Radio). Unlike commercial radio, a community radio station is run by a not-for-profit organisation which, in turn, is answerable to all of the members of the community it serves. In theory, so too is RTÉ. However, the scale of operation of a national broadcaster and the appointment of the RTÉ authority by a government minister mean that most people do not recognise, let alone claim, ownership of the station. Even more important than the issue of scale is the question of participation in ownership, management and production. Unlike national or local commercial stations, a community radio station is run by members of the community, and programming is scheduled, produced and presented by them. While a limited number of people in any community will take up the option to become involved in either management of or programming on their community radio station, their right to do so is enshrined in the very definition of what it means to be a community radio station and to be licensed as such. This is fundamentally different from the relationship which either commercial or public service broadcasters have with their audience. It is only in community radio that the listener can become, indeed is expected to become, the broadcaster. Some types of public access to the airwaves exist in all sectors, but only community media are capable of providing meaningful or genuine participation (Bordenave, 1994; White, 1994). The understanding of genuine participation for community media is far wider than that allowed for in narrow definitions of participation in the mass media.

Community radio claims participation as a primary and underlying principle and, unlike access and participation in other types of mass communication, the community radio listener is encouraged to participate in the work of the station at all levels. Through the process of participation he or she is empowered and in turn empowers and enhances the community in which he or she lives. Access to all levels is open, from full ownership, to management, to production, to the facilitation of individual voices being heard on air. Public service radio and commercial radio cannot and do not attempt to provide that extensive range of participation opportunities. Other fundamental principles dictate their ethos and work. For public service broadcasters this is often simplified to the Reithian ambition to 'inform, educate, entertain'. The participation of members of the public in broadcasting may be useful in achieving those aims sometimes, but it is not an end in itself. It is not possible for commercial media to provide this extent of participation, nor is it their aim (Crisell, 1994; Barnard, 2000). For commercial broadcasters the main aim is to maximise profit and participation is allowed only when it is seen as a mechanism for maximising the number of listeners that can be sold to advertisers. For community radio participation is a central goal in itself. Bordenave (1994) explains that participative communication calls for a radical inversion of the normal broadcaster/listener relationship where the flow of communications is almost totally one-way. Community media seek to provide equal opportunities for all people to take part in the communication process. The real aim of providing these opportunities is to enable people to improve the community in which they live by working co-operatively together and by communicating with each other. He explains

Participation communication can be defined as that type of communication in which all the interlocutors are free and have equal access to the means to express their viewpoints, feelings and experiences. Collective action aimed at promoting their interests, solving their problems, and transforming their society, is the means end. (Bordenave, 1994: 43).

Ownership of stations and, therefore, control over work practices, schedules and content, are seen as markers of genuine participation. White (1994) complains that the very word 'participation' is a kaleidoscope term that has become part of development discourse and which projects employ without any clear definition of what it might mean. She provides a useful general distinction between 'pseudo participation' and 'genuine participation' (White, 1994: 17). 'Pseudo participation' is tightly controlled, heavily mediated and is facilitated for reasons such as the provision of cheap and popular programming or the projection of an image of inclusivity and localness. 'Genuine participation' is enabling, relatively unmediated and is provided for its own sake. Commercial media and public service broadcasters in general tend to work at the level of 'pseudo participation' while community media aim for 'genuine participation'.

All sectors of the media provide access for listeners to phone in to chat shows, but this must be recognised as pseudo participation, as listeners' voices are used to provide colour and interest to a programme that is controlled by the presenter and producer in studio (Higgins and Moss, 1982; White, 1994). While it provides stimulating, entertaining and often exciting programming, it is essentially cheap programming which does little to empower the participants and is heavily controlled by the station (Higgins and Moss, 1982; Crisell, 1994; Barnard, 2000). Phone-in shows on any medium provide a degree of access which is heavily mediated. Here listeners speaking on air appear to be offered some measure of participation. All three sectors in radio broadcasting utilise the phone-in show as a way of getting citizen voices on air, but there is an expectation that community radios' use of the 'phone-in' show should be less manipulative than that of commercial or public service radio stations. In community radio, the 'phone-in' is only one of many access points and should be viewed as an initial introduction for individuals who will progress to further levels of participation.

The mass media generally broadcast in one direction. As Galeano explains

The communication media are monopolized by the few that can reach everyone. Never have so many been held incommunicado by so few. More and more have the right to hear and see, but fewer and fewer have the privilege of informing, giving their opinion and creating. The dictatorship of the single word and the single image, much more devastating than that of the single party, is imposing a life whose exemplary citizen is a docile consumer and passive spectator built on the assembly line following the North American model of commercial television. (Galeano, in Herman and McChesney, 1997: vi).

Idealists and theorists as long ago as Brecht (1983 [1930]) through Enszensberger (1974) to Splichal (2002) point out that this need not be the case. Communication technologies could be used to democratise the airwaves; the public could participate in making their own media. This would be a practical facilitation of the human right to communicate, a right which is enshrined in the UN declaration of human rights, Article 49, and which states

> Everyone has the right to freedom of opinion and expression; this right includes freedom to hold opinions without interference and to seek, receive and impart information and ideas through any media and regardless of frontiers. (Universal Declaration of Human Rights, 1948).

This right has not been promoted by governments or protected in legislation around the globe. Instead of access to the mass media becoming easier and more available, the public are excluded from the production process and feel powerless to influence the policies and practices of broadcasters, either in state or privately owned stations. In fact, the mass media are concentrated more and more in the hands of business. The break up of the monopoly of public state broadcasters in Europe throughout the 1980s has not led to greater diversity and empowerment for citizens. McQuail (1991), in discussing communication as a basic and universal human right, assesses the performance of the mass media in general in providing for this right and concludes that

> Most generally, if we suppose there to be 'right to communicate', then it implies an equal individual claim to hear and to be heard. The fact that the mass media have, in practice, appropriated and almost monopolised a good many of the real opportunities for public communication does not diminish this claim. (McQuail, 1991: 72–3).

Neither the commercial nor the public service sectors of broadcasting promote the right of members of the public to the airwaves, let alone the facility to create their own media.

A third sector has emerged in the media worldwide which strives to give a voice to the listener. The World Association of Community Radio Broadcasters (AMARC) aims to democratise the airwaves, to empower people by giving them the chance to create their own media or micro-public sphere (AMARC, 2006). The AMARC Europe Charter, formulated in 1994, to which all Irish community radio stations must subscribe as a condition of licensing, states as its first point that community radios 'Promote the right to communicate, assist the free flow of information and opinions, encourage creative expression and contribute to the democratic process and a pluralist society' (AMARC, 2006). In some places this is highly politicised. Revolutionaries and labour activists in Latin America have used community radio to successfully further their causes (Hein, 1984; O'Connor, 1990). Ecological and anti-globalisation activists have developed projects such as Indymedia. Sparked by distrust of the 'professional journalist', they rely on local eyewitnesses and activists to provide news which provides an alternative to mainstream media and is frequently counter hegemonic. Radical and alternative media provide a space where committed activists can spread their messages (Downing et al., 2000; Atton, 2001). In Ireland to date, community radios have proven less political than their counterparts in developing countries, but their work has a strong social dimension. Irish community radios provide the opportunity for members of geographic communities and of specific communities of interest all over the country to create their own media. Where people communicate with their neighbours, they can identify common problems and needs and begin to address them collectively. Working alongside others who differ from themselves, but who share a common space or interest (in effect, a community), helps people to foster and develop community spirit. While local and minority cultures are only ever a minority interest for mainstream media, on community channels they can take centre stage. The provision of a space to debate becomes political and fosters democratic communication. Over time community radio develops a space for civil society to discuss and debate: it provides a micro-public sphere. Where community development practices are consciously employed, participants are enabled to identify both the problems and the solutions to those problems for themselves. This is empowering and can result in significant social change in communities. So how do Irish community radio stations facilitate the human right to communicate? To what extent can members of the public participate in the broadcasting, administration and ownership of these stations? My own research found that Irish community radio stations believe in and depend on the participation of the members of their communities, the traditional audience if you like, in order to achieve their aim of developing their communities (Day, 2007). Public participation in communication can be difficult to evaluate. Guest spots and phone-ins to radio chat shows provide only a measure of pseudo participation (Higgins and Moss, 1982; White, 1994). To provide for meaningful, potentially empowering participation or genuine participation, much more must be facilitated. Elsewhere I have established a hierarchy of levels of access and participation in the mass media (Day, 2007) and find that the three markers of genuine participation are the extent to which members of the public are facilitated: to produce and present their own programming; to manage both that programming and the station; and the extent to which they are the legal owners of the station. In other words we must examine the extent to which Irish community radio stations are owned, managed and broadcast by their communities.

Ownership

Each of the community radio stations licensed in Ireland is owned by the community which it is licensed to serve. Sometimes this is in partnership, as with West Limerick Community Radio (WLCR), Co. Limerick, Radio Corca Baiscinn (RCB), Co. Clare and Radio Pobal Inis Eoghan (ICR), Co. Donegal. These were all founded by community development organisations as the communication arm of their projects and as another tool for developing their communities and constituents. Others are owned by co-operative societies (co-ops) which any person in the target community can join by paying a nominal fee. In each case a person or organisation can hold as many shares as they may want to buy, but these shares do not pay dividends. They are a way of fundraising for the station and each person or organisation has one vote only, regardless of the number of shares purchased. Examples of this type of station include NEAR FM and Dublin South Community Radio (DSCR), both in the capital city. When applying for their first licence in 1994, NEAR FM proposed a model of a co-op with four membership categories – individuals, community organisations, local businesses and others, including churches and statutory bodies. This was designed to ensure the participation of the community at the levels of ownership and management. As they explained at the time

> The rules of the co-operative are designed to ensure a balanced Management Board representing the four categories above. The station will be owned by the co-operative on behalf of the community, of which it is widely representative. As the Society is a co-operative with membership open to everybody in the area, ownership will effectively be vested in the community. (NEAR, 1994: 7)

Some community radio stations have opted to form limited companies but, again, shares, which do not pay dividends, are offered to all members of the community at a nominal price. In some of these instances, for example Connemara Community Radio, Co. Galway, WLCR, Co. Limerick and RCB, Co. Clare, the parent or funding partner maintains a controlling interest.

In 1994, the group which founded Community Radio Castlebar (CRC), Co. Mayo, described themselves as 'A group representing a range of community interests. It is also a partnership between the public and voluntary sector'

(CRC, 1994: 11). They proposed setting up a company limited by guarantee with a board of directors drawn from all the community groups active in the town of Castlebar and with representatives of statutory bodies, in particular the Vocational Education Committee (VEC). This is more or less the structure which survives today. Ownership of the station is a specific objective for the board and they believe that the structure of their organisation is effective in enabling a wide range of access to broadcasting and ownership by the community at large. Forty different local organisations are involved and have the right to elect directors to the Board of Management (CRC 1998: 4). This is seen by the station as a valuable and important strategy which enables the widening of access to a network of groups and individuals (CRC, 1998: 4).

Student community radio stations are generally owned by the students in partnership with the institution or the student union or both and Ireland currently has three of these, Flirt FM in Galway, Wired FM in Limerick, and Cork Campus Radio based in UCC.

No matter which model of ownership is employed, each community radio station has a board of management which has representation from the community. In every case the majority of board members are volunteers. A gender balance is ensured, as this is a requirement of licensing, but in almost all cases this is reflected in practice on the air and on the ground (Gibbons, 1998). Echoing other community media activists, Douglas (1994) has proclaimed that 'Freedom of the Press is Owning One' and in Ireland, all community radio stations are owned by the communities which they are licensed to serve.

Management

Passive ownership does little to empower members of the public. Irish community radio stations are required to provide the opportunity for participation in the management of their stations. Most try to do this, but levels of success vary. Some Irish community radio stations, through lack of resources and vision, fail to include their community sufficiently in the management of their projects. Stations which fail in this respect are found to be the least successful in sustaining other aspects of their projects such as community engagement, creating stimulating innovative programming and even the basic requirement of efficient administration and fiscal management (Day, 2007). Depending on volunteers to run an enterprise requires different skills to running a commercial business, and over the first ten years of licensed community radio broadcasting most stations came to recognise this. This was the result of their interaction with other stations through the Community Radio Forum of Ireland, now known as CRAOL; their observation of practice in stations deemed to be successful; and their exposure to the community radio ethos and movement, nationally through CRAOL, and internationally through AMARC. Today, almost all community radio stations recognise the necessity of managing their projects democratically, providing for participation in planning, daily management and evaluation. Stations which employed paid managers with a background in, or at least an interest in, community development, were found to facilitate the widest range of participation of community members in the management of their station. In each case, these stations proved to be the most successful in achieving their other objectives – a sense of ownership of and pride in the station by the community, participation and innovation in programming, and a higher proportion of off-air initiatives designed to build the community than those which stuck to traditional, hierarchical, business models of management (Day, 2007).

Every Irish community radio station has a board of management, democratically elected, which is in charge of the long-term policy and control of the station. In most cases, a paid manager, assisted by a sub-committee or executive nominated by this board, manages the day-to-day running of the station. In all cases, decisions can be, and are, challenged by volunteers and paid staff and, in the examples of best practice, decisions are taken by consensus rather than by formal vote. A former manager of Connemara Community Radio explains their style of management: 'Management is, we have agreed that it will be, by consensus for day to day operation, it's only expected that it's in a crisis situation that it will revert to a vote'. She credits their success in operating in a democratic and participative manner to the fact that most members of the board of management are actively involved in broadcasting and work in the station regularly, so that they are aware of the issues when decisions regarding policy or strategy need to be taken. This can also be seen as one of the benefits of open and participative practices – that management and administration are shared willingly by participants. What the manager of NEAR FM in Dublin had to say about getting basic maintenance done was equally true for persuading people to participate in the more mundane tasks of administration and management. He noted that 'You can get an awful lot more out of them when they're on air. It's difficult to get a carpenter who has a bit of spare time to come and volunteer his services, but a carpenter who's doing a blues programme, he's quite happy.'

West Dublin Area Radio (WDAR) and its predecessor West Dublin Community Radio (WDCR) provide an example of a non-hierarchical management style. Decision making is shared in an informal, unstructured, relaxed manner. This is described in their 1998 application for a licence as

Post heroic or marginal with emphasis on the development of personal responsibility by all members of the station. A genuine effort is made to create a positive atmosphere as opposed to any heavily rule bound framework. There is a keen awareness of the 'cause of community radio' supported by a group culture of co-operation considered necessary to create genuine community within the station itself. (WDCR, 1998: 4)

One former station manager explained this more simply by observing that 'Everyone works together, there are no rules, everyone has their fair say, we found that rules don't work'. He expanded on this by explaining

> We have a very easy-going atmosphere here. We try not to have tensions. We work with volunteers and if you have tensions they won't want to be here and there has to be a good feeling . . . people feel welcome when they walk into the station – it's a policy. It stems from us working here – we enjoy what we do and that flows through the whole system.

The best management plans need to be revised regularly. Irish community radio stations collectively devised a circular flow model of management which now forms part of BCI community radio policy (BCI, 2001), but not every station manages to avoid hierarchical forms of management. Paper plans need to be put into practice and this requires careful handling and constant evaluation. The Limerick city student community radio station, Wired FM, has changed its management structures several times as a result of student evaluations. WDAR went through an even more radical transformation. As WDCR, it started out life as a college-led project: it was to be a media lab for mature students in Ballyfermot Senior College. However, it quickly changed into a community-owned and managed enterprise when it began broadcasting. As a former station manager observes

> Well, the original plans that were sent in, let me tell you, what we're doing now is very different. The original proposal that was put in, I mean someone had this idea of ladies going lunching, I can always remember, that will stand out in my head – imagine, like an area where women have five and six kids pulling out of them, like ladies going lunching? I think they took the idea that time from radio as opposed to from community. They looked at a set of nice radio programmes and said 'This would be lovely'. It would have been the VEC originally who put in the proposal but since then they have become much more involved with the community and they're led by the community.

The West Dublin city station discovered very early on that they were of value to their community only if they were led by their community and they revised their ownership and management structures radically to promote participation at all levels.

Some community radio stations cling to the traditional hierarchal style of management favoured by many businesses. Their managers and board members find they suffer from exhaustion, alienation and even despair. This stems from too few people trying to do everything themselves and not trusting the owners of the station – the community itself – to share the responsibility of management. However, the mechanism to convene meetings, to discuss policy and management decisions and to act democratically, exists in all Irish community radio stations. As most stations have come to see the community development aspect of their work as the most important part of their projects, they are careful to work slowly and consultatively. They recognise the need to pause regularly and reflect on current experience, to evaluate their strategies and performance, in order to build for the future.

The employment of the appropriate personnel was found to be the single most important factor in managing community radio stations in a democratic and participative manner (Day, 2007). Managers need to be sensitive to the needs and expectations of volunteers, staff and board members and be able to delegate and motivate. Those with a background in community development were found to be the most successful in ensuring genuine participation in management and administration (Day, 2007). Perhaps this is best summed up by the West Dublin manager who explained why they do not work hierarchically but prefer to work consensually: 'There is no point in asking someone to do something they don't want to do – they'll do it badly – some do administration, some do programming, some news, we work it out together.'

Programming

Access to programming is probably the most obvious marker of public participation in any medium. It is placed third in the hierarchy of markers of public participation in the mass media (Day, 2007) as participation in ownership and management of the media provide for greater power and control. However, it is essential that a station which promotes the human right to communicate facilitates members of its community to communicate on the airwaves. Volunteers who live in the community comprise the majority of the voices heard on air. This is a deliberate policy in each case as the station is set up to be used by its owners. While programmers expect to have listeners, listeners are expected to be programmers. In some cases, people on long-term job initiative schemes and on the Community Employment Scheme (CE or FÁS workers) produce and present programmes but, generally, they are employed in stations as administrative and programme support. In Connemara Community Radio one such employee is in charge of developing the volunteer cohort and another is the technician who looks after the studio and also trains newcomers to become proficient in their broadcasting skills. The care of volunteers is a priority for all stations, although some succeed better than others. On average 80 people participate on at least a weekly basis in Irish community radio stations (Day, 2007), and this figure increases significantly if the numbers of former volunteers and shareholders are counted, as they form a pool from which they can be drawn. Although turnover of volunteers is high in student stations, it is not generally a critical issue for geographically based stations.

Provision of access to the airwaves on its own is not sufficient to ensure that members of the public get to be heard. International research (Berrigan, 1977; Bordenave, 1994) shows that, unless measures are taken to support and educate marginalised members of the community, it is the more articulate and privileged who will end up on air. Research from Germany and Australia in the late 1990s concluded that this is frequently well-educated, confident young men (Günnel, 2002; Beatson, 1999) who want to spin disks. In order to facilitate the ideal speech communication envisioned by Habermas (1983 [1962]), where each person has the right to be heard as an equal, community radio activists must target those who are most marginalised and disadvantaged. This entails putting training and education in place which equip individuals and groups in overcoming the barriers to communication which Irish society places in their path. Participants need to become aware of, and confident in, their own ability and right to communicate. They also need to be aware of the wider implications which this can have for the group to which they belong, the changes which they can begin to make in the social fabric of their community, and the fact that their participation in their local community radio station is part of a global new social movement (NSM). I term this process 'conscientisation' as it involves a measure of consciousness raising over and above the basic and necessary skills training for programme makers and it stimulates the conscience, both individual and collective (Day, 2007). This is not realised through the passive consumption of media products, but through active participation in their production. Splichal explains that

> Instead of providing only passive access to the consumption sphere, democratisation implies primarily the development of conditions for active participation, that is, a direct and indirect incorporation of citizens into the production and exchange of messages in different forms of communication from interpersonal communication to the mass media in which the individual can realise his interests and meet his needs in collaboration with others. (Splichal, 1993: 12)

Mere numbers of participants in the production of programmes will not ensure the democratisation of the media. Rather, it is necessary for new forms of communication and democracy to expand the social basis of communication and to include those who have been excluded heretofore, such as minorities, women, young people and the unemployed. Community radio stations can provide such a space, a micro-public sphere, but how alternative or emancipatory this proves to be is another matter. In order to be able to exercise the human right to communicate through broadcasting, access to the airwaves must be provided. To be able to communicate, to enable individuals and communities to be heard, mechanisms must be put in place to facilitate participation. Participation in communication as a human right means that it is not an extra benefit or a bonus which may or may not be granted or withheld (Bordenave, 1994). Unless the final goal for stations in their facilitation of access and participation is the empowerment of individuals and their communities, only a form of pseudo-participation is offered.

The care shown by community radio activists in West Dublin reaps dividends as participants, both paid and voluntary, respect the aims of the station and work to build their community collectively. Members of the management team aim to develop participants first personally and then collectively. The emphasis in this station is on the empowerment of individuals, on the provision of a space in which participants can grow and develop. One former station manager explains

> We're in an area that is very marginalised, we're also in an area where only 0.7% of people go to third level education. An awful lot of people, either the kids that I deal with or their parents, are people who dropped out of second level education. Most of their parents, a lot of their parents, cannot read or write. While radio can be a wonderful tool in that area, you also have to be very conscious in dealing with people that you are giving them the space that they need to be able to deal with you and that you're bringing them to a level that makes it better for them.

Some groups targeted by Irish community radio stations include women in the home, the elderly, disaffected youth, new immigrants and the disabled. The chairperson of NEAR FM believes that they are catering well for all types of members of their community. He says

> I think after that then, the mix is good, we have people who have disabilities . . . that woman I tapped on the shoulder, she's blind and comes in quite a bit . . . people in wheelchairs, in as volunteers. There's a good mix, young people and I'm happy to see we're now getting down to the school girls and they are coming in and are quite assertive so we brought them in through the transition year and now they're coming back. Two of those girls were on the transition year and brought two of their friends in, slightly older who had missed it and now they're being trained and we're getting some younger boys in about 14–15 age groups and we're trying to make them welcome as well. We want to make them welcome and you go right up to people in their eighties.

NEAR FM has a long track record of working with new immigrants. This started with the arrival of refugees from Bosnia in the mid-1990s but has grown now to include many ethnicities and languages. Apart from the programmes where these new immigrants broadcast to their own groups, in their own languages, NEAR FM have a number of initiatives to assist in promoting racial harmony and understanding, in the development of a multi-cultural community. One of these is known as 'Refugee Radio' where the entire schedule for the station is taken over by refugees for one week. Another policy of integrating new arrivals in the area into existing programming as members of teams with existing volunteers for the long haul is seen as a high priority by station management. The provision of English language programming, which introduces the host community to their new neighbours, also helps to break down myths and misconceptions which often lead to racism. Many other stations have followed the lead of NEAR FM. For example, Wired FM facilitates the Polish community in Limerick city and ICR in Donegal has a bilingual Chinese programme. Some stations work in partnership with state agencies and NGOs who already work with marginalised groups or in areas of difficulty and tension. These can often take the form of off-air training which culminates in a broadcast programme but goes beyond that product in the process of training, educating and empowering the participants in a process of conscientisation. Examples of this include the work done by NEAR FM with prisoners on release from Mountjoy Jail, the rehabilitation for drug abusers programme of WDCR, programmes to promote peace and reconciliation on Dundalk FM and ICR and the many community radio stations which work with young school leavers.

Connemara Community Radio was set up originally to reach those who are housebound and isolated. As a rural station based in difficult physical terrain, the station is primarily interested in improving the quality of life for members of its community and plays a role in connecting those who are isolated through infirmity or location to the wider community. One of the objectives it set itself at the outset in 1994 was 'To combat isolation and loneliness which is a feature of life in dispersed communities, especially for the elderly, disabled and housebound' (CCR, 1994: 4). The station organises regular outside broadcasts and personnel travel all over the remote, poorly serviced 300 square mile area to which they broadcast. They always ensure that their arrival is a social occasion and use the broadcast as an opportunity to recruit more participants. Based in the village of Letterfrack, they devised a distance-learning package which is now used by community radio stations across Europe and they have opened a second, on-air studio on the offshore island of Inis Bofin, with the town of Clifden soon to follow.

One of the ways in which community radio acts as a tool for the community activists is by creating and facilitating multi-flows of communication

(Day, 2007). Community radio is ideally placed to facilitate the formation of communications networks. This is done explicitly in the broadcasting of programmes to target groups in the community, which helps those who are similar to bond with each other. It also helps when marginalised people present themselves to the wider community on their own terms, as is the case with Traveller and Gay programmes in several stations. In Connemara Community Radio, ICR and RCB one of the primary aims of the stations is to relieve and redress the loneliness of many rural dwellers. In other stations, it is a case of enabling people to hear their own voices and through this to become engaged in the life of their community. Many stations try to employ the community development practice of enabling people to identify their shared needs through dialogue. They then facilitate further debate so that the people themselves can identify the solutions to their self-identified problems and set about collectively implementing the necessary changes. Sometimes a group which begins to broadcast with a single issue in mind develops and moves beyond that to the larger community development and communication projects. One example of this is the group of disabled people in West Dublin who no longer present a show on disability but produce and present a general magazine show. Another example is provided by young people with cerebral palsy who produce a music show on Wired FM. All of the Irish community radio stations see themselves as forming the central node or nexus for a number of communication networks which benefit their communities. CRC was initially founded to give a platform to the adult literacy and education programmes of Mayo VEC. They were so successful in this project that they provided the prototype for the national adult literacy programme broadcast on RTÉ, *Read, Write, Now,* in conjunction with the National Adult Literacy Association (NALA).

Not all groups targeted by community radio stations are marginalised. Irish speakers are not usually seen as economically disadvantaged as, today, they are frequently among the upwardly mobile, middle classes. However, they do face linguistic communication needs which are not adequately served by either the public service or commercial sectors. Raidió na Life in Dublin and Wired Luimnigh in Limerick were set up specifically to serve Irish speakers in the two cities. Similarly, today's students are among the most privileged members of society but they also have specific needs and the student radio stations of Flirt FM, Wired FM and Cork Campus Radio serve them. The diversity of stations contained within the group of over 20 is wide but, in each case, the station strives to cater for the needs of its community. The most successful among them manage to persuade the members of their communities to identify these needs for themselves and they assist them in establishing programmes on and off air to cater for them. On the rural peninsulas of Inishowen and Loophead, ICR and RCB battle against isolation and loneliness.

They are based in communities which have been left behind by the Celtic Tiger and it is interesting that both stations were founded by and are supported by their local community development bodies. In city stations, such as NEAR FM, DSCR and TCR, it is the communities that are most at risk and vulnerable in all urban areas that are prioritised for training, for example disaffected youth, immigrants, the unemployed, travellers and the disabled. Such marginalised groups can be seen as subsets of the larger community and their interests and lived experiences may often lead them into conflict with the wider community and with each other. Working in conjunction with other agencies that care for these marginalised groups within society, Irish community radio stations form part of the community development efforts to build a more inclusive and democratic society.

Conclusions

Irish community radio stations facilitate the human right to communicate and contribute to the democratisation of communication and the improvement of community life in the process. They do this by facilitating genuine participation but this must be rooted in an understanding of the radical potential for change, social and political which participation in the media can have for individuals, minorities and entire communities. The facilitation of genuine participation must be planned and supported by all those involved in the community radio station. This can happen only when participants undergo a process of education which has empowerment and conscientisation as well as basic skills training as its goals. Genuine participation occurs only when people participate at the levels of programme production, management and ownership of the station. These three levels of engagement require constant vigilance, evaluation and revision. None of these initiatives happens by accident. They all stem from the ethos and aims of community radio worldwide (Day, 2007). Irish community radio stations frequently fail to live up to their potential, yet they strive towards the provision of an ideal construct of public participation in mass communication. They provide the only example of licensed broadcasters in Ireland which try, as a matter of fundamental principle, to facilitate the human right to communicate. Only in this way will it be possible to democratise the airwaves, provide a micro-public sphere and build a sense of a responsible and caring community. It may be a tall order but it is worth asking the question Brecht asked when dreaming of a radio which could provide for two-way communication 'If you think that this is Utopia, then I would ask why you consider it is utopian?' (Brecht, 1983 [1930]: 169).

Appendix

Irish community radio stations mentioned, with abbreviations where used

CCR – Connemara Community Radio, serves 300 square miles of North West Galway and offshore islands.

Cork Campus Radio – student radio for Cork city, based in University College Cork (UCC).

CRC – Community Radio Castlebar, serves town and hinterland of Castlebar, Co. Mayo.

DSCR – Dublin South Community Radio, serves part of south Dublin – Rathfarnham, Dundrum, Stillorgan area.

Dundalk FM – serves town of Dundalk, Co. Louth.

FLIRT – Galway's student community radio station, initials are not an acronym.

ICR – acronym for Inishowen Community Radio, official name, Raidió Pobal Inis Eoghain, serves peninsula of Inishowen in Co. Donegal.

NEAR FM – North Side Access Radio, serves part of north Dublin – Coolock, Raheny, Donaghmeade, Artane.

Raidió na Life – serves the Irish speaking community of Dublin city (translates as 'Radio of the Liffey', the main river in Dublin).

RCB – Radio Corca Baiscinn, serves the community of the Loop Head peninsula in Co. Clare (translates as 'Radio of the people of Bascann').

TCR - Tallaght Community Radio.

WDAR – West Dublin Access Radio, serves part of west Dublin, Ballyfermot, Inchicore, city area and successor to WDCR.

WDCR – West Dublin Community Radio, forerunner to WDAR

Wired FM – Student community radio in Limerick, based in Mary Immaculate College, University of Limerick and Limerick Institute of Technology, (LIT).

Wired Luimnigh – Irish language programming for non-student Irish speaking community of Limerick city.

WLCR – West Limerick Community Radio.

Notes

Chapter 3 Recent and current trends in Irish language broadcasting

1   This is based on Committee for Language Attitude Research's survey in 1973, as well as the Institiúid Teangeolaíochta Éireann surveys in 1983 and 1993 and my own analysis of International Social Survey Programme data from the surveys on national identity in 1995 and 2003.

2   For example, while making the programme *No Béarla* for TG4 Manchan, the presenter of the programme, ordered a drink in Irish in a pub in Dublin and was asked to leave. Most Irish speakers have similar stories.

3   See the Departmental Committee to Consider the Question of Special Station/ Stations for Broadcasting in Irish, 1945, which is reprinted in Watson, 2003: 131–9.

4   While it makes sense to measure bureaucracies according to criteria of efficiency and effectiveness, sometimes this rigid bureaucratic approach oversteps the bounds of usefulness and is used, for example, in the relationship between hospital staff and patients.

5   See also Alex Honneth's article on how the goals of individualisation have been 'transmuted into a support of the system's legitimacy' (Honneth, 2004: 463). He illustrates the paradox of how the freedom which is expected to accompany individualisation results in pathologies.

Chapter 6 War and peace on the screen

1   One of the longest, but not the most costly. Between 1969 and 1998, over 3,600 people died in Northern Ireland as a result of the troubles, compared to 60,000 lives lost since 1983 in the continuing Sri Lanka conflict, and an estimated 150,000 deaths in the Algerian civil war 1991–2002. (http://news.bbc.co.uk)

2   In the mid 1960s, ITN and BBC bulletins (on which RTÉ's were modelled) were 12–15 minutes long. Cox (1995): 179–80; Horgan (2004): 26. The longer bulletins were a commercial half hour: usually 25–27 minutes.

3   Purdie (1990) suggests that Fred Heatley of NICRA was kneed in the groin.

4   The original material has been shown repeatedly in various documentaries, notably including Thames Television's *The Troubles* (1981).

5   The term loyalist is used to distinguish the extreme form of unionism that was prepared to use direct, non-state violent action to resist nationalist demands. Similarly, the term republican distinguishes the supporters of physical force from the mainstream of nationalism.

6   About 90 per cent of police officers were Protestants, in a society where more than a third of the population were Catholics. Darby (1978: 59).

7   Of course, the reliability of the media matters only if our model allows that citizens' views have at least some influence over the decisions of the elite who exercise power.

8   The 'propaganda model' does not coincide in meaning with propaganda as generally used in the sense of deliberate distortion.

9   This is another simplification. Galtung identified 12 common reporting styles that can exacerbate conflict; see Carter and Weaver (2003: ch. 1).

10 Unjustly convicted in 1975 of murder after 21 people were killed by bombs planted in pubs, their convictions were quashed in 1991.

11 For instance, Nelson and others (1997) presented groups of students with alternative television news reports of a Ku Klux Klan rally in Ohio, one of which emphasised the free speech aspects of the story, the other placing it in a law and order frame, emphasising the police role in preventing violence. Afterwards the two groups were asked to what degree they supported the right of the KKK to hold rallies; when averaged over a seven-point scale from 'strongly oppose' to 'strongly support', those who saw the free speech framing scored 3.96, those who saw the law and order version scored 3.31 (where a high number indicated more support for the rally). The difference between these numbers is statistically significant, though hardly persuasive of a substantial impact, especially when we note that local audiences were in fact able to see both versions if they wished. See also Bartels (1993) for the difficulty in establishing the impact of news broadcasts during election campaigns.

12 The 'cultivation effect' theory of media is beyond the scope of this chapter, but its origins and evolution may be explored in Gerbner et al. (1994).

13 The terms nationalism and unionism refer to the political expression of Irish and British identities.

14 Sky News was established in 1989, and in 2006 its share of the total viewing time was under one per cent in the UK and just over two per cent in the Republic. TV3 began broadcasting from Dublin in 1998 and had an audience share in 2005 of 13 per cent (figures from Barb and AGB Nielsen).

15 Combined share for BBC1, BBC2, UTV and Channel 4 in 2005 was about 20 per cent.

16 The peacekeeping frame was remarkably long-lived for some journalists. ITN reporter Desmond Hamill called his 1985 book on the army *Pig in the Middle.*

17 Two weeks later one of the prison officers interviewed for the programme was shot dead by the IRA.

18 Peter Heathwood's catalogue of programmes is available on the internet conflict archive maintained by the University of Ulster, as accessed 8 Dec. 2006: http://cain.ulst.ac.uk/heathwood/heathwoodnote.htm

19 There was one notable exception in the midst of national pay talks in 1987: the government turned a blind eye when the president of the Irish Congress of Trade Unions happened also to be a leading member of Sinn Féin; ministers could hardly

object to broadcast interviews with a trade union leader with whom they were themselves negotiating. Purcell (1991): 58

20 See Horgan (2002), Horgan (2004: ch. 6) and Gregg (2005) for accounts of how divisions in southern opinion about republican violence were reflected within RTÉ.

21 White (2005: 44). At that stage the peace process was under way, and the censorship order was entirely lifted a few months later.

22 Moloney (2003: 105–6).

23 Imposed by order of Home Secretary Douglas Hurd.

24   In the 12 months before the ban was imposed, Sinn Fein was interviewed on British television 29 times, and not at all in the following year. In the 12 months before the ban was lifted in 1984, there were 67 interviews. Lago (1998): 678. The ban did mean that such interviews had to be pre-recorded, depriving participants of the immediacy and drama of live exchanges.

25 'Border genocide' refers to the murders of young Protestants in rural areas.

26 Philo (2002: 186) says explaining conflict requires 'longer bulletins, in-depth interviews and more detailed accounts', but warns that 'audiences can get lost in detail and longer interviews with prevaricating politicians may simply add to the confusion.'

27 Parkinson (1998: 71–3); Greenslade (1998) also observes how IRA attacks in Britain tended to get far more prominence than equivalent incidents in the north. Various authors, including Curtis (1988 [1994]: ch. 5), have noted a general tendency to give less prominence to reports of violence by loyalists.

28 We should add that pictures alone can have multiple contradictory meanings, and require anchoring with commentary to be unambiguous.

29 An early example of 'citizen journalism': the pictures were shot by a passing amateur camera enthusiast.

30 A recurrent problem was selecting pictures that told the story without provoking distaste. Audiences generally do not like to see spilt blood. By the 1990s a BBC training video was using broadcast footage from the 1970s of body parts being shovelled up from the street after a bomb to illustrate what was not acceptable.

31 The main BBC news ran five items, using the opportunity to provide more context than usual.

32 Her niece and two nephews were killed by a runaway car driven by an IRA man who had been shot by the British army.

33 Social Democratic and Labour Party, representing the non-violent majority of nationalist opinion in the north at the time.

Chapter 7 Selling fear? The changing face of crime reporting in Ireland

1   Indictable crime was dealt with by judge and jury, non-indictable crime was dealt with at a summary level at the District Court. The same distinction applies to headline and non-headline offences.

2   See annual reports at www.garda.ie

3   Figures from www.cso.ie

4   The periodicals were: *World's Pictorial News and Competitor's Guide, News of the World, Empire News, The People, Thomson's Weekly News, Weekly Record.*

5   See also NAI SR22/36. The report was released to the public in 2000.

6   The four titles were: *Irish Times, Irish Press, Evening Herald* and *Daily Star.*

7   *The Irish Times* had a policy of not using criminals as sources for stories.

8   See annual reports at www.garda.ie

Chapter 9   Television as social history

1   In Sheehan (1987), part one elaborates on this approach to analysing television drama, while part two applies it to a history of Irish television drama from 1962 to 1987.

2   Sheehan (2004): this is a sequel to the previous book, taking the story from 1987 to 2002. It traces the evolution of *Fair City* from 1989 to 2002. Brennan (2003) looks at how the production process constrains the serial's representation of social reality.

3   *Tolka Row* was an RTÉ serial set in Dublin running from 1964 to 1968.

4   My review was in *The New Nation* 8, 1989. For more about the reviews at the time and throughout the serial, see Sheehan (2004).

5   Sheehan (1993) focuses on the history of soap opera and an analysis of *Glenroe* and *Fair City* up to 1993. There were a number of producers and writers of these serials in attendance and much argument about my analysis.

6   This was confirmed in an interview with *Fair City* chief script editor Kevin Mc Hugh 29 Aug. 2001.

7   This was also confirmed in the above interview.

8   Liam Lawlor was a Fianna Fáil politician who went to prison for contempt of court in connection with allegations of corruption.

9   The phrase comes from a speech made by Ombudsman Emily O'Reilly in 2004 where she advised the nation to turn from the new religions of sex and drink and shopping and to tiptoe back to the churches. See *Irish Independent*, 4 Nov. 2004.

10   This was in the television review column of Shane Hegarty in *The Irish Times*, 13 Dec. 2003.

Chapter 10   Characteristics of contemporary Irish film

1   The song 'The Wind that Shakes the Barley' by Robert Dwyer Joyce (1830–83) speaks of a young man agonising over the choice between settling down with his girl or joining the rebellion of the United Irishmen of 1798: 'of foreign chains around us. / And so I said: the mountain glen/ I'll seek at morning early/ And join the brave united

men/ while soft winds shake the barley'. Loach sees the period, like the Spanish Civil War as a 'pivotal moment'. Partition led 'inevitably' to the war in the north, with its suppression of civil rights. He saw a major challenge in finding the balance between period authenticities and keeping the film feeling contemporary and current. The well-seasoned polemicist in an interview claims that there are some parallels with the Irish War of Independence in 1922 and the current war in Iraq. In this hyper-globalised post-9/11 worldview, Irish film and its 'troubled' history can be dovetailed with the major global conflicts at present. In a revealing unpublished interview with Yvonne Hogan, a journalist with Independent newspapers, Loach affirms how he is fascinated by the 'psychology of occupation' and how they [the British] 'are still convinced that they are on a civilising mission'.

2   K. Hayes suggests in a chapter on Jordan that the 'canonisation of *Michael Collins*, his veneration in the film is a repair of the rupture of the Civil War with an undertow of apology to the (founding) fathers for not having been there' (in Roche, 2005: 206).

3   Symptomatic of this transformation is the recent Fianna Fáil political party's reaffir-mation of the 1916 memorialisation, which was suspended with the 'troubles' in the north. The film ostensibly fits into this reaffirmation and reclaiming of republican ideals.

4   Reminiscent of *Casablanca* (1942) and the singing of the French anthem, the rebels sing 'O Ró sé na bheatha abhaile' [which incidentally may not have been written by this period] as a growing anthem of solidarity.

5   Somewhat reminiscent of the 'maggot scene' in Eisenstein's *Battleship Potemkin* (1925), the sequence helps provide a simple cause and effect montage reaction to illustrate the roots of revolutionary zeal.

6   Certainly the war is effectively represented, if only by a series of skirmishes, as the conscripts wait continuously for notes to arrive to give instructions. There are unfor-tunately some very contrived attempts at humour to lighten the tone, like the boy losing a letter of instruction, which informs them that the truce is signed. Apparently, the rebels on the ground had no inkling of this impending cessation of hostilities.

7   Luke Gibbons (*Irish Times*, 18 June 2006) articulates a common response to criticism that films like *The Wind that Shakes the Barley* end up simplifying events, reducing the complex texture of historical explanations to matters of heroes and villains. Gibbons correctly affirms how the family takes central stage as the source of the most enduring loyalties and bonds between characters, with the 'grandmother Peggy (Mary O'Riordan), the mother, Bernadette (Mary Murphy) and both daughter and son, Sinead (Orla Fitzgerald) and Michael (Lawrence Barry) testifying to their ancestral loyalties. Peggy belongs to a generation that barely survived the famine and lived through the upheavals of the Land War in the late 19th century'. Gibbons incisively concludes that 'narrative closure fails to bring moral or political resolution, as feelings of injustice, outrage or even sorrow are not purged by the denouement of the plot' (2006: 7). Earlier, as Damien's girlfriend Sinead and her family are being attacked by the British army, the newly formed rebels can only look on in shock and

anger as their homestead is burnt. This abiding image continues as a powerful motif and symbol of Irish troubles through the film and is used for much of the familial action of the film, particularly as a spectre framing the final sequence – reaffirming the ultimate trauma of broken personal and national dreams.

8   Ging's recent cogent endorsement of the capacity of 1970s and 1980s Irish film-makers to accommodate and promote marginalised voices should be recognised. Many of which she argues 'rather than espousing the Ireland of official state nationalism, explicitly challenged it' (in Kirby, et al. 2002: 177).

9   Incidentally, Connolly (2003) maps these filmmakers' international influences through their affiliation with European political art movements.

10 Hugh Linehan, a journalist with the *Irish Times* accused the cinema of the Celtic Tiger of a 'lack of ambition or subversion' and suggested that 'conventional tigers of church and family are rolled out and knocked down with wearisome predictability' (Linehan, 1999: 46–9).

11 Hill (2006) captures the varying dilemmas while continuing to use the trope of the 'troubles' to frame northern Irish cinema in his conclusion:

> Films concerning Northern Ireland are faced with a number of obstacles. For the last 40 years, the 'troubles' has been *the* distinctive feature of the region and it is difficult to set a film in Northern Ireland that does not deal with the impact of the conflict in some way or other without appearing either naïve or wilfully evasive. . . . For while the prospect of 'peace' may have spurred the production of a new cycle of 'upbeat' 'troubles' films aimed at the popular audience, they nonetheless remain haunted by the realities of continuing social division and the absence of any 'quick fix' solution to the conflict (2006: 242).

12 Sheridan's production company Hell's Kitchen, formed with Arthur Lappin in 1983 has developed over 20 films, many of which dealt with themes around 'the troubles' (see Barton in Roche, 2005: 194).

13 This became particularly important within a revisionist agenda, resulting in part from the seismic shifts in nationalist politics, emanating from the difficulties dramatised by 'the troubles'.

14 Barton situates so-called heritage narratives in relation to Irish tourism imagery, which has tended to promote Ireland as a 'feel good' location and suggests that, though its cinematic and literary period dramas, Ireland has fashioned itself (and been fashioned) as a 'symbol of a living imagined history, a country hanging suspended in a pure and permanent past' (1997: 85).

15 One rightly disgruntled Irish film-maker complains of an 'urban form of fascism' with regard to film scripts. This is borne out by numerous reviews of his art-feature *Country* which suggests a very strong antipathy to any contemporary Irish narrative dealing with the rural past as being de facto unsophisticated and uninteresting. I would counter that rural landscape alongside historical narratives can still produce a unique insight into a contemporary Irish mindset.

16 Farming as a primal rural profession, oscillating between nurturing and exploitation of the land, can, I argue (2006), be used as a barometer of core ecological land
ethics. For example, films like *The Field* and *How Harry Became a Tree* foreground
farming and by extension ecology and at the same time dramatise a psychotic form of
agency, reflecting an unhealthy preoccupation with land and by extension identity.

17 Yet one finds even in very early gritty realist and urban-based narratives like
Joyriders (1989) a valorising of farming. The mature joyriders gravitate to the west and
a farm on which an ageing widower (David Kelly) lives, more asleep than awake. The
city dwellers need a refuge in the country and their redemption comes from hard
work on the farm and this is also where the erstwhile urban delinquent Perky Rice
(Andrew Connolly) realises his need for a family. According to Shaun Richards it
'irresistibly evoke[s] John Ford westerns' as the 'land is resettled as a garden is planted'
which serves to revitalise what is dying (in Graham and Kirkland, 1999: 114).

18 Incidentally, one of the obvious questions raised by the current high profile of
Irish leading males in Hollywood, is why no female stars have attained similar success.
It is certainly not owing to an absence of charisma or performative ability. Barton
draws on the work of Hamid Naficy and his study of an 'accented filmmaker' to
explain how they reproduce 'their own identity formation through their fictional
subjects' (in Barton, 2006: 6).

19 See forthcoming 2007 special issue of *Convergence: Journal of New Media* on
DVD add-ons which includes a report 'Pleasure and Pedagogy: The consumption
of DVD add-ons among Irish teenagers' by Brereton and O'Connor on research
carried out by the Centre for Society, Information and the Media (SIM) in secondary
schools during 2006.

20 The add-ons on *Man of Aran* provide a useful series of interviews with the director
and others, involved in the making of the film and help frame the text's continued
importance over the years. For example, we are told the island natives were shy at first,
according to Flaherty and others, with suspicions that the interlopers were Protestants
intent on converting them from Catholicism. They uncovered the historical
cautionary tale of the 'soupers' – shorthand for how during the famine, some starving
families gave up their religion for some food from their charity. Furthermore,
interesting realistic images of transporting cattle off the island were not used in
Flaherty's final 'documentary'. The reason of course for this omission was because
such sequences would not contribute to the director's universal thesis of the conflicts
embodied by 'man versus nature', which was commercially driven to maximise
potential audiences. Furthermore, representations of religion were also avoided for
similar reasons, ensuring the film's longevity and universality.

21 However, I found strong criticism of a postmodern/smart aesthetic in the authorial
voiceover by the Irish director of the film, where in an audio commentary he painfully
underlines every filmic reference in illustrating his homage to classics from Ford and
Godard in particular, rupturing the film's self-referential humour somewhat. So
rather than increasing the intertextual allure of the comedy, the voiceover commen-

tary almost patronises the listener, while slavishly listing the filmic references. Of course the DVD is first and foremost a means of promoting the film. And there is no predetermined reason to believe that the director is the most knowledgeable about either their own role in the filmmaking process or the finished film itself.

22 Martin Barker and Kate Brookes (1998) provide a broad list of suggestions which are a good start to help investigate the cultural significance of Irish film:

- investigate the relations between the vocabularies of involvement and pleasure, and the histories and socio-cultural characteristics of particular audiences;
- investigate the relations between established production imperatives and the wider operations of cultural industries;
- investigate the relations between the patterns and form of the film, and the wider generic and other traditions (1998: 142).

Chapter 12 *Big Brother* meets the Celtic Tiger?

1 Although RTÉ the national public service broadcaster has been screening Irish reality programmes since 2001 and viewers in Ireland have had access to it through other channels, there has been very little academic analysis to date. However, see Callery (2006) and Duffy (2006).

2 It is not possible to give precise ratings for reality TV, because Irish viewers watch British and American shows that are screened on non-Irish television channels. It is also worth noting that most of the reality programmes spontaneously mentioned in my own research and in Callery (2006) and Duffy (2006) were either British or American, so ratings for the genre as a whole are much higher than the figures for Irish-produced shows indicate.

3 It is of interest to note that the more negative assessment of reality TV is by far more common in macro studies of production and political economy than in audience studies.

4 One of the main criticisms of reception studies is that reported viewing may not match actual viewing because audiences are either not aware of their 'real' pleasures/ attitudes (subconscious and ideological factors operating here) or they are unwilling to admit in an interview or focus group to some of the more 'negative' pleasures such as voyeurism. This difficulty is not unique to reality TV but to self-reporting of socially sanctioned attitudes and behaviours in social science research generally. The issue of focus group participants performing narratives of the self has also been addressed by Buckingham (2000) and by Hill (2005). These narratives are germane to the method and cannot be eliminated. However, it is important that researchers remain sensitive to the performance contexts in which the focus group discussions occur. Finally, I would concur with Hall (2003: 638) that ' [t]he social context may shape participants' comments but it does not necessarily make them misleading'.

5   The discussion here is based on five focus groups comprising a group of Communications Studies graduates (CS) with three participants (one male and two female) in their early twenties; a group of accountants with seven participants (four male and three female) in their mid to late twenties; a group of four students (all female) in their second year of secondary school and with an average age of 14; a group of two MA students (MTV) (one male, one female) in their early twenties, and a group of four (two male and two female) working in an IT company in their mid to late twenties. There are no verbatim quotes from the latter group as the data was written from memory immediately after the discussion rather than recorded on audio. The discussions took place in Dublin in the summer of 2006. They were relatively open-ended and focused on motivations for viewing, contexts of viewing, viewing patterns, viewing preferences across a range of sub-genres, and levels of inter-activity. The names used in the text are pseudonyms. I would like to take this opportunity to thank the participants and group organisers who gave so generously of their time and energy.

6   The 'ethic of charity' was strikingly evident in the recent Irish-produced *Celebrity, You're a Star* (2006) where the viewing audience consistently voted for John Aldridge, a former star soccer player, who went on to win the competition despite the fact that he was not a good singer but who was raising funds for a well-known and long-established Dublin children's hospital.

Chapter 13 New lads or protest masculinities?

1   According to Fejes (1992), what has happened at the level of the cultural represen-tation of men is best explained as a trajectory from the consideration of 'masculinity as fact' to the 'facticity of masculinity'.

2   Also known as 'dude cinema' (Troyer and Marchiselli, 2005).

3   Twoccing' refers to car-theft or taking without owner's consent.

4   More information about the Youthreach programme can be found at http://www.youthreach.ie/index.htm.

5   The Junior Certificate is a national examination normally taken by students aged 14–15, after three years of post-primary education.

6   The club is engaged in the indigenous games of Hurling and Gaelic Football, for whose revival and maintenance the Gaelic Athletic Association was originally established in 1884.

7   Intermission was on theatrical release for 18 weeks in the Republic of Ireland and played on 30 screens in the first week of its release. It premiered at number one on its rental release and is Irish video rental chain Xtravision's most rented video/DVD in a six-week period ever (statistics from Moira Horgan, Head of Marketing, Bord Scannán na hÉireann / the Irish Film Board).

8   According to Liebes and Katz (1990), real engagement occurs at the intersection of referential and closed, whereby the text's characters and their values are treated as 'given' and are frequently argued with.

Chapter 14   Teachers and the consumption of ICT

1   The bulk of the research for the Wired for Learning project was conducted by the author for her PhD, awarded in 2002. Following completion of her PhD the author was commissioned by the National Centre for Technology in Education (NCTE) to prepare an evaluation study for the Department of Education and Science and IBM covering the total period of the pilot project from 1999–2002 which involved additional fieldwork not included in the PhD. The full evaluation report entitled *Wired for Learning in Ireland: Final Evaluation* (2003) is available from the NCTE, located at DCU.

2   During the start-up phase of the project in 1998 and 1999 both the NCTE and IBM engaged teachers in an intensive series of meeting and workshops to develop the scope of the project in Ireland, to outline the process of localising the software for the Irish education system and to train teachers in both ICT skills and the Wired for Learning software. During the Autumn of 1998 extensive consultation was carried out by IBM, the NCTE and the DES, with the first three pilot schools to come on board. The consultation exercise with schools was based on facilitated workshops delivered in each school and attended by a steering group of teachers. As the project progressed, substantial investment was made in further training involving the delivery of a 'Change Management' workshop for school principals and ICT co-ordinators, and courses in 'Train the Trainer', 'Network System Management and Maintenance' and 'Project Management' for IT co-ordinators and their assistants. Skills training in ICT and WFL specific training was made available to all teachers on a voluntary basis. The take-up of training was very high with in excess of 70 per cent of teachers partici- pating. In addition, to facilitate in motivating staff to use the WFL system teacher release time equivalent to .45 days for primary schools and approximately 10 hours per week for secondary schools was provided by the DES. Schools could use these days for planned WFL work. Some schools allocated all or the bulk of the teacher release days to the IT co-ordinator while other schools allocated the time among the teaching staff in such as way as to encourage mainstream teachers to use WFL in a collaborative way by releasing groups of teachers to work together on different aspects of WFL.

3   Fullan (1991), who has written extensively on the process of change and innova- tion in schools, makes an important distinction between real change and illusory change. He maintains that many change efforts in schools fail because there is an overemphasis on the *objectives* of the proposed innovation or reform effort without due acknowledgement of the *subjective realities* of teachers who are caught up in the

change process. Consequently new programmes are frequently introduced and described in terms of programme goals and supposed benefits rather than of how the change will affect teachers personally when it comes to their classroom activities and the amount of extra work required outside class. Because many change efforts or innovations fail to take cognisance of this subjective reality, a stalemate ensues resulting in at best, superficial change, and at worst, no change.

4   In 1996, women comprised 78 per cent of the teachers and 46 per cent of principals in primary schools. In the secondary school sector, laywomen comprised 54 per cent of teachers while only 14.7 per cent of the principals were laywomen. Religious women accounted for 4.3 per cent of all teachers but held two thirds of the female held principalships. In vocational schools, where 47 per cent of the teachers were women, 11 per cent of the principalships were held by women; within the community and comprehensive schools, although half of the teachers are women only 6.1 per cent of principalships are held by lay women with religious women accounting for 2.4 per cent of principalships (Lynch, 1999).

Chapter 15 Listen to yourself

1   The bulk of this research was conducted under the supervision of Professor Farrel Corcoran, of the School of Communications, DCU, as the fieldwork for a PhD which was awarded in 2004. The project examined the work of six Irish community radio stations first licensed in 1994 and the thesis was entitled 'Community radio in Ireland: building community, participation and multi-flows of communication'. It employed a multi-method approach including long-term observation, interviews and analysis of station literature, meetings and schedules. The research was subsequently extended and published as a book (Day, 2007)

Bibliography

Ackerman, B. (1983) 'Form and function in children's understanding of ironic utterances', *Journal of Experimental Child Psychology* 35: 457–508.

Acland, C. (1995) *Youth, Murder, Spectacle: The Cultural Politics of 'Youth in Crisis'.* Boulder, CO: Westview.

Ahlstrom, D. (2003) 'New funds buy our way to the top of the world class', *Irish Times* (Science Technology Engineering special report), 8 Apr.

Ahlstrom, D. (2006), *Flashes of Brilliance: The Cutting Edge of Irish Science.* Dublin: Royal Irish Academy.

Alexa Internet (2007) *Top Sites Ireland.* http://www.alexa.com/site/ds/top_sites?cc=IE&ts_mode=country&lang=none [accessed 13 Jan.]

Allen, G. (1999) *The Garda Síochána: Policing Independent Ireland 1922–82.* Dublin: Gill & Macmillan.

Allen, S. (2005) 'News on the Web: the emerging forms and practices of online journalism', pp. 67–84 in S. Allen (ed.), *Journalism: Critical Issues.* Maidenhead: Open University Press.

Allon, Y., Cullen, D. and Patterson, H. (eds) (2001) *Contemporary British and Irish Film Directors: A Wallflower Critical Guide.* London: Wallflower.

AMARC (2006) http://www.amarc.org. [accessed 29 Sept.]

Anderson, B. (1991) *Imagined Communities: Reflections on the Origin and Spread of Nationalism*, revised edn. London and New York: Verso.

Andrejevic, M. (2002) 'The kinder, gentler gaze of Big Brother: reality TV in the era of digital capitalism', *New Media and Society* 4 (2): 251–70.

Andrejevic, M. (2004) *Reality TV: The Work of Being Watched.* Lanham: Rowman & Littlefield.

Ang, I. (1985) *Watching Dallas: Soap Opera and Melodramatic Imagination*, trans. Della Couling. London: Methuen.

Ang, I. (1996) *Living Room Wars: Rethinking Media Audiences for a Postmodern World.* London: Routledge.

Appadurai, A. (1990) 'Disjuncture and difference in the global cultural economy', pp. 259–310 in Featherstone, M. (ed.), *Global Culture: Nationalism, Globalisation and Modernity.* London: Sage.

Appadurai, A. (1996) *Modernity at Large: Cultural Dimensions of Globalization* (Minneapolis: University of Minnesota Press).

Article 19 (1996) *Broadcasting Genocide: Censorship, Propaganda and State Sponsored Violence in Rwanda 1990–1994.* London: Article 19.

Aslama, M. and Pannti, M. (2006) 'Talking alone: Reality TV, emotions and authenticity', *European Journal of Cultural Studies* 9 (2): 167–84.

Atton, C. (2001) *Alternative Media.* London: Sage.

Baker, K. (1996) 'Reporting the conflict', pp. 118–26 in McLoone, M. (ed.), *Broadcasting in a Divided Community.* Belfast: Institute of Irish Studies.

Barker, M. and Austin, T. (2000) *From Ants to Titanic: Reinventing Film Analysis.* London: Pluto.

Barker, M. and Brooks, K. (1998) *Knowing Audiences: Judge Dredd, Its Friends, Fans and Foes.* Luton: University of Luton Press.

Barnard, S. (2000) *Studying Radio.* London: Arnold.

Barrett, A., Bergin, A. and Duggy, D. (2006) 'The labour market characteristics and labour market impacts of immigrants in Ireland', *Economic and Social Review* 37: 1–26.

Bartels, L. M. (1993) 'Messages received: the political impact of media exposure', *American Political Science Review,* 87 (2): 267–81.

Barto, T. (1996) 'A global perspective on technology integration in education; problems and strategies', *Educational Media International* 33 (4): 155–8.

Barton, R. (1997) 'From history to heritage: Some recent developments in Irish cinema', *Irish Review* 21: 41–56

Barton, R. (2002) *Jim Sheridan: Framing the Nation.* Dublin: Liffey.

Barton, R. (2004) *Irish National Cinema.* London: Routledge.

Barton, R. (2006) *Acting Irish in Hollywood: From Fitzgerald to Farrell.* Dublin: Irish Academic Press.

Barton, R. and O'Brien, H. (eds) (2004) *Keeping it Real: Irish Film and Television.* London: Wallflower Press.

Bauer, M. (1998) 'The medicalisation of science news – from the 'rocket-scalpel' to the "gene-meteorite" complex', *Social Science Information* 37 (4): 731–51.

Bauman, Z. (1996) 'From pilgrim to tourist – or a short history of identity', pp. 19–36 in Hall, S. and Du Gay, P. (eds), *Questions of Cultural Identity.* London: Sage.

BCI (2001) *BCI Policy on Community Radio Broadcasting.* Dublin: Broadcasting Commission of Ireland.

Beatson, J. (1999) 'Developing community radio in advanced democracies: participation, access and equity versus public accountability'. Paper presented at Radiocracy Conference, University of Wales, Cardiff, November.

Beck, U. (1992) *Risk Society: Towards a New Modernity.* London: Sage.

Belfast Agreement (1998) http://www.nio.gov.uk/agreement.pdf [accessed 29 Mar.].

Bell, D. (1973) *The Coming of Post-Industrial Society: A Venture in Social Forecasting.* New York: Basic Books.

Bell, The (1942) 'Crime in Dublin', 5 (3): 173–83.

Berker, T., Hartman, M., Punie, Y. and Ward, K. (eds) (2006) *Domestication of Media and Technology.* Maidenhead: Open University Press.

Berrigan, F. (ed.) (1977) *Access: Some Western Models of Community Media.* Paris: UNESCO.

Beynon, J. (2002) *Masculinities and Culture.* Buckingham: Open University Press.

Birt, J. (1975) 'Can television news break the understanding-barrier?' *The Times*, 28 Feb.

Bloomberg News (2006) 'News Corp. to start selling video online', www.nytimes.com [accessed 15 Aug.].

Boczkowski, P. J. (2004), *Digitizing the News: Innovation in Online Newspapers*. Cambridge MA: MIT Press.

Bonner, F. (2003) *Ordinary Television*. London: Sage.

Bordenave, J. D. (1994) 'Participative communication as a part of building the participative society', pp. 35–48 in White, S. A., Nair, S. and Ascroft, J. (eds), *Participatory Communication: Working for Change and Development*. London: Sage.

Bourke, S. (2004) *Taking the Free-Speech Temperature: Irish Libel Law and Newspaper Journalism*. Dublin: DCU.

Boyd-Barrett, O. (2005) 'A different scale of difference', *Global Communication and Communication* 1 (1): 15–19.

Brady, C. (2004) 'Low standards in high places', *Village*, 16–22 Oct.: 32–3.

Brady, C. (2005) *Up With The Times*. Dublin: Gill & Macmillan.

Brandenburg, H. (2005) 'Political bias in the Irish media: a quantitative study of campaign coverage during the 2002 general election', *Irish Political Studies* 20 (3): 297–322.

Brecht, B. (1983 [1930]) 'Radio as a means of communication: a talk on the functions of radio', pp. 169–71 in Mattelart, A. and Siegelaub, S. (eds), *Communication and Class Struggle: 2, Liberation, Socialism*. New York: Bagnolet.

Breen, J. (1996) *Times They Are a Changin'*. Dublin: The Irish Times.

Brennan, E. (2003) '*The Fair City* production line', PhD thesis, UCD.

Brenton, S. and Cohen, R. (2003) *Shooting People: Adventures in Reality TV*. London: Verso.

Brereton, P. (2001) Review of Martin Barker et al., *From Ants to Titanic* (2000) in www.film.philosophy.com, Nov.

Brereton, P. (2006) 'Nature tourism and Irish film', *Irish Studies Review* 14 (4): 407–20.

Brunsdon, C. (2003) 'Lifestyling Britain: the 8–9 slot on British television', *International Journal of Cultural Studies* 6 (1): 5–23.

Buckingham, D. (2000) *The Making of Citizens: Young People, News and Politics*. London: Routledge.

Buric, A. (2000) 'The media, war and peace in Bosnia', pp. 64–99 in Davis, A. (ed.), *Regional Media in Conflict*. London: Institute for War and Peace Reporting.

Butler, D. (1991) 'Ulster unionism and British broadcasting journalism 1924–89', pp. 99–121 in Rolston, B. (1991) (ed.), *The Media and Northern Ireland*. Basingtoke: Macmillan.

Byrne, T. *Power in the Eye: An Introduction to Contemporary Irish Film*. Langham, MD: Scarecrow Press, 1997.

Callahan, C. (2003) *A Journalist's Guide to the Internet: The Net as a Reporting Tool*, 2nd edn. Boston: Allyn & Bacon.

Callery, B. (2006) 'Everybody is talking about it!: an investigation into teenagers' responses to reality television'. MA dissertation, DCU.

Carrel, S. (1994) *Language Rights, Individual and Collective*. Dublin: European Bureau for Lesser-Used Languages.

Carter, C. and Weaver, C. K. (2003) *Violence and the Media*. Buckingham: Open University Press.

Castells, M. (1996) *The Rise of the Network Society*. Oxford: Blackwell.

Castells, M. and Himanen, P. (2002) *The Information Society and the Welfare State: The Finnish Model*. Oxford: Oxford University Press.

Cathcart, R. (1984) *A Most Contrary Region: The BBC in Northern Ireland 1924–1984*. Belfast: Blackstaff.

Caughie, J. with Rockett, K. (1996) *The Companion to British and Irish Cinema*. London: Cassell.

CCR (1994) 'Application by Connemara Community Radio to the IRTC for a licence to broadcast'. Unpublished.

Chalaby, J. (2006) 'American cultural primacy in a new media order: a European Perspective', *International Communication Gazette* 68 (1): 33–51.

Chibnall, S. (2001) 'Underworld England: Guy Ritchie and the British gangster film' *Filmhäftet* 118 (6) [http://www.filmint.nu/pdf/english/118/underworldengland.pdf]

Chibnall, S. and Murphy, R. (eds) (1999) *British Crime Cinema*. London and New York: Routledge.

Chubb, B. (1984) 'The political role of the media in contemporary Ireland', pp. 75–8 in Farrell, B. (ed.), *Communications and Community in Ireland*. Dublin, RTÉ.

Clark, F. and Illman, Deborah L. (2006) 'A longitudinal study of the *New York Times* Science Times Section', *Science Communication* 27 (4): 496–513.

Coakley, J. (2005) 'Society and political culture', pp. 36–71 in Coakley, J. and Gallagher, M. (eds), *Politics in the Republic of Ireland*, 4th edn. London: Routledge.

Collis, B., Knezek, G., Miyashita, K., Pelgrum, W., Plomp, Tj. and Sakomoto, T. (1996) *Children and Computers in School*. Mahwah, NJ: Erblaum.

Commission of the European Communities (1994a) *Europe and the Global Information Society: Recommendations to the European Council* ['Bangemann Report']. Brussels: EC.

Commission of the European Communities (1994b) *Growth, Competitiveness and Employment: Challenges for Entering in the 21st Century* [White Paper, 'Délors Report']. Luxembourg: EC.

Commission of the European Communities (1994c) *Strategy Options to Strengthen the European Programme Industry in the Context of the Audiovisual Policy of the European Union*. Brussels: EC [Com (94) 96 final].

Commission of the European Communities (1995) *Europe's way to the Information Society: An Action Plan*. Brussels: EC

Commission of the European Communities (2000a) *Five Year Assessment Report Related to the Specific Programme: User-Friendly Information Society, 1995–99.* Brussels: EC.

Commission of the European Communities (2000b) *eEurope, An Information Society for All: Communication on a Commission Initiative for the Special European Council of Lisbon,* 23 and 24 Mar.

Commission of the European Communities (2002) *Information Society, 1995–99.* Brussels: EC [Last Accessed via Europa website, 13 Dec. 2002].

Commission on the Newspaper Industry (1996) *Report of the Commission on the Newspaper Industry.* Dublin: Stationery Office.

Connell, R. W. (1995) *Masculinities.* Sydney: Allen & Unwin.

Connell, R. W. (2005) 'Change among the gatekeepers: men, masculinities, and gender equality in the global arena', *Signs: Journal of Women in Culture and Society* 30 (3): 1801–25.

Connolly, M. (2003) 'An archaeology of Irish cinema: Ireland's subaltern, migrant and feminist film cultures', unpublished PhD thesis, DCU.

Coopers and Lybrand (1992) *Report on Indigenous Audiovisual Production Industry for IDA/Temple Bar Properties.* Dublin: Coopers & Lybrand.

Corcoran, F. (2004) *RTÉ and the Globalisation of Irish Television.* Bristol: Intellect Books.

Corcoran, M. (1993) *Irish Illegals: Transients between Two Societies.* Westport, CT: Greenwood.

Corcoran, M. P. (2004) 'The political preferences and value orientations of Irish journalists', *Irish Journal of Sociology* 13 (2): 22–42.

Corcoran, M. P. and O'Brien, M. (eds) (2005) *Political Censorship and the Democratic State: The Irish Broadcasting Ban.* Dublin: Four Courts.

Corner, J. (2002) Performing the real: documentary diversions', *Television and New Media* 3 (3): 255–71.

Corrigan, C. (2006) 'Crime: "out of control" once again', *Magill,* Sept.: 14–16.

Cox, G. (1995) *Pioneering Television News.* London: John Libbey.

Crawdus, G. (1997) 'The screenwriting of Irish history: Neil Jordan's *Michael Collins*', *Cineaste* XXII (4): 14–23.

CRC (1994) 'Application by Community Radio Castlebar to the IRTC for a licence to broadcast'. Unpublished.

CRC (1998) 'Application by Community Radio Castlebar to the IRTC for a licence to broadcast'. Unpublished.

Crisell, A. (1994) *Understanding Radio,* 2nd edn. London: Routledge.

Cuban, L. (1993a) *How Teachers Taught: Constancy and Change in American Classrooms 1890–1980,* 2nd edn. New York: Teachers College Press,

Cuban, L. (1993b) 'Computers meet classroom: classroom wins', *Teachers College Record,* 95 (2): 185–210.

Cullingford, E. B. (2001) *Ireland's Others: Ethnicity and Gender in Irish Literature and Popular Culture.* Cork: Cork University Press.

Cullingford, E. B. (2003) 'Re-reading the past: *Michael Collins* and contemporary popular culture', pp 174–88 in Savage, Robert J. Jr (ed.), *Ireland in the New Century*. Dublin: Four Courts.

Cunningham, S. (2001) 'Popular media as public "sphericules" for diasporic communities', *International Journal of Cultural Studies* 4 (2): 131–47.

Curran, J. (2002) *Media and Power*. London: Routledge.

Curran, J. and Gurevitch, M. (1996) *Mass Media and Society*. London: Arnold

Curran, J. and Seaton, J. (1988) *Power without Responsibility: The Press and Broadcasting in Britain*, 3rd edn. London: Routledge.

Curtis, L. (1998 [1984]) *Ireland the Propaganda War* (1st edn, London: Pluto). Belfast: Sásta.

Darby, J. (1978) *Conflict in Northern Ireland: The Development of a Polarised Community*. Dublin: Gill & Macmillan.

Davis, E. and Sinnott, R. (1979) *Attitudes in the Republic of Ireland Relevant to the Northern Ireland Problem*. Dublin: ESRI.

Day, R. (2007). *Community Radio in Ireland: Building the Community, Participation and Multi-flows of Communication*. Cresskill: Hampton Press.

De Valera, S. (mimeo) (1999) Speech delivered at the launch of the final Report of the Film Industry Strategic Review Group, Shaw Room, National Gallery of Ireland, 4 Aug.

Department of Arts, Culture and the Gaeltacht (1995) *A Strategy for Success Based on Economic Realities: The Next Next Stage of Development for the Film Industry in Ireland* [The Indecon Report]. Dublin: Indecon.

Department of Arts, Heritage, Gaeltacht and the Islands (1999) *Report: Film Industry Strategic Review Group (1999), The Strategic Development of the Irish Film and Television Industry 2000–2010* [The Kilkenny Report]. Dublin: Department of Arts, Heritage, Gaeltacht and the Islands.

Des Forges, A. (1999) *Leave None To Tell The Story: Genocide in Rwanda*. New York: Human Rights Watch.

Deuze, M. (2003) 'The Web and its journalisms: considering the consequences of different types of newsmedia online', *New Media and Society* 5 (2): 203–30.

Devereux, E. (1998) *Devils and Angels: Television, Ideology and the Coverage of Poverty*. Luton: John Libbey Media.

Devlin, M. (2000) 'Representations of Irish youth', unpublished PhD thesis, NUI Maynooth.

Doolan, L., Dowling, J. and Quinn, B. (1969) *Sit Down and be Counted: The Cultural Evolution of a Television Station*. Dublin: Wellington.

Dorfman, A. and Mattelart, A. (1975) *How to Read Donald Duck: Imperialist Ideology in the Disney Comic*. New York: International General Editions.

Dornan, C. (1990) 'Some problems of conceptualising the issues of "science in the media"', *Critical Studies in Mass Communication* 7: 48–71

Douglas, T. (1994) 'Freedom of the press is owning one', pp. 91–5 in O'Donnell, P. and Cunningham, S. (eds) (1994) *Who's Telling the Story? A Conference on Media and Development in Australia and the Region.* Sydney: UTS, Community AID Abroad.

Downing, J. D. with Ford, T. V., Gil, G. and Stein, L. (2000) *Radical Media: Rebellious Communication and Social Movements.* Thousand Oaks: Sage.

Driscoll, P. D., Salwen, M. B. and Garrison, B. (eds) (2005) *Online News and the Public.* Mahwah NJ: Lawrence Erlbaum.

Druckman, J. N. (2001) 'The implications of framing effects for citizen competence', *Political Behaviour* 23 (3): 225–56.

Drudy, S. and Lynch, K. (1993) *Schools and Society in Ireland.* Dublin: Gill & Macmillan.

Duffy, L. (2006) 'Just entertainment: An exploration of reality TV and its audiences', unpublished BA project, School of Communications, DCU.

Duncombe, S. (ed.) (2002) *Cultural Resistance Reader.* London and New York: Verso.

Dunwoody, S. and Ryan, M. (1987) 'The credible scientific source', *Journalism Quarterly* 64: 21–7.

Dwyer, M. (2003) 'That's a wrap', *The Irish Times* (*The Ticket*), 21 Aug.

EGFSN (Expert Group on Future Skills Needs, Ireland) (2006) *Future Skills Requirements of the International Digital Media Industry: Implications for Ireland.* Dublin: Forfas.

ENSCOT Team (2003) *ENSCOT: The European Network of Science Communication Teachers, Public Understanding of Science* 12: 167–81.

Enzensberger, H. M. (1974) 'Constituents of a theory of the media', pp. 95–128 in Enzensberger, *The Consciousness Industry, On Literature, Politics and the Media,* ed. Roloff, M. New York: Seabury Press.

Eurobarometer (2005) *Statistical Bulletin of the European Community.* Brussels: EU Commission

Fayard, P. M. (1993) *Sciences aux quotidiens: l'information scientifique et technique dans les quotidiens nationaux européens.* Nice: Z'Editions.

Fejes, F. J. (1992) 'Masculinity as fact: a review of empirical mass communication research on masculinity', pp. 9–22 in Craig, S. (ed.), *Men, Masculinity, and the Media.* London: Sage.

Film Makers Ireland (1992) *The Independent Television Production Sector.* Dublin: FMI.

Fisher, D. (1978) *Broadcasting in Ireland.* London: International Institute of Communications.

Fisher, D. (2005) 'Getting tough with RTÉ', pp. 61–72 in Corcoran, M. P. and O'Brien, M. (eds), *Political Censorship and the Democratic State: The Irish Broadcasting Ban.* Dublin: Four Courts.

Fishman, M. and Cavender, G. (eds) (1998) *Entertaining Crime: Television Reality Programs.* New York: Aldine DeGruyter.

Fiske, J. and Dawson, R. (1996) 'Audiencing violence: watching homeless men watch Die Hard', pp. 297–316 in Hay, J., Grossberg, L. and Wartella, E. (eds), *The Audience and Its Landscape*. Boulder CO: Westview.

Flynn, Arthur (2005) *The Story of Irish Film*. Dublin: Currach Press, 2005.

Flynn, James (2005) 'Chairman's report', *Film and Television Production in Ireland Review 2005*. Dublin: IBEC

Forfas (2002) *A Strategy for the Digital Content Industry in Ireland*. Dublin: Forfas.

Forfas (2004) *Wireless Communications: An Area of Opportunity for Ireland*. Dublin: Forfas.

Friedman, S., Dunwoody, S. and Rogers, C. (eds) (1999) *Communicating Uncertainty: Media Coverage of New and Controversial Science*. Mahwah NJ: Lawrence Erlbaum.

Fullan, M. (1991) *The New Meaning of Educational Change*. New York: Teachers College Press.

Fursich, E. and Lester, E. P. (1996) 'Science journalism under scrutiny', *Critical Studies in Mass Communication* 13: 24–43.

Galtung, J. and Ruge, M. (1973) 'Structuring and selecting news', pp. 62–72 in Cohen, S. and Young, J. (eds), *The Manufacture of News*. London, Constable.

Garcia Canclini, N. (1995) *Hybrid Cultures: Strategies for Leaving and Entering Modernity*. Minneapolis: University of Minnesota Press.

Gauntlett, D. (2002) *Media, Gender and Identity: An Introduction*. London and New York: Routledge.

Georgiou, M. (2005) 'Diasporic media across Europe: multicultural societies and the universalism-particularism continuum', *Journal of Ethnic and Migration Studies* 31: 481–98.

Gerbner, G., Gross, L., Morgan, M. and Signorelli, N. (1994) 'Growing up with television: the cultivation perspective', pp. 56–73 in Bryant, J. and Zillman, D. (eds) *Media Effects*. Hillsdale, NJ: Lawrence Erlbaum.

Gerbner, G. and Siefert, M. (eds) (1984) *World Communications*. New York: Longman.

Gibbons, L. (1996a) 'Engendering the state: narrative, allegory and Michael Collins', *Eire-Ireland* 31 (3–4): 261–9.

Gibbons, L. (1996b) *Transformations in Irish Culture*. Cork: Cork University Press.

Gibbons, L. (2002a) 'The cracked looking glass of cinema: James Joyce, John Huston and the memory of *The Dead'*, *Yale Journal of Criticism* 15 (1): 142

Gibbons, L. (2002b) *The Quiet Man*. Cork: Cork University Press.

Gibbons, M. (1998) *Breaking Glass Walls: Gender and Employment Patterns in the Independent Radio Sector in Ireland: A Report to Women-on-Air*. Dublin: Nexus.

Giddens, A. (1990) *The Consequences of Modernity*. Cambridge: Polity.

Gillespie, M. (1995) *Television, Ethnicity and Cultural Change*. London: Routledge.

Gillmor, D. (2006) *We the Media: Grassroots Journalism by the People, for the People*. Sebastopol CA: O'Reilly.

Ging, D. (2005) 'A "manual on masculinity"? The consumption and use of mediated images of masculinity among teenage boys in Ireland', *Irish Journal of Sociology*

14 (2): 29–52.

Giroux, H. and Szeman, I. (2001) 'Ikea boy fights back: Fight Club, consumerism, and the political limits of nineties cinema', pp. 95–104 in Lewis, J. (ed.), *The End of Cinema as We Know It: American Film in the 90s.* New York: New York University Press.

Glaser, B. and Strauss, A. (1967) *The Discovery of Grounded Theory.* Chicago: Aldine.

Goffman, E. (1966) *The Presentation of Self in Everyday Life.* London: Pelican.

Goldsmith, M. (1986) *The Science Critic: A Critical Analysis of the Popular Presentation of Science.* London: Routledge & Kegan Paul.

Gotz, M. (2004) '"Soaps want to explain reality": daily soaps and big brother in the everyday life of German children and adolescents', pp. 65–81 in Von Feilitzen, C. (ed.), *Young People, Soap Operas and Reality TV.* Goteborg: International Clearing House on Children, Youth and Media, Nordicom, Goteborg University.

Government of Ireland (1995) *Green Paper on Broadcasting.* Dublin: Stationery Office.

Government of Ireland (1996) *White Paper on Science Technology and Innovation.* Dublin: Stationery Office.

Government of Ireland (2003) Official Languages Act. Dublin: Stationery Office.

Government of Ireland (2006) *Strategy for Science, Technology and Innovation: 2006–2013.* Dublin: Stationery Office.

Graham, B. (ed.) (1997) *In Search of Ireland: A Cultural Geography.* London: Routledge.

Graham, C. and Kirkland, R. (eds) (1999) *Ireland and Cultural Theory.* Houndmills: Macmillan.

Greenslade, R. (1998) Damien Walsh memorial lecture, 4 Aug. http://cain.ulst.ac.uk/othelem/media/greenslade.htm

Gregg, G. (2005) 'Emotional blackmail', *Magill,* June 2005: 28–36.

Greven, D. (2002) 'Dude, where's my gender? Contemporary teen comedies and new forms of American masculinity', *Cineaste* 27 (3): 14–21.

Günnel, T. (2002) 'Counteracting the gap: strategies for teaching media competence', pp. 333–58 in Jankowski, N. W., and Prehn, O. (eds), *Community Media in the Information Age: Perspectives and Prospects.* Cresskill: Hampton.

Gunter, B. (2003) *News and the Net.* Mahwah, NJ: Lawrence Erlbaum.

Habermas, J. (1971) *Toward a Rational Society.* London: Heinemann.

Habermas, J. (1979) *Communication and the Evolution of Society.* London: Heinemann.

Habermas, J. (1983 [1962]) *The Structural Transformation of the Public Sphere: An Inquiry into a Category of Bourgeois Society,* trans. Burger T. with F. Lawrence. Cambridge: Polity.

Halcli, A. (2000) 'Social movements', pp.463–75 in Browning, G., Halchli, A. and Webster, F. (eds), *Understanding Contemporary Society: Theories of the Present.* London: Sage.

Hall, A. (2003) 'Reading realism: audiences' evaluations of the reality of media texts' *Journal of Communication* Dec.: 624–41

Hall, S. (1992) 'The question of cultural identity', pp. 273–327 in Hall, S., Held, D. and McGrew, T. (eds), *Modernity and its Futures*. Cambridge: Polity/Open University Press.

Hall, S., Held, D. and McGrew, T. (eds) (1992) *Modernity and its Futures*. Cambridge: Polity /Open University Press.

Hall, S. S. (1996) 'Wired for learning', *IBM Research Magazine* 34 (3): 1–6.

Hamill, D. (1985) *Pig in the Middle*. London: Methuen.

Hanke, R. (1998) 'Theorizing masculinity with/in the media', *Communication Theory* 8 (2): 183–203.

Hansen, A. (1994) 'Journalistic practices and science reporting in the British press', *Public Understanding of Science* 3: 111–34.

Hartley, J. (1999) *The Uses of Television*. London: Routledge.

Harvey, D. (1989) *The Condition of Postmodernity*. Oxford: Basil Blackwell.

Hawkins, G. (2001) 'The ethics of television', *International Journal of Cultural Studies*, 4 (4): 412–26.

Hazelkorn, E. (1996) 'New technologies and changing work practices in the media industry: the case of Ireland', *Irish Communications Review* 6: 28–38.

Hein, K. (1984) 'Popular participation in rural radio: Radio Baha'I, Otavalo, Ecuador', *Studies in Latin American Popular Culture* I (3): 97–101.

Henderson, L., Miller, D. and Reilly, J. (1990) *Speak no Evil: The British Broadcasting Ban, the Media and the Conflict in Ireland*. Glasgow: Glasgow Media Group.

Herman, E. S. (2000) 'The propaganda model: a retrospective', *Journalism Studies* I (1): 101–12.

Herman, E. S. and Chomsky, N. (1988) *Manufacturing Consent*. New York: Pantheon.

Herman, E. S. and McChesney, R. W. (1997). *The Global Media: The New Missionaries of Corporate Capitalism*. London: Cassel.

Hesmondhalgh, D. (2002). *The Cultural Industries*. London, Sage.

Higbee, W. (2001) 'Screening the "other" Paris: cinematic representations of the French urban periphery in *La Haine* and *Ma 6–T va crack-er*', *Modern and Contemporary France* 9 (2): 197–208.

Higgins, C. S. and Moss, P. D. (1982) *Sounds Real: Radio in Everyday Life*. St Lucia: University of Queensland Press.

Higgins, M. D. (1995), speech to British National Heritage Parliamentary Committee. Mimeo.

Hill, A. (2005) *Reality TV: Audiences and Popular Factual Television*. London: Routledge.

Hill, J. (2006) *Cinema and Northern Ireland: Film, Culture and Politics*. London: BFI.

Hill, J. and Gibson, P. C. (eds) (1998) *The Oxford Companion to World Cinema*. Oxford: Oxford University Press.

Hill, J. and McLoon, M. (1996) *Big Picture, Small Screen: The Relations between Film and Television*. Luton: John Libby Press.

Hill, J., McLoone, M. and Hainsworth, P. (eds) (1994) *Border Crossing: Film in Ireland, Britain and Europe*. London: BFI.

Hjort, M. and MacKenzie, S. (eds) (2000) *Cinema and Nation.* London: Routledge.

Hobson, D. (2004) 'Everyday people, everyday life: British teenagers, soap opera and reality TV', pp. 129–47 in Von Feilitzen, C. (ed.), *Young People, Soap Operas and Reality TV.* Goteborg: International Clearinghouse on Children, Youth and Media, Nordicom, University, Goteborg.

Holliman, R. et al. (2002) 'Science in the news: a cross-cultural study of newspapers in five European countries', Paper presented to Seventh International Conference on Public Communication of Science and Technology, Dec. 2002, Cape Town, http://www.saasta.ac.za/scicom/pcst7/holliman1.pdf

Hollywood Reporter (1997) 'Irish arts czar commissions screen office', 6 June.

Holmes, S. and Jermyn, D. (2003) *Understanding Reality Television.* London: Routledge.

Hooks, B. (1994) *Outlaw Culture: Resisting Representations.* New York: Routledge.

Hooper S., and Rieber, L. (1995) 'Teaching with technology', pp. 155–70 in Ornstein, A. C. (ed.), *Teaching Theory into Practice.* Boston: Allyn & Baker.

Horgan, J. (2001) *Irish Media: A Critical History Since 1922.* London: Routledge.

Horgan, J. (2002) 'Journalists and censorship: a case history of the NUJ in Ireland and the broadcasting ban 1971–94', *Journalism Studies* 3 (3): 377–92.

Horgan, J. (2003) 'Churches, governments and the media: confronting their own and each Other's Responsibilities', pp. 228–40 in Mackey, J. and McDonagh, E. (eds), *Religion and Politics in Ireland at the Turn of the Millennium.* Dublin: Columba.

Horgan, J. (2004) *Broadcasting and Public Life.* Dublin: Four Courts.

Hoskins, C., McFadden, S. and Finn, A. (1997) *Global Television and Film.* Oxford: Oxford University Press.

Hourigan, N. (2001) *Comparison of the Campaigns for Raidio na Gaeltachta and TnaG.* Maynooth: Department of Sociology, NUI Maynooth.

Hutcheon, L. (1994) *Irony's Edge: The Theory and Politics of Irony.* London: Routledge.

Independent Estimates Review Committee on Estimates for Public Services (2002) *Report.* Dublin: Stationery Office.

Irish Film Board (2006) 'Minister John O'Donoghue meets the stars of *Becoming Jane*'. Mimeo.

Irish Times (1994) 'Maintaining law and order should be seen as community responsibility', 19 Sept.

Irish Times (1996a) 'Litany of repressive measures emanating from the airways is not an appropriate response', 28 June.

Irish Times (1996b) 'Media are the greatest enemy of crusading journalists', 22 Oct.

Irish Times (2003a): 'Discovering science (Editorial)', 11 Nov.

Irish Times (2003b) 'INLA link suspected in bomb hoax', 15 Nov.

Irish Times (2006a) 'New disciplinary code for gardai after Morris reports', 20 May.

Irish Times (2006b) 'Final bill for abuse in care may be €1.2 bn', 13 Oct.

ITAP (Information Technology Advisory Panel) (1983) *Making a Business of Information.* London: Cabinet Office.

Jones, J. M. (2003) 'Show your real face: a fan study of the UK *Big Brother* transmissions (2000, 2001, 2002): investigating the boundaries between notions of consumers and producers of factual television', *New Media and Society* 5 (3): 400–1.

Katz, E. and Liebes, T. (1986) 'Mutual aid in the decoding of Dallas: preliminary notes from a cross-cultural study', pp. 187–99 in Drummond P. and Patterson, R. (eds), *Television in Transition*. London: BFI.

Kawamoto, K. (2003) *Digital Journalism: Emerging Media and the Changing Horizons of Journalism*. Lanham, MD: Rowman & Littlefield.

Keane, J. (1995) 'Structural transformation of the public sphere', *Communication Review* 1 (1): 1–22.

Keating, A. (2002) 'Secrets and lies', PhD thesis, DCU.

Keegan, J. (1993) *A History of Warfare*. London: Hutchinson.

Kelly, A. (2002) *Compulsory Irish: Language and Education in Ireland 1870s–1970s*. Dublin: Irish Academic Press.

Kelly, M. and O'Connor, B. (eds) (1997) *Media Audiences in Ireland*. Dublin: UCD Press.

Kenny, C. (2006) 'Time to call a halt to the lip service behind TG4 "success"', *The Irish Times*, 27 Aug.

Kerr, A. (2000) 'Media diversity and cultural identities: the development of multimedia content in Ireland', *New Media and Society* 2: 286–312.

Kerr, A. (2003) 'Súil Eile: an Irish perspective on the mass media and globalization', pp. 125–76 in Samatar, A. (ed.), *Prometheus's Bequest: Technology and Change*. St. Paul, Minnesota: Macalster College.

Kerr, A., Kücklich, J. and Brereton, P. (2006) 'New media: new pleasures?', *International Journal of Cultural Studies* 9 (1): 63–82.

Kerrigan, G. and Shaw, H. (1985) 'Crime hysteria', *Magill*, Apr.: 10–21.

Kevin, D., Ader, T., Fueg, G., Pertzinidou, E. and Schoenthal, M. (2004) *Final Report of the Study on 'The Information of the Citizen in the EU: Obligations for the Media and the Institutions Concerning The Citizen's Right to be Fully and Objectively Informed'*. Dusseldorf/Paris: European Institute for the Media.

Khagram, S. and Levitt, P. (2004) *Towards a Sociology of Transnationalism and a Transnational Sociology*. Social Science Research Network Electronic Paper. http://ssrn.com/sol3/papers.cfm?abstract_id=556993 (accessed 1/08/06).

Kiberd, D. (1997) 'Have media practitioners a brief to change society?', pp. 33–40 in Kiberd, D. (ed.), *Media in Ireland: The Search for Ethical Journalism*. Dublin: Open Air.

Kiberd, D. (ed.) (2002) *Media in Ireland: Issues in Broadcasting*. Dublin: Four Courts.

Kilborn, R. (1994) 'How real can you get? Recent developments in "reality" television', *European Journal of Communication* 9: 421–39.

Kilborn, R. (2003) *Staging the Real: Factual TV Programming in the Age of Big Brother*. Manchester: Manchester University Press.

Kilborn, R. and Izod, J. (1997) *An Introduction to TV Documentary: Confronting Reality*. Manchester: Manchester University Press.

Kimmel M. (2008 forthcoming) *Guyland: The Inner Lives of Young Men*. New York: HarperCollins.

Kirby, P (2002) *The Celtic Tiger in Distress: Growth with Inequality in Ireland*. Basingstoke: Palgrave.

Kirby, P., Gibbons, L. and Cronin, M. (eds) (2002). *Reinventing Ireland: Culture, Society and Global Economy*. London: Pluto.

Kirkland, R. (1999) 'Gender, nation, excess: reading hush-a-by baby', pp. 109–21 in Brewster, Scott et al. (eds), *Ireland in Proximity: History, Gender, Space*. London: Routledge, 1999.

Kirschke, L. (1996) *Broadcasting Genocide: Censorship, Propaganda and State Sponsored Violence in Rwanda 1990–1994*. London: Article 19.

Klinenberg, E. K. (2006) 'Mega-merger mania', *The Nation*, 3 July.

Knuffer, N. (1993) 'Teachers and educational computing: changing roles and changing pedagogy', pp. 163–79 in Muffoletto, R., and Knuffer, N. (eds), *Computers in Education: Social, Political and Historical Perspectives*. Cresskill NJ: Hampton.

Kropiwiec, K. and Chiyoko King-O'Riain, R. (2006) *Polish Migrant Workers in Ireland*. Dublin: National Consultative Committee on Racism and Interculturalism.

Kua, E., Reder, M. and Grossel, M. J. (2004) 'Science in the news: a study of reporting genomics', *Public Understanding of Science* 13: 309–22.

Kubicek, H., Williams, R. and Dutton, W. H. (eds) (1997) *The Social Shaping of Information Superhighways: European and American Roads to the Information Society*. New York and Frankfurt: St Martins Press and Campus.

Kyle, K. (1996) 'The media and Northern Ireland – some personal recollections 1969–80', pp. 105–17 in McLoone, M. (ed.), *Broadcasting in a Divided Community*. Belfast: Institute of Irish Studies.

Lacey, J. (2002) 'One for the boys? The Sopranos and its male British audience', pp. 95–121 in Lavery, D. (ed.), *This Thing of Ours: Investigating the Sopranos*. London: Wallflower Press.

Lago, R. (1998) 'Interviewing Sinn Féin under the new political environment: a comparative analysis of interviews with Sinn Féin on British television', *Media Culture and Society* 20 (4): 677–85.

Lang, K. and Lang, G. E. (1966) 'The mass media and voting', pp. 455–72 in Berelson, B. and Janowitz, M. (eds), *Reader in Public Opinion and Communication*. New York: Free Press.

Lee, J. J. (1989): *Ireland 1912–1985: Politics and Society*. Cambridge: Cambridge University Press.

Leigh, D. (2000) 'Get smarter', *Sight and Sound* July: 22–5.

Levinson, P. 1999, *Digital McLuhan: A Guide to the Information Millennium*. London/New York: Routledge.

Liebes, T. and Katz, E. (1990) *The Export of Meaning: Cross-Cultural Readings of Dallas.* Cambridge: Polity.

Linehan, H. (1999) 'Myth, mammon and mediocrity: the trouble with recent Irish cinema', *Cineaste* 24 (2): 46–50.

Livingstone, S. (1996) 'On the continuing problem of media effects', pp. 305–24 in Curran, J. and Gurevitch, M. (eds), *Mass Media and Society.* London: Arnold.

Lull, J. (1995) *Media, Communication, Culture: A Global Approach.* Cambridge: Polity.

Lumby, K. (2004) 'Out of the slipstream: the creation of celebrities', *On line Opinion: e-journal of social and political debate,* http//:www.onlineopinion.com.au/print.asp?article=2541 [30 Dec. 2006].

Lynch, K. (1999) *Equality in Education.* Dublin: Gill & Macmillan.

Lynch, K. and Lodge, A. (2002) *Equality and Power in Schools.* London: RoutledgeFalmer.

McBride, S. (ed.) (1980) *Many Voices, One World.* Paris: UNESCO.

McBrierty, V. J. and Kinsella, R. P. (1998) *Ireland and the Knowledge Economy: The New Techno-Academic Paradigm.* Dublin: Oak Tree.

McCafferty, N. (1991) 'At the edges of the picture: the media, women and the war in the North', pp. 207–13 in Rolston, B. (ed.), *The Media and Northern Ireland.* Basingstoke: Macmillan.

McCann, E. (1993) *War and an Irish Town.* London: Pluto.

McChesney, R. W. (2006) 'Fight for a free press', *The Nation,* 3 July.

McCombs, M. (2004) *Setting the Agenda: the Mass Media and Public Opinion.* Cambridge: Polity.

McCombs, M. E., and Shaw, Donald L. (1972) 'The agenda setting function of mass media', *Public Opinion Quarterly* 36 (2): 176–87.

McConnell, D. (1994) *Implementing Computer Supported Co-operative Learning.* London: Kogan Page.

McCullagh, C. (1996) *Crime in Ireland: A Sociological Introduction.* Cork: Cork University Press.

McDonald, H. (1997) 'How the BBC dances to an IRA tune', *Sunday Times,* 19 Jan.

McIlroy, B. (1998a) *Irish Cinema: An Illustrated History.* Dun Laoghaire: Anna Livia.

McIlroy, B. (1998b) *Shooting to Kill: Filmmaking and the 'Troubles' in Northern Ireland.* Trowbridge: Flick Books.

MacKenzie, D. and Wajcman, J. (eds) (1999) *The Social Shaping of Technology,* 2nd edn. London: Oxford University Press.

MacKillop, J. (ed.) (1999) *Contemporary Irish Cinema.* Syracuse: Syracuse University Press.

McLoone, M. (1996) *Broadcasting in a Divided Community.* Belfast: Institute of Irish Studies.

McLoone, M. (2000) *Irish Film: The Emergence of a Contemporary Cinema.* London: BFI Press.

McLoone, M. and MacMahon, J. (eds) (1984) *Television and Irish Society*. Dublin: RTÉ–IFI

McNair, B. (2006) *Cultural Chaos: Journalism and Power in a Globalised World.*

McPhail, T. (1986) *Electronic Colonialism*. London: Sage.

McQuail, D. (1991) 'Mass media in the public interest: towards a framework of norms for media performance', pp. 68–81 in Curran, J. and Gurevitch, M., (eds), *Mass Media and Society*. London: Edward Arnold.

Maeroff, G. (1988) *The Empowerment of Teachers: Overcoming the Crisis of Confidence*. New York: Teachers College Press.

Mathjis, E. (2002) 'Big brother and critical discourse: the reception of big brother Belgium', *Television and New Media* 3 (3): 311–22.

Mayne, J. (2002) 'Paradoxes of spectatorship', pp. 28–45 in Turner, G. (ed.) *The Film Cultures Reader*. London and New York: Routledge.

Mazzonetto, M., Merzagora, M. and Tola, E. (2005) *Science in Radio Broadcasting: The Role of the Radio in Science Communication*. Milan: Polimetrica.

Means, B. (1994) 'Using technology to advance educational goals', pp. 191–222 in Means, B. (ed.), *Technology and Education Reform: The Reality behind the Promise*. San Francisco: Josey-Bass.

Mendible, M. (2004) 'Humiliation, subjectivity and reality TV', *Feminist Media Studies* 4 (3): 335–8.

Messner, M. A. and Montez de Oca, J. (2005) 'The male consumer as loser: beer and liquor ads in mega sports media events', *Signs: Journal of Women in Culture and Society* 30 (3): 1879–1909.

Miller, D. (1994) *Don't Mention the War: Northern Ireland, Propaganda and the Media*. London: Pluto.

Miller, D. (1995) 'The media and Northern Ireland: censorship, information management and the broadcasting ban', pp. 45–75 in Philo, G. (ed.), *Glasgow Media Group Reader*, vol. 2. London: Routledge.

Miller, D. (2002) 'The media, propaganda, and the Northern Ireland peace process', pp. 114–29 in Kiberd, D. (ed.), *Media in Ireland: Issues in Broadcasting*. Dublin: Four Courts.

Miller, T., Govil, N., McMurrin, J., Maxwell, R. and Wang, Ting (eds) (2005) *Global Hollywood 2*. London: BFI.

Moloney, E. (1988) 'The media: asking the right questions', pp. 134–46 in Farrell, M. (ed.), *Twenty Years On*. Dingle: Brandon.

Moloney, E. (1991) 'Closing down the airwaves: the story of the broadcasting ban', pp. 8–50 in Rolston, B. (ed.), *The Media and Northern Ireland*. Basingstoke: Macmillan.

Moloney, E. (2003) *A Secret History of the IRA*. London and New York: W.W. Norton.

Monk, C. (1999) 'From underworld to underclass: crime and British cinema in the 1990s', pp. 172–88 in Chibnall, S. and Murphy, R. (eds), *British Crime Cinema*. London; NY: Routledge.

Morley, D. (1986) *Family Television.* London: Comedia.

Morley, D. (1996) 'The geography of television: ethnography, communications and community', pp. 317–42 in Hay, J., Grossberg, L. and Wartella, E. (eds), *The Audience and Its Landscape.* Boulder, CO: Westview.

Morley, D. and Robins, K. (1995) *Space of Identity. Global media, Electronic Landscapes and Cultural Boundaries.* London: Routledge.

Morley, D. and Silverstone, R. (1990) 'Domestic communication: technologies and meanings', *Media, Culture and Society* 12: 31–55.

Morrissey, M. and Smyth, M. (2002) *Northern Ireland after the Good Friday Agreement.* London: Pluto.

Mulvihill, M. (1987) 'Science and technology in the Irish media', *Technology Ireland,* May: 6

Naficy, H. (1993). *The Making of Exile Cultures: Iranian Television in Los Angeles.* Minneapolis, University of Minnesota Press.

Naficy, H. (2001) *An Accented Cinema.* Princeton NJ: Princeton University Press.

NEAR (1994) Application by North East Area Radio to the IRTC for a licence to broadcast. Unpublished.

Negroponte, N. (1996) *Being Digital.* London: Hodder & Stoughton.

Neil, G. (2006) 'Assessing the effectiveness of UNESCO's new Convention on Cultural Diversity', *Global Media and Communication* 2 (2): 257–62.

Nelkin, D. (1995) *Selling Science: How The Press Covers Science and Technology,* 2nd edn. New York: W. H. Freeman.

Nelson, T. E., Clawson, R. A. and Oxley, Z. (1997) 'Media framing of a civil liberties conflict and its effect on tolerance', *American Political Science Review* 91 (3): 567–83.

Nixon, S. (1997) 'Exhibiting masculinity', pp. 291–330 in Hall, S. (ed.), *Representation: Cultural Representations and Signifying Practices.* London: Sage.

Nordenstreng K. and Schiller, H. (eds) (1993) *Beyond National Sovereignty: International Communication in the 1990s.* Norwood, NJ: Ablex.

Nordenstreng, K. and Schiller, H. (eds) (1979) *National Sovereignty and National Community.* Norwood, NJ: Ablex

North Leitrim Men's Group (2001) *Research Project: A Study of the Situation of the Single Rural Man.* Manorhamilton: North Leitrim Men's Group.

Nye, R. A. (2005) 'Locating masculinity: some recent work on men', *Journal of Women in Culture and Society* 30 (3): 1937–62.

O'Brien, H. (2004) *The Real Ireland: The Evolution of Ireland in Documentary Film.* Manchester: Manchester University Press.

O'Brien, M. (2005) 'Disavowing democracy: the silencing project in the south', pp. 48–58 in Corcoran, M. P. and O'Brien, M. (eds), *Political Censorship and the Democratic State: the Irish Broadcasting Ban.* Dublin: Four Courts.

O'Connell, D. (2005) 'Narrative strategies in contemporary Irish cinema 1993–2003', PhD thesis, DCU.

O'Connell, M. (1999) 'Is Irish public opinion towards crime distorted by media bias?' *European Journal of Communication* 14 (2): 191–212.

O'Connell, M. and Whelan, A. (1996) 'The public perception of crime prevalence, newspaper readership and "mean world" attitudes', *Legal and Criminological Psychology* 1: 179–95.

O'Connor, A. (1990) 'The miners' radio stations in Bolivia: a culture of resistance', *Journal of Communication* 40 (1): 102–10.

O'Donnell, H. (1999) *Good Times, Bad Times: Soap Operas and Society in Western Europe.* London: Leicester University Press.

O'Donnell, I. (2004) 'Patterns in crime', *Irish Criminal Law Journal* 14(2): 2–7.

O'Donoghue, J. (2006), Speech at Cannes Film Festival, 21 May 2006. Mimeo.

OECD (1991) *Reviews of National Policies for Education: Ireland.* Paris: OECD.

OECD (1999) *Economic Survey of Ireland.* Paris: OECD

OECD (2006) *Economic Survey of Ireland.* Paris: OECD

O'Farrell, John (1998) 'Divided people, divided press', *Media Studies Journal* Spring/ Summer: 96–103

Ofcom (2006) http://www.ofcom.org.uk/research/cm/icmr06/ [9 Jan. 2007].

O'Halloran, M. (2004) 'Major film studios "shun" Ireland', *Irish Times,* 2 July.

O'Hearn, D. (1998) *Inside the Celtic Tiger: The Irish Economy and the Asian Model.* London: Pluto.

Ó Muirí, P. (2005) 'Molann RTÉ fograiocht a bhaint de TG4', *Irish Times,* 2 Nov.

O'Regan, T. (1996) *Australian National Cinema.* London: Routledge.

Ó Riagáin, P. and Ó Gliasáin, M. (1984) *The Irish Language in the Republic of Ireland 1983: Preliminary Report of a National Survey.* Dublin: Institiúid Teangeolaíochta Éireann.

Ó Riain, S. (2004) *The Politics of High-Tech Growth: Developmental Network States in the Global Economy.* Cambridge: Cambridge University Press.

O'Reilly, E. (1998) *Veronica Guerin: The Life and Death of a Crime Reporter.* London: Vintage.

O'Rourke, A. (2006) 'Planned legislation not the answer to privacy concerns', *Irish Times,* 8 July.

O'Sullivan, E. (2001) '"This otherwise delicate subject": child sexual abuse in early twentieth-century Ireland', pp. 176–201 in O'Mahony, P. (ed.), *Criminal Justice in Ireland.* Dublin: IPA.

O'Sullivan, J. (2005a), 'Delivering Ireland: journalism's search for a role online', *Gazette* 67 (1): 45–68.

O'Sullivan, J. (2005b), 'Ireland: newsprint colonizes the web' pp. 158–71 in Van der Wurff, R. and Lauf, E. (eds), *Print and Online Newspapers in Europe: A Comparative Analysis in 16 Countries.* Amsterdam: Het Spinhuis.

O'Toole, F. (2006) 'Brand leader', *Granta* 53: 45–75

Outing, S. (2004) *Eyetrack III: What News Websites Look Like Through Readers' Eyes* http://www.poynter.org/content/content_view.asp?id=70472 [Dec. 4, 2006].

Papathanassopoulos, S. (2005) 'Europe: an exemplary landscape for comprehending globalisation', *Global Media and Communication* I (I): 46–50.

Parkinson, A. F (1998) *Ulster Loyalism and the British Media.* Dublin: Four Courts.

Pavlik, J. V. (2001) *Journalism and New Media.* New York: Columbia University Press.

Peripheral Vision. Oxford: Oxford University Press.

Peters, H-P. (1995) 'The interaction of journalists and scientific experts – co-operation and conflict between two professional cultures', *Media, Culture and Society* 17: 31–48.

Pettitt, L. (2004) '"We're not fucking Eye-talians": the gangster genre and Irish cinema', pp. 25–38 in Barton, R. and O'Brien, H. (eds), *Keeping It Real: Irish Film and Television.* London: Wallflower Press.

Pettitt, L. (2000) *Screening Ireland: Film and Television Representation.* Manchester: Manchester University Press.

Pfeil, F. (1995) *White Guys: Studies in Postmodern Domination and Difference.* New York: Verso.

Philo, G. (1995) *Glasgow Media Group Reader,* vol. 2. London: Routledge

Philo, G. (2002) 'Television news and audience understanding of war, conflict and disaster', *Journalism Studies* 3 (2): 173–86.

Preston, P. (1990) *Measuring the Information Economy: Proposals for Updating the ISIC* Oxford: Economic and Social Research Council, PICT Research Papers.

Preston, P. (1995) 'Ireland and the European information society: a scoping study', Consultancy report.

Preston, P. (1997a) 'The info superhighway and the less developed regions and smaller entities', pp. 277–98 in Kubicek, Herbert et al. (eds), *The Social Shaping of Information Highways: Comparing US and EU Action Plans.* New York: St Martin's; Frankfurt: Campus.

Preston, P. (1997b) 'Beyond the information society: selected atoms and bits of the national strategy in Ireland', *Economic and Social Review* 28 (3): 185–212.

Preston, P. (2001) *Re-shaping Communications: Technology, Information and Social Change.* London and Thousand Oaks, CA: Sage.

Preston, P. (2003) 'The European Union's ICT policies: neglected social and cultural dimensions', pp 33–58 in Servaes, J. (ed.), *The European Information Society.* Bristol, UK and Portland, OR: Intellect Books.

Preston, P. (2005) 'ICTs in everyday life: public policy implications for "Europe's way to the information society"', pp 195–212 in Silverstone, R. (ed.), *Media Technology and Everyday Life.* Aldershot: Ashgate.

Preston, P. (2006) 'Mapping media and creative industries in Ireland's KbE', unpublished report.

Preston, P. and Cawley, A. (2004) 'Mis-understanding the "knowledge economy' in early 21st century: lessons from innovation in the media sector', *Communication and Strategies Journal* 55: 119–45.

Preston, P., Cawley, A. and Metykova, M. (2007) 'Broadband and Rural Areas in the EU: Recent Research Findings and Implications', *Telecommunications Policy* 31.

Preston, P. and Kerr, A. (2001) 'Digital media, nation-states and local cultures: the case of multimedia "content" production', *Media, Culture and Society* 23: 109–31.

Price Waterhouse Cooper (2003) *Realising the Potential of the Irish Film and Television Industry: A Unique National Asset.* Dublin: SPI.

Purcell, B. (1991) 'The silence in Irish broadcasting', pp. 51–68 in Rolston, B. (ed.), *The Media and Northern Ireland.* Basingstoke: Macmillan.

Purdie, B. (1990) *Politics in the Streets: The Origins of the Civil Rights Movement in Northern Ireland.* Belfast: Blackstaff.

Quin, R. (2004) 'From Beverly Hills to Big Brother: how Australian teenage girls respond' in Von Feilitzen, C. (ed.), *Young People, Soap Operas and Reality TV.* Goteborg: International Clearinghouse on Children, Youth and Media, Nordicom, Goteborg University.

Quinn, G. and Trench, B. (2002) *Online News Media and Their Audiences.* Mudia: International Institute of Infonomics.

Raftery, M. and O'Sullivan, E. (1999) *Suffer the Little Children: The Inside Story of Ireland's Industrial Schools.* Dublin, New Island.

Rantanen, T. (2005) *The Media and Globalisation.* London, Sage.

Reuters (2006) 'MTV focuses on the digital frontier at 25', www.nytimes.com [27 Aug. 2006].

RnL (2006) 'Guth na Cathrach', www.bci.ie [accessed 9 Oct. 2006].

Robertson, R. (1992) *Globalisation: Social Theory and Global Culture.* London: Sage.

Robins, K. and Aksoy, A. (2001) 'From spaces of identity to mental spaces: lessons from Turkish-Cypriot cultural experience in Britain', *Journal of Ethnic and Migration Studies* 27: 685–711.

Roche, A. (ed.) (2005) *The UCD Aesthetic: Celebrating 150 Years.* Dublin: New Island.

Roche, J. P. and Muskavitch, M. A. T. (2003) 'Limited precision in print media communication of West Nile Virus', *Science Communication* 24: 353–65.

Rockett, E. and Rockett, K. (2003) *Neil Jordan: Exploring Boundaries.* Dublin: Liffey.

Rockett, K. (1978–9) 'Irish cinema: notes on some nationalist fictions', *Screen* 20 (3–4): 115–23

Rockett, K. (1999) 'Irish cinema: the national in the international', *Cineaste* XXIV (2–1): 23–5.

Rockett, K. and Hill, J. (eds) (2004) *National Cinema and Beyond.* Dublin: Four Courts.

Rockett, K., Gibbons, L. and Hill, J. (eds) (1988) *Cinema and Ireland.* London: Routledge.

Rodden, T. (1991) 'A survey of CSCW systems', *Interacting with Computers* 3 (3): 319–53.

Rolston, B. and Miller, D. (eds) (1996) *War and Words: A Northern Ireland Media Reader.* Belfast: Beyond the Pale.

Roscoe, J. (2001) '*Big Brother* Australia: performing the "real" Twenty-four Seven', *International Journal of Cultural Studies* 4 (1): 473–88.

Rosenfeld, L. and Morville, P. (2002) *Information Architecture for the World Wide Web,* 2nd edn. Sebastopol, CA: O'Reilly Media.

RTÉ (2005) Submission to European Commission on Television Without Frontiers Issue papers. Available at: ec.europa.eu/comm./avpolicy/docs/reg

Ryan, L. (1990) 'Irish emigration to Britain since World War II', pp. 45–67 in Kearney, R. (ed), *Migrations: The Irish at Home and Abroad*. Dublin, Wolfhound.

Sandholtz, J. and Ringstaff, C. and Dwyer, D. (1997) *Teaching with Technology: Creating Student Centered Classrooms*. New York: Teachers College Press.

Sarason, B. (1996) *Revisiting The Culture of the School and the Problem of Change*. New York: Teachers College Press.

Savran, T. (1998) *Taking it Like a Man: White Masculinity, Masochism and Contemporary American Culture*. Princeton NJ: Princeton University Press.

Scannell, P. (2002) 'Big brother as a television event', *Television and New Media* 3 (3): 271–83.

Schiller, H. (1969) *Mass Communication and American Empire*. New York: Augustus M. Kelley.

Schiller, H. (1976) *Communication and Cultural Domination*. New York: International Arts and Sciences Press.

Schiller, H. (1981) *Who Knows: Information in the Age of the Fortune 500*. Norwood, NJ: Ablex.

Schiller, H. (1991) 'Not yet the post-imperial era', *Critical Studies in Mass Communication* 8: 13–28.

Schlesinger, P. (1987) *Putting Reality Together: BBC News*. London: Methuen.

Schlesinger, P. (1991) *Media, State and Nation*. London: Sage.

Schlesinger, P., Boyle, R., Dobash, R. E., Haynes, R., McNair, B. and Dobash, R. (1998) *Men Viewing Violence*. London: Broadcasting Standards Commission, http://www-fms.stir.ac.uk/research/mvv/ [14 July 2005].

Schlesinger, P., Elliott, P., and Murdock, G. (1983) *Televising Terrorism*. London: Comedia.

Schultz, T. (2000) 'Mass media and the concept of interactivity: an exploratory study of online forums and reader email', *Media, Culture and Society* 22 (2): 205–21.

Science, Technology and Innovation Advisory Council (1995) *Making Knowledge Work for Us*, 3 vols. Dublin: Stationery Office.

Sconce, J. (2002) 'Irony, nihilism and the new American "smart" film', *Screen* 43 (4): 349–69.

Seaton, J. (1988) 'The sociology of the mass media', pp. 221–45 in Curran, J. and Seaton, J. (1988) *Power without Responsibility: The Press and Broadcasting in Britain*, 3rd edn. London: Routledge.

Seaton, J. (2005) *Carnage and the Media*. London: Allen Lane.

Shary, T. (2005) 'Bad boys and Hollywood hype: gendered conflict in juvenile delinquency films', pp. 24–5 in Pomerance, M. and Gateward, F. (eds), *Where are the Boys? Cinemas of Masculinity and Youth*. Detroit: Wayne State University Press.

Sheehan, H. (1987) *Irish Television Drama: A Society and Its Stories* Dublin: Radio Telefís Éireann.

Sheehan, H. (1993) 'Soap opera and social order', paper delivered at the *Imagining Ireland* conference at Irish Film Centre, Dublin 31 Oct. www.comms.dcu.ie/sheehanh/itvsoap.htm

Sheehan, H. (2004) *The Continuing Story of Irish Television Drama: Tracking the Tiger.* Dublin: Four Courts.

Shingler M. and Wieringa, C. (1998) *On Air: Methods and Meanings of Radio.* London: Arnold.

Siklos, R. (2006) 'Not in the real world anymore', *New York Times,* 18 Sept.

Silber, L. and Little, A. (1995) *The Death of Yugoslavia.* London: Penguin/BBC.

Silverstone, R. (1984) 'Narrative strategies in television science', *Media, Culture and Society* 6: 377–410.

Silverstone, R. (1999) *Why Study the Media?* London: Sage.

Silverstone, R. (ed.) (2005) *Media Technology and Everyday Life.* Aldershot: Ashgate.

Silverstone, R. and Hirsch, E. (eds) (1992) *Consuming Technologies: Media and Information in Domestic Spaces.* London: Routledge.

Sinclair, J., Jacka, E. and Cunningham, S. (1996) *New Patterns in Global Television:*

Singer, J. B. (2005) 'The political j-blogger: "Normalizing" a new media form to fit old norms and practices', *Journalism: Theory Practice and Criticism* 6 (2): 173–99.

Slide, A. (1988) *The Cinema and Ireland.* North Carolina: McFarland Press.

Sparks, C. (2005) 'The problem of globalisation', *Global Media and Communication* 1 (1): 20–3.

Special Working Group on the Film Production Industry (1993) *The Film Production Industry in Ireland: A Report to An Taoiseach, Albert Reynolds.* Dublin: Stationery Office.

Spencer, G. (2000) *Disturbing the Peace: Politics, Television News and the Northern Ireland Peace Process.* Aldershot: Ashgate.

Spencer, G. (2004) 'The impact of television news on the Northern Ireland peace negotiations', *Media, Culture and Society* 26 (5): 603–23.

Spicer, A. (2001) *Typical Men: The Representation of Masculinity in Popular British Culture.* London and New York: I. B. Tauris.

Splichal, S. (1993) 'Searching for new paradigms: an introduction', pp. 3–18 in Splichal, S. and Wasko, J. (eds) (1993) *Communication and Democracy.* Norwood: Ablex.

Splichal, S. (2002) 'Rethinking publicness: the precedence of the right to communicate' *Javnost: The Public* IX (3): 83–105.

Sreberny-Mohammadi, A. (1996) 'The global and the local in international communications', pp.177–203 in Curran, J. and Gurevitch, M. (eds), *Mass Media and Society.* London: Arnold.

Standard, The (1929) 'Fined under censorship', 26 Oct.: 2.

Starr, P. (1996) 'Computing our way to educational reform', *The American Prospect* 27 (July–Aug.): 50–9.

Steinman, C. (1992) 'Gaze out of bounds', pp. 199–214 in Craig, S. (ed.), *Men Masculinity and the Media*. London: Sage.

Sterne, J. and Trench, B. (1994) 'Science and technology: the media's blind spot', *Irish Communications Review* 4: 18–29.

Surette, R. (1998) *Media, Crime and Criminal Justice: Images and Realities*. Belmont, CA and London: Wadsworth.

Sweeney, P. (1998) *The Celtic Tiger: Ireland's Economic Miracle Explained*. Dublin: Oak Tree.

Tasker, Y. (1993) 'Dumb movies for dumb people: masculinity, the body, and the voice in contemporary action cinema', pp. 230–44 in Cohan, S. and Hark, I. R. (eds), *Screening the Male: Exploring Masculinities in Hollywood Cinema*. London and New York: Routledge.

TG4 (2006) 'TG4 Annual Report 2005' www.tg4.ie [accessed 6 Oct.].

Thompson, J. B. (1995). *The Media and Modernity: A Social Theory of the Media*, Cambridge: Polity; Stanford: Stanford University Press.

Thompson, M. (1999) *Forging War: The Media in Serbia, Croatia and Bosnia-Hercegovina*. Luton: Article 19/University of Luton Press.

Thussu, D. K. (1998) *Electronic Empires: Global Media and Local Resistance*. London: Arnold.

Thussu, D. K. (2006) *International Communication: Continuity and Change*, 2nd edn. London: Hodder Arnold.

Thussu, D. K. and Freedman, D. (eds) (2003) *War and the Media*. London: Sage.

Tincknell, E. and Raghuram, P. (2002) 'Big brother – reconfiguring the "active" audience of cultural studies', *European Journal of Cultural Studies* 5 (2): 199–215.

Titley, G. (2003), 'Cultivating habitats of meaning: broadcasting, participation and interculturalism', *Irish Communications Review* 9: 1–11.

Titley, G. (2006) 'Red, white (and blue about it): the transnational field of Polish media in Ireland', Paper presented at the Irish Media Research Network Conference, Dublin Institute of Technology, June 2006.

Tobin, J. (2000) *Good Guys Don't Wear Hats: Children's Talk about the Media*. Stoke on Trent: Trentham Books.

Tomlinson, J. (1991) *Cultural Imperialism*. London: Continuum.

Tomlinson, J. (1997) 'Cultural globalisation and cultural imperialism', pp. 170–90 in Mohammadi, A. (ed.), *International Communication and Globalisation*. London: Sage.

Trench, B. (2006) 'Science communication and citizen science – how dead is the deficit model?' Paper presented to Scientific Culture and Global Citizenship, Ninth International Conference on Public Communication of Science and Technology, May 2006, Seoul, Korea, http://www.pcst2006.org/Upload/WB1.PDF

Troyer, J. and Marchiselli, C. (2005) 'Slack, slacker, slackest: homosocial bonding practices in contemporary dude cinema', pp. 264–76 in Pomerance, M. and

Gateward, F. (eds), *Where are the Boys: Cinemas of Masculinity and Youth*. Detroit: Wayne State University Press.

Truetzschler, W. (2002) 'The Irish media landscape', *European Media Landscape* (Online). European Journalism Centre. http://www.ejc.nl/jr/emland/ireland.html [13 October 2004].

Truetzschler, W. (2004) 'Ireland', pp. 115–25 in Kelly, M., Mazzoleni, G. and McQuail, D. (eds), *The Media in Europe*, 3rd edn. London: Sage.

Turner, G. (2002) 'Audiences and consumption', pp. 379–81 in Turner, G. (ed.), *The Film Cultures Reader*. London and New York: Routledge.

Turner, G. (2006) 'The mass production of celebrity: "Celetoids", reality TV and the "demotic turn"', *International Journal of Cultural Studies* 9 (2): 153–65.

Turner, G., Bonner, F. and Marshall, P. D. (2000) *Fame Games: The Production of Celebrity in Australia*. Melbourne: Cambridge University Press.

Ugba, A. (2002) *Mapping Minorities and their Media: The National Context – Ireland*. London: EMTEL II/LSE.

Universal Declaration of Human Rights (1948) http:www.un.org/rights/ (accessed 29.09.06).

Van der Wurff, R. and Lauk, E. (eds) (2005) *Print and Online Newspapers in Europe: A Comparative Analysis in 16 Countries*. Amsterdam: Het Spinhuis.

Van Veen, K., Sleegers, P., Bergen, T. and Klasen, C. (2001) 'Professional orientations of school teachers towards their work', *Teaching and Teacher Education* 17: 175–94.

Van Zoonen, L. (2001) 'Desire and resistance: big brother and the recognition of everyday life', *Media, Culture and Society*, 23: 669–77.

Vertovec, S. (2001) 'Transnationalism and identity', *Journal of Ethnic and Migration Studies* 27 (4): 573–82.

Von Feilitzen, C. (ed.) (2004) *Young People, Soap Operas and Reality TV*. International Clearinghouse on Children, Youth and Media, Nordicom, Goteborg University.

Wajcman, J. (1991) *Feminism Confronts Technology*. University Park PA: Penn State University Press.

Walkerdine, V. (1986) 'Video replay: families, films and fantasy', pp. 167–99 in Burgin, V., Donald, J. and Kaplan, C. (eds) *Formations of Fantasy*. London and New York: Methuen.

Wall, M. (2005) '"Blogs of war": weblogs as news', *Journalism* 6 (2): 153–72.

Wang, Y. Y. and Chiyoko King-O'Riain, R. (2006) *Chinese Students in Ireland*. Dublin: National Consultative Committee on Racism and Interculturalism.

Ward, L. (2006) 'Baffled about how to quell your toddlers' tantrums? Try TV classes, families are told', *Guardian*, 21 Nov.

Waterford Standard (1929a) 'Serious charge against Mr Laurence Breen', 28 Sept. 1929.

Waterford Standard (1929b) 'Censorship of publications act', 26 Oct. 1929.

Watson, I. (1996) 'The Irish language and television: national identity, preservation, restoration and minority rights', *British Journal of Sociology* 47 (2): 255–74.

Watson, I. (2002) 'Irish-language broadcasting: history, ideology and identity', *Media, Culture and Society* 24: 739–57.

Watson, I. (2003) *Broadcasting in Irish*. Dublin: Four Courts.

Watt, P. (2006) 'Part of the bigger picture: positive actions in Census 2006', *Spectrum, Journal of the National Consultative Committee on Racism and Interculturalism* 11: 3–5.

WDCR (1998) 'Application by West Dublin Community Radio to the IRTC for a licence to broadcast.' Unpublished.

Whelehan, I. (2000). *Overloaded: Popular Culture and the Future of Feminism.* London: Women's Press.

White, A. (2005) 'Section 31: ministerial orders and court challenges', pp. 34–47 in Corcoran, M. P. and O'Brien, M. (eds), *Political Censorship and the Democratic State: the Irish Broadcasting Ban.* Dublin: Four Courts.

White, H. (1973) *Metahistory: The Historical Imagination in Nineteenth-Century Europe.* Baltimore: Johns Hopkins University Press.

White, S. A. (1994) 'Introduction: the concept of participation: transforming rhetoric to reality', pp. 15–35 in White, S. A., Nair, K. S. and Ascroft, J., *Participatory Communication: Working for Change and Development.* London: Sage.

White, V. (1997) 'The arts of consultation', *Irish Times*, 9 July 1997.

Williams, A. (2002) (ed.), *Film and Nationalism.* Piscataway, NJ: Rutgers University Press.

Wilsdon, J., Wynne, B. and Stilgoe, J. (2005) *The Public Value of Science.* London: Demos.

Wolfsfeld, G. (2004) *Media and the Path to Peace.* Cambridge: Cambridge University Press.

Wood, B. (2004) 'A world in retreat: the reconfiguration of hybridity in 20th-century New Zealand television', *Media, Culture and Society* 26 (1): 45–62.

Wynne, B. (1991) 'Knowledges in context', *Science, Technology and Human Values* 16: 111–21.

Wynne, B. (1995) 'The public understanding of science', pp. 361–88 in Jasanoff, S., Markle, G. E., Peterson, J. C., and Pinch, T. (eds), *Handbook of Science and Technology Studies.* Thousand Oaks, CA: Sage.

Index